MANAGING AN ALLIANCE

I. M. DESTLER HIDEO SATO
PRISCILLA CLAPP HARUHIRO FUKUI

MANAGING AN ALLIANCE

The Politics of U.S.–Japanese Relations

THE BROOKINGS INSTITUTION
Washington, D.C.

Copyright © 1976 by

THE BROOKINGS INSTITUTION

1775 Massachusetts Avenue, N.W., Washington, D.C. 20036

Library of Congress Cataloging in Publication Data:

Main entry under title:
Managing an alliance.
  Bibliography: p.
  Includes index.
  1. United States—Foreign relations—Japan.
2. Japan—Foreign relations—United States.
I. Destler, I.M.
E183.8.J3M3 327.73'052 75-44501
ISBN 0-8157-1820-9
ISBN 0-8157-1819-5 pbk.

1 2 3 4 5 6 7 8 9

THE BROOKINGS INSTITUTION is an independent organization devoted to nonpartisan research, education, and publication in economics, government, foreign policy, and the social sciences generally. Its principal purposes are to aid in the development of sound public policies and to promote public understanding of issues of national importance.

The Institution was founded on December 8, 1927, to merge the activities of the Institute for Government Research, founded in 1916, the Institute of Economics, founded in 1922, and the Robert Brookings Graduate School of Economics and Government, founded in 1924.

The Board of Trustees is responsible for the general administration of the Institution, while the immediate direction of the policies, program, and staff is vested in the President, assisted by an advisory committee of the officers and staff. The bylaws of the Institution state: "It is the function of the Trustees to make possible the conduct of scientific research, and publication, under the most favorable conditions, and to safeguard the independence of the research staff in the pursuit of their studies and in the publication of the results of such studies. It is not a part of their function to determine, control, or influence the conduct of particular investigations or the conclusions reached."

The President bears final responsibility for the decision to publish a manuscript as a Brookings book. In reaching his judgment on the competence, accuracy, and objectivity of each study, the President is advised by the director of the appropriate research program and weighs the views of a panel of expert outside readers who report to him in confidence on the quality of the work. Publication of a work signifies that it is deemed a competent treatment worthy of public consideration but does not imply endorsement of conclusions or recommendations.

The Institution maintains its position of neutrality on issues of public policy in order to safeguard the intellectual freedom of the staff. Hence interpretations or conclusions in Brookings publications should be understood to be solely those of the authors and should not be attributed to the Institution, to its trustees, officers, or other staff members, or to the organizations that support its research.

Foreword

NEGOTIATIONS between governments are sometimes regarded as encounters in which diplomats on each side press clearly defined national objectives, adjusting them only as the positions and tactics of those across the table make compromise essential. But the conduct of diplomacy is often much more complicated. Negotiators have to bargain not only with their foreign counterparts, but also with officials of their own government—to establish basic policy and to ensure that agreements reached abroad have support at home.

The authors of this book find such a pattern in relations between the United States and its most important single ally—Japan. They trace the manner in which misunderstanding of the constraints binding leaders and officials can disrupt particular negotiations and provoke domestic political crises that damage bilateral relations on a broader range of issues. To shed light on how such setbacks can be avoided, the authors analyze the politics of Japanese-American relations since 1945, examining the causes of failure and the lessons to be drawn from success. They focus on the security treaty revision of 1957–60 and later negotiations, but also touch on events before the Second World War to illustrate specific points.

The book stems from a project conceived and organized by Morton H. Halperin in 1971, when he was a Brookings senior fellow. To reflect attitudes and viewpoints on both sides of the Pacific, the project brought together two Japanese and two American scholars to pursue parallel, collaborative research and analysis. They concentrated first on specific negotiations, interviewing many participants in Tokyo and Washington. Particular attention was given to the Okinawa reversion question and the textile dispute of 1969–71. They then applied their findings to a general study of U.S. and Japanese domestic decision-making and its influence on bilateral issues, of which this book is the result.

All four authors were Brookings research associates while working on the project. Their individual contributions cannot be defined precisely, because the ideas and analysis that emerged result from several years of teamwork. Priscilla Clapp focused on the historical and case background in chapter 2, with important contributions from Haruhiro Fukui. I. M. Destler was responsible for the comparative analysis of Japanese and American policymaking in chapter 3, also with important contributions from Fukui. Hideo Sato developed most of the analysis of misperceptions in chapter 4 and a large part of the analysis of Japanese-American interaction in chapter 5. In addition, Destler assumed the major coordinating and final writing responsibility. In the course of revision, however, all four authors influenced each chapter, and all participated in the case studies—Destler, Fukui, and Sato in that on the textile dispute, and Clapp and Fukui in that on Okinawa reversion.

The study was financed by the National Endowment for the Humanities, the Ford Foundation, and the Rockefeller Foundation. The authors thank Morton H. Halperin, Henry Owen, William P. Bundy, Joseph S. Nye, Leon V. Sigal, and Philip H. Trezise for their comments on drafts. They are also grateful to Laurel Rabin, who reviewed the manuscript for clarity and accuracy; to Donna Daniels Verdier for her administrative support as the study took shape; to her and Delores Burton for deciphering and typing successive drafts; to Alice M. Carroll for editing the book; and to Florence Robinson for preparing the index.

The views expressed here are solely those of the authors and should not be ascribed to the trustees, officers, or other staff members of the Brookings Institution, or to the National Endowment for the Humanities, the Ford Foundation, or the Rockefeller Foundation.

GILBERT Y. STEINER
Acting President

June 1976
Washington, D.C.

Contents

1. Introduction   1

2. Three Postwar Cases   8
   The Postwar Setting *10*
   Revision of the Security Treaty *12*
   Okinawa Reversion *23*
   The Textile Dispute *35*
   Conclusions *45*

3. Foreign Policymaking in Japan and the United States   48
   Japan's Political System: The Major Actors *49*
   Institutions of Political Leadership *60*
   The Bureaucracies *68*
   Conclusions *86*

4. Misperceptions Across the Pacific   89
   Misperceptions Rooted in Politics as Usual *90*
   Misperceptions Rooted in Cultural Differences *100*
   Conclusions *121*

5. The Interplay of National Systems   125
   Initiation of Bilateral Issues *126*
   The Politics of Interaction *130*
   Resolution of Issues *142*
   Conclusions *164*

6. Managing Future U.S.-Japanese Relations   167
   The Importance of U.S.-Japanese Relations *168*
   The Relevance of Past Cases to Future Problems *170*
   Explaining Success and Failure *171*
   Japan as a Typical Large Ally *176*
   Japan as a Special Case *184*
   Increasing U.S. Government Sensitivity to Japan *190*

Bibliography   197

Index   203

CHAPTER ONE

Introduction

JAPAN'S ECONOMIC expansion since 1945 is one of the remarkable and least expected success stories of the past thirty years. A related success story, the U.S.-Japanese alliance, has likewise exceeded the hopes of most participants and observers. Just as Japan's shattered industries and demoralized population seemed unlikely sources of an economic miracle, the prospects for a close, mutually beneficial relationship between two bitter wartime enemies were not exactly encouraging. Yet such a relationship emerged and has persisted. Japanese leaders found the United States to be a dependable and generally beneficent patron as they built new policies founded on cooperative relations with the nations of the West. For American leaders, Japan proved to be a vital geographical link in the Pacific network of defenses, as well as a loyal ally willing to follow the American lead in international policy.

Achieving and maintaining such a partnership has required sustained effort by leaders and officials on both sides of the Pacific, because of the ever-present potential for serious misunderstanding and disagreement. Deep divisions within Japan about the virtue of the American connection fueled a severe crisis in 1960 when the bilateral security treaty was revised. A decade later, just as a similar crisis was being avoided by agreement on returning Okinawa to Japanese control, the two countries became engaged in a bitter three-year dispute over textiles. And before this was resolved, the alliance was further shaken when the United States made its surprise opening to China in July 1971 and when President Nixon suspended the dollar's convertibility into gold a month later and imposed a temporary surcharge on imports. As the imbalance in trade—a major target of Nixon's economic measures—grew to $4 billion in Japan's favor in 1972, Japanese-American tension continued. But

1

after Japan established diplomatic relations with Peking late that year, and a sharp upsurge in U.S. exports closed the trade gap, the tension subsided. By the mid-seventies it was clear that the alliance had survived these crises and entered a new if somewhat uncertain era. Gerald Ford, in the fourth month of his presidency, undertook as his first overseas venture the visit to Tokyo that protest demonstrations had forced President Dwight Eisenhower to cancel in 1960. And Emperor Hirohito's return visit in 1975 was even more symbolic of the ability of both countries to look beyond past conflicts.

Yet problems—actual and potential—continue. Americans inevitably worry about whether Japan will one day choose to acquire nuclear arms and about the impact of such a choice on world power relationships. And although Japan's particular vulnerability to the recent economic ills of the industrialized world has tempered visions of an economic superstate, Americans worry about the possibility of future Japanese trade offensives. Underlying these genuine substantive concerns is a widespread anxiety about what "the Japanese" really want, who "the Japanese" really are. For many Americans, the cultural gap raises questions about the foundations of the relationship and the extent of mutual understanding, about what officials on the other side of the negotiating table are really thinking. And in Japan, where the psychology of the junior partner still prevails, concern about "the Americans" is far more pervasive. Opposition Communists and Socialists have long challenged American policies; now conservative politicians and bureaucrats worry about the dependability of U.S. policies. The "Nixon shocks" of 1971 suggested to them either a purposive U.S. administration determined to shake up and loosen the alliance, or else a willful, capricious giant paying little heed to U.S.-Japanese relations as it pursued matters of current preoccupation. The communist victory in Indochina in April 1975 raised further concerns about the American security commitment.

All of these uncertainties seem related to a deeper change in the international economic and political structure, for the U.S.-Japanese alliance of the fifties and sixties flourished under circumstances that clearly no longer exist. The American policy of isolating and containing China then made the Japanese connection, and Japanese bases, critically important; they seem less crucial in a multipolar world. Until the 1960s the Japanese economy had limited impact internationally, so that remarkably effective growth and export policies could be pursued— and encouraged by the United States—without threatening the domestic markets of too many American industries; now the sheer size of Japan's economy demands attention to how its domestic policies affect the international order. Furthermore, the oil embargo of 1973 and the ensuing fourfold oil price increase illustrated dramatically the limitations of American ability and determination to protect Japan from her economic vulnerabilities, and resulted inevitably in differing national policy responses. Obviously, the U.S.-Japanese relationship must be reshaped to fit the new realities, to manage and mediate economic rivalry, to maintain basic trust and mutual confidence while independent overtures to third powers are being undertaken by both sides. By 1975, leaders in both countries were showing sensitivity to this requirement, recognizing both the value and the vulnerability of the relationship. But there remains the ever-present need to translate such general predispositions into concrete, mutually beneficial cooperation within an altered world environment.

An important determinant of the future of the relationship will be how the American and Japanese governments deal with one another on the major policy issues that arise between them. Ideally, the actions of each should be based on careful, rational calculations of the impact of such actions on the other and the other's likely response. But powerful political facts of life work against this—the inevitable existence of other policy goals that compete with good U.S.-Japanese relations; the dispersion of power within the two governments and societies that makes coherent central policies difficult for leaders to achieve whatever their priorities may be. Thus the major foreign policy actions that emerge from both governments have their roots in politics at home, both bureaucratic politics within each government and the broader national interplay labeled domestic politics.[1] The politics of U.S.-Japanese relations involves far more than the direct dealings of Japanese and American officials with one another. Constructive U.S.-Japanese relations require far more than mutual understanding and effective

1. While this book is not an explicit effort to determine either the utility or the limitations of the bureaucratic politics approach to the study of foreign policy, our basic orientation owes much to works such as Graham Allison, *Essence of Decision: Explaining the Cuban Missile Crisis* (Little, Brown, 1971); and Morton H. Halperin with the assistance of Priscilla Clapp and Arnold Kanter, *Bureaucratic Politics and Foreign Policy* (Brookings Institution, 1974). Like those writers, we consider politics and decisionmaking inside each government as part of a broader national political process, and in our study we give considerable attention to such broader domestic politics. On this general point, see Halperin, *Bureaucratic Politics*, pp. 4–5.

communication between the officials who specialize in maintaining them. For these officials must also work within their own governments and societies to reach solutions to particular problems that will have sufficient domestic support. Otherwise, officials with quite different perspectives and priorities are likely to gain the upper hand.

In the dispute over textiles in 1969–71, for example, the objectives of industrialists and their government supporters came to dominate the bilateral negotiating process. Those in Washington who argued for compromise in order to avoid a disruption of bilateral relations could not win the support of the President, who was determined to honor his pledge to protect the U.S. textile industry against the influx of Japanese synthetic and wool textiles. Those whom the President assigned to negotiate textile quotas with the Japanese had little stake in the objective of maintaining good relations with Japan and even less sensitivity to the fact that a demanding American approach was likely to stiffen Japanese resistance. Thus in 1969, instead of using quiet diplomacy with Japan to pursue his objective of textile quotas, the American official in charge of the issue, Secretary of Commerce Maurice Stans, led a highly visible mission to Europe seeking to line up support for a multilateral agreement aimed at Asian textile products. Inevitably Japanese national pride was aroused, and when Stans arrived in Tokyo a month later to deal directly with Japanese negotiators he was greeted with a unanimous Diet resolution opposing an agreement on textile quotas, as well as by a foreign minister whose opening statement expressed official unwillingness to discuss the problem.

Why were American official actions of the sort that would trigger the very kinds of Japanese policy responses that U.S. officials wished to avoid? U.S. tactics did not, of course, create the substantive difference between the two governments. The fact that Nixon wanted thoroughgoing quotas and Japanese leaders no more than a very loose restrictive arrangement was bound to make resolution difficult. But why transform textiles from a tough negotiating problem into a confrontation before negotiations had even begun, and a confrontation, moreover, with an atypically unified and unusually adamant coalition of Japanese actors and interests? How might American officials have done better? Could they have understood enough about Japanese politics and decisionmaking to facilitate U.S. policy choices aimed at resolving or preventing crisis rather than precipitating it? Or were Japanese politics and decisionmaking too alien, too "Oriental" for Westerners to comprehend?

Do Japanese decisionmakers do any better in understanding the U.S. system, or in shaping their actions consciously to affect it? Or are officials in each country so preoccupied with the politics of their own system that they have no time to comprehend the other? If so, then how does one explain the successes like Okinawa reversion?

For even as the secretary of commerce was bringing the textile issue to a point of confrontation with Japan, U.S. and Japanese officials were reaching an amicable agreement in principle to return Okinawa to full Japanese sovereignty. Indeed the Okinawa question in itself was more complex and held greater potential for creating bilateral animosity than textiles. The Okinawa question reached far more deeply into Japanese politics and national consciousness than textiles and held crucial implications to Japanese for the sincerity of American professions of partnership and alliance. Until 1967, the American government had consistently held a more rigid and less compromising position on the Okinawa issue than it had on earlier negotiations for textile quotas. How was a satisfactory settlement reached? Why would the two governments allow an interest as narrow as textiles (a modest and declining portion of the total trade relationship and the two domestic economies) to diminish the gains for the alliance which reversion was bringing?

These are the types of problems this book seeks to address. Although it does not assume that adequate official American understanding of Japanese politics and policymaking—or vice versa—would in itself resolve difficult policy issues, it does assume that misunderstanding is likely to compound the real problems that already exist. Although it does not claim that improving the process of U.S.-Japanese relations would in itself eliminate the significant substantive differences that are bound to arise, it does rest on the belief that how communications and negotiations between the two countries are handled will affect the prospects for relatively expeditious and amicable resolutions of substantive differences that arise in the future, just as it has in the past.

Chapter 2 introduces the three main cases that are used illustratively throughout the book. These three cases—the revision of the security treaty, the reversion of Okinawa, and the textile dispute—span a twenty-year period and required the attention of both governments at all levels. Chapter 3 opens our more general discussion by focusing on the national political and bureaucratic institutions through which policy decisions and actions are taken. Here the emphasis falls overwhelmingly on Japan, since we are writing mainly for Americans who are already familiar with their own system. One important purpose of the chapter is to demonstrate that many of the institutional differences can be explained by political concepts and variables with which Americans are very familiar. The general discussion moves next, in chapter 4, to a consideration of how officials in each government tend to perceive actions taken by the other—and particularly to recurrent patterns of misperceptions. Some of these seem common to any bilateral relationship between large, complex democracies. Others, however, stem from cultural differences and, in treating them, we give attention to elements of Japanese culture that seem particularly prone to American misunderstanding.

Chapter 5 takes a more comprehensive look at the interplay between the two governments. Here our focus is on the origin and communication of initiatives, the types of negotiating channels brought into play, and some of the ways that actions by actors in one system have an impact on decisionmaking in the other—whether or not the effect is intended. For example, we examine how the specific steps that officials in one country take can strengthen or weaken potential allies in the other.

And finally, in chapter 6, we develop and summarize our conclusions and our policy recommendations. Here we continue to focus particularly on U.S. relations with Japan. But we organize our analysis so as to indicate which of our findings might also be applicable to other U.S. relationships with large allies.

In basing our study on a set of specific cases, we inevitably oversimplify some of the negotiating problems involved. Managing the relationship requires more than resolving individual, bilateral negotiating issues; actors on both sides are always involved in a range of U.S.-Japan issues at the same time, bilateral and multilateral, with each affecting the others. Indeed, the U.S.-Japan relationship itself cannot be fully understood outside its broader international context; the recent oil crisis, and the Japanese government's tilt toward the Arab countries, diverging sharply from the U.S. stance, is a case in point. But focusing on bilateral issues helped make our research manageable, and simplifies the presentation of the analysis. Furthermore, a look at the postwar record will show such specific cases have been very important in shaping broader U.S.-Japan dealings in the past. Chapter 6 includes our argument for the relevance of our findings to current multilateral issues as well.

Another kind of problem arises from the potential evolution of Japanese policymaking. Postwar policies have been shaped by conservative, Liberal Democratic party (LDP) cabinets working with senior bureaucrats who shared their general assumptions about international issues. The cases we have studied all reflect this pattern. If the LDP were to lose its diminished Diet majority, and especially if a Socialist-Communist coalition were to take power, this pattern would undergo major change, much more fundamental than shifts between parties in the United States. It would affect many of the specific institutional relationships analyzed in this study. Nevertheless, even in the case of sharp leadership shifts, an understanding of the institutions currently dominant would be important for predicting and interpreting the institutional changes most likely to occur under basic political change. In the more probable case of either a continuing LDP majority government or a trend toward LDP-led coalitions, the future would bear much greater resemblance to the present.

Finally, for the reader close to policymaking in either government, our single-minded focus on the U.S.-Japan relationship may seem a bit artificial, since actors in both countries necessarily have to take account of other values as well. We recognize, of course, that no U.S. president and no Japanese prime minister could adopt this focus in its absolute form—there is no reason, after all, why the claims of "good U.S.-Japanese relations" should take priority in every case over other policy interests and goals of groups and governments. Indeed, the very existence of substantive differences that need to be resolved attests to the importance of these other goals and interests. Yet constructive overall U.S.-Japanese relations are an important goal, fully worthy of an analysis of how they can be politically and procedurally advanced. Thus for purposes of this book, we are only secondarily concerned with the specific substance of particular U.S.-Japan questions—what types of export or import quotas there should be, if any; what changes should take place, if any, in security obligations and arrangements. Instead, we seek to emphasize how the way these issues are perceived and managed by influential policy actors in both countries can affect the prospects for mutually acceptable resolutions.

CHAPTER TWO

Three Postwar Cases

THREE MAJOR postwar negotiations illustrate the interplay between domestic politics and U.S.-Japanese relations: revision of the bilateral security treaty (completed in 1960); the reversion of Okinawan administrative rights to Japan (agreed to in 1969); and the dispute over quotas for Japanese textile exports to the United States (resolved in 1971). Each became a major political issue between the two countries. Each involved not only dealings between foreign offices, but struggles over national politics and policy in Tokyo and Washington.

Security treaty revision and Okinawa reversion were both deeply significant bilateral issues involving Japan's basic alignment in world politics and her territorial integrity. The public demonstrations and political turmoil surrounding ratification of the revised security treaty in 1960 were unprecedented in postwar Japan. The policy community in Washington was surprised at the depth of controversy in Japan over an alliance that Americans saw as so generous and beneficial.

The lessons of the treaty revision remained in the minds of policymakers in Washington and Tokyo as they began to grapple with the highly complex problem of Okinawa several years later. To Japanese, Okinawa represented the unresolved status of Japanese sovereignty, a reminder of the war and defeat, an anachronism in times of surging Japanese economic power and renewed national pride. To Americans, Okinawa was a thorny security problem. As a sprawling collection of bases had developed on the island, so had the attitude that American administrative control was essential to maintaining the bases. There was significant resistance in Washington to the idea of compromising larger U.S.

security interests simply for the sake of returning to Japan the administrative rights over a few outlying islands. It took a long, complex process of domestic bargaining—on both sides—to recast the issue and reach an equitable solution that averted repetition of the 1960 crisis.[1]

The textile dispute, by contrast, was significant not because of what was directly at stake, but because of the political crisis it provoked. In substance it was a market struggle between two declining national textile industries carried out through their governments. But its resolution became equated with the commitment and effectiveness of the two countries' top leaders. Because this dispute coincided with a series of dazzling Japanese economic successes, it tended to reinforce American perceptions that Japanese economic advances were rapidly becoming a threat to American interests. And frustrations arising from this particular negotiation were an important cause of the shock treatment applied to Japan by the Nixon administration in 1971.[2]

Together these three cases provide a convenient means of exploring nearly a twenty-year span in the postwar U.S.-Japanese relationship. The histories of all three overlap, most significantly those of Okinawa reversion and textiles. A description of how each arose and was resolved affords a view of the politics of U.S.-Japanese relations and the general perspectives of each country during the postwar period. But our purpose in describing them here is less to offer history for its own sake than to build a foundation for the chapters that follow. In our subsequent efforts to generalize about the politics of U.S.-Japanese relations, we shall draw mainly—though not exclusively—on these three cases for illustrative examples and supporting evidence. And introducing the cases at this point has one further purpose. While they are interesting as self-contained stories, many of their specific episodes are difficult to understand without the broader analysis of policymaking patterns and interaction that follows. Thus we hope that their presentation will both establish the need for such analysis and develop the reader's interest in the questions that analysis will treat.

1. The discussion of Okinawa in this study is drawn from Priscilla Clapp and Haruhiro Fukui, "Decisionmaking in U.S.-Japanese Relations: Okinawa Reversion" (1976; processed).

2. The discussion of the textile dispute in this study is drawn from I. M. Destler, Hideo Sato, and Haruhiro Fukui, "The Textile Wrangle: Conflict in Japanese-American Relations 1969–71" (1976; processed).

The Postwar Setting

On September 8, 1951, Japan and forty-eight other nations affixed signatures to a treaty of peace ending the state of war that had existed officially for nearly ten years. The set of understandings and agreements that evolved between the United States and Japan as a prelude to the peace settlement did much to define the relationship between the two countries for the next twenty years. The peace settlement was nonpunitive (and economically supportive) by design, and these generous terms helped foster bonds of alliance and friendship between the former enemies. But Japan was compelled to sacrifice certain areas of sovereignty to accommodate American security interests, and the unusual arrangements devised for the purpose became sources of domestic resentment and friction in Japan.

For American leaders—as President Truman instructed his special negotiator John Foster Dulles in January 1951—the principal purpose of the peace settlement was to "secure the adherence of the Japanese nation to the free nations of the world, and to assure that it will play its full part in resisting the further expansion of Communist imperialism."[3] To this end, Dulles won the acquiescence of other World War II allies to Japan's reentry into the international community, despite their preference for strong reparations requirements and other sanctions. And the United States worked in the ensuing years to open access to world markets for the Japanese, whose products had been discriminated against before the war. The United States sponsored and pressed the case for Japan's membership in the postwar General Agreement on Tariffs and Trade (GATT) structure aimed at nondiscriminatory international commerce.

The United States also negotiated a mutual security treaty with the Japanese, which came into effect simultaneously with the peace treaty. Dulles's goal here was an alliance modeled on the principles of the North Atlantic Treaty Organization, with each member contributing to the common defense according to its abilities. During the initial stages, Japanese security would be guaranteed by the continued presence of American forces in Japan, but Japan would rebuild its own forces as

3. Quoted in Townsend Hoopes, *The Devil and John Foster Dulles* (Little, Brown, 1973), p. 105.

rapidly as possible to replace and augment American strength. Japan's eventual contribution would be toward insuring the security of neighboring Asian countries. But for a Japan still reeling from the devastation of war and the psychological agony of national self-recrimination, that was an unwelcome prospect. Dulles soon modified his demand for immediate large-scale rearmament not only in response to the pleas of the Japanese premier, but under pressure from nervous Asian allies and dissenters within the American government. He settled for assurance from Prime Minister Shigeru Yoshida that Japan would undertake a gradual program of rearmament within the limits of economic capability and constitutional law.[4] In turn, the United States withheld an explicit commitment to Japan's security and pressed other provisions on Japan limiting its sovereignty.

Japanese territorial jurisdiction also fell victim to the pressing American concern for security. With the outbreak of the Korean War and the subsequent American commitment to that war, the American bases on Okinawa, like those in Japan, became active staging centers. There was a general feeling in Washington that continued U.S. administrative control over Okinawa and other outlying Japanese islands would prove a valuable strategic asset in the long run. Japanese officials were understandably concerned that these territories not be permanently separated from Japan, although they may have recognized the strategic significance of the Okinawa bases. To satisfy the long-run interests of harmony with Japan and, at the same time, retain the flexibility of the Okinawa bases afforded by direct American administrative control, Dulles devised a unique formula whereby Japan would retain "residual sovereignty" over the outlying islands. When and if the islands would return to full Japanese sovereignty were questions to be answered by future generations.

Finally, with the division of China under a communist Peking government and a nationalist Taipei government there arose the question of which to include in the San Francisco peace conference as signatory to

4. Article Nine of Japan's constitution stipulates: "Aspiring sincerely to an international peace based on justice and order, the Japanese people forever renounce war as a sovereign right of the nation and the threat or use of force as a means of settling international disputes. In order to accomplish the aim of the preceding paragraph, land, sea, and air forces, as well as other war potential, will never be maintained. The right of belligerency of the state will not be recognized." However, this language has been construed by postwar governments as permitting the creation of limited military forces for self-defense.

the treaty with Japan. The United States was, by 1951, heavily committed against Peking. Great Britain, however, had recognized the
communist regime and favored her participation in the settlement. It was
decided that neither China would be invited and Japan would be left to
settle the question of peace with China later. However, the powerful
pro-Nationalist China lobby in the U.S. Congress was not satisfied with
this disposition of the issue and demanded assurances from Japan that
it would indeed conclude a peace treaty with the Taipei government.
Against his preference that Japan take a less committed position on the
China question, Prime Minister Yoshida acceded to Dulles's request for
assurances that would satisfy Congress. To have refused would have
jeopardized Senate ratification of the peace treaty. On April 28, 1952,
the day such ratification took place, Japanese officials signed a separate
peace treaty with Nationalist China. This episode came to symbolize
American unreadiness to accept the normalization of Japanese relations
with mainland China. It symbolized also Japan's dependence on the
United States, the asymmetry of the relationship which colored all three
of the postwar cases treated here.

Revision of the Security Treaty

The revised security treaty signed in January 1960 was the product of
the first major postwar negotiation between Japan and the United
States, and American officials tended to view it as a demonstration to
Japan of American faith in the alliance. The negotiation had been primarily aimed at meeting conditions of mutuality that Japanese leaders
had argued were essential for their country's security and sovereignty.
These conditions had apparently been satisfied, and the new treaty had
the approval of a political majority in Tokyo. Why, in the months after
its signing, was the opposition so successful in using the treaty to create
an extreme political crisis in Japan? As surprising to many Americans as
the furor of the storm was the rapidity with which it faded after mid-
year. Conservatives consolidated their rule and gained in subsequent
elections; the U.S. alliance survived intact, if not strengthened.

The origins of the 1960 crisis lie, at least partially, in the terms of the
security treaty included in the peace package of 1951. Because of American disappointment over Japan's contributions to free world defense,
there were no explicit provisions for mutual security: the United States

was "presently *willing* to maintain certain of its armed forces in and about Japan," forces which "*may* be utilized to contribute to the maintenance of the international peace and security . . . in the Far East . . . and to the security of Japan against armed attack from without."[5] Indeed, the treaty even authorized the use of these U.S. forces, "at the express request of the Japanese government," to control externally instigated insurrection within Japan. There were no other provisions for mutual consultation on the deployment or use of U.S. forces in Japan, except whatever "conditions" might be "determined by administrative agreements." The treaty also called upon Japan "increasingly [to] assume responsibility for its own defense against direct and indirect aggression," and it prohibited Japan from granting any base rights to a third power without the consent of the United States. In sum, the treaty was—for the Japanese—only a modest step from occupation. And it was very different from other security treaties concluded by the United States in the forties and fifties.

The small circle of Japanese politicians and officials who negotiated the security treaty nonetheless favored a security arrangement with the United States because they shared, to some extent, American concern about the communist threat in Asia, particularly the possibility of a communist victory in South Korea. They accepted the continued presence of American forces in or around Japan as a means of guaranteeing Japanese security against such an external threat. In return for this guarantee, they were willing to allow American bases to be used to guarantee the larger security of Asia. For them, this contribution to the free world cause was a reasonable quid pro quo for an explicit American commitment to ensure Japanese security, which would provide the basis for a *mutual* security pact.

American leaders, on the other hand, particularly John Foster Dulles, viewed mutual security fundamentally as a parallel commitment by two or more governments to the defense of each other. This implied parallel contributions by each country, according to ability, in material resources and explicit concern for collective defense. What the Japanese viewed as their contribution to mutuality—commitment to the free world and the provision of Japanese bases—Americans did not consider equal or parallel to their own contribution. Under the Japanese equation, the

5. For the text of the treaty, see Martin E. Weinstein, *Japan's Postwar Defense Policy, 1947–1968* (Columbia University Press, 1971), pp. 137–38. Emphasis added.

United States would be providing most of the resources for Japanese security. As long as Japan was unwilling to contribute materially to collective security or to make an explicit commitment to the security of its neighbors, Americans could see no justification for offering a comprehensive guarantee for Japan's security. Even if American officials could grasp the significance and intrinsic value of the Japanese quid pro quo, they felt they could never convince Congress, which was always looking for the direct return on dollars spent. Thus the same Dulles who had negotiated the security treaty continued to press for major Japanese rearmament after he became President Eisenhower's secretary of state. On at least one occasion he even disparaged Japanese defense efforts by comparing the size of her forces with those in neighboring South Korea, which had been fighting a war for three years.[6] For Dulles and most Americans, however, that war underscored the fundamental struggle between the free world and its communist adversaries; and they saw the strengthening of anticommunist military forces in Europe and Asia as essential because of that struggle.

Japanese leaders were fearful of undertaking rearmament so soon after the war, not only because of the memories of Japan's prewar expansionism it would evoke among its Asian neighbors, but because of the intolerable domestic division it would create. Premier Yoshida and his advisers knew that to commit Japan to the level of rearmament that Dulles had requested in 1951 would cause enough of a drain on reconstruction to cause widespread social unrest. Furthermore, rearmament might lead to a revival of Japanese militarism, if it were undertaken so quickly that the prewar generation of military officers had to be brought back to power. There might be international economic repercussions as well. If other countries, particularly Asian neighbors, saw Japan rebuilding its military machine to become the strong partner in an Asian collective security arrangement, they would be reluctant to provide the markets and raw materials on which Japan's economic reconstruction depended. For this would awaken memories of the prewar Japanese scheme for a Greater East Asian Co-Prosperity Sphere.

Even the quid pro quo defined by Japanese governmental leaders met considerable domestic opposition. There was broad support for Japanese neutrality in international relations, extending beyond the So-

6. See John M. Allison, *Ambassador from the Prairie: or Allison Wonderland* (Houghton Mifflin, 1973), p. 242.

cialist and Communist party opposition to include many articulate intellectuals. Advocates of neutrality saw a commitment to the free world as increasing the risk that Japan would be needlessly drawn into conflict—either directly or by implication. At the very least, such a commitment would seriously inhibit Japanese relations with communist countries. And it was hard for conservatives to counter the argument that American bases in Japan were simply a revised form of American occupation, for in substance the security treaty seemed little more than an arrangement for continued stationing of U.S. troops. Thus any Japanese government, no matter how it defined the international situation and Japan's security needs, would pay a domestic political price for a security treaty with the United States.

The gap in approaches to the security relationship was dramatically illustrated when three senior Japanese leaders met with John Foster Dulles in August 1955, carrying with them Prime Minister Ichiro Hatoyama's request for revision of the security treaty. They cited domestic discontent with Japan's "unequal" status under the 1951 arrangement, and argued that without changes Japan's conservatives would be hard pressed to stay in power. Dulles sternly rejected their request and apparently lectured them on Japan's refusal to make a significant contribution to regional defense.[7] At the conclusion of the discussion Foreign Minister Shigemitsu signed a joint communiqué committing Japan "to contribute to the preservation of international peace and security in the Western Pacific." In Japan the Hatoyama government was quickly accused by both conservative and opposition politicians of violating Japanese law and the constitution by agreeing to such a commitment. And the government found it necessary to deny that this was the intention of the communiqué, forcing Shigemitsu to retreat from the position he had taken in Washington.

Nevertheless, substantial policy adjustments by both governments were already under way. The United States had begun reducing the number of troops stationed in Japan; they dropped from almost 200,000 in late 1954 to about 90,000 in December 1956. Successive Japanese governments had been taking significant strides toward rearmament. In

7. Interview, Ichirō Kōno, a member of the delegation, Sept. 30, 1964 (Dulles Oral History Library, Princeton University). See also Asahi Shimbun Staff, *The Pacific Rivals: A Japanese View of Japanese-American Relations* (Weatherhill/Asahi, 1972), pp. 231–32; Allison, *Ambassador from the Prairie*, pp. 266–67; and Dan Kurzman, *Kishi and Japan: The Search for the Sun* (Obolensky, 1960), p. 288.

1952 the National Police Reserve, which had been formed by the American occupation to assume responsibility for internal security, was reorganized (with the Maritime Safety Force) into a National Security Force and designated for gradual expansion. In 1954, legislation was passed to establish national Self-Defense Forces, composed of separate ground, air, and naval arms. Their authorized strength reached 214,182 men by late 1956,[8] well under the 350,000 that Dulles continued to seek, but a substantial rise nonetheless. By 1957, moreover, the Japanese and U.S. governments had reached a series of understandings on limitations to the security treaty that were not contained in the document itself. Generally, these understandings evolved from consultations between the two governments on details about the deployment and use of U.S. forces in Japan which had not been made explicit in the security treaty or administrative agreement.

Even more important for the security relationship, however, was the adjustment in Japan to postoccupation self-government. With the release of those prewar leaders who had been purged from political activity during the occupation, the number of competing forces within the Japanese conservative leadership increased dramatically. Prime Minister Yoshida was forced to resign in late 1954 with the advent of renewed factional rivalry. Almost overnight the task of rising to and maintaining the position of prime minister became an incredibly complex problem of balancing factional coalitions and outmaneuvering numerous actual and would-be rivals. Conservative politicians aspiring to party leadership would seize upon salient foreign policy issues, safely removed from immediate domestic impact or informed public scrutiny, to gain valuable publicity and an advantage over their competitors.

Such maneuvering was evident in the August 1955 delegation to Washington. It was apparently a device for Prime Minister Hatoyama to demonstrate concern about the security arrangements to his domestic audience; if he could initiate revision of the treaty it would be an additional political plum. Because the senior Japanese representative in the delegation, Foreign Minister Shigemitsu, was not considered forceful enough to impress American leaders with Japan's position, Hatoyama had asked Nobusuke Kishi, chairman of the ruling Democratic party, to accompany Shigemitsu. Kishi was reluctant to appear in Washington

8. This and U.S. troop figures are from Weinstein, *Japan's Postwar Defense Policy*, p. 77.

as Shigemitsu's aide, because he already saw himself as a contender for top leadership. But he agreed to go in return for Hatoyama's endorsement of his campaign for merger of the two conservative parties, the Democrats and the Liberals, which Kishi saw as enhancing his premiership prospects.[9]

And indeed, Kishi did rise in early 1957 to the presidency of the newly consolidated Liberal Democratic party.[10] He was now clearly the strongest of the conservative leaders. He was certainly not the most popular, however, either within the party or with the public more generally. He was openly contemptuous of the press, and the dislike was reciprocated. His maneuvering within the party to advance and solidify his own position did not win him the affection of his conservative colleagues. And his identification with the prewar Japanese government (he had been minister of commerce in the Tōjō cabinet and was subsequently jailed as a war criminal) made him an easy target for an opposition seeking to arouse public anxiety about his "undemocratic" behavior. Kishi seems to have felt that only through personal forcefulness could he lead the nation in the direction he calculated to be best. But among other Japanese political actors there was an undercurrent of suspicion that whatever Kishi was pushing was more directly relevant to his own personal advancement than to the national interest.

Kishi addressed the security treaty question directly at his first press conference as prime minister: "From the point of view of national sentiment, the Japanese people desire that the present security treaty and administrative agreement between Japan and the United States should be abolished."[11] Those arrangements had become the more irritating as Japan recovered her economic strength and national self-confidence. The large number of American troops in Japan was causing multiple frictions with the local population and providing a constant

9. Kurzman, *Kishi and Japan*, p. 288. Kishi further used the Washington trip to push his cause when he returned to Tokyo, by arguing that only conservative unification would make it possible for Japan to improve its relations with the United States.

10. The Liberal and Democratic parties managed to effect a merger in November 1955. In December 1956, Tanzan Ishibashi narrowly defeated Kishi for the LDP presidency, and thus succeeded Hatoyama as prime minister. Kishi, who had been appointed deputy prime minister and foreign minister, took over two months later when Ishibashi was forced by illness to resign. Kishi was formally elected party president in March 1957.

11. As cited in George Packard III, *Protest in Tokyo* (Princeton University Press, 1966), p. 44.

reminder of defeat and occupation. Yet as far as the public could see, Yoshida's security treaty gave Japan no choice in the matter. Although there was no single mind on how best to achieve security, there appears to have been a consensus that the treaty was a temporary device, which must eventually be revised or eliminated, and that it was highly undesirable to become involved in an alliance that would bring Japan into conflict where its own interests were not at stake.[12]

In moving to take the matter up with the American government, Kishi had reason to presume that he might make headway. The substantial increase in size of the Japanese Self-Defense Forces under the Hatoyama government was practical evidence of Japan's awareness of and contribution to its own defense needs. Furthermore, Kishi had spent considerable effort before his ascendancy to convince American officials of his own commitment to a strong U.S.-Japanese alliance (as well as to educate them to the realities of what was and was not politically acceptable in Japan). Moreover, there had emerged within the U.S. government a strong, increasingly influential opposition to the Dulles-Pentagon stress on maximum Japanese military effort. Officials concerned with Japan at the U.S. embassy in Tokyo and the State Department in Washington argued for modification of the stern Dulles conditions. They developed a more political approach to the Japanese alliance, identifying U.S.-Japanese relations with the future of Kishi and the new Liberal Democratic party, favoring steps that might strengthen them domestically. Under their influence, Dulles personally seems to have softened his stance by the spring of 1957. Thus when Kishi traveled to Washington to meet President Eisenhower in June 1957, the situation was far more propitious than it had proved two years earlier.

For Japan the most important result of the 1957 summit meeting was mutual recognition of the "understanding that the Security Treaty of 1951 was designed to be transitional in character and not in that form to remain in perpetuity." Furthermore, a joint committee was established "to study problems arising in relation to the Security Treaty," which, as Kishi pointed out after his return to Japan, did not exclude matters relating to revision.[13] In return, Premier Kishi recognized the "major threat"

12. Ibid., pp. 31–32.
13. For his own purposes, Secretary of State Dulles indicated that revision was not in fact under way and that the joint committee had not been established expressly for revision of the treaty. Needless to say, Kishi was confronted with Dulles's comments at home.

of international communism and acknowledged the "deterrent power of the free world" in preventing aggression in Asia. Although the prime minister may actually have hoped to achieve an American commitment to revision at the summit meeting, from the American perspective an agreement in principle would not be possible until there was clear mutual understanding of the specific issues involved. Kishi himself has acknowledged a conversation with Secretary of State Dulles—probably during this visit—in which they discussed the pros and cons of merely amending the current treaty to avoid the legislative process or going ahead with full revision and accepting the political consequences. The latter course was taken.[14]

A year later Foreign Minister Aiichiro Fujiyama began discussions with American Ambassador Douglas MacArthur II that were clearly preliminary to an explicit plan for negotiation. In September 1958, Fujiyama and Dulles officially agreed to undertake negotiations, and talks began in Tokyo. At this point, however, factionalism within the Liberal Democratic party forced Kishi to suspend official negotiations until he reestablished his position and developed some base of agreement among party leaders. Although none of his LDP colleagues and rivals were taking a stand against revision of the treaty, several publicly criticized details in the government's approach. This apparently was more a reflection of anti-Kishi feeling and factional rivalry than of deep conviction, but the effect was to delay progress in the negotiations and force Kishi to spend considerable time building consensus and buttressing his strength within the party. Clear party unity was never achieved on the terms of revision and the continuing intraparty struggle sapped Kishi's power over time and left him at a psychological disadvantage in the matter of treaty revision. "The treaty was clearly to be his 'last act' as far as all the other LDP leaders were concerned."[15]

Debate within the LDP seems also to have increased the broader public anxiety about the American alliance, an anxiety that the opposi-

14. Interview, Nobusuke Kishi, Oct. 2, 1964 (Dulles Oral History Library, Princeton University). When the revision question was formally raised the first American response was to suggest three possibilities: (1) a simple base-lease agreement; (2) amendment of the current treaty; and (3) a new treaty. Kishi apparently chose the third over the advice of the Foreign Ministry that amendment was preferable because there would be strong popular resistance to a new treaty. (See Packard, *Protest in Tokyo*, p. 70.) Similar differences arose between Sato and the Foreign Ministry on Okinawa reversion several years later.

15. Packard, *Protest in Tokyo*, p. 81.

tion parties both reflected and fanned. Premier Hatoyama had struck a responsive public chord by negotiating a peace agreement with the Soviet Union in 1956; many Japanese favored a similar opening toward China and saw the American alliance as the major roadblock. The late fifties, moreover, was a period of recurrent cold war tension—over Berlin and across the Taiwan straits. The latter were patrolled by the U.S. Seventh Fleet, and a Japan tied to the United States could in no way assume a neutral position. Not only did it look more likely that military alliance with the United States might draw Japan into useless conflict, but the strength of the Soviet Union seemed clearly on the rise and the United States no longer looked like an unassailable protector. Thus, even as Japanese negotiators were winning major concessions from the Americans, a deeper Japanese uneasiness with the U.S. relationship persisted and grew.

In January 1960, Kishi flew to Washington to sign the revised treaty negotiated by Foreign Minister Fujiyama and Ambassador MacArthur over the previous fifteen months. In substance, the premier could claim considerable achievement. The new treaty was fully mutual in form, with each party committed to join in resisting "armed attack against either Party in the territories under the administration of Japan." Japan did not have to assume any broader collective security responsibilities in the region. The condescending tone of the earlier agreement was not duplicated, nor were its specific infringements on Japanese sovereignty. And in an exchange of diplomatic notes accompanying the treaty, agreement was reached on a "prior consultation" formula: "Major changes in the deployment into Japan of United States armed forces, major changes in the equipment, and the use of facilities and areas in Japan as bases for military combat operations to be undertaken from Japan other than those conducted under Article V [in response to an attack against Japan], of the said Treaty, shall be the subjects of prior consultation with the Government of Japan."[16] To symbolize the new relationship, it was announced that President Eisenhower and Crown Prince Akihito would exchange state visits, with the President to arrive in Tokyo the following June.

The treaty was submitted to the Diet for ratification in April and it became the subject of renewed debate. The responses of Prime Minister

16. Weinstein, *Japan's Postwar Defense Policy*, p. 96. For the text of the treaty, see ibid., pp. 139–41.

Kishi and his cabinet to opposition questions only exacerbated the tension. When the Socialist party disrupted the Diet session in order to stall ratification, Kishi counterattacked on May 19 with a series of maneuvers that resulted in ratification of the treaty by the LDP members of the lower house, in the absence of the opposition members.[17] Under the Japanese constitution, this meant that the treaty would automatically take effect thirty days thereafter—the precise day of Eisenhower's planned arrival in Japan. The whole sequence looked a little too clever to be publicly acceptable. Widespread anger focused on Kishi, "whose insolence," in the words of a Japanese observer, "typified the worst aspects of prewar bureaucracy."[18] Not a few critics saw Kishi's arbitrary exploitation of his Diet majority and failure to take heed of opposition concerns as threats to Japanese democracy. Demonstrators, urged on by Communist and Socialist opposition, descended in ever-increasing numbers on Kishi and the Diet building. Their objective quickly became the cancellation of Eisenhower's visit.

In part, this was due to unhappiness with the treaty, but even more, it was anti-Kishi. The Eisenhower visit became the test-crucible of the premier's tenure in office. Not only did Kishi himself so identify it, but the opposition and the demonstrators also did and began planning for disruption of the visit as the ultimate means to discredit Kishi. When Eisenhower's press secretary, James Hagerty, led an advance party on June 10 to make final preparations, the limousine taking him from the airport was surrounded by a crowd that trapped Hagerty for about an hour before he could be rescued by helicopter. Nonetheless, Kishi remained determined to welcome Eisenhower, and neither the U.S. embassy nor the White House seemed to wish a postponement.

For the embassy, the problem was partly protocol—it was the Japanese government's responsibility to protect a state visitor, or to request a postponement if it could not do so. A cable from Ambassador Mac-Arthur shortly after the lower house action argued that "it would be great mistake for President to take initiative in postponing his visit to Japan," though a change in timing might be acceptable if "initiative be

17. Opposition members of the Diet had tried physically to keep the speaker of the lower house in his office so that he could not initiate a vote on the treaty ratification before the time ran out on that Diet session. They were removed from the building bodily by the police and when the vote was initiated, they did not know the Diet had reconvened. The majority LDP members, however, were present and voted for ratification.

18. Quoted in Packard, *Protest in Tokyo*, p. 246.

that of GOJ [Government of Japan]."[19] But the embassy's support of
the Kishi government encouraged sticking with the trip on policy
grounds as well, especially since cancellation would damage both national leaders. And MacArthur feared that if the Kishi government were
to collapse, final ratification of the new security treaty would be "very
seriously jeopardized"[20] (though all that was now legally required was
that the Diet remain in session for thirty days after May 19). And if
treaty ratification were thus blocked, it would be "the greatest victory
communists could gain in Asia" and a devastating blow to Japanese
democracy.[21] Thus for the embassy, persevering with the Eisenhower
visit was essential to hold the line against communist encroachment in
Asia.

President Eisenhower also remained ready to proceed. He wanted
to end his career as president on a note of international peace and a
reconfirmation of the strength of the free world alliance. Thus in 1959
he had embarked on a series of state visits that would take him to Asian
and European allies and also, he had hoped, to the Soviet Union. The
visit to Tokyo would be the most important stop on his Asian itinerary.
Then, in May 1960, the Russian invitation was dramatically withdrawn
after an American U-2 plane was shot down over Russia. Eisenhower
did not wish a second such public humiliation, and when he left on
June 12 for the Philippines—his first Far Eastern stop—he hoped that
the Tokyo visit would still be possible. But on June 15 the Tokyo
demonstrations provoked a major battle between police and demonstrators, during which a young woman student was crushed to death. Despite
the fact that Japanese public opinion was now moving against the left,
Kishi concluded that the President's safety could not be guaranteed;
indeed, Kishi himself could not move about freely. So on June 16 in
Manila, Eisenhower learned that the invitation had been withdrawn.

A week after the cancellation, Premier Kishi resigned. The wave of
public emotion and demonstrations in Tokyo quickly subsided, and the
conservatives actually made gains in the Diet elections the following
November. Controversy over the security treaty also receded into the

19. Cable no. 3825, U.S. Embassy, Tokyo, to Secretary of State (eyes only),
May 25, 1960. This is one of a number of State Department documents on the
period declassified in 1975 under the Freedom of Information Act.

20. Cable no. 3798, U.S. Embassy, Tokyo, to Secretary of State, May 23, 1960.

21. Ibid.; and cable no. 4017, U.S. Embassy, Tokyo, to Secretary of State, June
4, 1960.

background and Japanese politicians, both conservative and opposition, expressed regret that the crisis in Tokyo had taken on such a strong tone of anti-Americanism.

The initial White House comment on the cancellation of Eisenhower's trip was "that a small organized minority, led by professional Communist agitators acting under external direction and control, have been able by resort to force and violence to prevent his good-will visit."[22] Later, a more subtle interpretation began to emerge at higher levels in Washington. Senator Sparkman concluded, for example, that one cause of the crisis was Kishi's failure to engage in public discussion and develop public support for his policies, and he warned that "it served notice on our country that Japan cannot be taken for granted."[23] A respected expert on Japan, Harvard professor Edwin O. Reischauer, wrote that this current of discontent in Japan "cannot be disregarded, for it is made up, not just of the formally organized Socialist opposition, centering around the trade-union movement, but also the bulk of Japan's intellectuals and college students—that is, the would-be ideological pathfinders and the generation to which the future of Japan belongs."[24] Within a year, Reischauer was named U.S. ambassador to Japan by the new Democratic President John F. Kennedy, specifically "to establish ties that might reach deeper into Japanese society than the Foreign Office."[25] And for years to come the lessons of 1960 remained vivid in the minds of policymakers, conditioning the approach of both American and Japanese officials to matters concerning the security treaty.

Okinawa Reversion

On May 15, 1972, the U.S. military administration of Okinawa ended and full sovereignty was returned to Japan. On the Japanese side, the issue of reversion not only reopened public debate about the security

22. A. Merriman Smith, *A President's Odyssey* (Harper, 1961), p. 222.

23. Senator John Sparkman, *The Far East and the Middle East,* Report to the Senate Committee on Foreign Relations, 86:2 (Government Printing Office, 1960), pp. 1–9. Eisenhower himself later expressed the view, according to Smith, that Kishi "generated trouble for himself the way he rammed the defense treaty with the United States through the lower house of the Diet." (*A President's Odyssey,* p. 258.)

24. Edwin O. Reischauer, "The Broken Dialogue with Japan," *Foreign Affairs,* vol. 39 (October 1960), p. 13.

25. W. W. Rostow, *The Diffusion of Power, 1957–1972* (Macmillan, 1972), p. 237.

alliance with the United States but raised sensitive questions of national sovereignty. On the American side, and within official Japanese circles, the Okinawa decision required a strategic reassessment, which inevitably produced severe resistance from those whose operations and missions were likely to be affected by change. The question had all the potential for a repetition of the crisis of 1960. Moreover, Okinawa became directly linked to the tenth anniversary of the mutual security treaty, for after 1970 either side could cancel the treaty on a year's notice. If Okinawa's status was not renegotiated before 1970, it was widely feared that Japanese resentment would lead to major demonstrations against maintaining the treaty.

Thus the issue to be resolved through bilateral negotiation was highly complex. In Japan and Okinawa there was strong public reaction against U.S. military ventures in Southeast Asia and the possible implication of Japan. In Washington there was severe military resistance to giving up Okinawa. How was it possible to reach an amicable decision in time to avert a crisis? What was required on the U.S. side to avoid resistance from military leaders and to gain their acquiescence to a decision that also acceded to Japanese antinuclear sentiment? How did the Sato government in Japan manage to withstand the political consequences of engaging in public debate about the security alliance, the issue that had brought Kishi's downfall in 1960?

Although he was the first Japanese premier to pledge himself to the resolution of the Okinawa question, Sato was not the first to discuss the issue with American officials. When Premier Hayato Ikeda visited Washington in 1961, he expressed concern to President John F. Kennedy that his most difficult domestic political problem arising from Japan's relations with the United States was the continued American military administration of the Ryūkyū[26] and Bonin islands. For during

26. The terms *Okinawa* and *Ryūkyū Islands* are used interchangeably in this study; they refer to those islands under postwar U.S. administration that reverted to Japan under the agreement effective in May 1972. Geographically, *Okinawa* can also mean just the main island and *Okinawa Islands* can mean that plus the small group of islands immediately around it. *Ryūkyū Islands* can include other islands not included in the U.S. administration (*Ryūkyū Rettō*), or be limited (as in this study) to the area of that administration (*Ryūkyū Shotō*). More important, the alternative designations have a political significance. When the territory was separated administratively from Japan in 1945, Americans (inclined to deemphasize the islands' ties to Japan) reverted to the old Chinese designation, Ryūkyū Islands, and called only the largest island Okinawa. Japanese continued to call them the Okinawa Islands after the former prefecture of Okinawa.

the 1950s the United States had clung steadfastly to the position that reversion of these administrative rights to Japan could not be considered as long as tension and aggression in Asia persisted. Discussions with the Japanese had never been allowed to go beyond this position. The U.S. Department of the Army, invested with the responsibility of governing Okinawa and the Bonins, had followed blueprints developed for the occupation of Europe after World War II. Under Dulles, the Department of State strongly supported military estimates of the importance of maintaining total control over Okinawa and the notion that Japan's "residual sovereignty" would continue into the indefinite future. (The State Department did not participate in the U.S. administration.)

Nevertheless, Ikeda's suggestion to President Kennedy fell on fertile ground. On Okinawa, pressures against the U.S. bases had been rising and it was generally believed in both the White House and State Department that at least part of the solution to this problem might be sought in negotiation with Japan (the rest would be in increased U.S. aid to Okinawa). In 1961, probably in response to Ikeda's concern, a special U.S. government commission was formed to study the matter. Its objectives were to find means of relieving pressures against the Okinawa bases and demonstrating good faith to the Japanese of American intentions to return the islands one day; consideration of reversion was not included. The few officials who saw a base rights agreement for Okinawa similar to that in Japan as a workable alternative were not willing to challenge unified military claims that such an arrangement would seriously impair American military operations. Furthermore, without the support of the military for whatever measures were to be taken, it was thought that Congress would not approve increased aid to Okinawa, which was the Kennedy administration's most important objective.[27] Acting on the commission's recommendations, President Kennedy announced the intentions of the U.S. government "to discharge more effectively our responsibilities towards the people of the Ryūkyūs, and to minimize the stresses that will accompany the anticipated eventual restoration of the Ryūkyū Islands to Japanese administration." He proposed that Congress increase aid to Okinawa, that arrangements be made for Japanese cooperation in economic assistance to Okinawa, and

27. Previous appropriations from Congress for civil aid to Okinawa had not been adequate to meet the needs, and there was hope that increased aid and economic growth would make the local population less inclined to disrupt base operations.

that a civilian be appointed to fill the position of civil administrator in the U.S. administrative structure on Okinawa.[28]

This unilateral gesture by the American President was received with renewed hope in Japan, although very little substantive change in the administration of Okinawa resulted. Within the American government it lent credence to the concept of Japanese residual sovereignty and emphasized the impermanence of American control. Furthermore, the commission's work created awareness of the Okinawa problem among middle-level officials in both the Pentagon and the State Department; they now saw a need to pay close attention to developments on the islands. However, it also drew out the opposition—the belief that Okinawa was no longer Japanese and should never return to Japan was represented eloquently by the high commissioner, General Paul W. Caraway. Although he could agree wholeheartedly with the need for increased U.S. aid to Okinawa, he was firmly set against any Japanese aid contributions. And until Caraway was replaced in 1964, there were none.[29] For the time being, Washington hesitated to enforce the intent of the President's recommendations. From this point, opinion appears to have polarized within the U.S. government between those who advocated concessions to local sentiment in order to preserve harmony with Japan and those who insisted that even a single concession would lead to a series of concessions, resulting eventually in total degradation of the strategic value of the Okinawa bases.

In the LDP presidential elections of 1964, one of the candidates, Eisaku Sato, chose to speak out boldly on the issue of Okinawa reversion as a means of distinguishing his platform from those of his opponents, but, as characteristic of political gambits, with no particular strategy for fulfilling his promise. Although Sato lost the election to Ikeda, he did come to office four months later when illness forced Ikeda's resignation. He renewed his pledge to pursue the matter of Okinawa reversion with American leaders. Sato had picked up the issue almost casually, but as premier he became increasingly attached to it emotionally as well as politically, and the final Japanese position on the terms of reversion bore the stamp of his personality.

Sato had risen through the ranks of the Liberal Democratic party

28. Statement by the President Upon Signing Order Relating to the Administration of the Ryūkyū Islands, March 19, 1962, in *Public Papers of the President, 1962*, p. 247.

29. The 1964 appointee, General Albert Watson, was far more conciliatory.

as a protégé of Shigeru Yoshida, and his political style was one of extreme patience and caution. Once Sato had defined the issue of Okinawa reversion as an important foreign policy objective, he almost immediately stepped back and began a waiting game that was to last for more than three years. As a former bureaucrat, he was inclined to lean heavily on the counsel of the Foreign Ministry professionals, but he consistently weighed this against the views and recommendations of individuals and groups outside the government, whom he considered more in tune with domestic politics.

Career officials in the Japanese Foreign Ministry (the Gaimushō) in the postwar period have probably been most concerned with maintaining and strengthening the basic framework of cooperation with the United States that was defined at the time of the peace treaty. Although they recognized in 1951 the inherent difficulties of the peace package, they worked more consistently and methodically than any other group in Japan over the next twenty years to remove those aspects of the arrangement that might turn the Japanese public against the United States, and to avoid weakening the security and economic relationship with the United States, which they considered essential to Japan's well-being.[30] One of their greatest concerns was balancing the vagaries of LDP factional politics, which tended to raise contentious issues prematurely, with what they calculated to be feasible in negotiations with the United States.

In 1957, when Premier Kishi chose to pursue treaty revision with American leaders, the Foreign Ministry had already succeeded in establishing with American officials a series of understandings that made revision almost the next logical step. When Premier Sato brought up the subject of Okinawa reversion in 1965, none of the incremental steps had yet been taken and, as far as the Foreign Ministry was concerned, Japan was far from prepared to assume the responsibility for administering Okinawa or to work out the complex arrangements that would have to be made to accommodate the operations of the American bases on Okinawa. Above all, it was important to avoid creating a domestic political situation that would lead to a rupture in the existing security structure between Japan and the United States. Until 1967, when public

30. For example, Gaimushō officials tended to view the prior consultation formula arrived at in the revised security treaty of 1960 as insurance against an abrupt American withdrawal from Japan, as much as it was cast publicly as insurance against American introduction of unwanted troops or weapons.

pressure for an early solution of the problem was steadily growing and Sato began to search for a concrete diplomatic strategy to bring it about, senior Foreign Ministry officials deliberately avoided personal involvement. But the initial steps toward moving Okinawa into a position for reunion with Japan had begun in 1966, and after 1967 the momentum was consciously sustained through a series of negotiated adjustments that in effect Japanized Okinawa.

There had been considerable discussion within the American government before 1966 about the need to begin planning for reversion. Diplomats anticipated initiatives by the Japanese government to negotiate a settlement of the problem and military officials could see merit in the argument that 1970 might be the crucial decision point. The expiration of the security treaty would offer a clear opportunity for the opposition parties in Japan to mount a major offensive against the entire security relationship and renew the horrors of 1960. If the United States did not take steps to return full Japanese sovereignty over Okinawa by 1970, the opposition could rouse public sentiment against the security treaty, jeopardizing the entire alliance with Japan.

Recognition of this threat did not affect the formal position of the Joint Chiefs of Staff on reversion, however. Apparently, they would not endorse Ambassador Reischauer's recommendations that the U.S. government begin discussion of the problem with the Japanese government, nor would they consider reversion as a real option for discussion within the American government. Their reluctance to accept the State Department's sense of urgency stalled attempts in late 1965 and early 1966 to focus on the problem within a small interdepartmental forum. Finally it was agreed that a special study group, chaired by the State Department's country director for Japan, should analyze the local pressures in both Japan and Okinawa before any consideration was given to the possible effects of reversion on base operations.

The formation of this group marked the beginning of American consensus building. Concerned with the potential of local discontent for disrupting the operations of American bases on Okinawa, representatives of the State Department, the Joint Chiefs of Staff, the Department of the Army, and the Office of International Security Affairs (part of the secretary of defense's staff) were able to agree that 1970 was indeed a crucial year. Whatever problems existed would demand a solution within five years. The objective for the American government, they decided, should be to retain maximum flexibility for using the Okinawa bases and yet accommodate Japanese public demands in order to preserve the larger security arrangement with Japan proper. The bases on Okinawa were highly valued, but the alliance with Japan was much more important.

From their agreement that there was an urgent local problem requiring immediate consideration of reversion, the interdepartmental group went on to define a need for better coordination between the American administrative organ on Okinawa and the embassy in Tokyo, as well as between these two entities and Washington. All of the parties to this highly complex problem would have to communicate effectively, if the issue were to be resolved systematically by the crucial deadline. They recommended that both the high commissioner and the ambassador report regularly to Washington on the mounting local pressures and their recommendations for dealing with them. This would serve the dual purpose of educating Washington and monitoring the field operations.

In late 1966 a new ambassador to Japan and a new high commissioner for Okinawa were named with conscious recognition that the reversion to Japan of administrative rights over Okinawa would be the next major agreement between Japan and the United States. Ambassador U. Alexis Johnson and High Commissioner General Ferdinand Unger met in Washington before they left for their posts and agreed to work together to prepare the way. The effect of this conscious planning by two high U.S. government officials was felt most strongly on Okinawa. Shortly after his arrival, Unger announced to the Okinawan legislature that it was time for them to begin preparing for return to Japanese administration. It was the first time an American military leader had broached the subject publicly in anything but a negative sense.

During 1967 the Washington study group produced a second report aimed at establishing an American position preparatory to the summit meeting between the Japanese prime minister and the American president scheduled for the autumn. This report compared the conventional operational capabilities of the American bases on Okinawa with the capabilities they would have if their status were the same as that of the bases in Japan. The conclusion was that very little would be lost if Okinawa reverted to Japanese administration.[31] Thus with the full par-

---

31. The strategic role of the bases, in particular as a depot for storing nuclear weapons, was not considered in this evaluation.

ticipation of the Joint Chiefs of Staff the widely entertained idea that
reversion would render the bases virtually useless began to dissipate.
The foundation had now been laid for direct discussions with Japanese
officials.

In the months before the 1967 summit meeting Japanese Foreign
Ministry officials began to perceive that Washington's wall of resistance
to the return of Okinawa had begun to crack. Possibilities suddenly
appeared for negotiating the incremental steps that would lead to full
reversion. It soon became evident that the summit would at least produce agreement on the return of the Bonin Islands. When Premier Sato
learned this, he decided that he would seek to go a step further and
achieve agreement in principle on the early reversion of Okinawa.
Shortly before the summit he signaled his wishes to the White House
through a private emissary. The answering signal from Washington
was that the U.S. government was not prepared for an agreement in
principle until the exact status of the Okinawan bases after reversion
had been discussed and agreed upon bilaterally.[32] Neither Sato, nor
his unofficial advisers, nor the Foreign Ministry were prepared to make
such a detailed commitment. There had been no serious public discussion and there was no way of defining the specific terms that would
settle well in Japan, particularly if the Americans were seeking special
status for these bases, as their position seemed to suggest. The compromise finally reached in hectic last-minute negotiations was a recognition by President Johnson of the Japanese desire for the return of
administrative rights over Okinawa within a few years.[33] Meanwhile,
negotiations for the return of administrative rights over the smaller
and less strategic Bonin Islands would begin as soon as possible.

In Tokyo, the reaction to Sato's negotiating achievements was equiv-
ocal, but not ultimately damaging to his position. There was satisfaction with the explicit arrangements in the communiqué for bringing

32. When Sato's proposal for agreement in principle on early reversion arrived,
President Johnson asked that it be discussed with key senators and congressmen. The
chairman of the Senate Armed Services Committee objected adamantly and Sato's
proposal was rejected. Apparently, senior State Department officials—and perhaps
President Johnson himself—saw a subtle connection between congressional reactions
and the attitudes of military leaders. In other words, they suspected that the interdepartmental bargaining process had not produced a full expression of military sentiments and that Congress would provide the public sounding board.

33. In the Japanese version of the joint communiqué the word *few* was interpreted
as *two to three*, so that Sato could point to a positive move toward reversion of
Okinawa as a result of his trip to Washington.

Okinawa into line with Japan economically and socially in preparation for reversion, because this was recognized as a means of maintaining momentum through concrete measures. However, the ambiguity of the American position on reversion itself was suspect and argument continued on whether the American government had actually committed itself to early reversion.

But for American officials who had been working toward reversion the 1967 summit represented a breakthrough. The absence in the communiqué of the standard rhetoric on retaining control of Okinawa until tensions in the Far East subsided—especially considering that tensions were actually at a peak in 1967—indicated to the careful observer that substantial movement had been made in the U.S. bureaucracy toward the reversion of Okinawa. Furthermore, the language devised for the agreement on the return of the Bonins set the precedent for negotiations on the reversion of Okinawa with the Joint Chiefs of Staff and it avoided the sticky issue of nuclear weapons storage, which was best left to the president himself. To the Japanese public and media, the reversion of the Bonins was related only indirectly to the reversion of Okinawa. Moreover, the opposition claimed that it was a substitute for, rather than a prelude to, the return of Okinawa. Only the specialists in the Foreign Ministry shared the American view of its significance.

On his return from Washington Sato initiated a year of debate on "defense-mindedness" in Japan. In a speech before both houses of the Diet on December 5, 1967, he declared that, "if the people become determined to defend their own country in unity and to take realistic steps toward that end, not only the international stature of our country will rise and we shall be better able to contribute to the stability of Asia, but, I am convinced, it will bring about the reversion of Okinawa in the near future."[34] Although Sato publicly held to his position that the terms of reversion were as yet a "blank sheet" on the Japanese side, he also indicated that the Japanese people would have to consider the possibility that the reversion of Okinawa could not be achieved without Japanese acceptance of a special status for the Okinawan bases allowing the continued presence of nuclear weapons. Voices outside the government began to rise in favor of nonnuclear status for the bases under the same restrictions that applied to the American bases in Japan proper, the so-called home-level formula. Within the Foreign Ministry

34. *Yomiuri*, Dec. 25, 1967.

the view continued to prevail that the Americans would not agree to open negotiations if Japan ruled out entirely the possibility of basing nuclear weapons on Okinawa.

In late January 1969, Foreign Minister Aichi announced that he had arrived at a two-step formula under which the current status of the bases would be maintained without modification for a certain period after reversion and, when the specific period was over, the bases would be reduced to home-level status. Almost immediately there was a strong reaction from within the LDP, and the movement favoring home-level status for the Okinawan bases grew quickly, threatening to become a partywide revolt against the prime minister. This indication of opinion from within his own party undoubtedly was the final sign to Sato that a public consensus had jelled. In early March 1969 Sato stated in the Diet that he would try to persuade the American government that the continued presence of nuclear weapons on Okinawa would alienate the local population to the point where the usefulness of the American bases would be jeopardized.

In the United States, 1968 was a presidential election year that brought the Republicans back to the White House. Richard Nixon, perceiving a need for strong, centralized presidential control over foreign policymaking, designed, even before his inauguration, a new National Security Council (NSC) system and ordered a series of studies on specific foreign policy problems. Two key members of the interdepartmental study group on Okinawa became members of the new NSC staff, and one of the first studies ordered was of U.S. relations with Japan. Thus at the same time that the Japanese premier was moving into a definitive position on the postreversion status of the bases, the American government was making its final calculations on whether the loss of nuclear storage facilities on Okinawa would seriously affect U.S. strategic operations in Asia. By now, American military leaders had become aware of the momentum in Japan toward a reversion arrangement and the fact that the President would have to come to a decision before the 1969 summit meeting with the Japanese prime minister.[35]

35. The State Department was arguing that to retain the long-term usefulness of the bases in both Japan and Okinawa there was a need for the United States to demonstrate its commitment to a strong alliance with Japan. Specifically, the Sato group within the Liberal Democratic party was the most pro-American and most firmly committed to preserving the U.S.-Japan relationship over the long run. Sato had staked his reputation on Okinawa reversion and, if he did not achieve this within his term as premier, he would not be in a position to determine his successor.

Although they were inclined to believe that some sort of nuclear storage arrangement could be negotiated with the Japanese government, they were also prepared to defer to the President's judgment if he ruled otherwise. Careful analysis had shown that the value of such nuclear storage was marginal. But when the President authorized the State Department to begin negotiations with the Japanese government in the late spring, he reserved his position on the issue.

The Japanese Foreign Ministry, once the premier had declared himself on the side of nuclear-free reversion, could now begin formulating a concrete negotiating position. On the basis of conversations with American officials during the last year, Gaimushō officials knew that the American side was most interested in Japanese concessions on the understanding on prior consultation, and specific commitment to security interests outside Japan. The Japanese government had been taking the position publicly that the prior consultation formula under the 1960 treaty meant a Japanese veto over any American request for major troop or weapons movements into Japan. If the Japanese government were willing to indicate that it would respond favorably to an American request in an emergency and to express Japanese interest in the security of other Asian countries, the strategic flexibility of all the American bases in Japan would be increased. Foreign Ministry negotiators believed these to be reasonable concessions in return for home-level status for the Okinawa bases, which only a few months earlier they had believed to be highly improbable. Thus the two sides went into the communiqué negotiations with similar perceptions of the fair exchange to be achieved; the differences between them were only a matter of degree.

Throughout the five-month negotiation, the Japanese officials were given no indication from the American side about its disposition toward the matter of nuclear weapons.[36] As they proceeded to negotiate their

---

If the United States, having already committed itself in principle to early reversion, were to impede the process at this point, it would appear to be a conscious judgment on the part of the U.S. government to alter the relationship with Japan. This would add fuel to the public hostility that already existed toward the U.S. bases in Japan and Okinawa, and would hasten the day when the United States would have to pull out altogether.

36. According to Armin H. Meyer, U.S. ambassador to Tokyo, "no Okinawa negotiating session would pass without a Japanese appeal for the incorporation of clear assurance in the communiqué that no nuclear weapons would be stationed on post-reversion Okinawa. Just as often, the American negotiators would parry the

own concessions to reversion, they (and the premier) became increasingly anxious that other factors were going to be brought into play by the American government—from one quarter or another—to force upon Japan a higher price in return for nuclear-free reversion than would be publicly acceptable. Above all, they did not want to become involved in a secret agreement on nuclear storage. Apparently to make doubly sure that the negotiations would produce nuclear-free reversion, and realizing that the real authority for decision was not in the State Department, Premier Sato opened up his own private channel to the president's assistant for national security affairs, Henry Kissinger. This appears to have produced the desired assurance, although at the price of a promise to agree to restrict textile exports to the United States.

On November 19, 1969, Premier Sato arrived in Washington. Two days later the joint communiqué was released to the public, announcing that he and President Nixon had agreed on the reversion to Japan of administrative rights over Okinawa, consistent with the policy of the Japanese government with regard to nuclear weapons. The communiqué included Japanese recognition of some common interest in the security of Korea, and possibly Taiwan. (No common position on Vietnam was taken, except for a mutual expression of hope that the war would have ended by the time reversion occurred.) American officials were still concerned, however, that the connection between the Japanese commitments and the status of the bases in Japan after reversion be made clear to the military audience to insure against a reaction from Congress. Thus both Under Secretary of State U. Alexis Johnson and the Japanese prime minister explained to the press the significance of the new Japanese commitments to Asian security and the relaxation of the meaning of prior consultation. In effect the Japanese commitment was overstated for American consumption.

In Japan reactions were mixed, with the opposition parties taking a predictably negative stand. Premier Sato and the Foreign Ministry had to answer publicly in Tokyo for his postcommuniqué assurances to the American public. There was little prospect, however, for the opposition to arouse widespread public emotion about the issue, because the basic domestic concerns had been satisfied. Okinawa would return

---

question. Actually a decision had been made within the top levels of the American government some months earlier, but it was to be left to the President to convey the good news to Prime Minister Sato in November." (*Assignment: Tokyo* [Bobbs-Merrill, 1974], pp. 37–38.)

to full Japanese sovereignty, without the continued presence of American nuclear weapons, and with the same restrictions on the bases as applied to those in Japan under the security treaty.

With this basic decision as a framework, the detailed negotiations for the return of Okinawa to Japanese administration took place in 1970–71. Among the myriad thorny questions to be resolved were not only issues between the two governments, but also matters vital to the future interests of the Okinawan population, including the desire of private American businesses to retain a preferential status on Okinawa. Agreement was reached in mid-1971 and the treaty was submitted for legislative ratification. On May 15, 1972, Okinawa returned to Japan.

The Textile Dispute

Even as the United States and Japan were reaching an amicable solution to the territorial question that had clouded Japan's political sovereignty for nearly twenty years, one of the most severe bilateral confrontations of the postwar period was emerging. In his race for the presidency, Richard Nixon had pledged his support to the cause of the American textile manufacturers, as part of his quest for southern votes at the Republican nominating convention and the November election. Once in office, President Nixon proceeded to make good on his promise, pressing for the stringent controls on imports of Japanese synthetic and wool textile products that were being sought by the American manufacturers.

As a domestic political issue useful in an aspiring leader's campaign, the textile question paralleled Okinawa. It was parallel in several other respects as well. Each was a prime U.S.-Japan issue for at least two years and each had a major broader impact on the relationship. Each dominated summit conferences and the attention of those officials most concerned with U.S.-Japanese relations. And the resolution of each required concessions by a specific interest (the U.S. military, the Japanese textile industry) that would not be easily won. Yet a fundamental political difference between the issues facilitated resolution of Okinawa while rendering textiles more intractable. Okinawa reversion represented, for almost all Japanese, a deeply felt "national interest" of the most fundamental sort; its importance in Tokyo politics stemmed from the basic belief that Okinawa was part of the Japanese nation and should, by rights, be under Japanese control. Textiles in U.S. politics was the very opposite, a narrow, particular interest of the industry's management and workers, and of a politician in securing their political and financial support. Many Japanese considered U.S. textile demands in a certain sense illegitimate; this was not the sort of serious, important U.S. national interest that they would feel obligated to accommodate. Okinawa, by contrast, was recognized as a legitimate and important Japanese interest by almost all American actors. Without such recognition, its status would not have been so constructively resolved.

The very contrast between the two issues—the "high politics" of Okinawa versus the "low politics" of textiles—makes even more astounding the political prominence that the textile issue attained and the bitterness it created, not just between the respective textile interests but among officials and even national leaders. Nixon had recognized the need for concessions to Japanese domestic politics and national aspirations in agreeing to return Okinawa to Japanese sovereignty. How could he turn around and make rigid, uncompromising demands on the Japanese premier for textile export quotas that would place him under strong political attack? When the extent of domestic resistance in Japan became fully apparent, why did Washington continue to pursue an uncompromising position? And why, since textile exports had long been declining in importance to Japan, did the government in Tokyo resist so adamantly for so long? How could the same two governments that were skillfully negotiating the return of Okinawa for the sake of a harmonious, long-term relationship be unable to negotiate a seemingly more simple and less consequential problem?

The impact of low-cost Japanese textiles on the U.S. market had been a source of minor friction even before the Pacific war. It arose again in the early fifties when the Japanese textile industry, having recovered from its wartime devastation with the help of American financial and technical aid, began to make substantial sales in the United States. These sales remained a small fraction of the overall U.S. textile market but were concentrated in specific product lines like cotton blouses and velveteen cloth. The textile industry, politically very strong in the southern states and New England, pressed for quota restrictions.

The Eisenhower administration resisted efforts to legislate quotas but supported voluntary Japanese export limitations, which were incorporated into a bilateral agreement in 1957. In 1961 the Kennedy administration sought broader restrictions from a group of exporting countries, leading to negotiation of the Long-Term Arrangement on Cotton Textiles (LTA) in February 1962. This fulfilled a campaign commitment by the new President, and also paved the way for the major trade liberalization initiative he was developing—the Trade Expansion Act of 1962—by eliminating textile industry opposition. The Japanese government went along with the agreement, partly because it seemed to offer Japan greater prospects for gradually increased exports to the United States than the 1956–61 bilateral agreements which had kept Japan's sales stagnant while those from Hong Kong and other Asian competitors shot dramatically upward. But implementation of the long-term arrangement required detailed, virtually continuous bilateral negotiations, and these proved increasingly contentious. The industries in both countries intensified their pressure on the governments, and their influence was enhanced by the increasing influence of their official spokesmen: in Japan, the Textile and General Merchandise Bureau of the Ministry of International Trade and Industry (MITI); and in the United States, the Commerce Department and the interagency textile committees which it chaired and staffed.

During the same period, the United States was also pressing Japan to limit exports in a number of other product lines. But the general thrust of U.S. policy was to encourage Japanese economic expansion. The predominant official American view was that a full-employment economy in Japan depended on trade and that Japanese democracy, in turn, depended on a healthy economy. It was also important that Western markets be open to Japanese trade so that Japan would not have to turn toward the communist countries. Furthermore, it was believed, if special barriers were erected against Japan and Japan were treated like an outcast, hostile forces might once again become dominant there. The United States strongly supported Japan's entry into the General Agreement on Tariffs and Trade (GATT) against the strong resistance of countries such as Britain. Also, because Japan was so vulnerable and weak economically, special measures to protect Japan's economy, such as import restrictions, were believed justifiable. Thus during the 1950s and well into the 1960s the attitudes of American and Japanese officials on free trade for Japan were basically parallel, stressing (except on special products) nondiscriminatory treatment of Japanese exports and not expecting Japanese reciprocity on imports. The United States did apply pressure on Japan, however, to minimize its trade with communist countries, particularly China.

Taking full advantage of postwar economic opportunities, Japan expanded her production and trade remarkably in the fifties, and even more rapidly in the sixties. Her economy came to bear little resemblance to the outdated American image of an economy dependent on cheap labor producing mainly handcrafted products and low-quality textiles. And as Japan's share of total U.S. cotton textile imports deteriorated through the 1960s, her overall trade with the United States was rapidly expanding. By 1969, sales of machine tools, appliances, motor vehicles, and so forth, had risen to 45 percent of Japan's total exports, and the trade balance with the United States had shifted from chronic deficit to what would become chronic surplus. Rapidly growing also, however, were sales of textiles from manmade fibers, whose importance was multiplied by a worldwide revolution in textile manufacturing. It was to controls on these products, which remained outside of the painfully negotiated restrictions on cotton products, that candidate Nixon pledged himself. And he promised to seek controls on wool textiles as well. He did so at a time of broad and growing American unhappiness with Japan's foreign economic policies—particularly the maintenance of import and capital restrictions well after Japan's economy had, to American eyes, outgrown the need for them. By this time, also, the capacity for considerable bilateral cooperation in textile relations, which had existed until the early sixties, had given way to intense competition and mutual resentment.

Presumably unaware of the recent antagonisms over textiles, but well aware of Kennedy's success in 1961 and 1962, Nixon sought to deliver quickly on his promise. Like Kennedy, he pursued his goal not by asking Congress to enact textile import quotas—this seemed likely to lead Congress to impose quotas on other products, which Nixon didn't want—but by the proven course of negotiating an agreement with the Japanese under which they would restrict their exports "voluntarily." He separated textiles from broader foreign and trade policy, assigning it as a special negotiating task briefly to a White House aide and then to his politically loyal secretary of commerce, Maurice Stans.

Stans's first major efforts came on a general trade mission to Europe in April 1969, when he urged officials in five countries to join in meeting the common threat of low-priced synthetic textiles from Asia. After meeting a cool reception there, he traveled a month later to Tokyo to confront a major political storm, as industry and political figures had already mobilized to resist what was seen as a new and flagrant effort to line up Western countries against Eastern products. From this and a subsequent discussion with Japan's minister of international trade and industry, Stans gained only an agreement to hold "fact-finding" talks in September 1969, which accomplished nothing. But President Nixon's evident concern about the issue led Premier Sato to fear that continued Japanese resistance on textiles might jeopardize his chances of gaining Nixon's agreement on Okinawa reversion without nuclear weapons at the forthcoming November summit. It had been made clear to Japanese negotiators that the nuclear question was being reserved for a presidential decision, and that the President had a personal stake in achieving a strong textile quota agreement. Thus before the summit meeting, Sato initiated talks through a private emissary that formed the basis for his discussions with President Nixon at the meeting. What resulted was an understanding—later portrayed as a misunderstanding—on how future negotiations for voluntary Japanese quotas would be carried on, and what their outcome would be.

Faced with elections shortly after his return to Tokyo, Sato answered public speculation about a "secret deal" on textiles by denial, and he resisted behaving in any way that would indicate publicly the existence of a private understanding. American officials, particularly those who had been privy to the details of the back-channel exchange, expected that the prime minister would be able to move his government to accommodate the President's request, and they became frustrated when official Japanese resistance failed to dissolve after the LDP triumphed at the polls in late December. Sato himself had met firm opposition from MITI and the Japanese textile industry. Hoping to break this resistance, he used a cabinet reshuffle to replace the MITI minister with a man who he felt would be more responsive to him personally. But the new minister, finding he could not persuade the industry and the MITI bureaucracy to seek accommodation with American demands, rather quickly began to espouse the MITI view. Contributing to his stand was an embarrassing fact that plagued the talks throughout—that the Americans were unable to demonstrate widespread, serious injury to the U.S. industry caused by imports. This was the accepted international criterion for quota restrictions, though it had not been applied in the cotton textile negotiations a decade earlier. Thus very few Japanese thought the U.S. case had much substantive merit.

By March 1970, nearly a year after the initial American requests, the two sides had become locked in irreconcilable opposition. The situation had become a cause for concern in both Washington and Tokyo. American textile leaders and their advocates in government were understandably dissatisfied at the failure to gain Japanese restraint. However, free traders in the United States—though opposed to the Nixon textile initiative on trade grounds—were now disturbed by signs that Congress, pressured by the textile firms and other import-affected industries, might enact highly restrictive general quota legislation. Failure to gain some textile concessions from Japan would make such protectionist legislation much more likely. Although the Japanese textile industry and most MITI officials were quite satisfied with the failure of the negotiations and tended to believe that the U.S. Congress would never actually enact comprehensive quotas, officials in the Ministry of Foreign Affairs and the Japanese embassy in Washington were very concerned about the quota campaign emerging in Congress.

Thus the circumstances were ripe for new initiatives aiming at compromise, and they began to spring up left and right during the spring of 1970. At this point, communications between the two governments became extremely confused, with official, semiofficial, and private spokesmen sending messages and proposing compromises. New American suggestions for solution proliferated, but none of the proposals met with success in Tokyo. Those that were directed into the Japanese system through the premier or the Foreign Ministry would meet with resistance in the MITI, where the formulas were considered too rigid, or where proof of injury was stressed as a precondition for restraint. One plan, put forward by free-trader Donald Kendall, that might have won eventual Tokyo acceptance lost its impetus when its revelation brought forth vehement industry objections in the United States, and considerable industry opposition in Japan as well.

In the midst of this confusion, U.S. Secretary of Commerce Maurice Stans and Japanese Minister of International Trade and Industry Kiichi Miyazawa began dealing through an intermediary of their own to see if they could find some ground for compromise. In late June 1970 Miyazawa visited Washington to meet directly with Stans. Despite the commerce secretary's belief that their back-channel communications made success probable, the talks with his Japanese counterpart failed. Thereupon the Nixon administration "reluctantly" endorsed proposed legislation for textile import controls that it had heretofore resisted, carefully pointing out that textiles was a special case and repeating its opposition to statutory quotas on other products.

Through the summer, the prospects of more general quota legislation in Congress seemed to brighten, creating widespread concern in the international trade community and increasing pressure on Japan for textile concessions that might stem the protectionist drive. In September 1970 President Nixon shifted textile responsibility from Stans to Presidential Assistant Peter Flanigan. During the same month, Tokyo requested a meeting with the American President during Sato's October visit to the United Nations. The Japanese embassy in Washington attempted to reopen communications on the textile issue in advance of the summit, but met with a new formulation of the hard-line position in the White House developed under the guidance of Flanigan and Henry Kissinger. The idea was to remain immovable in order to maximize the pressure on Sato, and it proved successful. Prime Minister Sato arrived at the summit meeting without having agreed to the terms on which the Americans were insisting, hoping perhaps to talk the matter out generally. But under strong pressure from Nixon and Kissinger, he left the meeting having agreed in substance to the American demands.

The negotiations that followed this summit agreement slowly began to show promise. Though the Japanese government was having trouble agreeing on a position at all close to what Sato had endorsed at the summit, progress was made in drafting an agreement with the impact Americans desired but in a form relatively palatable to Japanese. In the third week of December, however, just as the U.S. and Japanese negotiators felt they were on the verge of agreement, the U.S. textile industry reacted negatively to certain provisions, and this led to a presidential determination that the United States had to harden its position. After this, the negotiations once again became stalemated. The trade legislation died in the closing days of Congress, removing this immediate pressure. And the Sato government, subjected to vehement attacks from its textile industry and other critics of the mid-December formula, was hardly ready to make further major concessions.

The failure of the December negotiations led to still another inconclusive episode, this one intended by neither government and damaging to both. In early 1971, U.S. Congressman Wilbur Mills, the chairman of the powerful Ways and Means Committee who had been supporting protectionist legislation against his own free-trade instincts, decided to intervene directly to obviate the need for congressional action. By now leaders of the Japanese textile industry, concerned with the broader threat posed to exports by quota legislation, were seriously considering the possibility of designing and implementing their own voluntary quotas, applying criteria less stringent than the U.S. government had sought but perhaps significant enough to undercut the drive for something stronger. In March 1971 Mills and the Japanese industry leaders succeeded in reaching agreement on such a formula, which was then endorsed by the Japanese prime minister's office as resolving the problem. The U.S. textile industry was up in arms. So, apparently, was President Nixon, who saw himself not only upstaged on the textile issue but also undercut in his constitutional prerogative to negotiate trade agreements with foreign governments. Three days after the Japan Textile Federation announced its program, the President issued a strongly worded statement denouncing both its substance and the manner of its negotiation. There was dismay in Tokyo, because by now all major actors on the Japanese side had joined in support of the plan and there was no respectable way of abandoning it. Japanese decisionmakers found it inconceivable that a powerful member of the legislature could have taken major policy action without the knowledge and at least tacit approval of the chief of government. To President Nixon, on the other hand, it looked as if the Japanese premier had maneuvered to renege on his personal promises, by conspiring with a leading member of the Democratic opposition in a way that discredited and humiliated the Republican President.

This fiasco occurred against the background of mounting concern in the United States, both official and unofficial, about the widening imbalance in U.S. trade with Japan. Already, many Americans had begun to back away from the belief that the Japanese economy needed particularly benevolent U.S. economic policies for its survival, or even that Japanese economic expansion was in America's interest. They were uneasy about the U.S. deficit in the bilateral trade balance, about the shift in Japanese exports toward more technologically sophisticated products, about the growing imbalance in overall U.S. trade and payments, and about Japan's rapid rise to economic power.

By the third year of the Nixon administration, therefore, U.S. officials concerned with economic relations with Japan were divided into two groups with sharply divergent views of Japan. The more dramatic was reflected by the "Japan, Inc." concept espoused in the Commerce Department and by some on the White House staff. The Japanese, in this view, had developed a powerful, rapidly growing, purposively managed, and relentlessly self-interested economic juggernaut which was posing a fundamental challenge to U.S. economic supremacy.[37] Strong defensive action would be required by the United States if the world economy was to cope with this Japanese threat. The rival view, prevalent among Japan specialists both inside and outside the government, saw important limiting factors in Japanese economic growth and management, and warned that severe or insensitive pressure on Japan would destroy the cooperative political alliance which had been so carefully nurtured in the postwar period (and which was basic to preventing the conditions that had led to war in the first place). Adherents of this view, naturally, argued against forcing comprehensive textile quotas on the Japanese, although they did see the need for some Japanese export restraint. But they too found fault with Japanese slowness in dismantling the postwar system of import and investment restrictions. And they believed that the yen had become undervalued and thus gave Japanese products an unfair advantage in world markets.

In Japan, there were many in and out of government who felt policy changes in these areas were necessary. But movement toward liberalizing trade restrictions was slow, and on the yen nonexistent, thus adding to the frustration of American officials and American businessmen as well. Leaders of Japanese industry and government still presumed on American benevolence to maintain a somewhat unbalanced trade relationship in recognition of what they regarded as severe economic vulnerabilities peculiar to Japan. Moreover, economic growth had been accompanied by a resurgence of nationalistic sentiment and consequent resistance to the long-standing practice of yielding to specific American export control pressures, which had been Japan's side of the de facto postwar bilateral economic bargain. Thus on both sides of the Pacific, resolution of the textile dispute was complicated by the unraveling of the assumptions about the economic relationship under which earlier textile deals had been struck. And on each side, the textile issue generated strong resentment of the other. Japanese felt bitter about "unreasonable" U.S. economic demands for which they saw little substantive justification; Americans railed against an island nation that seemed

37. An unidentified member of the Nixon cabinet was quoted in *Time*, May 10, 1971, as saying: "The Japanese are still fighting the war, only now instead of a shooting war it is an economic war. Their immediate intention is to try to dominate the Pacific and then perhaps the world."

relentlessly on the make economically, unwilling to make trade concessions to the nation that had provided for her defense and "generously"
agreed to return Okinawa.

In the spring of 1971, after his denunciation of the Mills plan, President Nixon assigned responsibility for the textile issue to Ambassador-
at-Large David Kennedy, and granted him wide authority to pursue
agreement with Japan. In Tokyo, Premier Sato was arranging a cabinet
reshuffle that would result in a new MITI minister, future Premier
Kakuei Tanaka, who he hoped would take care of the problem once and
for all. For Sato, the textile issue threatened the success of what he saw
as his major historic achievement, the reversion of Okinawa.

Suddenly, on July 15, Tokyo was hit with the shock of Nixon's announcement of his plans to visit China. And in another dramatic decision, on August 15, Nixon announced plans to stimulate the sagging
U.S. economy and right the international imbalance through tax cuts, a
temporary freeze on wages and prices, the imposition of a temporary
10 percent surcharge on imports, and a floating of the dollar aimed at
forcing a readjustment of international exchange rates—especially that
of the yen. Just as the China shock seemed to challenge the foundations
of the international political structure, so the announcement of August
15 hit at the heart of the postwar economic structure. Japan took the
brunt of both blows, and nothing was done by those few U.S. officials
who had prior knowledge of either announcement to soften their impact.

Shortly thereafter the United States indicated that it would impose textile quotas by executive order under the tenuous authority of the
Trading with the Enemy Act if agreement were not reached by October
15.[38] Japanese government leaders, and leaders of industries other than
textiles, were now preoccupied with larger economic concerns, and saw
acceptance of an unpleasant textile agreement as necessary to help
salvage the larger U.S.-Japan relationship. Premier Sato and his advisers

---

38. Though the act was passed originally in 1917 when the "enemy" was
Germany, the authority to be invoked had last been clarified—and expanded—in an
amendment enacted just after Pearl Harbor. It provided that, "during the time of
war or during any other period of national emergency declared by the President, the
President may . . . regulate . . . any . . . importation or exportation of . . . any property
in which any foreign country or a national thereof has any interest." President Nixon
had declared a national emergency in his August 15 announcement. Moreover,
previous "national emergencies" had never been rescinded. But many lawyers thought
this authority insufficient because other, more recent legislation aimed specifically at
trade regulation did not give the president this power.

saw no reasonable alternative except to yield to the American pressure, so Tanaka negotiated the matter personally and forced the terms on a weary industry and bureaucracy. On the evening of October 15, after frenetic eleventh-hour negotiations in Tokyo, Tanaka and Kennedy initialed a memorandum of understanding bringing to a conclusion the bitter three-year controversy.

Ironically, Japanese exports of manmade textiles to the United States declined dramatically after 1971 for reasons largely unrelated to the quotas. Most Japanese textiles had long been losing their competitive advantage vis à vis those of other Asian countries, but revaluation plus Japanese domestic inflation sharply accelerated this trend. By 1973, Japan was importing more textile made-up goods than she was exporting (exports had been five times as great as imports in 1970). Not surprisingly, Japanese textile industry leaders concerned with protecting their home market became interested in the same types of international trade restrictions that they had for decades resisted. As revaluation of the yen began to take effect in 1973, moreover, and as Japan did finally liberalize her import regime, the balance of payments between the United States and Japan moved into relative equilibrium. Bilateral trade issues receded into the background, with multilateral questions centering about the energy crisis arising in their place. Still, the controversy of 1969–71 remained more than an unhappy memory. Its intractability and bitterness spurred larger doubts about the relationship on both sides of the Pacific, doubts that persist to this day. And the very fact that such an issue could escalate out of control was grounds for future concern.

Conclusions

The root problems in negotiating the security treaty were problems of Japanese domestic politics. As an exercise in adjustment between official government positions, the issue was dealt with quite intelligently: the existence of a problem (the old "unequal" treaty) became mutually recognized, and national policy positions were adjusted sufficiently to achieve a negotiated solution. Particularly important was the American willingness to yield on full reciprocity of obligations and to compromise on Japanese rearmament. But on both sides, officials underestimated the depth and potential impact of Japanese domestic opposition, particularly the combustible combination of a controversial treaty identified with an unpopular premier. And after the antitreaty movement had gathered strength, those in power fanned the flames further—Kishi by pressing his parliamentary majority and forcing ratification; both national leaders in holding to plans for the state visit which became, inevitably, the movement's new target.

Thus, most obviously, the treaty revision underscores the fundamental need for an alliance to maintain political support within its member countries. But the specific politics of the issue in Tokyo was quite different from what Americans encounter at home. Leading members of the ruling Liberal Democratic party fought publicly in 1958 and 1959 over the terms the government was negotiating; the greatest popular resentment was triggered when the prime minister insisted that a majority of the elected Diet be able to act on ratification. And behind these particular events were more enduring political institutions—the strength of factions within Japan's ruling party; the polarization between establishment conservatives and the left opposition; the place of consensus in Japanese cultural values and practices.

Okinawa and textiles stand, broadly, as the "success" and "failure" stories of the sixties and early seventies. Yet in some respects they were strikingly similar. Each was publicly controversial in Japan more than the United States. Each engaged a strong interest in the United States whose perceived needs—if pressed too far—could both make resolution difficult and weaken the alliance more generally. On Okinawa, however, the Japanese premier managed to keep on top of the issue, and the perceived needs of the U.S. military were both scaled down and satisfied. On textiles, that same premier faced enormous resistance inside and outside of his party, and the U.S. textile industry managed to control the U.S. position throughout; its demands were never significantly modified, and the issue was resolved only after severe damage was done to U.S.-Japanese trust and dealings on other issues. Why did the politics of the two issues lead to such opposite outcomes? And why was an Okinawa-for-textile-quotas trade, so inescapably logical as a bilateral bargain, so elusive in practice?

Succeeding chapters delve more generally into such questions: problems of politics and policymaking within the two countries; problems of perception and interaction between them. Why would Kishi's conservative rivals let factional strife affect relations with their major ally and protector? A fuller answer requires an analysis of Japan's ruling party and the political system within which it operates. Why did the U.S.

embassy (and the president) not pull back earlier from the aborted Eisenhower visit? An explanation requires a look at the political and cultural barriers affecting perception of events in one country by officials in the other. Why did proponents of a moderate settlement in both capitals succeed in supporting one another on Okinawa, while failing on textiles? What were the differences in how negotiations were conducted, in how steps taken in one capital affected the politics of the issue in the other? Fuller development of the partial, tentative answers offered in this chapter requires a more general effort to analyze these two national policymaking systems and their impact on one another.

CHAPTER THREE

Foreign Policymaking in Japan and the United States

THE OKINAWA and textile issues were brought to prominence by politicians, Sato and Nixon, who aspired to national leadership in 1964 and 1968 and raised these issues as part of their campaigns. Neither man sought first to discover whether reversion or new textile quotas would actually be negotiable with the other government. But once each issue was raised, success in resolving it would turn on whether, in that other government, political leaders and senior bureaucrats were willing and able to mobilize sufficient support for granting what the leader in the initiating country sought.

On Okinawa (a critical issue to Japanese), American officials proved willing and able to manage the process to achieve such an outcome. On textiles (not of comparable general importance to Americans), Japanese officials were not, at least not in time to avert a major crisis. But in both cases, an issue that arose from political interplay within one country could not be put to rest until it was confronted and resolved in the politics of the other.

In both cases, moreover, government officials played key roles in the politics of decisionmaking. On Okinawa, the U.S. decision to grant reversion by 1972 was the product of careful internal bargaining between State Department and Pentagon officials; the White House was favorably inclined toward reversion but unwilling to move if there were strong military or congressional opposition. On textiles, Japanese resistance owed no little to the stubbornness of Ministry of International Trade and Industry (MITI) bureaucrats operating in a domestic political climate of strong opposition to quotas, and to the limited leverage of a premier who sought repeatedly to win acquiescence to Japanese concessions. Security treaty revision was even more dominated in the negotiating

48

stage by inside actors both bureaucratic and political; ministers and foreign office officials in both capitals came together on a new security agreement which was, to them, the culminating achievement of the successful relationship they had constructed after the occupation. The fact that it triggered a major crisis in Japan underscores the importance of the broader domestic political arena. Consensus within governments may be necessary, but it is not sufficient. Major foreign policy agreements by democratic states require broader national support and consensus (or at least acquiescence) if these agreements, and the politicians who sponsor them, are to survive and prosper.

Understanding the politics of U.S.-Japanese relations, then, requires understanding the politics of policymaking within each country as it copes, internally, with issues important to that relationship. It requires particular attention to the governments that generate the decisions and actions, but attention also to the larger national political processes within which these governments operate.[1]

Japan's Political System: The Major Actors

In prewar Japan, under the imperial constitution, power was shared by several competing groups. The strongest of these were the emperor's personal advisers (elder statesmen called *jūshin* or *genrō*) and the military and civil bureaucracies, but the hereditary peerage who dominated the upper chamber of the Imperial Diet and the political parties that held precarious control over the lower chamber also had a role in shaping foreign policy. *Jūshin* spoke directly on current issues through the extra-parliamentary privy council, and their substantial influence on the actions of the cabinet was enhanced through the exercise of their customary right to appoint the prime minister. The military, on the other hand, had the important advantage of direct access to the throne under the principle of the "independence of military command." Both by law and by convention they also controlled the cabinet portfolios of war and

1. In describing these governments and processes, we have found it necessary to go beyond the case evidence which is the major basis for other chapters in this study. Thus we draw also on other sources as noted, and on our general research into foreign policymaking in both capitals. Since we write primarily for an American audience, and since the U.S. foreign policymaking system has been extensively analyzed elsewhere, we give particular emphasis to the Japanese side. Readers desiring more about the American system may wish to consult the books on foreign policymaking and organization in the bibliography.

the navy and through them manipulated cabinet decisions on foreign policy and security issues. By the late 1930s the military had clearly become the major force in Japan's foreign policy. They did not, however, dominate all major foreign policymaking decisions and actions. The Tōjō cabinet which presided over the decisions directly leading to Pearl Harbor in late 1941 was not a true military dictatorship but represented a form of collaboration and compromise between military and civil bureaucrats, with the elder statesmen ever-active behind the scenes.[2]

The structure of the Japanese government was drastically altered by the 1947 constitution. The emperor ceased to rule even in form; the *jūshin* and the privy council were abolished, as were the hereditary peerage and the House of Peers and the military services. The legal centerpiece of the new system was the reconstituted Diet ("the highest organ of state power"). The Diet was to oversee all actions of the cabinet, control the purse-strings of the state, and ratify international treaties. From its members the Diet designates the prime minister, who appoints his own cabinet, a majority of whom must be Diet members. The cabinet is responsible for administering the democratized civil service.

The Diet is composed of two houses, both popularly elected. The more powerful House of Representatives (lower house) is chosen in its entirety in elections held at least every four years—and more often if the cabinet so decides. The House of Councillors (upper house) has basically a checking and restraining function; its members hold office for fixed six-year terms, with half elected every three years. If the lower house votes a resolution of no confidence, the entire cabinet must resign unless new elections are promptly held. After such elections the new Diet must act either to renew the premier's mandate or to replace him.

In postwar practice, most of the Diet's power has been exercised by the Diet members belonging to the majority Liberal Democratic party (LDP), and particularly by the senior LDP members, who fill most cabinet positions and other leadership posts. And though the constitutionally defined role of the bureaucracy is to implement policies and legislation, bureaucrats have taken an active part in policymaking and legislative activities. Big businessmen (the *zaikai*) have also exerted a great deal of political influence in government policymaking by means

2. For extended discussion of Japan's prewar system, see Seiichi Imai, "Cabinet, Emperor, and Senior Statesmen," in Dorothy Borg and Shumpei Okamoto, eds., *Pearl Harbor as History: Japanese-American Relations, 1931–1941* (Columbia University Press, 1973), pp. 53–79.

of their close personal and financial ties to LDP politicians and working relations with government bureaucrats. Together, the party, bureaucracy, and business communities are frequently characterized as the "tripartite power elite" of postwar Japan.[3]

But other groups are active also—particularly on foreign policy matters. For a pervasive feature of postwar Japanese politics has been the domestic divisiveness of major foreign policy issues in general and U.S.-Japan issues in particular. Opposition Diet members and intellectuals have questioned the very basis of the establishment's foreign policy, and their recurrent criticism—reported and sometimes headlined in the media—has brought a particular pattern to the politics of foreign policy issues in Tokyo, especially those involving U.S. security ties.

The Conservative Establishment

The Liberal Democratic party has held absolute (though diminishing) majorities in both houses of the Diet ever since it was created in 1955, and has been generally able to maintain party discipline in parliamentary voting. Thus the LDP president has always been elected premier, and his government prevails on legislation when it comes to be voted on. The LDP is correctly labeled "conservative": leaders and members support economic growth based on private, capitalist enterprise domestically, and a foreign policy founded on the alliance and security treaty with the United States. However, the party is anything but dogmatic. There is considerable diversity of view within the party, and its leaders have proved flexible and pragmatic on particular issues (like the 1972 establishment of diplomatic relations with mainland China).

The major components of the LDP are its factions—well established, formally organized groups of Diet members, each headed by a senior LDP leader. Factions are sometimes identified with substantive policy orientations: in 1975, that of Deputy Premier Takeo Fukuda was generally considered conservative, whereas the faction under Prime Minister Takeo Miki was identified with its leader's progressive, reformist positions. But the main cement holding factions together is reciprocal personal political interests. A member needs the leader's help in winning party endorsement of his candidacy, in obtaining campaign funding

3. For a discussion of the prevalence of this concept in studies of recent Japanese politics, see Haruhiro Fukui, "Foreign Policy-Making in Japan: Case Studies for Empirical Theory" (paper prepared for delivery at 1974 meeting of the Association for Asian Studies; processed), pp. 4–8.

and other election help, and in seeking particular posts in the Diet, the party, and (eventually) the cabinet. The leader needs a solid group of supporters to enhance his political power and his quest for the premiership or other senior cabinet positions.

Aside from the president, the three major party officials are the secretary-general, the chairman of the executive council, and the chairman of the policy affairs research council (PARC). The PARC organizes the party's participation in debate on current policy issues through a series of standing and special policy committees under its jurisdiction. The standing committees correspond both to the executive ministries and agencies and to the Diet committees. These party committees do not usually initiate foreign policy proposals of their own because they have neither the technical nor the manpower resources to do so. But they often react forcefully to foreign policy initiatives coming from the cabinet and bureaucracy, as on security treaty revision, Okinawa reversion, textiles, and China. And the government pays close attention to "party opinion," which can literally break or make a prime minister and his cabinet.

Because the party has received especially strong electoral support from rural areas, it is particularly responsive to agricultural interests. The drawing of electoral districts favors the LDP by giving disproportionate representation to rural voters. As if to compensate, however, the system of multimember electoral districts gives the opposition parties greater opportunities than winner-take-all, single-member districts like those in the United States, where a party with 40 percent of the vote would generally prevail over several smaller rival parties unless these latter could coalesce behind a single candidate.

The LDP leaders work in close cooperation with the permanent bureaucracy. As in other parliamentary democracies, Japan's cabinet system is supported by a strong and influential civil service. The ministries are dominated by career officers who know the details of policy issues and manage the specific instruments of governmental action. The cabinet ministers who lead them often serve for limited periods, and rather than recruiting their own subordinates, they rely on the career officials for most of the information, analysis, and advice they require. Many ministers enter politics after having served in the bureaucracy and for them relationships with ministry officials are enhanced by a sense of common profession. Also contributing to cooperation between politicians and bureaucrats is a shared consensus about basic policies. For like LDP leaders, senior bureaucrats have overwhelmingly favored strong, business-based growth policies at home and a foreign policy based on the U.S. alliance abroad.

Japan's big business community, a key component of the ruling establishment, also shares these values. Businessmen supply politicians needed funds and support, and the amounts of money spent in election campaigns are very large. In turn, they make use of many opportunities to influence government policies and internal LDP politics, and though they may not always prevail, their views and interests are given very full consideration, especially on issues where they have direct economic stakes. Businessmen also have close, reciprocal working relationships with bureaucrats on the many issues that affect their interests. These relationships are deepened by the frequent practice of bureaucrats retiring from high official posts to senior corporate positions.

The big business community also operates through several national organizations. The four major ones are Keidanren (Federation of Economic Organizations), Nikkeiren (Japan Federation of Employers' Associations), Keizai Dōyūkai (Japan Committee for Economic Development), and Nisshō (Japan Chamber of Commerce and Industry). Leaders of these groups seek to develop and promote a view of business interests—and Japanese national interests—that is broader than that of particular economic interests and firms. They do not always prevail, however; in 1969 and 1970, Keidanren efforts to soften the textile leaders' stance on quotas were repeatedly unavailing. Still, these organizations are considerably more prestigious and influential than American counterparts like the Chamber of Commerce and the National Association of Manufacturers.

Opposition Groups and Other Actors

Standing outside the ruling establishment, sharing neither their involvement nor their consensus about policy, are other political actors who represent many millions of Japanese. They include the opposition political parties and allied labor unions, and large segments of the intellectual community. Their influence on government policymaking is mainly indirect, but their impact has been significant, and may be more so if the LDP's Diet majorities continue to shrink. In the lower house election of 1960 the party gained 58 percent of the vote and 63 percent of the seats; in 1972, it won 47 percent of the vote and 55 percent of the seats. The 1974 upper house election saw the LDP win just 42 percent of the vote, and its majority was reduced to a bare 127 out of 251 seats.

The ruling party has been further beset by the formation of cross-factional groups of relatively junior members dissatisfied with both the policies of the leadership and the continuation of the same old faces in power. Also weakening the establishment coalition—and offering opportunities to the opposition—are policy predicaments rooted in the economic successes of the fifties and sixties. Rapid growth has been accompanied by environmental damage—but efforts to reverse such damage produce strains in the government-business coalition. And the economic crisis brought on by skyrocketing energy costs, double-digit inflation, and minimal real economic growth has halted—at least temporarily—the steady rise in economic well-being which has contributed no little to the LDP's public support. Also damaging to the LDP have been well-documented charges of high-level corruption and "money politics," the most dramatic of which drove Prime Minister Kakuei Tanaka from power in December 1974. These have not only provided ammunition for critics of the regime, but strained LDP-business ties by making businessmen reluctant to supply political funds, and forcing LDP politicians to demonstrate publicly that they are not simply captives of business interests.

OPPOSITION PARTIES. Even when the LDP Diet majority is large, the government leadership cannot totally ignore the opposition parties. Cabinet members, including the prime minister, must respond regularly to interpellations from all Diet members—and those from opposition members are particularly sharp and pointed. Their responses are attacked by opposition Diet members and reported in detail by a lively and frequently critical press. During the textile issue Socialists and Democratic Socialists pressed Premier Sato on whether he had made a secret textile-Okinawa deal with President Nixon. Each denial of such a deal by Sato only served to fuel the public suspicions.

Most Japanese opposition parties espouse leftist ideologies. The Japan Socialist party (JSP), the largest, has frequently appeared more radical than the Japan Communist party (JCP), its principal rival. Both the JSP and the JCP are particularly sensitive to foreign policy issues, favoring nonalignment and demilitarization, reduction or dissolution of the Japan Self-Defense Forces, and an end to the U.S.-Japan Mutual Security Treaty.[4] The more moderate Democratic Socialist party (DSP) does not

4. Over the years the two parties' attitudes toward national defense and the U.S. alliance have become somewhat more pragmatic and flexible. While still calling for the dissolution of the Self-Defense Forces, the JSP favors a gradual replacement of

oppose the security treaty but would allow stationing of U.S. troops in Japan only in case of emergency. The non-Marxist Kōmeitō (the political arm of the Sōka Gakkai Buddhist organization) calls for gradual dissolution of the security treaty. The JSP holds more Diet seats than the other three opposition parties combined. But it has declined sharply in relative terms since 1960, with the Communists and the Kōmeitō making significant gains.

The government has tried to minimize public discussion of security and foreign policy issues in order to avoid confrontation with the opposition. But the opposition parties actively seek public airing of such issues, mounting publicity campaigns against certain government policies both in and out of the Diet. Wide press coverage of heated Diet interpellations and press exposure of any controversial behavior of the government or of individual government leaders are helpful to them. In October 1974, for example, Japanese newspapers headlined the testimony of retired U.S. Admiral Gene LaRocque before a U.S. congressional subcommittee that American ships carrying nuclear weapons "do not offload them when they go into foreign ports such as Japan." The government, which had long sought to convey the impression that no U.S. nuclear weapons entered Japan, was immediately confronted with widespread public demonstrations and attacks from opposition Diet members. The generalized reassurances it hastily obtained from the U.S. government did not absolve the Japanese government of culpability in the eyes of its critics, and the opposition succeeded in rekindling public debate on an issue the LDP government wished to keep out of the spotlight.[5]

Once an issue becomes controversial in the public arena, it is difficult for the government to overrule the opposition for fear of being accused

---

the SDF by what they call a "peaceful land development force," supposedly a much less military-oriented organization. The JCP now recognizes the inherent right of self-defense for Japan and talks in terms of reducing the size of the SDF. See *Asahi nenkan* [Asahi almanac], *1956*, *1967*, and *1974*. Further softening of their formal and informal stands has been evident since 1974.

5. The United States assured Japan in a formal note that it had "faithfully honored its commitments to Japan." This was a reference to the "prior consultation" formula of 1960 covering any "major changes" in U.S. force or equipment deployments in Japan. The Japanese government insisted in turn that the United States had not asked for consultations on nuclear weapons transit. But this left unresolved the question of whether there had been a secret arrangement on nuclear transit reached in 1960, as reported in the press. (See *New York Times*, Oct. 8, 15, and 17, 1974; *Japan Times Weekly*, Oct. 19, 1974; *Washington Post*, Oct. 23, 1974; and T. J. Pempel, "Japan's Nuclear Allergy," *Current History*, April 1975, pp. 169–73.)

of "tyranny of the majority," particularly if Diet action is required. Despite their minority status, opposition members can also win concessions on policies developed in the legislative committees they serve on. And on a few upper house committees, non-LDP members have come into the majority owing to the thinning of overall LDP control.

LABOR UNIONS. None of the major labor unions in Japan supports the party in power. The largest and most influential is the Sohyo (General Council of Japanese Trade Unions) with 4.3 million members as of June 1973 from the public and private sectors. The Sohyo is the power base for the JSP (some of the Sohyo's affiliates also cooperate with the JCP). Its largest affiliate is the Jichirō (All Japan Prefectural and Municipal Workers' Union) with a little more than a million government workers, followed by the Nikkyōso (Japan Teachers' Union) with nearly 600,000 members. The second largest union grouping, the Dōmei (Japanese Confederation of Labor) with 2,277,900 members, officially supports the Democratic Socialist party. Its largest affiliate, the Zensen Dōmei (Japan Federation of Textile Workers' Union), has 543,000 members. The Chūritsu Rōren (Liaison Conference of Neutral Labor Unions) with 1,374,300 members is not affiliated with any specific political party but usually works jointly with the Sohyo and the Dōmei for advancing common labor objectives, including an annual wage hike.

Like the business organizations, these labor unions often articulate their demands through regular government channels (relevant divisions and bureaus of the ministries, such as Labor and Finance). And if the business groups work politically through the LDP, the labor groups work through the opposition parties, particularly those with which they have ties. Beyond this, the unions resort to street demonstrations, rallies, and strikes to influence government policies. Their actions range from annual wage demands (often called the "spring offensives") to opposition to the U.S.-Japanese defense alliance. Labor unionists played a key role in the mammoth demonstrations in 1960 against the revised U.S.-Japan mutual security treaty and against President Eisenhower's scheduled Tokyo visit. They sponsored a nationwide railroad strike in opposing President Ford's visit to Japan. The Zensen Dōmei was the focal point of the popular protest against the imposition of export controls during the U.S.-Japan textile negotiations.

ACADEMIA AND INTELLECTUALS. In Japan the government and academia have been for the most part mutually exclusive communities. The government seldom brings in professors for short-term service, and professional bureaucrats who see themselves as their society's elite do practically all policy research and planning for the government. The academic community, for its part, is suspicious of scholars maintaining close relations with the government, especially scholars in the social sciences. One reason is that older scholars have a sense of guilt over their collaboration with the government that eventually brought about the war and suppression of thought. And their natural desire for independent thinking has been reinforced by the polarized Japanese political system. Many intellectuals have identified with the opposition, though this commitment seems to have weakened in recent years.

Intellectuals' reluctance to identify themselves with the government has also been related to the strong influence of Marxism in academia in postwar Japan. Even if most scholars are not Marxist, many have been sympathetic. And others have refrained from "selling themselves" to the capitalist government for fear of being accused of helping the establishment by their colleagues and students, some of whose leaders are aggressive Marxists or Maoists belonging to the radical national student organization, the Zengakuren. As a result, only a very small circle of scholars has been willing to advise the government, and some of them prefer to do so anonymously.

Since academia is generally critical of government policies, and the bureaucracy is in any case a rather closed community, the government principally works with those like-minded scholars it considers "safe." This relationship between the government and the small circle of its "chosen" scholars (who are pejoratively called *goyō gakusha*, or "government's scholars," by other intellectuals) inevitably limits the range of new ideas or perspectives considered. In many cases, the scholars end up telling the government what it wants to hear. Nevertheless, these scholars can sometimes play a significant role. In January 1969, for instance, several Japanese scholars close to Premier Sato convened a U.S.-Japanese conference on Okinawa at Kyoto to try to make influential Americans more sympathetic toward the home-level reversion formula. They were among the few Japanese intellectuals able to communicate effectively and comfortably with Americans, and their major contribution on the issue was their service as interpreters of Japanese domestic sentiment to these Americans (and vice versa). But they were also useful to Sato because they were more sensitive to Japanese domestic politics than were Gaimushō officials advising the premier on the same issue.

THE PRESS. Japan has a truly national press, which influences policymaking through its sometimes-conflicting roles of purveyor of information (including many leaks), vocal critic of the government, and confidant of politicians and senior officials. The average Japanese reads at least one of the five dailies with national circulation (*Asahi, Mainichi, Yomiuri, Sankei,* and *Nihon keizai*), and the average family owns at least one television set. Most Americans, by contrast, read only local newspapers.

Only a limited number of top-ranking Japanese politicians and bureaucrats have access to confidential information channeled through the Foreign Ministry. Thus for most Japanese—LDP members and *zaikai* included—the press is the main source of information on what is happening outside the country. The Japanese press gives a great deal of play to news on the United States and it boasts the largest foreign press corps in the United States. Japanese views or images of the United States have been, to a large extent, shaped by these correspondents, whose reports are frequently prepared in a hurry and sometimes over-dramatized to appeal to the audience back home.

The press in Japan is also influential as the mirror of public opinion. The general political climate of the nation has an important constraining effect on the government, which is reinforced by the Japanese tendency to emphasize consensus. To some extent public opinion comes to be identified with press reports and editorials. Beyond this, public opinion in Japan is often made by the press. The press was instrumental in setting the anti-Kishi mood in 1959–60, in fueling Okinawa reversion sentiment during the 1965–69 period, and in promoting a sense of national resistance to textile quotas in 1969–71. Philosophically, the press perceives itself as filling a vacuum created by the lack of an effective and practical political opposition—in essence, checking "the government's Pisa-like leanings toward America."[6]

The press exerts further influence on policymaking because of its ability to expose individuals or groups in a position of power, often with cooperation from dissident government officials. Frequent leaks to the Japanese press of official or private proposals helped exacerbate the textile issue. Press exposure of the LaRocque testimony on nuclear weapons in the fall of 1974 was a serious blow to the government of Premier Kakuei Tanaka, which had already been weakened by an electoral setback the previous summer. And the detailed reports of *Bungei shunjū,*

6. Yukio Matsuyama, "Japanese Press and Japan's Foreign Policy," *Journal of International Affairs,* vol. 26, no. 2 (1972), p. 153.

a monthly magazine, on Tanaka's allegedly shady financial dealings precipitated a crisis that led to the end of his rule in December. The extent to which the press criticizes particular government leaders or their factions is sometimes limited, however, by its financial dependence on the banks having close ties with such leaders, and by the unwritten code of conduct and sense of reciprocal obligation between individual politicians or bureaucrats and news reporters on their beats. Indeed, Japanese papers did not give the *Bungei shunjū* revelations prominent play until twelve days after the article was published, when Tanaka was questioned about it at the Foreign Correspondents' Club in Tokyo.[7]

Frequently those journalists who maintain close relations with government leaders serve as informal advisers. Very often, decisionmakers turn to their journalist friends to sound out possible public reactions to different policy alternatives. This is usually done during informal nighttime chats (*yomawari*) that newsmen regularly engage in with important politicians and bureaucrats.

The Effect of Polarization

The overall pattern of Japanese national politics, then, is one of sharp differences over the fundamental lines of foreign policy. There is considerable consensus on basic policy directions among the ruling party leaders and senior foreign office officials. They have consistently favored alignment with the United States as the primary means of protecting Japan's security, accommodation to certain U.S. military interests (for example, bases in Japan) in order to maintain the alliance and fulfill its purposes, and moderate Japanese rearmament. The business community has favored these as well. But the opposition parties have opposed, with varying degrees of militancy, the U.S.-Japan security treaty and the American military presence on Japanese soil. And public reaction against rearmament and nuclear weapons—far from fading as many expected—has endured and emerged as a fundamental factor in Japanese foreign policy and international identity.

Domestic politics has imposed substantial limits on the security policies LDP governments could pursue. Full-scale rearmament was out, as was any military role for Japan's forces outside of Japanese territory. Special public sensitivity on the nuclear issue meant that Premier Sato had to negotiate nuclear-free Okinawa reversion, though personally he

7. On their long-time silence on this issue, see Don Oberdorfer, "The Lockjaw of Tokyo Dailies," *Washington Post*, Jan. 4, 1975.

might have accepted an agreement calling for continued presence of nuclear weapons on Okinawa after reversion.

As important, however, has been the impact of domestic politics on how Japan's leaders have handled security issues with the public. The lack of consensus has reinforced a tendency toward minimal disclosure and maximum secrecy, toward conveying a vague and sometimes misleading picture of the purposes and operations of the bilateral security relationship. Thus in public forums ruling politicians and senior bureaucrats have emphasized aspects of Japan's foreign policy (such as pacifism, economic intercourse, and rejection of nuclear arms) that elicited overwhelming domestic acceptance, and refrained from explaining their own conception of Japanese security interests except when internal or external political pressure made some such articulation unavoidable. In the immediate postwar years, Premier Shigeru Yoshida "shared with his advisers a predisposition against discussing the real elements of high policy in public."[8] This elitist approach, characteristic also of the Gaimushō from which Yoshida had come, was regularly reinforced by short-term political pressures. During the Korean War, Yoshida could not have spoken of important Japanese interests in military and political developments on the Korean peninsula—a constant of Japanese foreign policy—without seeming to echo the discredited imperial past. In the decades that followed, LDP leaders were most successful politically when they could emphasize domestic issues—above all, economic growth—and minimize or defuse U.S.-Japan security questions.

Such a closed leadership style has sometimes kept potentially volatile matters from the opposition and the press. But it has left the leaders vulnerable when evidence surfaces that appears to contradict repeated governmental reassurances, as the LaRocque episode demonstrated.

Institutions of Political Leadership

All of these actors must work within the postwar parliamentary system. How does that system distribute power in practice—over policy issues in general and foreign policy issues in particular? And how does this compare with the presidential system as it operates in the United States?

8. Martin E. Weinstein, *Japan's Postwar Defense Policy, 1947–1968* (Columbia University Press, 1971), p. 56.

Prime Minister and President

To win and keep his office, the prime minister must command the support of a majority of the Diet. In practice this has meant the Liberal Democratic party. A party conference composed mainly of LDP Diet members chooses a party president by a direct ballot; then the LDP unites in the Diet to elect him prime minister.[9] Since the party is divided into factions, the premier must win and maintain the support of a majority (or "mainstream") factional coalition. Thus he chooses his cabinet with the factional balance uppermost in his mind. In both gaining the premiership and keeping it, therefore, he must concentrate primarily on intraparty politics.[10] But the desires and values of the broad national political community have their impact too, since party politicians see the premier's public standing as an important influence on the party's electoral prospects. Before he succeeded Sato as premier in 1972, for example, Kakuei Tanaka developed a reputation as a man of "decision and action" who could capture the public's imagination and lead aggressively to new policies; this was seen as an attractive contrast to Sato's cautious, insider style. And Tanaka's departure from office was preceded by his fall to record lows in public opinion polls, when he came to be seen as an ineffective yet arbitrary leader and a prime practitioner of "money politics."

Once in power, the premier is in a relatively strong personal position vis à vis his cabinet colleagues. Unlike prewar premiers who were hostage to the *jūshin* and the military, he has sole power to designate and remove other ministers and he is clearly the central figure in his cabinet. He seldom directly fires a minister—this would be considered too blatant an exercise of authority (and would alienate the target, who as a senior party member might be needed one day as an ally). But he can—and frequently does—remove a minister as part of a cabinet reshuffle—and such reshuffles are almost annual.

9. The present general rule is to hold such a conference every three years; they were held every two years up to 1972. In special circumstances like the forced resignation of Tanaka in 1974, ad hoc procedures are followed. In that particular case, an LDP elder statesman—Etsusaburō Shiina—negotiated with major faction leaders and gained consensus support for Takeo Miki, who was then chosen without opposition by the party's Diet members. More typically, however, the selection is openly contested and the formal intraparty ballot is crucial.

10. This would change, of course, were the LDP to lose its majority. Then a premier's support coalition would have to include at least some of the Diet opposition. A broader coalition might also arise if the LDP were to split.

Yet the premier's authority over his ministers is far more limited and constrained than that of an American president. The president's cabinet members are clearly his subordinates, usually brought to prominence by him, usually lacking independent bases, and thus dependent on his support and confidence if they are to play leading roles in the administration. The prime minister's cabinet is composed of fellow politicians, long-time colleagues who frequently have their own political bases as leaders of rival factions. Presidents can, and do, act above and around cabinet members, depleting their authority. The Japanese premier is much less free to ignore ministers in their spheres of formally designated responsibility. And if a U.S. president is expected to exercise visible leadership, get out front on issues, the ideal prime minister is more often seen as the overseer of a broad participatory decision process, remaining at the center and somehow moving things forward, but avoiding "arbitrary" actions.

He also needs to keep relations with the opposition within tolerable bounds. As long as the premier stays in power, his numerical majority in the Diet is sufficient to enact any legislation the cabinet submits. However, the opposition parties can—and often do—employ a variety of tactics to delay legislation and to underscore their opposition. It is considered improper for the premier to use his majority bluntly, so the views and interests of opposition politicians are frequently considered and to some degree accommodated. When a premier seeks—as did Kishi in 1960—to force through a controversial matter like renewal of the U.S.-Japan security treaty, he risks a strong public reaction against such "coercive" tactics even if he has beyond question the necessary Diet votes, and even if it was the opposition that resorted to obstructionist tactics in the first place. Such a reaction drove Kishi from office. In fact, it was exploited by rivals within his party who forced his replacement by a competing faction leader, Hayato Ikeda.

As the Kishi example shows, LDP factional politics are never very far below the surface in Japanese foreign policymaking on publicly controversial issues. In some cases, they can bring new policy initiatives and commitments to the surface. Sato was competing for the LDP presidency-cum-premiership when he first asserted that the postwar period would not end for Japan until Okinawa reverted to Japanese administrative control. Tanaka used the China issue to his advantage in 1972 by lining up weaker faction leaders in favor of a thoroughgoing China policy shift against the more cautious stance of the other major contender, Takeo Fukuda. And each leader took action on his issue once he reached power.

Factionalism can also, however, lead LDP leaders to temporize on foreign policy questions. A leader may fear that too dramatic an action will put him in a politically exposed position. Masayoshi Ohira, minister of international trade and industry in 1969, resisted efforts to settle the textile issue at least partly out of fear that identification with unpopular concessions would hurt his prospects of one day becoming premier. In 1974, Ohira as *foreign* minister moved cautiously toward an aviation agreement with Peking—which he favored personally—because of opposition from LDP members oriented toward Taiwan; ultimately, however, he seemed to conclude it was in his interest to act decisively and demonstrate his ability to prevail over his intraparty opponents on a controversial issue. And sometimes, as in early 1959 on security treaty revision, LDP leaders take publicly conflicting positions in their maneuvering for the succession. Similar maneuvering—and similar disarray— was evident in the Japanese response to the Arab oil export cutbacks in the fall of 1973, as several ministers took conflicting stances in their search for initiatives that could enhance their prestige and party standing. By contrast, Sato successfully avoided major factional complications on Okinawa by his cautious handling of the issue after he came to power. He also changed foreign ministers at a crucial stage, replacing rival faction leader Miki with a loyal supporter, Kiichi Aichi.

But though in most respects the Japanese prime minister is more constrained—and certainly less autonomous—than the U.S. president, the power differences are not all in favor of the latter. In relations with his legislature, it is the Japanese chief of government who has the advantage.

The Diet and Congress

Linked with the prime minister's dependence on the Diet is its responsiveness to him—as long as it supports his regime, it can usually be counted on to back his legislation. The American president's autonomy cuts both ways too—many presidential programs die for lack of congressional action. The president's colleagues (whose power and roles he must take account of and accommodate) are the congressional power barons—chairmen of standing committees who remain in their posts year after year and develop close relationships with senior bureaucrats and major interest groups in their substantive bailiwicks. Sometimes also congressional party leaders attain such power as to require considerable presidential deference, as did Senate Majority Leader Lyndon Johnson during the Eisenhower administration and Senate Minority Leader Everett Dirksen in the 1960s.

The influence of Representative Wilbur Mills on the textile issue was based on his position as House Ways and Means Committee chairman and his use of that position to establish himself as the most influential congressman on taxation and trade policy.[11] Mills could not control the U.S. negotiating position on the issue, but he had decisive influence on whether Congress would: (1) credibly threaten to enact statutory import quotas (more damaging to Japanese exports than a negotiated arrangement) and thereby strengthen the leverage of Nixon's negotiators; and (2) actually enact such quotas if negotiations failed.

Mills strongly preferred a negotiated quota arrangement to quotas by legislation, fearing that any bill containing statutory textile import limits would be quickly amended to include quotas for other products as well. But he collaborated with the Nixon administration in 1969 and early 1970 by threatening to push a quota bill through the House of Representatives unless negotiations with Japan were successful. When the White House surprised the Ways and Means chairman in June of 1970 by actually endorsing Mills's bill, he was left with no choice (in his eyes) but to move on legislation he disliked and feared. Quotas for other products were added, and the bill passed the House, only to die on the Senate floor as the congressional session expired in December 1970. Mills was determined to avoid such quota legislation in 1971. So he seized upon and pressed the proposal that the Japanese textile industry adopt its own export quotas, in a form far less stringent than the administration was demanding. This in turn was deeply resented by President Nixon, who saw his negotiating stance and political credibility being undercut. But for Mills it was enough trade restraint to support a claim that he had done something for textiles, and he stood adamantly against quota legislation thereafter.

An earlier exercise of congressional power resulted in the "Yoshida letter" of December 1951; negotiator Dulles extracted from Premier Yoshida a commitment to recognize Nationalist China in order to assure

11. Recent House reforms have made it more difficult for a committee chairman to attain the dominance that Mills had achieved in 1971. Committee procedures have been opened up and democratized. On Ways and Means the chairman's power has been diluted by an increase in the committee's size and the establishment of formal subcommittees, actions that Mills had resisted during his chairmanship.

Senate ratification of the peace treaty. Anticipation of similar congressional pressure on Okinawa strengthened the U.S. military in intragovernmental debates and contributed to pressure on the Japanese government to be flexible on base arrangements and assume greater regional security responsibilities as part of the reversion package.

In U.S. politics Wilbur Mills was the nearest equivalent to a senior Japanese cabinet member who leads a competing faction. Possessed of a separate power base, he was a rival baron with whom the President had to negotiate if they were to work in harmony. Once Mills felt that their textile collaboration of 1969 and 1970 had taken a turn unacceptable to his interests and convictions, he acted on his own. Similarly, Ministers Fukuda and Miki left the Tanaka cabinet in July 1974 when—after the LDP suffered a setback in the upper house elections—they felt their interests, and their party's interests, were no longer served by their continued membership. And for Miki, of course, this action bore fruit when he succeeded the discredited Tanaka the following December.

Fukuda and Miki were, of course, major Diet members and LDP leaders. And it is the balance among LDP leaders (and among parties within the Diet) that determines the composition of the ruling cabinet. The Diet also exercises significant, behind-the-scenes restraining power on government policy through the extensive consultations typically conducted before legislation is formally submitted. These primarily involve LDP Diet members, but the general preference for a working consensus also gives opposition members some marginal legislative power through their membership on particular Diet committees.

Once issues reach the formal decision stage, however, debate—though often heated—tends to have more ceremonial than substantive significance. The Diet generally enacts legislation as submitted by the cabinet and the bureaucracy, with the ruling party voting as a bloc. Thus it has not usually exercised the kind of power that the U.S. Congress can exert through floor votes on appropriations, the details of particular legislation, confirmation of senior appointees, and ratification of treaties. But there have been recent exceptions to LDP solidarity—the abstention of eighty-eight party members in the ratification vote on the China aviation agreement in 1974; the resistance of the party's right wing to ratification of the nonproliferation treaty a year later. And the declining relative position of the LDP in the Diet may enhance the leverage of the legislature and its committees even if the party continues to dominate the cabinet.

The Diet, moreover, exercises an indirect influence on Japanese foreign policymaking through its ability to call ministers to account. The major Japanese daily newspapers tend to play up such questioning—reporting it daily, in detail, with a slant frequently critical of the government and its officials. Ministers tend to respond by speaking cautiously. And their tendency toward caution in action is reinforced as well. Indeed, almost any step taken in U.S.-Japanese relations is colored by concern about and anticipation of Diet reaction and interpellation, and how it will be reported in the press.

Staffs of Political Leaders

A final area where Japanese policymaking institutions differ from American is in the paucity of major staff officials and offices serving the prime minister or the cabinet as a whole. In the United States, the president has a White House staff of several hundred and an executive office staff numbering several thousand—the "institutionalized presidency." This includes numerous politically appointed White House assistants who have specific substantive issue mandates domestic and foreign, and a welter of councils, staffs, and offices with a wide range of policy leadership and coordination functions. These officials and units stand outside of the cabinet departments, and frequently stand between cabinet officers and the president.

There is nothing parallel to this in Japanese government. Nor, for foreign policy, has any Japanese premier had an aide remotely like the president's assistant for national security affairs—a central U.S. foreign policy figure in the sixties and early seventies—or his supporting staff of foreign policy professionals operating outside of and above departmental bailiwicks. The Japanese prime minister has some staffing outside the ministries. There is the Cabinet Secretariat of nearly two hundred officials, as well as a small number of private secretaries on detail from the ministries to assist the premier in particular issue areas, including foreign policy. But most of the Cabinet Secretariat staff handle routine matters (including internal security), with only a few focusing on international matters. And the private secretaries are relatively junior. Generally, the only senior political aides whose allegiance is mainly to the premier are the chief cabinet secretary and his deputy. The term *kantei* (prime minister's official residence) is used to refer to the small political circle personally loyal to the premier.

If Japan has no counterpart to America's large presidential staffing, one reason is that the United States has nothing parallel to the Japanese cabinet. The most important policy issues in Tokyo tend to be handled and decided not by the prime minister acting alone but ceremonially by regularly convened cabinet meetings and in practice by an ad hoc group including the premier, the chief cabinet secretary, ministers in charge of the issues at hand or with recognized prerogatives for influencing them, and, frequently, one or more of the major LDP officials. No such collegial decisionmaking constrains the U.S. president's personal authority. Since Eisenhower's administration, the full cabinet has met infrequently and considered major current policy business very rarely; it has not even a ceremonial, ratification function. The closest approximation to the Japanese cabinet in American government, rather, is the senior circle of foreign policy advisers who attend National Security Council (NSC) meetings—the secretary of state, the secretary of defense, the national security assistant, the chairman of the Joint Chiefs of Staff, and the director of the Central Intelligence Agency.[12] They are important, however, not because of their formal membership on the council; after all, the usually peripheral vice president is also a member. Rather, their substantive responsibilities sometimes make them the group that meets regularly with the president on critical foreign policy matters. (An example was the "Tuesday lunch" of Lyndon Johnson, which brought together the secretaries of state and defense, the national security assistant, and sometimes the CIA director, the JCS chairman, and the president's chief press aide.) But the president has greater flexibility than a Japanese premier to operate according to his preferred style. Richard Nixon preferred to talk foreign policy overwhelmingly with one man, Henry Kissinger. Nixon emulated Presidents Kennedy and Johnson in using the National Security Council as a base, even a cover, for the operations of the national security assistant and his staff. This gave the

12. The NSC, established in 1947, now has four formal members: the president, the vice president, the secretary of state, and the secretary of defense. The JCS chairman, the CIA director, and the director of the Arms Control and Disarmament Agency are statutory advisers to the council. The president's assistant for national security affairs is the council's chief staff official. Its primary official role is to offer the president integrated advice on issues combining defense and general foreign policy considerations. Its actual role has varied according to the preferences and styles of particular presidents. (See Richard Moose, "White House National Security Staffs Since 1947," in Keith C. Clark and Lawrence J. Legere, eds., *The President and the Management of National Security* [Praeger, for Institute for Defense Analyses, 1969], pp. 55–98; and I. M. Destler, *Presidents, Bureaucrats, and Foreign Policy* [Princeton University Press, 1972 and 1974], especially chap. 5.)

president an independent capability to monitor and coordinate the operating foreign policy agencies, and to provide analyses and sometimes to manage negotiations independently of the operating agencies. In Nixon's first term, dependence on the national security assistant and staff reached new heights.

For a Japanese premier such a strong separate staff is not possible. The constitutional framework and governmental traditions do not provide for it, and the cabinet—being chosen for factional balance—does not offer an appropriate base for it. White House aides are, in Japanese terms, "members of the president's faction"—their loyalty is to him. But both the Japanese cabinet and the central ruling party organization lack such coherence, because the Liberal Democratic party upon whose support the premier's tenure depends is not a cohesive central organization but a coalition of factions.

But if strong central staff organizations tied to political leaders are less possible in Japan, leaders are also less likely perhaps to perceive a strong need for them. For the LDP leadership group is composed of men with long governmental experience. Not only have they served in the Diet but, in many cases, their political careers were preceded by long service in the government bureaucracy. Thus they move into their current positions with long-standing patterns of relationships both among themselves and with influential senior bureaucrats. In the United States, however, it is typical for presidents (and frequently cabinet members) to come into office without prior experience in federal executive positions. They have little sense for how one gets action out of the federal bureaucracy, and thus feel a particular need to do what their authority and large staff organizations notably permit—to bring in their own people, loyal to them, to ride herd on the federal establishment. This is a major element in the somewhat differing roles and influence of the career bureaucracies in the two countries.

The Bureaucracies

A glance at the postwar course of U.S.-Japanese relations reveals the pervasive influence of career officials and permanent bureaucratic institutions. Pentagon resistance delayed the negotiation of the 1951 peace and security treaties and affected their substance. The State Department country desk and the U.S. embassy in Tokyo, working closely with civilian and military members of the Defense Department, dominated Okinawa reversion policy in the critical 1966–68 period. Their Gaimushō counterparts in Tokyo played a substantial role during this same period, as the sole agency capable of interpreting the evolving U.S. position on the Okinawa issue. And MITI bureaucrats repeatedly prevailed over Japanese political leaders in setting the government's stance in the textile negotiations.

None of this is to deny the leading and frequently dominant roles that political leaders can play. In both Japan and the United States, major initiatives for change tend to grow out of the interests and actions of senior political figures. And major issues can be resolved only when political leaders settle on a particular resolution or, at minimum, acquiesce in it. In the United States, presidential dominance of the bureaucracy has recently been highlighted by the Nixon-Kissinger foreign policymaking system. And political leaders frequently prevail in Japan as well. Donald C. Hellmann's study of Japanese decisionmaking leading to the 1956 peace agreement with the Soviet Union, for example, chronicles the futile efforts of the leading Gaimushō officials to prevent its negotiation.

But from this case Hellmann draws a more general conclusion—that "the peace agreement of 1956 marked the passing of an era. Unlike the pre-war period the Japanese Foreign Office proved incapable of directly competing with the ruling party in the making of policy. As intended in the 1947 Constitution the Prime Minister and his party were in control—the old gave way to the new, the politician replaced the bureaucrat."[13]

It is true that no contemporary Japanese career bureaucracy has power approaching that of the prewar military services, and party politicians are infinitely more powerful. Yet bureaucratic influence in Japan is considerably greater than Hellmann's language implies. This is due in part to the weaknesses in political leadership institutions, but even more to the sheer volume and complexity of international transactions, which can only be managed by large bureaucratic institutions. The power-dwarfing of the Japanese bureaucracy emphasized by Hellmann

13. *Japanese Domestic Politics and Foreign Policy: The Peace Agreement with the Soviet Union* (University of California Press, 1969), pp. 141–42.

seems to have been the exception rather than the rule.[14] And American bureaucracy, while weakened by the Nixon-Kissinger system, was never so reduced in power as appearances made it seem.[15]

The Soviet-Japanese peace agreement issue was so unusual, moreover, that it is hardly surprising that Hellmann's conclusion could not be automatically applied to Japanese policymaking toward the United States. For Soviet relations were outside the mainstream of postwar Japanese foreign policy—particularly in the period before regular diplomatic relations were reestablished. The agreement had more symbolic importance than substantive impact on major Japanese interests and policies, foreign or domestic. And since there was no regular embassy channel in operation, the Gaimushō was deprived of the types of leverage it derives from its inside role. Thus it stands to reason that the politicians would be less constrained.

One of the sources of bureaucratic power is the size of the institutions involved. This is both effect and cause of the complexity of foreign policymaking in each country, and it clearly limits the ability of political leaders in both countries to control all that goes on. In the Japanese executive branch there are about 1 million public servants; the U.S. total is about 2.5 million. The proportion of these working on foreign policy is small, but the absolute numbers are considerable. By a liberal estimate, there are close to 10,000 Japanese bureaucrats with foreign policy responsibilities, including 2,600 in the Ministry of Foreign Affairs, a large percentage of MITI's 6,600 officials, and others from such institutions as the Finance Ministry, the Defense Agency, the Economic Planning Agency, and the Ministry of Agriculture and Forestry.[16] In the U.S.

14. See Shigeo Misawa, "An Outline of the Policy-Making Process in Japan," in Hiroshi Itoh, ed. and trans., *Japanese Politics, An Inside View: Readings from Japan* (Cornell University Press, 1973), pp. 12–48.

15. See Destler, *Presidents, Bureaucrats, and Foreign Policy*, chap. 5; and Chester A. Crocker, "The Nixon-Kissinger National Security Council System, 1969–72: A Study in Foreign Policy Management," in National Academy of Public Administration, *Making Organizational Change Effective: Case Studies of Attempted Reforms in Foreign Affairs*, Appendix O to the Report of the Commission on the Organization of the Government for the Conduct of Foreign Policy (Government Printing Office, 1976).

16. See Haruhiro Fukui, "Bureaucratic Power in Japan," in Peter Drysdale and Hironobu Kitaōji, eds., *Japan and Australia: Two Societies and Their Interactions* (Oxford University Press, forthcoming); and Jinjiin Ninyokyoku [Personnel Agency, Employment Bureau], "Shōwa 45-nendo ni okeru ippanshoku no kokka kōmuin no ninyō jōkyō chōsa hōkoku" [Report on government employment, 1970] (n.d.; processed).

government, 12,604 Americans were employed by the State Department at home and abroad in 1974, another 9,346 in its sister agencies (the Agency for International Development, the Arms Control and Disarmament Agency, and the United States Information Agency), an estimated 15,000 by the Central Intelligence Agency, and 987,236 as civilian workers on military matters for the Department of Defense.[17] To all these must be added the many other officials whose day-to-day business is primarily international—in the White House national security and international economic policy staffs; and in the international arms of departments with predominantly domestic missions such as Treasury, Agriculture, Commerce, and Labor.

Controlling all these officials would obviously be a formidable task for political leaders even if this were their paramount objective. In fact, of course, these leaders have competing priorities as well—relations with other senior officials; partisan political success in elections; particular high-priority issues they feel they must handle personally. Thus bureaucratic management gets only a fraction of their time. Yet national policy is, in many areas, the sum of the countless day-to-day operational decisions and actions officials take at various bureaucratic levels. To the extent that top leaders (and subordinates responsive to their interests) cannot ride herd on these many decisions and actions, they must, in practice, yield power to institutions over which they reign but cannot completely rule.

On those issues that they can personally oversee, moreover, government leaders depend on bureaucracies for a range of services and skills— information about current issues and the broader political and economic variables that affect decisions on these issues; expertise and experience in dealing with these issues; communications processes and channels linking their own to foreign governments. If leaders cannot go elsewhere for these resources, they must go to bureaucrats; they will thus tend to see the facts of issues as bureaucrats see them, and their policy decisions will tend to reflect bureaucratic preferences. Moreover, in all policymaking systems bureaucrats will have standard policy-influencing roles and authorities—whether established by law, regulation, or custom— that political leaders will disregard at their peril. And they have one

17. Senate Committee on Government Operations, *Organization of Federal Executive Departments and Agencies* (Government Printing Office, 1975); and Harry Howe Ransom, *The Intelligence Establishment* (Harvard University Press, 1970), p. 87.

further advantage vis à vis politicians: their narrower roles and interests and group loyalties allow for a single-mindedness in promoting their views and interests that politicians, who must respond to a broader range of interests and groups, cannot normally match.

Thus, the size of bureaucracies and the nature of their established skills and services assure that they will have significant foreign policy impact in both countries. In Japan, permanent governmental institutions are further strengthened by the way officials are recruited and the unusual prestige of the career public servant. In institutions like the Foreign Ministry (and, above all, the Finance Ministry), the professional group that enters under highly competitive qualifying examinations is considered—and considers itself—an elite. Moreover, entry into these elites is virtually impossible except at the beginning of one's career. Once in, an elite bureaucrat rises through the organization until he retires, generally after holding a responsible senior position. This reflects a broad characteristic of modern Japanese society. Social mobility from generation to generation is very great, but if birth does not determine status, success in school and examinations generally does. How one enters which organization is the major determinant of one's ultimate accomplishments.

In the U.S. bureaucracy, too, most bureaucrats are careerists who will devote all—or the bulk—of their working lives to government service. Their prestige in the society, however, is several notches lower than that of their Japanese counterparts.[18] And in the U.S. government, a significant role is played by the "in-and-outers," those mobile individuals, usually with professional bases outside government (in law or academia, for example), who take official positions for limited periods, perhaps two to five years. They are frequently identified politically with the party in power, or personally with high officials of the administration. And they occupy not only a large proportion of positions in the political layer (assistant secretaries upward) of each department, but also some of the positions—both senior and junior—on general policy planning or analysis staffs that serve the White House assistant for national security affairs, the secretary of state, and the secretary of defense.

The Japanese government is very different. There, aside from the political minister and the generally insignificant parliamentary vice

18. An exception is the military. As a reaction to the wartime experience, members of Japanese Self-Defense Forces have very low prestige in their society, much lower than that of American military officers and servicemen. Civilian officials of the Japan Defense Agency also have less prestige than their Pentagon counterparts.

ministers, the top positions in the ministries are filled by career officials.
So also are the (generally very small) staff advisory and coordinating
units that serve the premier and the cabinet. And the Japanese politicians
who lead the bureaucrats tend also to be a rather stable grouping, drawn
from among the senior LDP Diet members and thus changing but slowly
year after year. The political figures brought in by a U.S. president, however, are likely to be less known to their colleagues and subordinates,
less predictable in their policy views and personal capabilities.

The comings and goings of such in-and-outers at both the near-
cabinet and the staff level make the U.S. government a far more open
and fluid place than the Japanese. Consequently the U.S. government
has a considerably weaker institutional memory, at least at the level of
those who have substantial influence over policy.

The Gaimushō and State

In the United States and Japan all *foreign* policy issues concern the
State Department and the Gaimushō (Foreign Ministry), and each is in
fact involved in most such issues. As the major action channels of foreign
policymaking within the bureaucracies, the two share many organizational and behavioral characteristics typical of foreign offices. The differences between them reflect mainly the larger political systems within
which they operate.

The Foreign Ministry's influence over Japanese policy is derived overwhelmingly from its inside role—as the operating agency that handles
diplomatic relationships; as the source for the bulk of information, analysis, and policy proposals on which the cabinet must make its decisions.
The U.S. State Department has similar levers for influence, but nothing
like the Gaimushō's near-monopoly of them. State has very strong competitors in intelligence, policy analysis, and policy implementation. By
contrast, neither the LDP party organization, nor the Diet and its committees, nor the Cabinet Secretariat possesses sufficient information, or
analytic or operational resources, to challenge the Gaimushō.

The two foreign offices are similarly staffed. The dominant role in
each is played by an elite corps of officials recruited in their twenties or
early thirties. These officials rise (and expect to rise) through the ranks
to reach senior positions—including ambassadorships—prior to retirement. In the U.S. State Department, this elite is the approximately three
thousand Foreign Service officers. In Japan, it is the nearly six hundred
Foreign Ministry officials with Higher Foreign Service Examination

(HFSE) certificates, and the seventy-five or so with the near-equivalent prewar Higher Civil Service credentials.[19]

The differences between the two personnel systems are differences in degree; in sum, however, they make the Gaimushō a considerably purer example of the closed bureaucratic organization. Major U.S. ambassadorships and Washington positions at the bureau (assistant secretary) level and above are often filled by in-and-outers; so—though less frequently—are more junior staff jobs. This almost never happens in Japan. Internally, the U.S. Foreign Service is also more overtly competitive. Those judged as best are promoted more rapidly earlier in their careers than are their peers, and an elaborate performance evaluation system provides the formal basis for promotion decisions. The Gaimushō lacks such a structured performance evaluation system. In fact, the elite services of the Gaimushō are promoted almost automatically, with each "class" group entering the service together raised in rank simultaneously. Lateral entry into the U.S. Foreign Service at the middle and upper ranks is exceptional, but it does happen, particularly in cases where specialized talents are required; in the Japanese foreign service, it is virtually unheard of. These relative differences—when added to the smaller size of the Japanese Foreign Ministry—give the Gaimushō a stronger cohesiveness and corps spirit.

The predominance of the business of managing bilateral relations tends to strengthen the geographic subunits of both foreign offices. In State, the regional bureaus prefer to treat policy toward particular countries and areas as "their" business, and tend to control it unless the White House, departmental leaders, or strong competing departments or offices assert an active interest. In the Gaimushō, the same phenomenon holds, but without the counterweights of the U.S. system. There is nothing in the Japanese Foreign Ministry like the large "seventh floor" staff (office of the secretary of state and his major subordinates and staff) that exists in the U.S. State Department. Officials outranking the regional chiefs are fewer in number, and coordinating staffs very limited. Structurally, the senior career official in the Gaimushō is the vice minister, who works directly under the political minister. He is supported by two deputy vice ministers. Beneath this top triumvirate are the bureaus, which are either geographic (like the American Affairs Bureau) or functional (like the Economic Affairs Bureau). Each bureau is in turn divided into divisions. Bilateral issues are generally assigned to the geographic

19. Fukui, "Bureaucratic Power in Japan," p. 7.

bureaus, whereas multilateral problems are assigned to the functional bureaus. Nor is there any strong staff for overall planning and coordination, though the Treaties Bureau does get involved in a wide range of issues as the general legal counsel and adviser for the entire ministry. Thus, the Foreign Ministry is notably decentralized. The bureaus and divisions are "the basic units of decision and action"; their chiefs enjoy a "large measure of freedom, within the limits defined by the rule of seniority, to map out their courses of action with regard to any specific policy issue at hand."[20]

Heads of these bureaus and divisions naturally tend to give priority to their policy interests, and the interests of their clients (which are usually the foreign countries with whom they deal daily). Such loyalties are kept within bounds, however, by rotation of career officials among geographic and functional divisions, and among different parts of the world in their overseas assignments. Similar rotation policies are practiced in the U.S. State Department, though this does not prevent many officials from becoming identified with particular regions or countries for considerable portions of their careers.

Finally, each career service has a similar "organizational essence." In each, "the view held by the dominant group of the organization" as to its appropriate "missions" and "capabilities"[21] stresses the day-to-day management of relations with foreign governments and the shaping of government policy insofar as it affects those relations. Foreign service officers view themselves as diplomatic professionals trained (mainly by practical experience) in the art of dealing with foreign governments, and the art of understanding such governments. They tend to equate wisdom in foreign policy with careful, undramatic reliance on their expertise. On issues of policy substance, however, it is the generalist who is valued over the specialist.

In the conduct of normal, routinized, and invisible foreign relations, State Department and Gaimushō bureaucrats have played dominant

20. Haruhiro Fukui, "Policy-Making in Japan's Foreign Ministry" (paper prepared for delivery at a conference on Japan's foreign policy, at Kauai, Hawaii, Jan. 14–17, 1974; processed), p. 17. Interestingly, John Creighton Campbell reaches similar conclusions about the Japanese budget process, finding its "subsystems" to be "very independent . . . at least when compared with the United States." (*Contemporary Japanese Budget Politics* [University of California Press, forthcoming].)

21. This concept is developed in Morton H. Halperin with the assistance of Priscilla Clapp and Arnold Kanter, *Bureaucratic Politics and Foreign Policy* (Brookings Institution, 1974), p. 28.

roles, usually with skill and self-assurance. They have given priority to the bilateral security and economic relationship, and laid much of its legal and political groundwork. So long as issues fall within their juris-dictional bailiwicks, they are generally handled with reasonable effi-ciency and orderliness according to well-established operational pro-cedures.

But most important foreign policy issues cannot be so neatly and ex-clusively treated. In practice, the foreign offices must share responsibility with two types of competitors—with politicians as issues become domes-tically visible, or important to powerful home interests; with other bureaucracies having security and economic responsibilities as issues affect these responsibilities.

Relations with Political Leaders

On the critical question of relations with the political leaders and groups ultimately responsible for foreign policy, foreign office officials in each country are inevitably ambivalent. As professionals, they tend to see political leaders as ignorant meddlers in complex diplomatic issues. But as practical men, they realize that their ability to influence foreign policy depends heavily on their ties with the political leadership, since neither career group has—or is likely to develop—a strong domestic constituency. They particularly need the help of political leaders on the really big issues, for these involve not only domestic politics, but usu-ally also interagency relationships which foreign office people have diffi-culty managing without support from political executives.

The U.S. State Department has been regularly found wanting by presidents and their White House aides.[22] The Gaimushō seems to have done considerably better in its relations with LDP politicians. It can hardly exclude them from issues where they have political stakes. Nor can foreign office officials always thwart policies that they oppose, as their 1956 failure on the Soviet peace agreement demonstrated. But though it is politicians, not bureaucrats, who play the prominent—and frequently dominant—parts on the politically most important issues, formal deference by the bureaucrats leaves room for substantial actual impact. Since there is no base for a strong, competing central staff at the

22. For the classic account, see Arthur Schlesinger, Jr., *A Thousand Days* (Houghton Mifflin, 1965), pp. 406–47. For an analysis of the major ways presidents have found State to be unresponsive, see Destler, *Presidents, Bureaucrats, and Foreign Policy*, pp. 154–60.

political level, the Gaimushō can, if it is skillful in reading and accommo-dating factional politics, maintain considerable influence through the operational support it provides to the foreign minister and the pre-mier, and through its day-to-day responsibilities for implementing for-eign policy and managing foreign relations. On China policy in 1972 and 1974, for example, key Gaimushō officials were cooperatively and sup-portively involved, shaping many of the critical details of Japan's new relationships with Peking and Taipei. The contrast with the State De-partment's noninvolvement in Nixon's basic China policy turn of 1971 is striking, though State's China desk played a significant support role thereafter.

On issues involving Japan, however, State's relative weakness vis à vis the political leadership has frequently been offset by the asymmetry of the bilateral relationship. Prior to the Nixon years, U.S.-Japan issues were of distinctly subordinate interest to American political leaders, whereas they were vital to Japanese political leaders. These issues tended to be as neglected in the U.S. media as they were dramatized in the Japanese. For these reasons (and also because on matters Japanese the White House and State were usually in basic agreement), Japan issues tended (again before Nixon) to be "left pretty much in the hands of the experts," particularly the "middle-level bureaucrats in both the State Department and Defense Department" with "a continuing interest in U.S.-Japanese relations."[23] Arthur Schlesinger, Jr.'s forty-page chron-icle of Kennedy administration complaints about State, for example, dealt at no point with Japan. In Tokyo, however, U.S. relations were politically crucial to LDP leaders and controversial in domestic politics. This made influence over these issues by Japanese political leaders greater than was the norm. Comparing relations with political leaders, then, the Gaimushō's relatively greater strength is counterbalanced by the far greater political importance of U.S.-Japan issues in Tokyo.

Interagency Relations

Considerable differences also exist between the two foreign offices in their dealings with other bureaucracies with interests in particular areas

23. Priscilla A. Clapp and Morton H. Halperin, "U.S. Elite Images of Japan: The Postwar Period," in Akira Iriye, ed., *Mutual Images: Essays in American-Japanese Relations* (Harvard University Press, 1975). See also I. M. Destler, "Country Expertise and U.S. Foreign Policy-making: The Case of Japan," in Morton A. Kaplan and Kinhide Mushakōji, eds., *Japan, America, and the Future World Order* (Free Press, 1976).

of foreign policy—though the same broad factors affect both governments.

The day has long passed when foreign offices could hope to monop-
olize all dealings with foreign governments. Well under half of the
officials attached to U.S. embassies are State Department personnel;
MITI and Finance officials are prominent on Japanese embassy staffs in
major countries. And international conferences and missions on subjects
such as defense, trade, finance, and agriculture bring senior officials and
specialists from domestic agencies in the two governments into frequent
contact.

Still less can State and the Gaimushō exclude other agencies from
influencing basically domestic issues that have some foreign policy content. The line between international and domestic matters is hard to
locate; the overlap is pervasive. In the economic area, problems such as
international energy supply and consumption, regulation of exchange
rates, and trade (in general and in particular commodities) are all
matters of major consequence to agencies that cannot effectively carry
out their domestic responsibilities without substantial influence over
international matters. Similarly, decisions and actions on security issues
affect the roles and capabilities of military organizations, whose leaders
naturally become involved in these matters. In general, a foreign office's
influence tends to wane on issues where its officials lack expertise, where
groups with strong domestic interests and ties to other agencies (or to
politicians) become engaged, and where the matter at stake is of major
concern to agencies that are responsible for domestic policy.

ECONOMIC ISSUES. In foreign economic policy the Japanese Foreign
Ministry faces formidable competition from two major ministries,
Finance and International Trade and Industry.[24] In the 1969–71 negotia-
tions on the financial terms of Okinawa reversion, for example, the
Gaimushō, like the State Department, had great difficulty influencing
either the progress or the outcome of the talks, though they were essen-

24. The discussion of these two ministries draws substantially on Philip H. Trezise
with the collaboration of Yukio Suzuki, "Politics, Government, and Economic Growth
in Japan," in Hugh Patrick and Henry Rosovsky, eds., *Asia's New Giant: How the
Japanese Economy Works* (Brookings Institution, 1976); Fukui, "Bureaucratic Power
in Japan"; Yōnosuke Nagai, "MITI and Japan's Economic Diplomacy" (paper prepared for delivery at a conference on Japanese foreign policy, at Kauai, Hawaii, Jan.
14–17, 1974; processed); Campbell, *Contemporary Japanese Budget Politics;* and
I. M. Destler, Hideo Sato, and Haruhiro Fukui, "The Textile Wrangle: Conflict in
Japanese-American Relations 1969–71" (1976; processed), chap. 2.

tial to the implementation of the Sato-Nixon agreement in 1969. They were dominated instead by the Finance Ministry (with its senior official Yūsuke Kashiwagi acting as a de facto one-man negotiating team) and the U.S. Treasury Department (with Anthony Jurich, special assistant to Secretary David M. Kennedy, acting as Kashiwagi's counterpart). Similarly on the textile negotiations, it was MITI that usually played the lead bureaucratic role. Especially during the last and critical phases of the negotiations in the fall of 1971, a few MITI officials working directly under the new MITI minister, Tanaka, almost completely monopolized the action on the Japanese side. The Gaimushō made only weak efforts to get into the act.

The Finance Ministry is the elite agency of Japan's bureaucracy, responsible for macroeconomic policy and the government budget. Thus, it combines in form, and to a considerable degree in practice, the powers of the U.S. Treasury Department, Office of Management and Budget, and Council of Economic Advisers. Until very recently its basic (and unusually consistent) domestic economic policy orientation was to combine a low-interest, quite expansionist monetary policy with tightness on the fiscal side. This not only proved an effective formula for facilitating rapid economic growth, but meshed nicely with the ministry's role of budgetary gatekeeper. In years when the revenue-expenditure balance seemed likely to prove too repressive, Finance preferred tax reduction to increased public spending.

In foreign policy views, the ministry tends to be loosely divided between a group centered in the International Finance Bureau and more domestically oriented officials elsewhere. On balance, Finance has been more internationalist than MITI, and its relationship with the Gaimushō has frequently been cooperative. It has opposed sharp increases in Japan's defense capabilities because of the possible impact on the budget, paralleling the Gaimushō's opposition to such expenditures on the grounds of likely adverse diplomatic repercussions. The two ministries were allied in supporting import liberalization against the opposition of MITI and Agriculture. They have tended to cooperate in international financial negotiations to their mutual benefit, with Finance—as in other countries—clearly the lead agency. But on economic aid, Finance Ministry officials have been strongly restrictive, directly at odds with Foreign Ministry—and MITI—officials who would like to expand such aid and soften its terms.

The Gaimushō-MITI relationship has been generally much less amicable, with their rivalry deeply rooted in the prewar period. In the twenties and thirties the Gaimushō faced aggressive competition from MITI's predecessor, the Ministry of Commerce and Industry. In fact, "reformist" Commerce bureaucrats (such as future Premier Nobusuke Kishi) often worked hand in glove with radical army officers against Foreign Ministry moderates to whittle away the latter's authority over the management of the overseas territories in northern China and Southeast Asia.

After the war was over, though the military suddenly ceased to be a significant force, the renamed Commerce bureaucracy not only survived but prospered beyond earlier dreams. And the preoccupation of the successive postwar cabinets with economic expansion at home and abroad has worked to MITI's advantage in the interministry rivalry.

The role of the Ministry of International Trade and Industry is to promote and strengthen Japan's industrial development and foreign trade. The policy stands of MITI bureaucrats tend to follow rather directly from this role; their solicitude toward Japanese domestic economic interests leads to frequent, predictable differences with Gaimushō officials. In dealings with the United States, the Foreign Ministry will almost always be the advocate of trade concessions, with MITI urging a tougher stance.[25] Until very recently, the dominant view of MITI officials was that the Japanese economy remained weak and vulnerable. Its development, therefore, needed to be promoted by encouraging those industries and sectors with the best growth prospects, and protecting this development from overseas threats (such as excessive imports or possible domination by American capital investment). And in practice this spilled over into protecting the interests of slow-growing industries as well. At times, MITI officials have viewed international economic policy as simply an extension of domestic economic policy: seeing Japan's national interest as, essentially, the highest possible gross national product; arguing that foreign policy issues can be clearly divided into political and economic categories, with the latter to be resolved on technical grounds by specialists such as themselves. And these officials have felt that special protection for Japan was justified because they saw their country as

25. But MITI's concern with the domestic economy can lead to its advocacy of diplomatic concessions as well—in the oil crisis of late 1973, for example, MITI was inclined to favor concessions toward the Arabs on Israel to assure the flow of oil; Gaimushō officials were reluctant because of fear that it would damage what they considered most important, Japan's international prestige and reputation and the relationship with the United States.

weak; as one of them put it, "We cannot be optimistic about measures taken for unconditional free competition between Gulliver and the Lilliputians."[26]

Within MITI, however, there are spokesmen for a more international-ist policy orientation. The ministry is organized under the minister (a politician) and the vice minister (a career official), who are supported by a small secretariat. The line bureaus of the ministry, such as Heavy Industry, and Textiles and General Merchandise, are responsible for broad industrial sectors; the International Trade Bureau deals with foreign commerce. There is chronic tension on international issues be-tween the line bureaus, which are the heart of the organization, and the International Trade Bureau and the secretariat. These latter tend to be responsive to a broader range of policy considerations, and their stances on issues often approach those of the economic sections of the Foreign Ministry. This tension led one ranking MITI official to note: "MITI is no Goethe, but it is a unique government agency that has 'two souls.' One is nationalism and the other internationalism. Other agencies, such as Foreign Affairs and Defense, only have internationalism. Agriculture and Construction have only nationalism. MITI has both. When the wave of internationalism becomes too strong, nationalism asserts its identity, saying, 'What is my raison d'être?' "[27]

The ministry's influence on Japanese foreign policymaking derives, of course, from its influence on domestic economic policymaking. The con-cept of MITI as an all-powerful headquarters for "Japan, Inc." is clearly exaggerated. Nevertheless, MITI undoubtedly had a broad, many-faceted influence on Japan's postwar economic course in general, and even more on the day-to-day actions of particular firms. This influence has declined as the Japanese economy has become progressively decon-trolled, with industries less and less dependent on MITI for specific actions approving imports of goods and technology, or foreign exchange transactions. And as this has taken place MITI has become somewhat more internationally oriented, as if seeking to compensate in the foreign sphere for its decline in power domestically. But the ministry's power on particular issues remains closely related to its technical expertise on the Japanese economy, and to its network of relationships with Japanese businessmen. These relationships are important in securing information,

26. Naohiro Amaya, quoted in Nagai, "MITI and Japan's Economic Diplomacy."
27. Quoted in Daizō Kusayanagi, "Tsūsanshō: Tamesareru sutā kanchō" [MITI: Star agency on trial], *Bungei shunjū*, August 1974, p. 114.

and in gaining cooperation from businessmen on problems they must help to solve. This gives MITI a card to play in the larger political arena that the Foreign Ministry does not possess—the support, or threatened opposition, of business interests who are a major supporting group of the ruling party. This MITI-business relationship is strengthened by the frequent movement of ranking MITI bureaucrats to high-level positions in major industries after their retirement from the bureaucracy.

The types of stands taken by Finance and MITI, and the insistence of specialist agencies that policy issues are technical ones requiring their expertise, have clear parallels in American foreign economic policy-making. But if the U.S. State Department faces competition comparable to the Gaimushō's, it is not always as certain and consistent from whence the competition cometh. A larger number of institutions is involved, and their power waxes and wanes. The senior departmental competitor is Treasury, which is generally supreme in international monetary policy, but lacks Finance's macroeconomic dominance and its budget role. Instead, government spending is managed by the Office of Management and Budget, which is part of the president's executive office, and Treasury and OMB share the lead in national economic policy with the Council of Economic Advisers and the independent Federal Reserve Board. The balance of national economic policy influence depends significantly on the strengths, interests, and presidential relationships of politically designated executives in these organizations.

Multilateral trade negotiations are coordinated by the Office of the Special Representative for Trade Negotiations, which participates also in trade policy deliberations along with State, Commerce, Agriculture, and other departments. Since 1971, trade policy has also been coordinated to some degree by the staff of the White House Council on International Economic Policy (CIEP), whose formal writ covers all foreign economic matters. Interestingly, the Treasury's role on general trade policy has usually been minor, though recently strong secretaries like John Connally and George Shultz have made their marks in this area, and the department has particular trade regulation responsibilities—like that for countervailing duties.

The Treasury Department's international staff is quite small, totaling somewhat over two hundred. Its senior responsible official for monetary questions is the under secretary for monetary affairs; below him is the international office headed by an assistant secretary. A major concern of the department through the sixties and seventies has been the protection and improvement of the U.S. balance of payments. Treasury also, for historical reasons, has primary responsibility for U.S. policy vis à vis the multilateral development banks, though the Agency for International Development—an autonomous unit within State—retains responsibility for the shrinking bilateral aid program.

If Treasury thus differs from the Finance Ministry, it is even harder to find an American counterpart for MITI. The Commerce Department played a parallel role in the textile negotiations, but its leverage has not been comparable on other product issues, let alone other matters related to foreign policy. The Commerce Department's international staff numbers about thirteen hundred persons, concentrated particularly on export promotion services to U.S. businessmen, and on specialized problems of regulating trade with communist countries. On broader trade and investment policy issues, Commerce tends to be protectionist, responding to the interests of U.S. firms that feel threatened by international competition. But in general, Commerce is one of the weakest of the executive departments, and its role in determining U.S. economic policy is far more modest than its name implies. A stronger agency on issues relevant to it is the Department of Agriculture (USDA), with wide-ranging impact on domestic crop production and international trade. And in contrast to its Japanese counterpart, USDA in general is internationally oriented, reflecting the strong interest of U.S. agriculture in world markets.

Coordination of foreign economic policy is a recurring problem in the American bureaucracy, with the CIEP one in a series of imperfect organizational approaches. When coordination has been strong, it has generally come from individuals based in foreign policy agencies (State or the NSC staff) or economic policy institutions (mainly Treasury). In the Nixon administration, for example, strong leadership in this area came from economic policy czars like John Connally and George Shultz when it came at all.[28]

28. In the Kennedy and Johnson administrations a staff approach was employed: the president had a deputy special assistant for national security affairs whose mandate covered foreign economic policy and major overlapping political issues. In the late Eisenhower administration, Under Secretary of State Douglas Dillon proved an effective foreign economic policy czar operating from this line position. The Ford administration established a cabinet-level Economic Policy Board in September 1974 to coordinate foreign and domestic economic policy, and the CIEP has been subordinated to the new structure. But the Kissinger State Department has been unusually assertive on economic issues, and friction has been frequent between it and the domestic economic advisers and institutions.

Because of the concentration of authority in key ministries, the Japanese government has had neither the coordinating offices and committees that exist in the United States, nor any comparable shifting of power among individuals and institutions. There is no Office of the Special Trade Representative in the Kantei; no cabinet Council on International Economic Policy to coordinate (or at least try to coordinate) government activity in this sphere. But the absence in Japan of a body above the ministerial level does not prevent considerable coordination between ministries. On most noncontroversial matters, relevant divisions and bureaus in different ministries do cooperate with one another and coordinate views successfully enough. For instance, the Second North American Division in the Foreign Ministry's American Bureau maintains regular contact with the First Overseas Market Division in MITI's International Trade Bureau regarding economic relations with the United States. Moreover, the Japanese tendency toward consensus decisionmaking[29] may help to compensate for the lack of a supraministerial coordinating mechanism. This is not to deny that once a serious conflict does arise between ministries, it may be harder in the Japanese system to keep it under control or for top policymakers to resolve it. For smooth working relations within ministries are frequently accompanied by strong, sometimes bitter rivalry between them.

SECURITY ISSUES. In security matters it is the U.S. government that features strong career organizations with continuing major roles and responsibilities. The weight of these bureaucracies is illustrated (though not caused) by those in regular attendance at the National Security Council, including the secretary of defense, the director of central intelligence, and the chairman of the Joint Chiefs of Staff. For Americans, the blending of diplomatic, military, and intelligence activities has been the overriding problem in the formulation of postwar foreign policy, particularly on those issues that get the most sustained high-level attention. And control of the military services (and sometimes the CIA) has been perceived as the most crucial challenge to government foreign policy leaders.[30]

There is nothing comparable to the U.S. national security structure in postwar Japanese foreign policymaking. In fact, the weakness of the

29. Consensus decisionmaking is treated on pp. 101–08, below.

30. For detailed treatment of the roles and interests of the armed services and other security agencies with an influence on foreign policy, see Halperin, *Bureaucratic Politics and Foreign Policy,* chap. 3.

military establishment today is as remarkable as its dominance was in the thirties and early forties. After the war the Japanese military establishment was promptly liquidated by the occupation authorities. And the 1947 constitution prohibited, in the famous Article Nine, the nation's remilitarization and engagement in acts of war. But this constitutional proscription was modified in practice (and under pressure from the United States) to allow the development of substantial Self-Defense Forces (SDF) and progressively more sophisticated armament. Today the Defense Agency overseeing these forces is a reasonably large organization and a bureaucracy in itself. The management of nearly 250,000 troops and an annual budget of about $3.6 billion is a very substantial operation.[31] Compared to the formidable defense and security establishment of postwar America, however, Japan's Defense Agency and SDF do not look impressive at all. Moreover, there is no important foreign intelligence organization even remotely comparable to the American CIA. The Cabinet Research Office (Naikaku Chōsa-shitsu), the closest Japanese analogue, has been a very modest operation, interested predominantly in intelligence-gathering on communist bloc nations, especially the Soviet Union, China, and North Korea.

The difference between the politics of national security policymaking in the two governments is well illustrated by the Okinawa reversion case. In the United States, the key bureaucratic concern was the interests and stands of the military services, particularly the Army. Unless the military were prepared to go along, U.S. officials could not even discuss the question seriously with the Japanese government. Gradually, the U.S. military came to believe that reversion (1) was probably inevitable, and (2) could be accomplished in a way that would not damage the U.S. security position in the Far East. Only because of this accommodating military position was President Nixon able to decide on reversion in 1969 without precipitating a major bureaucratic (and, in consequence, congressional) fight. On the Japanese side, however, the Defense Agency was essentially out of the picture, even on issues like whether Japan would assert a security stake in Korea and Taiwan. These were all taken care of by the responsible segments of the Foreign Ministry—the North American Affairs and Security divisions of the American Affairs Bureau in cooperation with the Treaties Bureau. The critical politics in Japan on this issue was not that inside the government, but the broader national controversy

31. *Asahi nenkan* [Asahi almanac], *1974.*

over security policy and the potential impact of Okinawa on this controversy.

Conclusions

In its general structure and institutions, the Japanese government
differs from the American in several important respects. There is the
basic difference between parliamentary and presidential systems, and
thus between prime ministers and presidents, with the particular impact
on the former caused by the structure of Japan's ruling party and the
character of the opposition. There is the related difference in staff support for political leaders and bureaucracies, with the Tokyo government
featuring few of the high-level coordinating staffs or the in-and-out officials who are found in abundance in Washington. There are differences
—which reflect postwar policy priorities and constraints—in the identity
and influence of the major institutional actors in the two main policy
spheres—economics and national security. And there are differences
between the broader national communities interested in foreign policy,
most notably the continued polarization between ruling and opposition
parties in Tokyo.

These differences are varied and sometimes subtle, yet they are typical of the variation one might expect between any two large governments. Yet miscalculation based on misunderstanding of these differences helped bring crisis in security treaty revision, then later in the
textile negotiations. In both cases, Americans overestimated the ability
of the prime minister to control the issue.

In the first instance, what was underestimated was the leverage the
opposition could exercise on a politically controversial matter. The decision to negotiate a new security treaty requiring Diet ratification, and
the plans for an Eisenhower visit to cement and symbolize the new
relationship, both assumed that Premier Kishi could handle his domestic
politics. They assumed he could use his Diet majorities to get the treaty
ratified in a way that would vindicate and strengthen the conservative
leadership, upon whose continued rule American policy hopes rested.
But popular opposition to the treaty and to Kishi was strong, and the
combined effect of his and the opposition's tactics led the premier to a
situation where he could get the treaty ratified in time for Eisenhower's
visit only by violating procedural norms, which undercut his legitimacy

as a democratic leader. The outcome was the humiliation of both national leaders.

On textiles, the major miscalculation involved an overestimation of Sato's power within the cabinet and the conservative establishment. Sato was pressured by the Nixon White House to accept the American position on the terms of an agreement, and he agreed to do so. It was almost two years, however, before he could bring his government to carry out his wishes. He replaced one minister of international trade and industry with a man he thought more amenable, only to find that he had to replace this second minister eighteen months later. He sought to negotiate outside of official channels, and to convey all sorts of indirect signals of his intentions and his sincerity to both Americans and Japanese. But he met resistance from both the MITI bureaucracy and the Japanese textile industry and its supporters in the Diet, resistance dramatized by a national press that considered Japanese rejection of American proposals a long-overdue exercise of "autonomous diplomacy."

The White House response was to blame Sato personally—he had promised but had not delivered. A wiser reaction would have been to reevaluate the usefulness of pressing a Japanese premier to make promises he was likely to prove unable to keep. Sato was certainly not blameless—he seems to have dealt with the White House in a way that led Nixon to believe he could deliver. Kishi bore even more responsibility for the crisis in 1960, since it was his government that had pressed for the new treaty in the first place and pushed it through the Diet. But in both cases, American misreading of the politics of Japanese policymaking was a major contributor to a serious U.S.-Japan crisis.

American policymaking on Okinawa avoided such overestimation of the premier's power. Indeed, those who led in bringing the U.S. government around on the issue were moved by a sense of the vulnerability of Sato and the ruling Liberal Democratic party on the issue. These Americans feared that unless reversion on mutually acceptable terms were negotiated before the initial ten-year term of the security treaty expired in 1970, a new crisis threatening the ruling regime and the U.S.-Japanese alliance would arise. Because of this fear, the U.S. government proved willing to make substantive concessions aimed at clearing Sato's domestic path, rather than assuming that the premier could prevail at home with such terms as he signed onto. For example, Sato could probably have been brought to accept—as a price for reversion—a status for U.S. bases on Okinawa different, and more favorable to the U.S. military, than that of bases on the main Japanese islands—a status allowing greater flexibility for their military use, conceivably even the storage of nuclear weapons there. He was not pushed this far because responsible officials—including President Nixon—saw that what counted was not getting the maximum in specific concessions but an agreement that Sato and his successors could live with at home, one that would therefore really resolve the Okinawa issue. And special status for Okinawan bases would have meant, at minimum, a continuing domestic controversy for years to come.

Had the same American restraint been applied to the textile negotiations, much strife would have been averted. Yet the overestimation of Sato's power was only one of many political miscalculations by both sides in that unfortunate episode. And policy mistakes arising from misinterpretation of the politics of policymaking in the other capital have been frequent in other bilateral cases as well. This suggests the need for a general analysis of misperceptions in U.S.-Japanese relations, a look at some recurrent ways that officials in one capital have tended to misunderstand and misconstrue events and actions in the other capital. That is the purpose of chapter 4.

CHAPTER FOUR

Misperceptions across the Pacific

"LOOKING BACK on the mass of evidence that was available at the time," wrote journalist A. Merriman Smith a year later, "it becomes all the more unbelievable that Eisenhower thought he could go to Japan in June, 1960."[1] But apparently he did think so, and so also did American diplomats who advised him in the days and weeks before his plane was scheduled to land. A bit over nine years later, another Republican president was convinced that a Japanese premier would deliver him a stringent textile agreement. And fifteen months after that, politicians and bureaucrats in Tokyo were convinced that Congressman Wilbur Mills would not be negotiating a textile limitation agreement if he did not have White House acquiescence.

In these, as in all instances of relations between governments, officials in one capital had to make judgments about what would transpire in the politics of the other. They had to interpret what their counterparts had said and were doing, and predict how they might subsequently behave. They had to make certain assumptions about the broader political arena abroad and the abilities of particular leaders to prevail in that arena. They had to make at least some crude calculations as to how particular negotiators would respond to different types of personal negotiating styles and appeals. Often their perceptions and calculations were reasonably accurate, and seldom did their errors have such serious consequences as the three cited above. Yet misperceptions have been frequent enough in U.S.-Japanese relations to pose continuing problems for the relationship, and at times very serious problems.

One way of attacking the problem of misperception is to strike at one of its causes—lack of basic knowledge of one another's systems. To provide such information was one of the major purposes of chapter 3. But it

1. *A President's Odyssey* (Harper, 1961), p. 209.

is useful also to analyze misperceptions as they have actually occurred, to explore and attempt to categorize what kinds of mistakes are most frequently made by officials in reading the other government. And doing so requires consideration not only of political and institutional complexities and differences of the sort already introduced, but also of difficulties rooted in the two nations' quite different cultures. For a look at episodes of misperceptions in recent U.S.-Japanese relations suggests that they fall rather clearly into two general categories. The first type is those that arise inevitably in relationships between any two major democratic countries with complex and differing political and institutional structures. These flow directly from the existence of bureaucratic and broader political divisions and struggles within the countries, and seem to be characteristic of U.S. relations with European allies as well. The second type finds its causes in those divergent cultural values and styles peculiar to the U.S.-Japan relationship—for example, in the particular role that consensus plays in decisionmaking in Japan and the ways it is sometimes misconstrued by Americans.

Misperceptions Rooted in Politics as Usual

In his study of Anglo-American relations Richard E. Neustadt finds that crises between counterpart officials follow a recurrent pattern of "muddled perceptions, stifled communications, disappointed expectations, and paranoid reactions. In turn, each 'friend' misreads the other, each is reticent with the other, each is surprised by the other, each replies in kind."[2] This pattern he finds in dealings between two countries where the cultural and the language differences are markedly small, but where officials (as everywhere) are preoccupied with domestic and bureaucratic politics in their respective home capitals. This suggests that politically based misperceptions are endemic in relations between any two large countries.

In U.S.-Japanese relations, this kind of misperception may arise when actors in one country fail to recognize the existence of political divisions and conflicts in the other, seeing the target government as if it were a

2. *Alliance Politics* (Columbia University Press, 1970), p. 66. For application of this formulation to the 1969–71 textile negotiations, see Morton H. Halperin, "Comment," *Foreign Policy*, no. 14 (Spring 1974), pp. 155–56; and Yōnosuke Nagai, "Dōmei gaikō no kansei" [Trap of alliance diplomacy], *Chūō kōron*, January 1972.

unified, rational actor making a series of carefully calculated decisions (for example, "the Japanese" are trying to make us do x). Or officials may recognize that the other side also has its domestic political complexities and divisions, but then interpret them in terms of the particular features of their own political system. A third source of misperception is the particular interests and stakes of actors in one country, which may limit and distort their perception of events abroad.

Seeing the Other Government as Unified

Writing about official misperception, Robert Jervis concludes that, in general,

actors see others as more internally united than they in fact are and generally overestimate the degree to which others are following a coherent policy. The degree to which the other side's policies are the product of internal bargaining, internal misunderstandings, or subordinates' not following instructions is underestimated. Seeing only the finished product, they find it simpler to try to construct a rational explanation for the policies, even though they know that such an analysis could not explain their own policies.[3]

And because they see a particular action as a deliberate and calculated attempt by the foreign government to influence the behavior of their own, they tend sometimes to overreact, creating or increasing tension between the two countries.

This type of misperception was present in two decisive episodes during the slide toward war in 1941. The first was in July, when in response to the movement of Japanese troops into southern Indochina, President Franklin D. Roosevelt issued a "freezing order" which led ultimately to an embargo on U.S. oil exports to Japan. This embargo, in turn, forced Japanese leaders to choose either to make political and military concessions to the United States to negotiate its removal, or to strike out militarily to gain control of alternative oil sources before their reserve stocks became too depleted for full-scale military operations.

How united was the U.S. government on the embargo issue? It was, in fact, sharply divided. In ordering a freeze on Japanese assets in the

---

3. "Hypotheses on Misperception," *World Politics*, no. 3 (April 1968); reprinted in Morton H. Halperin and Arnold Kanter, eds., *Readings in American Foreign Policy: A Bureaucratic Perspective* (Little, Brown, 1973), pp. 134–35. On this same point, see Graham T. Allison and Morton H. Halperin, "Bureaucratic Politics: A Paradigm and Some Policy Implications," in Richard H. Ullman and Raymond Tanter, eds., *Theory and Policy in International Relations* (Princeton University Press, 1972) (Brookings Reprint 246).

United States Roosevelt was taking, he apparently thought, a middle course that explicitly rejected the immediate oil embargo desired by U.S. "hawks" like Treasury Secretary Henry Morgenthau and Assistant Secretary of State Dean Acheson. The chief of naval operations also opposed an embargo, fearing it would lead to a war with Japan before U.S. forces were ready to fight it. Whether the freezing order would in fact bring about an embargo depended on "how it was administered";[4] there were "weeks of wavering" about whether the U.S. government should "be lenient or severe in the issue of licenses to use 'frozen' dollars to pay for Japanese purchases."[5] But Japanese leaders seem to have concluded almost immediately that the freezing order was part of a coherent policy, essentially the total oil embargo which they had long feared. Hawks argued that this made it essential to press ahead with war plans for securing Southeast Asian oil before Japan's two-year oil stocks were too much depleted; "doves" were moved to redouble efforts to negotiate a modus vivendi. The Navy, which had been opposed to risking war with the United States, was now moved by the impending oil squeeze to harden its position, thus depleting the ranks of the doves in Tokyo.[6] No one there seems to have recognized the extent of the division and uncertainty within the U.S. government and the opportunity this might have offered to secure further oil in significant quantities if specific applications for export licenses were astutely contrived. Of course, Japanese officials' limited understanding of the U.S. government, and the lack of sympathetic U.S. officials with whom to work, would have made such an approach difficult.[7]

Four months later, President Roosevelt similarly overestimated *Japanese* unity at a particularly crucial point. As December approached, the Japanese government was divided in both its views and its lines of activity. Military forces were preparing steadily for war; Premier Hideki Tōjō and Foreign Minister Shigenori Tōgō—supported by the emperor

4. Dean Acheson, *Present at the Creation* (Norton, 1969), p. 24.

5. Herbert Feis, *The Road to Pearl Harbor* (Princeton University Press, 1950), p. 242.

6. See Kōichi Kido, *Kido Kōichi nikki* [Kōichi Kido diary], vol. 2 (Tokyo: Tokyo University Press, 1966), p. 896; and Teiji Yabe, *Konoye Fumimaro* [Fumimaro Konoye] (Tokyo: Jiji Press, 1958), pp. 154–55.

7. In fact, Acheson suggests that the way, presumably accidental, that the Japanese actually tested the freezing order played into the hands of Americans like himself who wished to use the freeze to enforce an oil embargo. (*Present at the Creation*, pp. 25–27.)

and his entourage—were striving to achieve some eleventh-hour U.S.-Japan agreement acceptable to the military that could avert a conflict. On the morning of November 26, Roosevelt was considering what response the United States should make to the most promising of Japan's proposals for a short-term modus vivendi; he had even drafted proposals of his own not too far from those Tokyo had put forward. Then he received a telephone call from Secretary of War Henry Stimson, a hawk. Stimson was passing on an intelligence report of Japanese troops heading south of Formosa. According to Roosevelt's biographer,

The President fairly blew up—"jumped into the air, so to speak," Stimson noted in his diary. To the President this changed the whole situation, because "it was evidence of bad faith *on the part of the Japanese* that while they were negotiating for an entire truce—an entire withdrawal (from China)—*they* should be sending *their* expedition down there to Indochina." Roosevelt's truce formula died that day. In its stead, Hull drew up a ten-point proposal that restated Washington's most stringent demands.[8]

In fact, "the Japanese" were pursuing no single coherent policy; the charge of "bad faith" presumed a unity that was absent. But the President's misperception triggered a hardening of the U.S. negotiating position that ended any chances for a peaceful settlement.

Another U.S. overestimation of the unity and purposiveness of Japanese policymakers came thirty years later, in March 1971. The Japanese textile industry unveiled its unilateral plan for moderate restrictions on exports to the United States, and the chief cabinet secretary announced that this plan made further intergovernmental negotiations on the subject unnecessary. A U.S. official deeply involved in the issue said he believed this was "the first time the Japanese had unilaterally broken off a negotiation with the United States since December 7, 1941"; he implied, once again, deliberate deceit, with "the Japanese" suddenly invoking their own desired solution as the Americans were still negotiating in good faith for another sort of outcome in a very different channel. And President Nixon himself seems to have held Premier Sato directly responsible for the industry's actions. In fact, however, Sato and other high Japanese officials had played only very limited and passive roles in the events leading to the plan's adoption by the textile industry; the driving force came from the unusual alignment of that industry with Congressman Wilbur Mills.

8. James MacGregor Burns, *Roosevelt: The Soldier of Freedom* (Harcourt Brace Jovanovich, 1970), p. 157. Emphasis added.

In the late sixties and early seventies, the "Japan, Inc." image held by many Americans reinforced their tendency to view the Japanese government as more united and purposive than it really was. For example, there was widespread exaggeration of the extent to which the Japanese government effectively controlled the development of its domestic economy and international trade.[9] And throughout the textile negotiations, U.S. officials repeatedly blamed "Japanese arrogance" or "delaying tactics" for Japanese actions that were unresponsive to the U.S. desire for an agreement. But in many cases, minimal, temporizing responses to U.S. proposals were caused rather by the sharp divisions among Japanese officials and industrialists involved.

Seeing the Other Government as Parallel to One's Own

A more sophisticated pattern of misperception arises when officials project assumptions derived from their own political framework onto the politics of the other country. They recognize political complexities and divisions in the counterpart government, and yet still err by assuming that the details of the other country's decisionmaking are like those at home.

This form of misperception is so natural that it is particularly difficult to avoid. For the process of policymaking in Japan is in many ways similar to that in America; each government is (as Neustadt says of America and Britain) "constitutional in character, representative in form, limited in scope, confined by guarantees of private right . . . and legitimatized by the symbols of popular sovereignty."[10] If misperceptions frequently arise between British and American leaders due to misreading of fine details or nuances where those two systems diverge, they seem even more likely in U.S.-Japanese relations. Thus, "intellectual conditioning as well as governmental gamesmanhip makes it extraordinarily difficult to transcend one's own frame of reference and to avoid assuming, by analogical reasoning, that the frame of reference of counterparts in Tokyo is comparable to the political environment in Washington, and vice versa."[11]

9. See Philip H. Trezise with the collaboration of Yukio Suzuki, "Politics, Government, and Economic Growth in Japan," in Hugh Patrick and Henry Rosovsky, eds., *Asia's New Giant: How the Japanese Economy Works* (Brookings Institution, 1976).

10. *Alliance Politics*, p. 79.

11. Michael H. Armacost, "U.S.-Japan Relations: Problems and Modalities of Communications," *Department of State Bulletin*, Jan. 15, 1973, p. 68.

Perhaps the most prominent postwar misperception of this type has been Americans' overestimation of the Japanese premier's power. In the textile case (where this mistake proved most costly), the United States not only sought commitments at summit conferences, but Presidential Assistant Henry Kissinger repeatedly tried to achieve a breakthrough by negotiating directly with the premier's personal office, the Kantei. Such efforts could have worked only if the Kantei were able to make prompt decisions, as the White House sometimes could, before cabinet or bureaucratic consensus had jelled. Its powers were not parallel, so the result was further White House frustration. White House misperception may have been fueled, however, by the repeatedly expressed Japanese desire to negotiate on textiles with someone other than Secretary of Commerce Maurice Stans. Sato himself signaled the White House on this point on at least three occasions. And some Japanese felt that moving Stans to one side on the issue might lead to significant U.S. substantive concessions. Thinking in terms of their own system, they apparently assumed that Stans's Commerce Department portfolio and industry constituency were the main sources of his hard line. In fact, Stans was—like most American cabinet officials—heavily dependent on the President. His views and actions generally reflected the President's political objectives, as was particularly likely on any "special issue" to which the President gave high priority. Thus, though Stans was replaced as U.S. negotiator in the fall of 1970, the U.S. negotiating position changed only marginally.[12]

And one of the greatest political miscalculations in postwar U.S.-Japanese relations occurred when Tokyo political leaders acquiesced in the import control plan that Japanese industry leaders had negotiated with Congressman Mills, in the expectation that President Richard Nixon would acquiesce also. Here too projection of homeland political assumptions onto the other system was an important source of error (though some important American actors misjudged this one as well). In Japan, with a parliamentary system dominated by the LDP, the pre-

12. A similar misperception in the other direction occurred in June 1970, when MITI Minister Kiichi Miyazawa came to Washington to negotiate with Stans, accompanied by Foreign Minister Kiichi Aichi. Kissinger sought to work around the former and strike a deal with the latter. He was right in assuming that the foreign minister would be more receptive than the MITI minister to U.S. interests. But he was wrong in assuming that Aichi could negotiate around Miyazawa as Kissinger was operating around Stans. Textiles was clearly within the organizational jurisdiction of the MITI, and the foreign minister could not simply bypass the MITI minister.

mier and his cabinet seldom view the Diet and its committees as independent competitors. And to the degree that Japanese actors did recognize that separation of powers made Mills something of a rival baron to Nixon, it was assumed that their mutual dependence would prevent either from risking a major public fight. Mills would not move without being sure the President could live with the arrangement; Nixon would not break with Mills on the issue because his Ways and Means Committee controlled so much of the President's priority legislation. And Mills—very much a widely consulting, consensus-style legislative leader —personally assured those Japanese who asked that he did have reason to believe the White House would go along. Thus, they were shocked when Nixon denounced the deal. To the President, however, Mills's action amounted to an attempt to undercut him politically and to challenge his basic constitutional prerogative of negotiating agreements with foreign governments.

The Stakes of the Beholder

In government, "where you stand depends on where you sit."[13] Officials' "comprehension of the other [government's] actual behavior is a function of their own concerns."[14] Moreover, "decision-makers tend to fit incoming information into their existing theories and images . . . actors tend to perceive what they expect."[15] This universal tendency for individuals to perceive the world in terms of their own day-to-day concerns and expectations, from their own vantage points, in part reflects political interests—officials see events in the context of their particular stakes in the policy actions to which such events may be relevant. They view the world from particular "perspectives." But it reflects also the apparent need for each human mind to view specific events within broader conceptual frameworks which change but slowly. Specific events or signals are perceived not independently, as pure new facts; they are interpreted —sometimes distorted—so that they may fit in with what the mind already knows.[16]

13. Graham Allison, *Essence of Decision: Explaining the Cuban Missile Crisis* (Little, Brown, 1971), p. 176.

14. Neustadt, *Alliance Politics,* p. 66.

15. Jervis, "Hypotheses on Misperception," p. 115.

16. For an extensive analysis of these cognitive phenomena and their relation to foreign policymaking, see ibid.; and, in particular, John D. Steinbruner, *The Cybernetic Theory of Decision: New Dimensions of Political Analysis* (Princeton University Press, 1974), especially chap. 4.

Once again the textile case offers illuminating examples. In the spring of 1969, the Japanese reaction to U.S. pressure for comprehensive export controls was uniformly negative. To State Department officials, who felt that such thoroughgoing restrictions were unnecessary, this was evidence that they were unattainable; they concluded that less stringent trade restrictions should therefore be sought. But Commerce Department officials who were committed to the comprehensive approach had a rather different reading. As one of them told the press, "The first thing the Japanese say to new negotiations is no. But this is just their way of opening."[17] Several months later, after Japan's Minister of International Trade and Industry Ohira had agreed to send a technical mission to Washington to discuss the textile problem, American officials differed again as to whether he had also agreed that the mission would discuss potential solutions. Predictably, Commerce bureaucrats (who had developed a proposal that the talks include discussion of solutions) argued that Ohira had acceded to this; their State Department colleagues believed he had acceded to no such thing.

The Japanese government made similar miscalculations. In the fall of 1970, with intergovernmental textile negotiations stymied and with restrictive import quota legislation making progress on Capitol Hill, the Japanese government needed to judge how likely the legislation was to pass, in order to determine whether they needed to makes concessions in order to prevent the bill's enactment. Gaimushō (Foreign Ministry) officials, who favored compromise to avert a further increase in general U.S.-Japanese tensions, judged that Congress was likely to pass the bill, and that Nixon was likely to sign it. Their MITI counterparts, who did not want to be pressured into major concessions on textiles, argued the opposite conclusion: that the "Christmas tree phenomenon" (the tendency of quota bills to attract a large number of restrictive amendments favoring various domestic interests) would either lead to congressional failure to enact the legislation, or force President Nixon to veto it. Thus for MITI officials the situation did not require Japan to soften its negotiating position.

In the treaty revision case, a look at the particular vantage points and stakes of major American actors helps to explain why "Eisenhower thought he could go to Japan in June 1960." The White House was anything but unaware of the street protests in Tokyo against the new secu-

17. *Daily News Record* (New York), March 24, 1969, p. 16.

rity treaty and the means Premier Nobusuke Kishi had used to force Diet action. Within four days of the controversial lower house vote on May 19, Secretary of State Christian Herter cabled Tokyo on the President's behalf raising the possibility of postponing the trip to late July or early August, so that Eisenhower's arrival would not coincide with final Japanese ratification of the treaty on June 19. The question of postponement was raised again, with considerably greater force, after the car carrying Press Secretary Hagerty's advance party was surrounded by demonstrators at Haneda airport on June 10. Eisenhower certainly wanted to go to Japan. It was to be the major Asian stop in his extended "journey for peace," his quest for diplomatic and goodwill gains abroad and a vindication at home in the form of a Republican victory in the 1960 election. Already his Moscow invitation had been withdrawn in the wake of the U-2 fiasco; the last thing he wanted was a second public rebuff, particularly one that would appear as backing down before communist pressure. But there was also an awareness in the White House and the State Department, expressed in a cable to the embassy on June 10, of the "need to face squarely the possibility of the grave damage which could result at home and abroad from either failing to make certain of an orderly visit or unwisely persisting in the visit."[18] There was also some concern within the administration that the fall of the Kishi government might be inevitable "regardless of whether the President visits Japan," and consequently with "why the prestige of President Eisenhower and the United States should be so deeply committed to so precarious and uncertain a cause."[19]

Given such recognition of the complexity of the situation, why did Eisenhower persist in his plans? A crucial reason was that he perceived the situation, in the final analysis, through the eyes of the U.S. embassy in Tokyo and Ambassador Douglas MacArthur II. There was no lack of information flowing through other channels—in the twenty-eight days before Kishi's eleventh-hour withdrawal of the invitation, events in Japan made the front page of the *New York Times* sixteen times. But for interpretation of what this all meant and how the United States should respond, the President depended, not surprisingly, on the ambas-

18. Assistant Secretary of State J. Graham Parsons, "Chronology of Ambassador MacArthur's Meetings with Prime Minister Kishi and Other Japanese Government Officials Prior to Postponement of President's Visit" (memorandum to Secretary of State Christian Herter, June 27, 1960).

19. *New York Times*, June 16, 1960.

sador. And while MacArthur did raise the question of postponement with Japanese leaders when instructed to do so, he accepted and supported, time after time, Kishi's determination to proceed.

The ambassador's position and his personal stakes made him far more an advocate and promoter of the trip than an objective evaluator of whether it should take place. On the day in May that Herter's cable arrived suggesting possible postponement, MacArthur was arguing vehemently (and for public effect) with the Japan Socialist party leader who had just delivered him an open letter to Eisenhower asking postponement.[20] Not surprisingly, he cabled back that "for President to take initiative in postponing his visit to Japan" would be a "great mistake" and "could be mortal blow for Kishi."[21] And not only did his personal identification with the success of the trip encourage him to persevere; he saw U.S. interests as tied very closely to the Kishi regime. This reflected not just the normal identification of a diplomat with the leaders with whom he deals, but the fact that the new security treaty—the prime accomplishment of his ambassadorship and of U.S.-Japanese relations since the occupation—had been negotiated with that regime and was being defended by that regime. Thus—in a turbulent political situation impossible to predict with certainty—his perceptions and recommendations reflected these priorities and preoccupations, and merged above all with the hope that—with steadfastness and perseverance—the President could make a triumphal visit that would vindicate the United States and the Kishi government. Positive evidence was highlighted—the press was giving signs it would put aside its animosity toward Kishi ("whom they hate blindly") and "soon begin to call on Japanese people to welcome President warmly."[22] Negative evidence was minimized—though "Japanese security authorities were very inadequate in handling Hagerty arrival," the fault was partly that of "White House and Embassy security people" who did not press the Japanese hard enough about the specific arrangements.[23] As late as a day before the massive, violent encounter between demonstrators and police that led to Kishi's withdrawal of the invitation, the ambassador reported and endorsed the Japanese

20. Ibid., May 25, 1960.
21. Cable no. 3825, U.S. Embassy, Tokyo, to Secretary of State (eyes only), May 25, 1960.
22. Cable no. 4082, U.S. Embassy, Tokyo, to Secretary of State, June 8, 1960.
23. Cable no. 4139, U.S. Embassy, Tokyo, to Secretary of State (eyes only), June 11, 1960.

government's assurances that "the security measures that they have in-
stituted plus changes in the climate of public opinion" offered "reasonable assurances" of a successful visit.[24] The result of all this perseverance,
of course, was the humiliating eleventh-hour cancellation which the embassy, the President, and the Kishi government wanted least of all. In
retrospect, the postponement suggested in late May would have been far
preferable, but it was not vigorously pursued because an ambassador
both set on the visit and staked to the Kishi government perceived sticking to the plan as the politically necessary course.[25]

Like other examples of misperception cited here, the U.S. mistake in
persisting with the trip can be explained by the sort of political interplay
within governments present in any bilateral relationship, by politics as
usual. But there also are deep cultural differences between Japan and
the United States, which are both reflected and reinforced by their two
very different languages. And these too have affected the perceptions
and expectations of officials as they looked across the Pacific.

Misperceptions Rooted in Cultural Differences

In its relations with Japan the United States faces a wide cultural gap
not present in its dealings with other major allies. An assistant secretary
of state pinpointed one key element of the problem:

Perhaps it is fair to say that both Americans and Japanese are poorly prepared
for cross-cultural understanding. We both developed, in rather isolated cir-

24. Parsons, "Chronology." For more on how officials' interpretations of particular
situations are typically "biased in the direction of supporting plans that had been built
on the basis of other considerations," see Joseph de Rivera, *The Psychological Dimension of Foreign Policy* (Merrill, 1968), p. 71.

25. The perceptions of the embassy and Washington were also substantially
colored by the "shared images" of a bipolar, cold-war world that shaped American
attitudes generally. Kishi was anticommunist, his opponents were communists and
socialists and vehement critics of the American connection. Thus MacArthur, like
most Americans, exaggerated the extent of foreign instigation in the antitreaty, anti-
Kishi movement ("Moscow and Peking are committing all their available reserves to
present internal struggle in Japan to defeat security treaty" [Cable no. 4082, U.S.
Embassy, Tokyo]). He concluded that "the very survival of Japanese democracy"
depended on thwarting the campaign by "minority groups" against Kishi, the treaty,
and the visit (paraphrased in Parsons, "Chronology"). And in language that fore-
shadowed a widespread official interpretation of another Asian nation's internal crisis,
he warned that "backing down to Communists will create domino reaction in free
Asia" (Cable no. 4082, U.S. Embassy, Tokyo). On the concept of "shared images,"
see Morton H. Halperin with the assistance of Priscilla Clapp and Arnold Kanter,
Bureaucratic Politics and Foreign Policy (Brookings Institution, 1974), chap. 2.

cumstances, relatively free from entanglements with other cultures and encroaching nations. We have both grown up in societies that until recently have emphasized cultural homogeneity as the desirable goal of national and human existence. It was the other fellow whose duty it was to understand us, if such understanding was even considered relevant, or necessary, or possible.[26]

The line between what is political and what is cultural is not easy to draw. But certain characteristics of Japanese and American policy behavior appear to be based on deep-rooted cultural values and patterns of interpersonal relationships; thus they are not adequately explained by the structures of the two political systems. And these lead to certain types of misperceptions that appear peculiar to the U.S.-Japan relationship (though some of them may also appear in Japan's dealings with other Western countries).

Consensus

American business leader Donald Kendall, frustrated in his attempt to mediate the controversial textile issue, concluded that consensual decisionmaking in Tokyo was the main barrier to smooth U.S.-Japanese relations. "So long as this basic decision-making remains predominant in Japan, U.S.-Japanese economic (as well as political) relations will continue to require a great deal of understanding on both sides, because Japan can never make a timely shift in policy."[27] Decisions either take too long, or they are not made. Many other Americans have had difficulty getting timely, responsive action out of the Japanese government.

This emphasis on consensus is, in part, a product of Japanese values and expectations about how human relations within groups should be maintained. Japanese culture attaches great importance to avoidance of direct confrontation. As a noted psychiatrist puts it, "The Japanese hate to contradict or to be contradicted—that is, to have to say 'No' in the conversation. They simply don't want to have divided opinions in the first place."[28] To Americans, a decision by a majority overruling a minor-

26. Testimony by Assistant Secretary of State John Richardson, Jr., in *Japan-United States Friendship Act*, Hearings before the Senate Commitee on Foreign Relations, 93:2 (Government Printing Office, 1974), p. 66.

27. Interview confirmed in letter to Hideo Sato, from Donald Kendall, Jan. 16, 1976. For a description of Kendall's textile experience, see pp. 137 and 138, below.

28. Takeo Doi, "Some Psychological Themes," in John C. Condon and Mitsuko Saito, eds., *Intercultural Encounters with Japan: Communication—Contact and Conflict* (Tokyo: Simul Press, 1974), p. 22. Students of Japanese culture sometimes stress the impact of a crowded environment on social relationships: the existence of a large population on small islands, secluded from the rest of the world, limited until recently

ity is legitimate, and the minority is supposed to adhere to it even if its views and needs are not accommodated. To Japanese, maximum effort should be made to involve and accommodate a potentially dissident minority in the process of decisionmaking; something decided by a majority and imposed without such an effort at accommodation is viewed as arbitrary and overbearing. Americans also believe, formally, that hierarchical rank gives its holders the right to make decisions and have them obeyed. By contrast, Japanese values emphasize the obligation of a senior officeholder to take due account of the views and sensitivities of his subordinates, even where this borders on rubber-stamping their recommendations.

These Japanese values lead logically (and practically) to a preference for broad participation as organizations debate their objectives and means of attaining them. They also lead to heavy reliance on substantive initiatives from persons lower in the hierarchy. When excessive delay can be avoided, and when the interests of those involved can in fact be accommodated by a policy accepted (though not necessarily preferred) by potential dissidents, then implementation can be remarkably smooth since those who must carry out the decision already understand and are committed to it.[29] And even where decisions are made by smaller

---

in geographic and social mobility even within those islands, seems to have induced Japanese to make special efforts to avoid friction and confrontation among themselves, particularly within the groups and communities where they would be spending their entire lives.

29. Richard Tanner Johnson and William G. Ōuchi, in "Made in America (Under Japanese Management)," *Harvard Business Review*, September–October 1974, pp. 61–69, discuss the advantages of a consensus, participatory management style within particular business firms. "Contrary to what many Westerners think, the Japanese system does not demand that all participants 'sign off.' Those who affix their seals to the document containing the decision are indicating their consent, which is not the same as their approval. Each participant is indicating satisfaction that his point of view has been fairly heard, and while he may not wholly agree that the decision is the best one, he is willing to go along with and, even more, to support it. In this manner, the Japanese sidestep the nearly impossible task of obtaining unanimity." (Ibid., p. 66.) Thus, the fact that he is consulted may bring a Japanese participant to acquiesce in a decision about which he retains substantive reservations, whereas had he not been consulted he might well have resisted. A related means by which the consensual style sidesteps the unanimity problem is through standards, also consensually determined, by which the parties "qualified" and "eligible" to influence a given issue are separated from the "unqualified" and "noneligible." These standards are usually based on seniority, general achievement, or specific responsibility and competence.

circles, there is often exceptionally broad consultation and information-sharing across jurisdictional and organizational lines. Japanese business and government leaders, for example, seem much more aware of important decisions being taken in each other's spheres than is the case in the United States, where the government-business relationship is more an adversary one.

There are also, however, very practical and pragmatic political reasons for Japanese leaders to apply a consensual style to broader political issues. In any society there are certain types of issues on which interests and opinions are so sharply and deeply divided that leaders risk major unrest if they initiate decisive actions on them. Decisions that are taken have to be based on compromise supported by at least an apparent consensus. Most frequently, decisions are avoided or deferred as long as the circumstances permit. In postwar Japan this has been true of many foreign policy issues—as well as some more basic constitutional issues.

In the United States, postwar disagreements on foreign policy issues have seldom been strictly along party lines. Majorities on foreign policy issues tend to be ad hoc, and U.S. senators and congressmen habitually cross party lines in their votes. In Japan, by contrast, the Liberal Democratic party is assured of the needed votes in every major legislative battle. If the rule of majoritarianism were strictly followed, the views of a large portion of the Japanese populace would be ignored. Their reaction would be to question the very legitimacy of the system and the ruling regime, as many Japanese did when Kishi used his numerical majority to push the revised security treaty through in 1960. Thus in a one-party dominant system like that of postwar Japan, pragmatic concern for democracy dictates that a pure and simple majoritarianism be tempered by considerations for minority interests and opinion.

The Japanese emphasis on consensus procedures in arriving at decisions can be thus attributed in part to the divisive nature of certain foreign policy issues and the lack of prior substantive consensus on them. And this applies not only to national political divisions, but those within the government as well. Japanese policymaking institutions are exceptionally closed. Bureaucratic and political elites are self-contained and slowly changing; issues tend to be dominated, where feasible, by organizational subsystems of middle-level specialists. But the cohesiveness of particular groups means that conflict between them can be notably bitter—as between MITI and the Gaimushō on textiles.[30] Consensus decisionmaking is a means of bridging these internal gaps. The existence of political as well as cultural roots for consensus decisionmaking is suggested also by its presence in other countries. In the United States even policies with full presidential sponsorship are much more easily implemented, much less subject to assaults, if they are backed by a broad coalition inside and outside the executive branch—indeed, they often cannot succeed without one. Similarly, bureaucrats must establish broad interagency participation and agreement if they are to pursue policy courses requiring a wide range of official actions, and to maintain the broad working-level communication and trust essential to effective operations. Thus, an analysis of U.S. policymaking in the early postwar period stressed the "strain toward agreement," the "need to build a consensus that includes, as it were, one's enemies as well as one's friends."[31] And in cases like Okinawa, efforts to build such consensus have been successful.

Nor should one assume that the Japanese preference for consensus means that policymaking on controversial issues is always immobilized by the need to get incompatible actors to agree. Shigeru Yoshida virtually dictated his policy on the 1951 peace treaty and the accompanying security treaty. His times were indeed quite exceptional and afforded him much greater freedom of action than any other postwar premier has enjoyed. In 1956, however, his successor Ichiro Hatoyama accomplished the peace settlement with the Soviet Union despite strong and sustained opposition of many of his colleagues in the Liberal Democratic party as well as that of the Foreign Ministry. And Nobusuke Kishi, of course, breached the rule of consensual decisionmaking by pushing the revision of the U.S.-Japan Mutual Security Treaty through the Diet.[32]

30. Chie Nakane argues that the traditional emphasis on vertical interpersonal relationships in Japan often militates against horizontal coordination and harmony between organized groups, such as government ministries and political party factions (*Japanese Society* [University of California Press, 1970]).

31. Warner R. Schilling, "The Politics of National Defense, Fiscal 1950," in Warner R. Schilling, Paul Y. Hammond, and Glenn H. Snyder, *Strategy, Politics, and Defense Budgets* (Columbia University Press, 1962), p. 23.

32. In those cases where the Japanese government makes major policy departures, it seems to operate very much as the American government operates in such cases: A small, ad hoc group develops, usually combining political and career officials; and this group has considerable day-to-day latitude in what steps to take and whom to consult, provided that due regard is paid to the major interests involved. (See Haruhiro Fukui, "Foreign Policy Making in Japan: Case Studies for Empirical

Nonetheless, on issues involving deep conflicts among interests, decisions do often come more slowly in Japan than in the United States. On textiles, for example, it was President Nixon who decided the basic U.S. negotiating stance, ignoring or overriding substantial opposition in the process, maintaining his position until finally successful. In Japan, however, political leaders and senior bureaucrats were repeatedly deferring to their colleagues, to business leaders, and to subordinates. They seemed unwilling to force a position on them, reluctant to move toward decisive action to settle the issue until the other interested parties, including especially the textile leaders, were "on board." The premier, the MITI minister, senior officials, business leaders—all deferred strong moves time and again because a consensus had not jelled.

Strong action on textiles was, of course, easier for Nixon than for Sato. The President was aligned with the most interested party—the textile industry. In Japan, decisive action meant going against that industry's interests. This maximized the political risks for any Japanese politician who stepped forward and proposed such action, and encouraged all to seek the protection of collective responsibility. Yet cultural styles and expectations were clearly a factor, also, in Sato's reluctance to press his ministers too forcefully for particular solutions, despite his deep personal stake in reaching a textile accord. Conversely, perceived breaches of the principle of consensus created ill feelings between Sato and the Japanese textile industry and damaged the prospects for agreement. Sato believed that industry concessions were vital to serve the overriding Japanese interest in the U.S. relationship. He felt that the industry was not behaving properly—was putting its selfish interests above the interests of the collectivity—when it failed to come around after he personally emphasized the need for agreement. The textile leaders, on the other hand, suspected that Sato had made secret concessions about which they had not been consulted, which they saw as a major breach in the proper procedure for handling such issues.

The value placed on consensus in Japan is reflected also in the effort

---

Theory" [paper prepared for delivery at 1974 meeting of the Association for Asian Studies; processed]). This pattern is very similar to that of the "ad hoc groups" which a recent senior participant describes and recommends for the management of important *United States* foreign policy issues. (See the testimony of Francis Bator, deputy special assistant to President Johnson for national security affairs, in *U.S. Foreign Economic Policy: Implications for the Organization of the Executive Branch*, Hearings before the House Committee on Foreign Affairs, 92:2 [GPO, 1972], p. 114.)

to avoid having obvious winners and losers on issues, and in the reluctance of officials in leadership positions to visibly move out front and
summon support overtly in the public arena, or even in private cabinet
meetings. Even Tanaka as MITI minister, who forced a textile agreement
on his bureaucracy in a notable departure from the consensus style,
continued to voice his resistance to such an agreement in press conferences—and even, apparently, in cabinet meetings—until long after he
had determined to force through a solution on U.S. terms. And unlike
Kishi in 1960, Tanaka was able to handle his issue without overriding
textile quota opponents in a winner-loser fashion. Rather he bore the
brunt of a *national* loss that many Japanese now felt essential to put an
end to the issue. By so doing Tanaka gained politically from textiles,
whereas Kishi undercut his legitimacy by winning on the security treaty
and was forced to resign.

This Japanese emphasis on consensus often irritates American negotiators, for such decisionmaking necessarily becomes time-consuming
and sometimes produces minimal, temporizing decisions. Americans are
likely to attribute these unsatisfactory results to political weakness or
conscious delaying tactics. In November 1970, for example, MITI and
Foreign Ministry officials had to revise the Japanese stance on textiles
after the second Sato-Nixon summit, where the premier had endorsed
a rather specific restriction formula. But they were unable to get textile
industry representatives to acquiesce in even a considerably looser
formula. So rather than presenting a proposal over industry opposition,
MITI Minister Miyazawa and Foreign Minister Aichi cabled Ambassador Nobuhiko Ushiba a summary of the MITI-industry discussions
and representative positions. When Ushiba presented this "position
paper" at the first session of the resumed talks Peter Flanigan, the
U.S. negotiator, was taken aback. He expressed extreme unhappiness
with the failure of the Japanese government to take a clear stance. And
there were many other instances in the talks when Americans were frustrated by Japanese delays and failure to come up with a counterproposal; these tended to be attributed to a conscious central decision to
avoid or delay an agreement—an outcome, of course, that some Japanese
actors did seek.

Japanese consensus values can also cause American officials to mis-
read Tokyo politics more generally. In the crisis of 1960, much of the
intense, widespread anti-Kishi feeling in Japan grew from the premier's
breaches of consensus values—his forcing the treaty through the Diet,

his ignoring or disregarding of public sentiment. But Ambassador Mac-Arthur interpreted the domestic confrontation as an essentially two-sided contest in which one side or the other, Kishi or the antitreaty coalition of the left, would have to prevail. Thus his cabled reports emphasized how "democracy in Japan now stands at crossroads," and his exhortations to Japanese moderates to do battle with the left stressed that "as a believer in Christian principles he saw no possibility of compromise between right and wrong."[33] Given such an interpretation, it was hardly surprising that MacArthur saw potential disaster if the leftist parties and demonstrators achieved any of three objectives—preventing Eisenhower's visit, forcing Kishi's resignation, reversing ratification of the treaty. In fact, they achieved two of them. But the result was not the fundamental setback for U.S. interests that MacArthur feared, for Kishi was replaced by a more moderate LDP premier, Hayato Ikeda, who stuck by the treaty and still won electoral endorsement and general domestic support. This middle-road solution reflected consensus values in several ways. By the end of May there was an overwhelming sentiment in Japan that Kishi would have to go because his "arbitrary" and "undemocratic" behavior had violated procedural norms; many LDP members and adherents shared in this view. But this did not mean most Japanese wanted or expected the Socialists to come to power; indeed, after the demonstrations took a violent turn, there was a reaction against the left as well. Similarly, MacArthur's cold-war-style, right-and-wrong formulation was at variance with the substantive Japanese consensus for minimal involvement in the ideological confrontation, a consensus that included supporters of the security alliance with the United States as well as opponents. Under all of these circumstances, what was necessary for resolving the crisis was that it be defused, which required Kishi's departure from power and a public deemphasis of security and ideological issues by his successor.

Related to the emphasis on consensus is the tendency of the Japanese to formulate their stands on issues during—rather than before—negotiations; they tend to *adapt* themselves to initiatives taken by others. And even when they initiate a negotiation, they have difficulty presenting particular proposals until there is not only domestic consensus but a basis for telling what the other side will accept. In contrast, Americans tend to emphasize initiatives and direction and work for agreement on

33. Cable no. 4081, U.S. Embassy, Tokyo, to Secretary of State, June 8, 1960, and an Embassy cable of June 11, 1960, as paraphrased in Parsons, "Chronology."

a specific proposal they set forth at the outset of negotiation.[34] On Okinawa, Sato made a specific request for home-level, nuclear-free reversion by 1972 only after several years of bilateral interaction on the issue; in the textile case, the U.S. government developed a specific substantive proposal very early and insisted on it throughout the dispute with very little modification.

These contrasting styles—Americans taking the initiative and Japanese adapting—may seem complementary. But the Japanese, in trying to accommodate the other side's position, expect their negotiating counterparts to respond in kind. They may be driven to strong resentment and resistance by efforts of the other side to force a settlement from a position of superior strength, just as they resent breach of consensus or "tyranny of the majority" in their domestic system. Exactly this sort of resistance arose repeatedly on the textile issue. However, in the case of Okinawa—where the Japanese were doing the asking—this difference in styles of negotiation worked to the advantage of both sides. The slow emergence of the Japanese position on specific terms gave American actors sympathetic to reversion time to bring their government around; indeed, the consensus on possible terms that was emerging in Washington fed importantly into Japanese decisionmaking and the consensus that emerged there.

Amae and Sincerity

Another cultural source of misperception in U.S.-Japanese relations is the Japanese psychological and cultural orientation known as *amae*. Essentially, *amae* refers to the attitude and expectations of the inferior or weaker party in a relationship of dependence with a superior party.

34. Kinhide Mushakōji calls the American style one of *erabi* (choosing) and the Japanese one of *awase* (adapting) (*Kokusai seiji to Nihon* [International politics and Japan], [Tokyo: Tokyo University Press, 1967], pp. 155–75). This difference in style is related to divergent attitudes toward the environment. Japanese culture shares with some non-Western cultures an emphasis on harmony with external environments, be they human or natural. Man is supposed to adjust or adapt himself. In Western society, on the other hand, man is supposed to control and change his external environment for his own purposes. For development of this contrast, see ibid.; Charles A. Moore, ed., *The Japanese Mind: Essentials of Japanese Philosophy and Culture* (Honolulu: University Press of Hawaii, 1967); and Hajime Nakamura, *Ways of Thinking of Eastern Peoples: India-China-Tibet-Japan* (Honolulu: University Press of Hawaii, 1964). Certainly the American tendency to emphasize initiatives and direction and the Japanese tendency toward passive adaptation derive also from the asymmetry of the power relationship between the two countries. The asymmetric relationship seems to reinforce this difference in cultural style.

It involves an assumption that the stronger will have indulgence for the weaker party, that the stronger will recognize an obligation to take care of and protect the weaker without requiring a reciprocal obligation.[35] Americans, by contrast, tend to think of relationships in terms of reciprocity—particularly when the parties are formally equal.

Amae explains in part why leaders in Japanese organizations may feel obligated to their followers. Leaders of the textile industry, for example, had to take care of the interests of the smaller firms, whereas the latter had no reciprocal obligation to place their demands within the framework of the overall interests of the industry. That kind of expectation sometimes carries over into international relations. The United States fits into the role of the superior partner vis à vis Japan, the older brother from whom much has been received and from whom much continues to be expected. Prime Minister Sato, for example, was apparently indulging in amae-type optimism when he hoped, on several occasions, that Nixon would be sympathetic to his domestic predicament on textiles. He seems to have assumed that Japan's patron, the United States—perhaps even Richard Nixon personally—would somehow accommodate Japan's and Sato's political needs because the United States was the stronger party. To Nixon, however, what was right and proper was that Sato should reciprocate politically for Nixon's agreement to return Okinawa.

Closely related to amae in Japanese society is the importance placed on demonstrating sincerity. The spirit in which a person approaches another is likely to be as important in achieving a favorable response as the substance of what is sought. Two people in a negotiating situation may not agree at first, but once one of them can demonstrate that he is sincerely doing his best to accommodate the other's interests, the other person will be inclined to reciprocate his sincerity by making reasonable concessions. Particularly if the former is the weaker of the two, the latter is more likely to make such concessions. This contrasts with Americans' tendency to place emphasis on what each party actually concedes.

In early summer 1941, Ambassador Kichisaburō Nomura and Secretary of State Cordell Hull were engaged in talks seeking a political accommodation that might arrest their countries' move toward war. On July 12, Japanese leaders were discussing how to respond to Hull's stiff counterproposal, which had included an oral statement indicating that

35. See Takeo Doi, The Anatomy of Dependence, trans. John Bester (Tokyo and New York: Kodansha International, 1973).

recent public statements of the Japanese foreign minister might pose "an insurmountable roadblock to the negotiation." Tōjō, then war minister, suggested to his colleagues that they should keep negotiating with America even if there seemed to be little hope. "Naturally the Oral Statement is an insult to our *kokutai* [national essence] and we must reject it. . . . But what if we *sincerely* tell the Americans what we hold to be right? Won't this move them?"[36]

In the postwar era, the most dramatic public example of the Japanese *amae* mentality and sincerity cult was the acceptance of Article Nine of the constitution of 1947 authored by the American occupation authorities. This renunciation of war and arms was founded, for many Japanese, on faith in the power of Japanese sincerity to dissuade potential aggressors from attacking. They felt such sincerity in pursuit of world peace would be rewarded by understanding from cooperative "peace-loving" nations of the world, who would help protect Japan not only by refraining from themselves committing aggression, but also by defending her—if necessary—with their own troops and arms through the United Nations peace-keeping machinery.

Such faith appeared increasingly naive to Americans becoming inured to the cold war. Many Japanese political leaders and senior foreign policy bureaucrats were also skeptical. The problem, as with less sweeping manifestations of this style in interpersonal negotiations, was that the other side might perceive it as an indication of weakness. When MITI Minister Ohira accepted Commerce Secretary Stans's proposal of July 1969 to hold "technical discussions" on the textile issue between expert representatives of the two countries, he apparently did so as a demonstration of his sincerity and willingness to give consideration to Stans's political needs even though he was convinced the Americans did not have a good substantive case. He apparently hoped that Stans's face would be saved and America's "unreasonable" push for controls would be significantly modified. For the Americans, however, the predominant interpretation was that now that the Japanese had conceded something, they were likely to concede more if pressure were maintained. Some considered the "technical discussions" label to be a face-saving device for Ohira and believed (incorrectly) that the discussions as carried out would include consideration of U.S. proposals.

On several occasions Prime Minister Sato acted as if he felt a demon-

36. John Toland, *The Rising Sun: The Decline and Fall of the Japanese Empire, 1936–1945* (Bantam, 1971), p. 97. Emphasis added.

stration of sincerity on his part could bring American concessions on a resolution of the textile impasse. One dramatic example was in June 1970, when MITI Minister Miyazawa flew to Washington for three days of private talks with Stans. Sato's method of making his "utmost efforts" to resolve the issue was not to intervene directly in the substantive debate within Japan for major modification of Japan's negotiating position in the direction Washington desired. Instead, he dispatched his foreign minister, Aichi, to join Miyazawa in Washington, and sent with Aichi a personal message to Nixon expressing Sato's desire to be helpful to the President on this issue and indicating he was doing all that he could. When Miyazawa did not concede on the substance, however, American leaders were not particularly mollified by Sato's letter or the fact that he had sent Aichi also; indeed, they do not seem to have understood his message at all.

An effort to demonstrate sincerity can even provoke bitter American reaction if found wanting on substantive grounds. In March 1970 a Japanese aide-mémoire on textiles was transmitted to the American government in an effort to break the impasse. It was, for those Japanese officials in Tokyo (and at the Washington embassy) who pressed it, a sincere effort to be as responsive to American needs on the issue as the politics of the issue in Japan would allow. It arrived at the Commerce Department, however, during a meeting of the Management-Labor Advisory Committee on textiles, an active, assertive group of textile industry and union leaders who had pressed for restrictive U.S. proposals and were frustrated by the lack of results. They angrily denounced the document as "arrogant" and unhelpful, because it did not come close to their terms on substance, and it suggested a U.S. Tariff Commission investigation of the extent of import-induced injury to the American textile industry. The Tariff Commission had been unsympathetic to the industry's case in the past and the committee members could only assume it would continue to be.

Haragei Bargaining

Related to the emphasis on sincerity is the frequent Japanese preference for sorting out issues by gut, nonverbal (*haragei*) bargaining, a time-consuming talking around a problem until a consensus begins to develop and each participant can work out his own individual way to adapt to it. *Haragei* can also be used to signal resistance, as MITI bureaucrats did during the 1969–71 negotiations when they emphasized "maintaining a spirit of confidence" between the government and the textile industry—meaning that the former should not act against the latter's wishes. However used, *haragei* reflects a cultural difference: "Americans do not grasp the fact that language plays an unusual role in Japan. Americans set great store by the literal meaning of words; Japanese are much more interested in the relationships and impressions that go unspoken."[37] According to Masao Kunihiro, "the art of *haragei* is very much a Japanese technique of communication. . . . In the use of this word there exists a feeling of a community of emotions, that is, a desire to be given special consideration (again related to *amae*) since the other man is considered to be your friend, a member of your group."[38] The problem, as Kunihiro goes on to explain, is that *haragei* communication works well only among members of an intimate group brought up in the same culture. Thus in cross-cultural dealings this style of communication often causes confusion or misunderstandings.[39]

In the pre-Pearl Harbor negotiations, Japanese leaders who were anxious to avoid war with the United States proposed a summit conference between President Roosevelt and Premier Fumimaro Konoye. They believed that agreement could be reached if such high-level person-to-person talks were "carried out with broadmindedness." Konoye apparently thought that if he personally met with Roosevelt and was able to convey his "gut" situation and sentiments (*hara o waru*),[40] his weaknesses and needs as a human being, the President would somehow understand his (and Japan's) position and seek a way to accommodate it. But the proposal was not accepted. President Roosevelt seemed in-

37. Bernard Krisher, *Newsweek*, Aug. 6, 1974.
38. Masao Kunihiro, "U.S.-Japan Communications," in Henry Rosovsky, ed., *Discord in the Pacific: Challenges to the Japanese-American Alliance* (Columbia Books for American Assembly, 1972), p. 167.
39. *Haragei* is not limited to Japan. A similar type of communication exists elsewhere among people of homogeneous background, including the United States. Here again the difference is in the realm of degree. And even in Japanese domestic politics, *haragei* does not work where very deep conflicts of interest or opinion exist, as between the Liberal Democratic party and the Japan Communist party.
40. In 1956, Ichirō Kōno, one of the most powerful LDP leaders, conducted direct personal negotiations with Premier Nikita Khrushchev in Moscow without the help of a Japanese interpreter. His rationale was that the language barrier could be overcome by the mutual trust generated if he "opened his heart." Prime Minister Hatoyama's Russian trip that followed also had a *haragei* flavor, though to a lesser degree.

clined to meet Konoye, but did not push the matter in the face of strong skepticism among his key advisers: Secretary of War Stimson, who wrote in his diary that "the invitation to the President is merely a blind to try to keep us from taking definite action"; Secretary of State Hull, who seems to have recognized that Konoye might be personally sincere, but "doubted the Premier's capacity to bring the military into line." So the Americans insisted that the summit must be preceded by "a meeting of minds on essential points," and in turn, Japanese military leaders—who felt they had yielded a good deal in acquiescing in the idea of a summit meeting—saw Washington's coldness as new evidence of the futility of negotiating with the Americans.[41]

Prior to his departure for Washington for his second summit textile discussion with President Nixon in October 1970, Prime Minister Sato reportedly stated: "Since Mr. Nixon and I are old friends, the negotiations will be three parts talk and seven parts *haragei*."[42] Although the premier was not sure he could make all the substantive concessions the Americans were demanding, he apparently believed that something would be worked out if only he personally talked to Nixon again. A personal meeting, a chance to convey his gut situation as one man to another, might help Nixon understand why he had been unable to deliver on his promise of a year earlier, so the President would not think Sato had designedly deceived him. For Nixon, however, what mattered was the terms of settlement; he refused to engage in any *haragei*-style discussion, insisting instead on Sato's personal endorsement of an explicit American five-point proposal as the basis for agreement.[43] And when Sato assented and then failed to deliver, further damage was done to relations between the two men and the governments they headed.

41. Feis, *Road to Pearl Harbor*, pp. 258–60; Burns, *Roosevelt: Soldier of Freedom*, pp. 134–37 and 144; Toland, *Rising Sun*, pp. 102–10.
42. Kunihiro, "U.S.-Japan Communications," p. 167.
43. Keidanren President Kogorō Uemura apparently made a similar mistake when he visited the United States in October 1970 to sound out major U.S. officials and business leaders on textiles prior to this second summit. He thought discussions conducted on general terms might lead to a way out of the textile impasse and apparently concluded that just because he emphasized a "spirit of mutual concession" and the Americans did not particularly object to it, they were actually prepared to make necessary concessions. For the Americans the "spirit of mutual concession" had no serious substantive implications. But for Uemura, who was used to *haragei* communications, a tacit understanding of such a general posture was very important. Consequently, he advised Sato to resume the negotiations.

Form versus Substance

In his 1973 foreign policy report to Congress, President Nixon chided Tokyo for placing such emphasis on Washington's having undertaken major policy changes in 1971 on China and international trade without prior consultation with Japan. A "mature alliance relationship," Nixon wrote, "means seriously addressing the underlying causes, not the superficial public events."[44] Such a relatively gentle rebuke might have been accepted quite calmly—or dismissed as mere verbiage—by a Western nation. But Japanese reacted as if they had been slapped. "The underlying thought of the statement," one ranking Japanese official said, "is 'what matters is the substance not the form.' For Japanese, where 'face' is involved, the form is as important and sometimes more important than the substance."[45]

In Japan, officials and politicians pay considerably greater respect to formal jurisdictions than do their American counterparts. To bypass those with formal responsibility for all or part of an issue is to humiliate them, whether they be subordinates or superiors or those in other offices. So formal prerogatives are carefully observed, even while active informal networks make it possible to move issues forward. If due respect is paid to an official's position, he may well not insist on exercising his substantive prerogatives.

One manifestation of this emphasis on form arose in mid-1945 when the Suzuki cabinet was trying to bring about Japan's surrender on terms that could be considered honorable. What really mattered to them— and to Japanese more generally after the surrender—was not so much the "substance" of imperial divinity and sovereignty, but rather the "form" of maintaining the imperial institution. Thus there was remarkably little resistance from his loyal subjects when the emperor, following occupation orders, renounced his divinity and was then reduced in the new constitution to the status of merely a "symbol" of national unity.

On the Okinawa reversion issue, American officials recognized the importance of form to the Japanese and were able to meet this need. The form of the decision that Japanese wanted—home-level reversion— was understood early in the game as the probable political requirement in Japan. Those in the U.S. government who recognized this were able

44. *U.S. Foreign Policy for the 1970s: Shaping a Durable Peace: A Report to the Congress by Richard Nixon* (GPO, 1973), p. 104.
45. *Newsweek*, Aug. 6, 1974, p. 35.

to put the substantive terms important to Americans into a home-level package suitable in form to Tokyo. The issue of nuclear weapons was left unresolved until the November 1969 summit meeting because it was feared that their removal might not be negotiable within the Washington bureaucracy; yet their retention would breach the form, since nuclear storage was not allowed on Japan's main islands. So it was left to the President to make a separate decision on nuclear storage; by the time he did, the balance of argument was clearly against it and his decision reflected this. (Of course, Japanese concern about nuclear weapons had strong substantive roots as well.)

In the textile negotiations, however, Japanese emphasis on form led to confusion and misunderstanding. At a bilateral Geneva conference in November 1969, the Japanese delegates insisted that any textile restraint agreement must maintain the form of "objective proof of injury" to the U.S. industry caused by imports. So they placed particular emphasis on establishing multilateral machinery for injury investigation, but gave signals that this would be rather flexibly applied. In fact, a directive from Tokyo on November 19 specified: "Even if proof of injury was absent, a Working Group consisting of the four Far Eastern countries might still consider some sort of export control, including the creation of a 'trigger mechanism' to alleviate the potential threat of imports to the United States industry."[46] However, the Americans wanted to first make sure that such a working group would in fact act favorably on American proposals for import restrictions. They either did not understand—or thought it insufficient—that if the United States accepted the Japanese-proposed form, the latter would feel they had an obligation to take American substantive interests fairly into account.

The issue became more complicated when, two months later, the Japanese government was unable to follow through on its suggestions that formal American concessions would lead to substantive Japanese ones. In mid-January 1970, the newly designated MITI minister, Miyazawa, suggested that once the United States presented information purporting to prove injury to the U.S. textile industry from imports, Japan might consider it as establishing actual injury even if the evidence was

46. This is described further in I. M. Destler, Hideo Sato, and Haruhiro Fukui, "The Textile Wrangle: Conflict in Japanese-American Relations 1969–71" (1976; processed), chap. 6. The "trigger mechanism" was a device by which sharp rises of exports in particular textile categories would automatically bring quantitative restrictions into play.

not convincing. The Americans did submit detailed injury materials, but Japanese actors who were strongly opposed to concessions on substantive grounds withheld their assent, and Miyazawa was unable to make the positive response he had suggested.

In December 1970, however, American concessions on matters of form came close to settling the issue. The U.S. negotiators accepted the format of an agreement (export ceilings based not on individual product categories but on groups of categories) that the Japanese government had developed, but proposed changes in its details that would make its practical effects very close to what the Americans had persistently sought. The Sato government responded positively, and the two sides moved to the verge of agreement. Had the White House not then toughened its stance under industry pressure, the textile issue might have been settled at this point.

As these examples indicate, attention to form is closely related to consensus decisionmaking. Respect for form includes efforts to assure that all relevant actors are properly consulted. It can also include adoption of a principle important to certain policy actors ("objective proof of injury" on textiles), but with adjustments in its practical application that result in an actual outcome at variance with their preferences. In both cases, attention to form gives potential dissidents a face-saving way out: they have a chance to participate in the decision; they win acceptance of their principle. And just as consensus and form are closely related, both are linked to *haragei* and *amae*. *Haragei* minimizes unnecessary verbal exchanges that might lead to confrontation; consensus is thereby approached as contestants feel each other out, read one another's minds. *Amae* facilitates *haragei*-type communications, particularly if one side (or both) reveals its weaknesses to the other. And the emphasis on consensus and form can fulfill an *amae* expectation of weaker parties that others will at least listen to them and seek to accommodate them. Moreover, by eventually conforming to the general sentiment of the group, dissidents can enhance their *amae* expectation that the group will take care of their interests more generally, in other ways.

None of these cultural patterns is unique to Japan; they probably exist in some form in all societies. But their particular importance to Japanese means that Americans dealing with that country need to be especially sensitive to these procedures and expectations, just as Japanese need to recognize that such sensitivity will not always be present in international negotiations. On most of the instances noted here, for example, accurate American perception of Japanese attention to form proved productive. This was not, of course, always the case, and none of the differences in cultural style highlighted here will necessarily prove the decisive barrier to an agreement in any given case. But they are relevant and potentially important factors in all such negotiations. Officials will ignore them at their peril.

Universalism and Cultural Arrogance

Not all culturally based misperceptions and misunderstandings have Japanese roots. Indeed, the very idea that when the two cultures differ it is the Japanese who are unusual reflects a general American cultural tendency that creates continuing problems in dealings with Japan, and with other countries as well.

Many students of American foreign policy have pointed out the tendency of Americans to believe that the policies they pursue reflect not just U.S. interests, but universal interests—if not of all countries, at least those that are allied with the United States. Thus American officials and political leaders are inclined to believe either that people in other countries share U.S. perceptions of common threats and common goals, or that they need to be persuaded that American policies fully reflect their own interests. On cold-war-related issues in particular, Americans have tended to resist the notion that allies have distinct sets of interests, or that the conceptual framework of leaders in other countries may be markedly different from their own.

In postwar U.S.-Japanese dealings, the guardian-ward relationship offered unusual opportunities for the expression of such universalism. During and after occupation, Americans saw their country as the benefactor of Japan, and on many security or economic issues Japanese in turn relied on the United States either to protect their interests or to speak for them in international forums. To many Americans, the occupation had reformed Japan along the lines of American values. This belief led some Americans to treat Japanese with condescension. One manifestation of this sense of superiority was the notion that "our military leaders somehow had a better grasp of the potential threats to Japan than the Japanese themselves";[47] those who did not share U.S. perceptions were militarily naive and required educating. And the popular criticism of the 1960s, that the Americans were shouldering a dispropor-

47. George R. Packard, "A Crisis in Understanding," in Rosovsky, *Discord in the Pacific*, p. 120.

tionate burden of the "common defense," implied that the magnitude and shape of U.S. security efforts in Asia served Japanese interests as much as American.

All of these characteristics were further reinforced by postwar Japanese reticence in articulating any clear conceptions of national security interests, let alone conceptions distinct from the Americans'.

Intertwined with this universalism is a cultural arrogance, historically familiar, that assumes—explicitly or implicitly—that the values and practices of one's own culture are the standard by which others' behavior should be judged. In American foreign relations, this has given rise to a messianic belief that the United States was setting an example for all peoples. In the words of one Japanese analyst, Americans who had pioneered in creating a new world felt "their faith and values were the best in the world, and the values of different cultures were regarded as inferior."[48] And for many Americans, he might have added, others' inferiority was the greater the more they deviated from the American standard.

When cultural arrogance becomes acute and focuses on distinctions based on ethnic origins, it is appropriate to call it "racism." Racism is hardly an exclusively American characteristic; many ethnic or larger groups, including Japanese, conceive of themselves as superior to certain other groups.[49] But American racism can cause particular difficulties because of (1) American power and (2) American universalism, which tends to mask for Americans some aspects of such racism even as it makes it particularly unpalatable to others. Such racism was particularly evident in the anti-Japanese immigration legislation early in this century, and in public campaigns against the sale or purchase of Japanese textiles and other products in the postwar period. Nor has it entirely

48. Hiroshi Kitamura, *Psychological Dimensions of U.S.-Japanese Relations*, Occasional Papers in International Affairs, no. 28 (Center for International Affairs, Harvard University, 1971), p. 21. Stanley Hoffmann emphasizes a different aspect of Americans' cultural biases: "Americans, whose history is a success story, tend to believe that the values that arise from their experience are of universal application, and they are reluctant to recognize that they are tied to the special conditions that made the American success possible." ("The American Style: Our Past and Our Principles," *Foreign Affairs*, vol. 46 [January 1968], p. 363.)

49. Japanese racism is important for understanding that country's relations with groups and nationalities to whom Japanese have tended to feel themselves superior— for example, Koreans. But because the typical Japanese attitude toward Americans since World War II has been closer to the opposite, it does not bear on the bilateral relationship the way that U.S. racism does.

disappeared; many observers saw racism in the way Maurice Stans approached the textile issue and felt that the Nixon administration's handling of the issue was more brutal than would have been the case had a European power been the target.

Americans' cultural arrogance can lead to underestimation of Japanese capabilities—as many American officials did prior to World War II. And when Japanese perform well by American standards, as on the world economic scene in the late sixties and early seventies, this refutation of American notions of superiority provides a ready market for explanations that the Japanese succeeded because they were somehow unfair, or did things in some fundamentally different way—charges never without some supporting evidence as cultural differences mean, by definition, some playing by different rules. Hence, many Americans have conceived of "Japan, Inc." as an integrated government-business economic juggernaut moving relentlessly forward to capture larger and larger shares of world markets, with even an aura of unstoppability. Thus an American cabinet official could say in 1971: "The Japanese are still fighting the war, but it is no longer a shooting war." And the recurrent concept of a "yellow peril," usually reserved for Chinese because of their large numbers, is applied also to Japan.

Reflecting the shallowness of American cultural exposure to Japan, such stereotyping is susceptible to quick change. Thus Japanese can be docile and hard-working, or relentless and inscrutably overpowering in economic enterprise; or they can be deceitful and untrustworthy, essentially impossible to deal with except through direct coercion. President Nixon, who came to office generally sympathetic to Japan and her conservative political leaders, reacted to Sato's failure to deliver on the textile issue by holding up Japan and Japanese cultural traits to contempt and ridicule.[50]

Language Differences

Underlying all of the differences in cultural values and styles, all of these causes of misperception, is the language barrier. Not only do America and Japan not share a common tongue; their two languages represent very different ways of thinking, in two very different civilizations. Reminiscing about the textile dispute in January 1973, former Premier Sato remarked that "if only Japan and the United States had a

50. See, for example, Marvin Kalb and Bernard Kalb, *Kissinger* (Little, Brown, 1974), p. 255.

common language things would have worked out smoothly." Whether this is true for that case is doubtful, but Sato's observation is a very apt general illustration of the sense of frustration, of communications difficulty, that American and Japanese officials often feel because they must talk through interpreters.

Interestingly, there are few decisive examples of mistranslation in the postwar period.[51] In 1941, after U.S. cryptographers broke the Japanese diplomatic codes, American mistranslation of the Japanese internal communications that U.S. leaders had gained access to seems to have exacerbated that deepening crisis. And after the Allied powers issued the Potsdam Declaration of July 1945 on the terms of Japanese surrender, Premier Suzuki's ill-worded response had the effect of converting a wait-and-see decision by a divided Japanese cabinet into an apparent rejection.[52] But on the textile negotiations, what Sato apparently meant to suggest—that his difficulties with Nixon were mainly the result of the errors of his translator at their first summit meeting—does not seem in fact to have been the case.[53] And occasionally, language differences can

51. Packard cites one moderately important case: "When Japanese Foreign Minister Takeo Fukuda visited Washington in September 1971, he held a press conference at which he was asked whether Japan would support the U.S. position on China at the United Nations General Assembly meeting that fall. His answer was 'not for the time being.' The interpreter missed the nuance of 'for the time being' and rendered the answer as a flat 'No' in English. Newspapers across the U.S. played the story as if Japan had harshly rebuked the United States. Later, it turned out that Japan did support the United States position at the U.N." ("A Crisis in Understanding," pp. 125–26.)

52. For many prewar examples, see Toland, Rising Sun, especially pp. 153–57. The Potsdam misunderstanding arose when Premier Suzuki spoke with Japanese reporters about the government's reaction to the Allied message. He was actively seeking some route to peace, and the cabinet had decided to withhold any response for the time being. Unfortunately, Suzuki characterized the official stance toward the declaration by using the word mokusatsu, whose literal meaning is "treat with silent contempt." The news agencies broadcast this language in their reports, and interpreters (Japanese as well as American) translated it directly. Thus, one week before Hiroshima, American leaders concluded that the Japanese government was set against surrender whereas in fact there was considerable support for it. However, the misperception was not so much a result of mistranslation as of Suzuki's poor choice of words. (See William Craig, The Fall of Japan [Dial, 1967], pp. 67–68; Herbert Feis, The Atomic Bomb and the End of World War II [Princeton University Press, 1966], p. 109; Robert J. C. Butow, Japan's Decision to Surrender [Stanford University Press, 1954], pp. 143–49; and William J. Coughlin, "The Great Mokusatsu Mistake," Harper's, March 1953, pp. 31–40.)

53. For the general story, see chap. 2, above. It receives detailed treatment in Destler, Sato, and Fukui, "The Textile Wrangle," chap. 6.

be used consciously to mutual advantage—as in the 1967 summit communiqué, where the English text pointed to Okinawa reversion within a "few years" (a general phrase chosen to avoid the impression of imminence), and the Japanese rendered the phrase as *"ryo-san-nen,"* literally "two to three years," to satisfy reversionist sentiment in Japan.

But more general language problems pervade U.S.-Japanese relations. Americans sometimes underrate such problems because they expect, generally, to deal in English and have others do so. Theirs has long been a predominant world language, and the power position and relative autonomy of the United States are such that Americans have never been forced to cope with another culture on its terms as the price of survival. But since relatively few Japanese know English, this means that Americans are in fact restricted in their informal contacts to a small circle, and those Japanese end up shielding them from broader exposure to their society even as they make possible what communication in fact occurs.

In bilateral negotiations, of course, the language problem is generally handled through the use of interpreters. But this creates subtle problems of its own. In U.S.-Japanese negotiations, it is particularly important for officials to try to perceive both the political and cultural framework of their negotiating counterparts. But ironically, speaking through an interpreter tends to relieve an official at a negotiation from the pressure to do so—he speaks in his own language, and it is his interpreter's job to make his meaning clear. The principal negotiators, on both sides, are thus likely to be much less attentive and sensitive to subtle messages than they should be. And the negotiating sessions tend to be exceptionally formal and impersonal, hampering the development of mutual trust and sympathy. Such mutual trust, of course, is hardly all that is required for agreements. Resolving difficult bilateral issues is not a simple question of winning over one's negotiating counterpart, but the far more complicated one of reaching a position that can be viable in two complex national (and bureaucratic) political arenas. But relationships of personal trust can be very helpful in developing solutions, and the language barrier all too often stands in the way.

Conclusions

Whether rooted in political or in cultural differences, the misperceptions of officials in each government have frequently led them to oversimplify the politics of the other country, and in ways that rendered effective negotiations more difficult. In many cases, expectations were unjustifiably high—Eisenhower would be able to visit Japan; Nixon would respond sensitively to Sato's *haragei* approach on textiles. In other circumstances, the perception was overly negative—"the Japanese" were irrevocably determined on war in November 1941; Japanese unresponsiveness on textiles reflected calculated delaying tactics rather than problems in achieving domestic consensus. But whether optimistic or pessimistic, these misinterpretations almost always made issues harder to resolve.

Too hopeful assessments postponed the facing of tough political problems by allowing an official to indulge in wishful thinking. The other country's officials and institutions might yet behave according to his domestic needs, eliminating or reducing any need for politically painful adjustments of his own. Thus Sato in the fall of 1970 postponed serious domestic political bargaining on textiles until after he saw his "old friend" Nixon, who would understand his political predicament and somehow accommodate it. Extremely negative interpretations, on the other hand, made agreement seem less attainable than it really was, and therefore reduced the incentive to search for political accommodation. If the dominant thrust of the other government's policies appears totally contrary to that of his own, then the quest for common ground seems hopeless; an actor will not then propose initiatives that are politically risky at home in order to test the international waters. Thus Roosevelt backed away from his modus vivendi proposal in 1941; he was not going to embark on a touchy political course at home if the Japanese seemed bent on making war anyway.

If such misperceptions have pervaded U.S.-Japanese relations, why did they not pose insuperable obstacles on an issue as difficult as Okinawa? Misperceptions were not entirely absent: Gaimushō officials, for example, underestimated more than once the extent of the concessions the U.S. government might make in order to accommodate Japanese domestic politics. And the state of bargaining on Okinawa reversion within the U.S. government often made American officials reluctant to communicate important information to their Japanese counterparts, thus limiting their understanding of where Washington stood on the issue and where it was heading. In 1966–67, internal discussions were closely held lest State and Pentagon civilians' attitudes toward reversion be revealed before military acquiescence was in sight. In 1969, the issue of nuclear weapons was reserved for separate presidential decision, so State Department negotiators were unable to discuss a solution of the question in the presummit negotiations. Thus Japanese officials were kept in the dark on a vital issue. Yet a satisfactory resolution was nonetheless achieved. Why?

One reason is that the misperceptions involved were not fundamental. Foreign Ministry men and other Japanese activists may not always have known exactly where the U.S. government was on this issue and where it would ultimately stand, but they understood, increasingly, who the key American actors were, what the critical arguments among them were, and how Japanese officials might influence the outcome by when and how they raised the issue. And since in their misperception they generally erred on the side of moderate pessimism, they brought pressure to keep Japanese political doors open to less desirable solutions if the U.S. government could not be moved beyond them. In this case, the slow process of consensus decisionmaking worked to their advantage, helping prevent a premature hardening of the Japanese stand. At the same time, their American counterparts were pressing in Washington for flexibility in considering Japanese political constraints. Thus neither government got locked into a position until mutually acceptable terms of agreement were beginning to emerge. On textiles, by contrast, both sides moved—because of intense domestic pressure—to fixed (and irreconcilable) positions long before any possible basis for mutual understanding had been established.

Part of the problem, on textiles, was that on neither side did those dominating policy place priority on understanding the politics of the issue in the other capital and making reasonable adaptations to it. Instead, they responded overwhelmingly to politics at home, holding to positions that would minimize their domestic and bureaucratic political vulnerability even though these positions were unacceptable across the Pacific. Thus the misperceptions that helped to exacerbate the textile crisis and to inhibit careful calculations of what outcomes might be politically viable in the other country were caused, in part, by the lack of serious concern about the politics of the other country's decisionmaking in the first place.

Thus, though misperception and misunderstanding seriously complicated resolution of the textile case, they did not cause the dispute, nor do they explain, by themselves, why it proved so intractable. The intractability, rather, was rooted in the domination of decisionmaking on both sides—particularly the American side—by men who not only were primarily concerned with what was good domestic and bureaucratic politics on the issue (this is not untypical, and is true in a sense of Okinawa as well), but who also failed to give much weight in their political calculations to the demands of politics on the other side of the Pacific. Such considerations, however, are part of the broader question of the overall political management of controversial bilateral issues.

CHAPTER FIVE

The Interplay of National Systems

CHAPTER 4 explored how politics in each capital can cause officials to misconstrue actions taken in the other, and how cultural differences create further problems of misinterpretation and misunderstanding. Yet the problem faced by officials who seek to resolve difficult bilateral issues is still more complex. For they must deal not just with the other system, but within their own at the same time. It was not enough that Japanese politicians and bureaucrats were astute in moving the U.S. government to negotiate a revised security treaty in the 1950s, if miscalculation of their own domestic scene meant that it produced a crisis in 1960. Nor could State Department officials in 1969 apply their Japan expertise very effectively on the textile issue as long as they were disregarded or overruled on the major policy decisions at home. For a particular settlement formula can win acceptance, and can endure, only if it can command enough political support within both the Japanese and the American domestic systems to be adopted, ratified if such is required, and implemented.[1]

Yet though these systems are in important respects inward-looking and relatively self-contained, they do not operate independently of one another. Actions of officials in one capital have varied effects on the politics of decisionmaking in the other—sometimes bringing agreement nearer, sometimes retarding it. Some such effects are consciously de-

1. How much support is enough for such purposes is a question without easy answer. The only fair response is that "it depends"—on the nature of the issue, the actors and institutions involved, the relevant policymaking procedures, the overall distribution of power. Frequently, broader consensus will be required in Tokyo than in Washington. This is true for cultural reasons, and also because of the lesser power of the prime minister, and the greater political visibility (and controversiality) of bilateral issues in Japan.

signed, but many come from signals originating in one country that influence the other without any particular intention that they do so. How then does the interplay of the two systems develop? Is there a pattern in the *initiation* of issues, in how they rise to prominence within one of the governments? How do they then become bilateral policy problems, of live concern in both capitals? Once an issue rises to importance, what are the patterns of *interaction* between national policymaking systems? What sorts of impacts do actions, proposals, and other communications and signals from one country have on the politics of the issue in the other? What is the effect of the asymmetry of impact—the fact that events in the United States have far more impact on Japanese policymaking than vice versa? Finally, what are the routes to *resolution* of issues? What role is played by informal *transnational alliances* in which actors from both countries work together to achieve particular negotiating outcomes? And what *official channels* are employed to negotiate U.S.-Japan issues, to what effects?

Issues do not, of course, move neatly through clearly delineated stages of initiation, interaction, and resolution. Interaction occurs continuously, with initiation and negotiation toward resolution two of its particular forms. And though the three postwar cases stressed in this study led eventually to negotiated resolutions, such is not always necessary or possible. Nevertheless, an analysis organized around these questions can shed further light on the politics of bilateral relations and the problems of officials who must manage them.

Initiation of Bilateral Issues

Each of the cases highlighted in this study was pressed by a politician seeking to enhance or solidify his position. Sato raised Okinawa as a candidate in the 1964 contest for the presidency of the Liberal Democratic party; Nixon embraced textiles as a competitor for the Republican presidential nomination in 1968. And security treaty revision—though an almost inevitable Japanese objective flowing out of the unbalanced treaty of 1951—first rose to become a live issue in 1955 when Premier Hatoyama "badly needed something in the nature of a diplomatic stunt to lend glamour to his new government." Thus, he sent three powerful ruling party leaders to Washington "to sound out Dulles' reaction to a revision of the security pact,"[2] which was widely resented in Japan as an "unequal treaty." After Dulles responded negatively, Hatoyama devoted his prime diplomatic energies to reaching a peace agreement with the Soviet Union. But the initiative was resumed in 1957 by Kishi, who had used his role as one of Hatoyama's emissaries on the 1955 trip to advance his own domestic political objectives.[3]

In the security treaty case, Hatoyama could gain little domestically unless he could get something from the Americans. Thus when he was rebuffed, he stepped back. Politicians who seize issues for campaign purposes, however, can often score gains in the electoral contest merely by advocating a change; they do not need a positive response from the other capital. On neither textiles nor Okinawa, in fact, was it in the aspiring leader's interests to think too carefully about whether the goal was politically attainable in the other country. Indeed, both Okinawa and textile quotas were available as domestic political issues precisely because they did not appear within reach to current leaders. In both cases, however, the aspirant soon won his office, reiterated his commitment, and thus reinforced his political stakes in attaining it. In each case the issue ultimately reached the point where failure to resolve it threatened to, or did, damage the broader relationship.

In the textile case, moreover, U.S. bureaucratic and domestic politics determined not only the priority given the issue, but how it was initially pursued and who would pursue it. Quotas were sought through international negotiations not because the Japanese were known to be receptive (they were not), but because the U.S. Congress was believed un-

2. Asahi Shimbun Staff, *The Pacific Rivals: A Japanese View of Japanese-American Relations* (Weatherhill/Asahi, 1972), pp. 231–32.

3. Of course, not all U.S.-Japan issues arise out of political leaders' needs for isues to ride. Some, like the differences in approaches to the oil crisis that began in 1973, stem from externally triggered events with unavoidable impact on both nations. Others appear more or less accidentally—like the reemergence of the nuclear weapons issue following the LaRocque statement of September 1974. Moreover, the fact that a politician exploits an issue does not necessarily mean that he lacks convictions on it. Sato certainly believed strongly in Okinawa reversion, particularly after his trip to the islands in the summer of 1965. But Nixon's convictions on textiles were hardly of comparable depth, nor did they reflect any deep national commitment on the issue. And the difference between the two cases in the type of domestic political interests involved affected the prospects for resolving them. The "low politics" roots of the textile issue in the United States undercut the legitimacy of the U.S. initiative in Tokyo, whereas the political urgency of reversion in Japan provided the principal impetus for American policy changes on that issue.

likely to enact restraints on textile imports without adding other products
as well. Secretary of Commerce Maurice Stans was assigned negotiating
responsibility not because he knew how to negotiate with Japan (he
did not), but because he was committed to the objective, loyal to the
President, and acceptable to the U.S. textile industry.

And just as politicians were in the vanguard on all three issues, foreign
office officials were counseling restraint. There were several reasons—
State Department coolness on textiles, for example, was partly a product
of a disinclination to give such priority to that kind of issue. But a common strand was the diplomats' relatively greater sensitivity to the constraints of the other country's politics, which made them reluctant to
force issues. Their concern for the bilateral relationship made them fear
that pushing an issue prematurely would lock the two governments into
positions that might prove irreconcilable and could not be changed because of domestic political forces, with textile-type crisis the consequence.[4]

Initiatives with strong political roots pose particular risks for the U.S.-
Japanese relationship unless handled with exceptional skill. For they
commit key actors in one government to an objective that can develop
a lot of domestic political steam, leaving them little room for compromise, when there is no assurance that the other political system can
arrive at a consensus on a solution acceptable to the initiators. Thus the
initiating politician can find himself out on a limb. Premier Sato's ultimate success on Okinawa came after years of uncertainty; by 1969 he
was a hostage to American leaders' willingness and ability to deliver a
reversion package he could accept. President Nixon's ultimate success
on textiles came only after the unacceptability of his demands in Japanese politics left him vulnerable to the alliance between Wilbur Mills
and the Japanese textile industry which confronted him in March 1971.

A problem important to one country's foreign policymakers becomes
a bilateral issue when the seriousness of their political concern is communicated to the other country in such a way that its officials must consider the issue and take some stance, however tentative, on it. Some

4. And such a deadlock can damage their roles as negotiators; giving them a
task of mediation that they cannot successfully perform undercuts their credibility
both at home and abroad. Officials thus caught in the middle risk losing the action
to others more committed to the substantive goal. And they appear to officials in the
other government either as unable to speak for their own government, or as unable
to move that government in the direction required for agreement.

THE INTERPLAY OF NATIONAL SYSTEMS 129

bilateral communication to this end is consciously directed by officials in the first country toward those in the other. But most Japanese-American communication on major issues is carried out not by purposive messages from one country's officialdom to the other's, but by *indirect communication*—a wide range of signals that pass from actors in one country to those in another without being explicitly directed or channeled to them.

The Okinawa issue, for example, became of concern to responsible American officials in the mid-sixties because of a particular form of indirect communication. Official Americans watching events in Japan and Okinawa had concluded that the issue was heating up politically, that it could not be postponed very much longer without substantial risk to the security relationship. They reached these conclusions from their reading of Tokyo's media, public statements and press conferences of political figures, from U.S. embassy reporting, and from other sources. There was also *informal direct communication* between Japanese and American officials from the early sixties: the discussions that President Kennedy's special commission held with Japanese officials in 1961 and 1962; consultations with Japanese officials by Ambassador Edwin Reischauer and his successor, U. Alexis Johnson; recurrent State Department–Gaimushō (Foreign Ministry) discussions in Washington and Tokyo.[5]

Such informal communication elicited a constructive U.S. response because those official Americans vitally interested in Japanese political developments were a relatively small group, whose members generally believed that continued conservative rule in Tokyo was crucial to the alliance, and that both the conservatives and the alliance would be threatened if Japan's territorial grievance remained unassuaged. By the time the 1967 Johnson-Sato summit conference approached, the issue had been a live one in both governments for over a year, and officials negotiating preliminary drafts of the summit communiqué knew that it would have to be treated in a way indicating some movement toward Japanese objectives.[6]

---

5. *Informal direct communication* is thus distinguished from *direct and formal communication*, involving either actual negotiations or the conveying of official stands from one capital to the other.

6. The favorable orientation of State and Defense civilians did not, of course, assure strong positive action by President Johnson. Sato seems to have perceived this well, and realized that he had to communicate effectively to Johnson not just that he wanted reversion—this no one doubted—but that he regarded its near-term attainment as very important. He needed to signal that he thought a serious bilateral crisis

The textile issue also became binational through indirect communications—flowing this time in the other direction. Candidate Nixon's commitment to new quotas was reported in Tokyo, as was Democratic presidential candidate Hubert Humphrey's parallel promise. Reported also were postinauguration public statements by Nixon and Stans, a major Stans speech on the subject to U.S. textile manufacturers, the views of other quota proponents (and opponents) in the United States, leaks from intragovernmental strategy meetings in Washington, and above all Stans's April trip to Europe where he sought support in restricting exports from Japan and other prime Asian producers. Broad Japanese attentiveness to any significant U.S. policy initiative toward their country assured that this news would appear frequently on the front page. Stans initiated direct and formal communication on the issue with Japanese when he went to Tokyo in May to convey personally the President's interest in quotas; the fact that he, a cabinet member, was heading a large interdepartmental mission was intended as a strong signal of U.S. seriousness that would encourage Japanese concessions. But the months of publicity that preceded his visit had spurred a fierce resistance campaign, mounted by Japan's textile industry, but drawing on a deep resurgence of nationalism as well. And Japanese wishing to resist "unreasonable" American trade demands could find hope in many of the signals they received, for the general trade policy community in Washington was clearly cool toward the initiative, as was the State Department. Even Stans's signal could be used against him—and was. Opponents of quotas in both countries expressed the view that the Nixon administration was making a lot of noise in order to impress the U.S. textile industry with the effort it was making; if Japan resisted firmly, the administration might then abandon or modify its initiative, emphasizing to the textile lobby how hard it had tried.

The Politics of Interaction

For an important issue to be seriously considered, it must rise to prominence in both governments. In so rising, however, it is likely to

---

might develop if progress toward reversion was not made, and thus that American actors needed to give serious consideration to meeting his needs in order to maintain a harmonious security relationship in the future. This priority Sato was able to communicate effectively through use of a private emissary, and though Johnson did not move as far as he might, sufficient progress was made to keep Sato on top of the issue at home.

engage a wide range of actors and interests in each country. On any given day, such actors will be saying and doing a variety of things with potential impact on the issue. They produce a welter of signals that pass from governmental and private actors in one country to actors in the other. Many of these signals are not intended as U.S.-Japanese communications, but rather are directed toward domestic targets. Thus the very process by which an issue gets taken seriously has the simultaneous effect of complicating its resolution—by plunging it into domestic political controversy that spills over into the international arena.

Moreover, even those signals meant to be bilateral communications are often not received as intended by the senders. For reception of signals is inevitably colored by the general policy views and concepts of the receiver, and by his specific interests and stakes in the issues the signal affects. The reception of signals between Japan and the United States is further clouded by cultural differences.

Sources of Signals within One Country

Signals are a product, of course, of the politics of decisionmaking in the country where they originate. If this politics were controlled by a dominant central actor, then each governmental action or signal could be assumed to be based on careful calculation as to how the articulation of an issue, the shape of a proposal, the means of its delivery, and the selection of a receptor in the other country could maximize the chances of a favorable response. Sometimes the behavior of a government approaches this—as in, apparently, the U.S. opening toward China in 1969–71. But usually the politics of policymaking in the initiating country is sufficiently competitive and complicated to preclude central control over communications. Individual actors may still calculate (and argue about) how best to communicate with the other side. But the sum of signals actually conveyed will not add up to a particular tactical plan.

One example of how governmental politics can produce particularly counterproductive signals was the set of decisions leading to Maurice Stans's April 1969 textile trip to Western Europe. Almost all U.S. actors felt, in retrospect, that this trip had been a mistake, feeding resistance and bitterness among Japanese resentful of the effort to create a unified Western front against them, making it politically impossible for Japanese leaders to make even a marginally helpful response to Stans's initiative. Moreover, the effort was unsuccessful in lining up European support. It resulted, however, not from any carefully planned textile negotiating strategy, but from a sequence of actions and pressures having little to do with Japan. In February 1969, before Stans assumed responsibility for the textile issue, President Nixon announced during a European visit that his secretary of commerce would follow him shortly to discuss trade issues that the President had not treated personally. Stans presumably welcomed this opportunity, since he was seeking the lead administration role in trade policymaking. In the six weeks between the trip's announcement and its taking, however, the secretary was losing his battle for general trade policy primacy but winning the textile mandate. Moreover, the administration had not developed very many other trade proposals, and the Europeans—still absorbing the tariff cuts negotiated in the Kennedy Round of the mid-sixties—were not very interested in further liberalization. Thus, once he got to Europe, textiles was what Stans emphasized—it was the issue for which he had responsibility, and on which he knew what he wanted. (And the initial means through which the administration sought quotas—a multilateral trade agreement among all significant textile importers and exporters—required that the issue be raised at an early stage with the Europeans.)

Twenty-eight years earlier, Japanese leaders sent a similarly unintended signal across the Pacific when they decided in July 1941 to move troops into southern Indochina. The action was not particularly designed to influence the United States. Rather, it was a response to Germany's invasion of Russia, which forced decision on the issue of whether Japan should join in attacking the Soviets. Japanese decisionmakers all favored some form of expansionist policy, and all were concerned that the country not "miss the bus" by failing to exploit the rapidly changing world situation to enhance Japan's security and position. In this context, the Indochina move was a limited step, one unlikely to bring major bloodshed because Vichy France (which ruled Indochina) would have to acquiesce. But Washington nevertheless received it as a strong signal that Japan was moving ahead with aggressive policies, and it led to the freezing of Japanese assets and—through that—to the embargo on oil.[7]

The decisions that led to Stans's textile trip to Europe focused mainly on other issues—how the new administration would deal with Europe on trade policy; who within the administration should become the leading trade policy figure. And the signals it conveyed to Japanese actors were largely indirect and unintended—reported through Japanese newspaper headlines to attentive readers. Similarly, Japan's decision to move into Indochina was not made in the framework of Japanese-

7. See pp. 91–92, above.

American relations. But domestic politics can also produce inappropriate bilateral signals even when actors are focusing directly on the issue at hand, and even when the communication is an official, intergovernmental message. Japan's March 1970 aide-mémoire on textiles,[8] for example, was triggered by two Japanese embassy officials in Washington who feared a complete breakdown of the dialogue on the issue unless Japan signaled a serious willingness to compromise. So they flew to Tokyo and succeeded in getting the aide-mémoire drafted and conveyed through diplomatic channels. But because the politics of the issue in Japan prevented major concessions, the aide-mémoire's substance was only a marginal improvement from the American point of view. And it was received in Washington not as a constructive initiative on which to build, but as what a U.S. industry leader called "the latest Japanese rebuff." Even State Department officials did not consider it very helpful at that point in the negotiations.[9]

In each of these examples, what was communicated proved counterproductive because officials' minds and pressures were mainly elsewhere —on domestic policy bargaining, on other foreign policy issues. The signals that were conveyed were compromises—the March 1970 aide-mémoire—or the result of bureaucratic happenstance—Stans's European textile visit. Yet each did affect, and negatively, the receptiveness of the other government to compromise. Could this have been anticipated? How, more generally, do signals from one country affect decisionmaking in the other?

The Impact of Signals in the Recipient Country

Signals from one country influence another, of course, through its politics. They may affect conceptions of what is at stake, or beliefs about the prospects, costs, or consequences of particular courses of action.

---

8. See p. 111, above.

9. A parallel—and far more consequential—occasion when an appropriate American signal was not sent because of domestic political pressures was in the Potsdam Declaration of July 1945 calling for Japanese surrender. To encourage this result, Secretary of War Henry Stimson and Under Secretary of State Joseph Grew argued that the declaration should include language suggesting Allied willingness to accept a continued role for the emperor under a "constitutional monarchy" following "policies of peace." Such language was included in the draft Truman took to Potsdam, but removed there partly because of contrary views of other officials, and mainly because Truman and Secretary of State James F. Byrnes felt that a publicly flexible attitude toward the emperor would appear as appeasement at home and engender strong U.S. domestic opposition. Of course, the United States did in fact accept retention of the emperor though he was required to renounce his divinity.

They may inject a closely held issue or proposal into the public arena. In these and other ways, they influence how officials must confront an issue in their own government, and often affect their leverage within that government as well.

ASYMMETRY OF IMPACT. In U.S.-Japanese relations, a key factor in how signals from one country affect the other is the asymmetry of the relationship. United States policies are far more important to Japan than vice versa; the same U.S.-Japan issues that are buried (or unreported) in the *New York Times* and the *Washington Post* make the front page of the *Asahi shimbun*. Thus, for example, every stage of the Okinawa reversion negotiations was closely followed in Japan, but these negotiations were barely noticed in the United States except by those with a particular interest. The main cause of the unbalanced relationship is the disparity in power and the (relatively) one-directional dependence during the postwar period; a further contributing factor is the unusual attentiveness of Japanese to how they are thought of in the United States (and in other major countries).

Thus the words and actions of U.S. policy figures have had far greater impact on Japanese politics than those of Japanese leaders have on American. Maurice Stans's statements and activities of early 1969 triggered emotional public resistance in Tokyo, but this resistance was not even prominently reported in the United States. Presidential visits, actual or aborted, are major political events in Japan; relatively few Americans are even aware of it when a Japanese premier comes to Washington. The Washington remarks of Japanese and American officials after high-level talks there seldom cause political problems for the Americans; the Japanese are usually confronted with them when they return to Tokyo.

Sometimes this asymmetry exacerbates difficulties, as it did on the textile issue. On Okinawa, however, it worked to the advantage of those favoring reversion. Limited U.S. attentiveness meant that reports of how the issue was heating up in Japan came mainly through persons sympathetic to the case for reversion. And American apathy made it possible for U.S. officials handling the issue to keep it largely out of the public arena. They feared that early public exposure would arouse potential opposition to reversion, activating an alliance between the military and conservative senators that could block a reversion treaty on any terms acceptable to Japan. But if public airing of the issue could be delayed, they could negotiate quietly with the military and work out a practical solution, a reversion package satisfying military base needs.

CHANGING THE BALANCE OF INFLUENCE. On controversial bilateral issues, the two governments tend to be divided between those inclined to make negotiating concessions and those who favor a more adamant stance. The internal debate is seldom simply a division between "hawks" and "doves," but on major issues there tends to be a group of moderates within each government who feel there are limits to how much the other government can concede, who wish to reach a settlement relatively soon, who feel a solution is possible on terms acceptable to the national interest, and who see mutual accommodation as the way to achieve it. Those favoring a tougher stance, by contrast, tend to place the substance of what is at stake (for example, how much control of textile trade) above the immediate need to resolve the issue. They typically prefer holding to a strong position, buttressed if possible by unilateral action. Often they believe that if such a stand is maintained the other government will come to understand its seriousness and yield to it, whereas modifying their own position will be seen as a demonstration of weakness, encouraging the other country not to make reciprocal concessions, but to hold fast and await further softening. And if the other government will not yield to firmness, they prefer no negotiated solution, and perhaps will press for unilateral action to achieve their ends (for example, textile quota legislation).

Behind these rationales are particular domestic orientations. Thus moderates tend to be foreign office officials and others who value international negotiation and accommodation; those taking a harder line will often reflect bureaucratic or private interests with major stakes in the substance of an issue—the U.S. military on Okinawa, both textile industries in 1969–71. But whatever the roots of their positions, much of the internal debate turns on how the other government is likely to behave, and how the actions of one's own can affect it. Officials whose predictions are borne out, whose intergovernmental initiatives bear fruit, tend to strengthen their credibility and influence at home. Those whose prove wrong or unsuccessful tend to be weakened.[10]

10. Of course, evidence will seldom be conclusive, and officials will if at all possible interpret it in ways consistent with their previous stands and arguments. In fact, either a tough or a conciliatory stand in one country is likely to be viewed by each faction in the other as a confirmation of its own assumptions. A concession, for example, will be seen by hawks across the Pacific as a reward for standing firm, and they will argue that more firmness will bring further concessions. Doves will likely see it as proving the possibility of agreement if their side reciprocates, but argue that failure to reciprocate will not win further concessions but rather undercut advocates of compromise in the other government.

In major deteriorations of bilateral relations, the typical pattern has been for each government's actions to undercut the moderates in the other. Allison and Halperin provide an interpretation of what each side's moderates needed—and did not get—in 1941.

In the months leading up to Pearl Harbor, competing groups in Japan and the United States needed different actions from each other's government in order to accomplish their objectives. In Tokyo those who opposed war with the United States needed to be able to show that the United States would not interfere with Japanese expansion by cutting off sources of scrap iron, oil, and other materials. They also needed the United States to avoid actions which would have enabled their opponents to argue that war with the United States was inevitable. . . .

. . . Roosevelt, who sought to avoid [a Pacific] war, . . . had to resist pressures within the government from those who wanted to go to war with Japan. At the same time he did not want to so demoralize them that they would resign or reduce their efforts to prepare for the war with Germany which he believed was necessary. Thus Roosevelt's purposes required that Japan avoid: (1) flagrant violations of international law, (2) linking up with Germany in ways that made it impossible to resist arguments that war with Japan was a part of the war against the Fascist alliance, and (3) threats to the British or Dutch colonies which could be seen as a threat to the Allies in Europe. . . .

In this context Japan moved to occupy all of French Indochina. This Japanese move . . . was incompatible with what Roosevelt needed from the Japanese government. He no longer felt able to resist the pressures to take some sort of action against Japan.[11]

And after he responded with the freezing order, which led to the oil embargo, "the Japanese leaders opposed to war did not have what they needed from the United States to pursue their objective."[12]

Similarly, the deletion of language about a role for the Japanese emperor from the Potsdam Declaration weakened the position of Japanese moderates favoring immediate surrender (Lord Keeper of the Privy Seal Kido, Premier Suzuki, Foreign Minister Tōgō, Navy Minister Yonai, and Emperor Hirohito himself), because they needed to be able to argue that yielding would not lead to utter destruction of the nation and its institutions.

The textile dispute was similarly characterized by failures of moderates on either side to get actions from their government that would

11. Graham T. Allison and Morton H. Halperin, "Bureaucratic Politics: A Paradigm and Some Policy Implications," in Richard H. Ullman and Raymond Tanter, eds., *Theory and Policy in International Relations* (Princeton University Press, 1972), pp. 66–67 (Brookings Reprint 246).

12. Ibid., p. 67.

strengthen moderates on the other side. One example of this was the failure of business executive Donald Kendall to win unambiguous Japanese support for the textile compromise he proposed in March 1970. Fearing the opposition of the U.S. textile industry and its governmental allies, Kendall and those working with him carefully limited their communications with Washington officials prior to his departure for Tokyo. They seem to have hoped that Kendall's personal relationship with President Nixon would make him credible as a negotiator in Tokyo, and that a strongly positive reaction from Japanese leaders might in turn strengthen his ability to win approval of his proposal in Washington. But though his plan bore marked resemblance to a recent Japanese official statement, Kendall was still unable in Tokyo to get the affirmative signal he sought, for reasons of Japanese domestic politics. Both government and industry leaders there were sympathetic to the plan, but each was reluctant to take the political heat of endorsing it first, particularly since U.S. commitment to the plan was uncertain. This undercut Kendall's ability to make the only argument at home that stood a chance of success—that his proposal was negotiable whereas the official administration stand was not.

By contrast, progress in resolving issues can be achieved when one government's actions serve to strengthen moderates on the other side. Thus, in the 1967 summit communiqué on Okinawa reversion, Premier Sato—who wanted to accommodate U.S. military needs insofar as domestic politics allowed—was given U.S. concessions sufficient to maintain his credibility at home as one who was, if gradually, achieving results. Thus during the last phase of the textile negotiations, Ambassador-at-Large David Kennedy and Minister of International Trade and Industry Kakuei Tanaka, both of whom wanted a settlement, were sensitive to one another's needs to maintain leverage at home.

Actors on one side can also seek to change the balance of decision power in the other government by trying to alter the views of key individuals. One major effort to do so on the Okinawa issue was the Kyoto conference of January 1969 sponsored by Japanese scholars who served as informal advisers to Sato on the question. Among those invited were two long-time American military leaders, General Maxwell Taylor and Admiral Arleigh Burke. The meeting was perceived by Japanese sponsors and participants as a vehicle for conveying the sincerity of Japanese feelings against nuclear weapons. They hoped their arguments would influence the American participants decisively toward a nonnuclear solution to the Okinawa problem and that the opinion of these participants, in turn, would have a direct impact on the decision process in Washington. This conference is often identified in Japanese accounts as a landmark in communication between Japan and the United States on the issue of Okinawa reversion, as the means by which popular Japanese feelings were conveyed effectively to Americans such as Taylor and Burke that perhaps led to significant modification of their views.[13] Whether this conference had any real effect on American thinking is a matter of debate. The record of the proceedings of the conference indicates very little movement by the American participants between the first and last meetings of the conference. It is even likely that they saw the conference as a means of educating Japanese participants about the relationship of Okinawa to Asian security needs and the state of opinion in Washington.

LIMITING OR WIDENING THE POLITICAL ARENA. Officials in one country can also affect policymaking in the other by influencing who knows in detail about an issue or a proposal, and thus the range of actors able to involve themselves. Kendall kept his compromise textile plan secret to prevent the U.S. industry from attacking it before he could mobilize support in Tokyo. But not only was he frustrated by the failure of Japanese moderates to lend active support; he was also undercut when four days after he brought it up there, it was leaked by dissident Japanese officials to the Tokyo press and thence to the textile press in the United States. This aroused American industry leaders and their governmental allies, ending any chance that the Nixon White House would put its weight behind the compromise.[14] A similar fate befell a compromise proposed at about the same time by Henry Kissinger. Its leak was apparently inadvertent, but nonetheless led to its being attacked (though more obliquely than Kendall's) in the United States and thereby undermined.

Another example of how action by one country's leaders can broaden the policy arena in the other was President Eisenhower's decision to visit Japan in 1960 to celebrate the new era in U.S.-Japanese relations. By increasing the visibility of the revised security treaty, by providing a target for demonstrations, and by threatening to strengthen Kishi in the

---

13. See, for example, Asahi Shimbun Staff, *Pacific Rivals*, pp. 228–29 and 11–13.

14. The leak had similar impact in Tokyo, subjecting those Japanese government and industry leaders sympathetic to the plan to vehement attack from smaller textile firms who saw their interests being sacrificed.

Japanese leadership struggle, the scheduled visit broadened the controversy in Japan, leading to the crisis of June.

Because exposure of a negotiating stand or a compromise proposal frequently subjects it to domestic attack, responsible officials usually favor keeping information on a particular negotiation closely held. American officials sought to keep the Okinawa issue out of the public arena lest a potentially popular case against reversion develop, encouraging resistance by the U.S. military before the issue could be negotiated within the bureaucracy. And they were notably successful in preventing leaks—partly, of course, because of limited public interest in the issue.[15] But Japanese-American cooperation in keeping the arena limited would have availed little unless broader support could eventually be secured—ultimately the U.S. government had to seek public backing in order to secure Senate ratification of a reversion treaty, and military interests had to be accommodated lest their Senate allies act to block it. And on textiles, even those secret efforts to negotiate an accord that were not leaked to the press were unsuccessful because they lacked necessary political backing in one country or the other. In the end, agreement was reached by negotiators who largely kept their dealings out of the press —but only because Tanaka was able to win broad enough acceptance of Japanese capitulation in the political and business community to counter textile industry opposition.[16]

IMPOSING A FAIT ACCOMPLI. Policy actors in one country frequently take unilateral action aimed at changing—in their favor—the range of possible outcomes on a bilateral issue. Thus the Japanese textile industry pushed to increase its exports to the American market while the negotiations were under way, since (according to standard international practice) these higher levels would then become the base from which any quota limits were calculated. Thus (far more consequentially) nations seek to strike decisive blows in war, as Japan sought at Pearl Harbor and the United States achieved through the two atomic attacks.

15. There seems to have been only one important Okinawa leak, a *New York Times* article of June 3, 1969, that revealed a U.S. negotiating position not yet officially raised with the Japanese. Not only did this not trigger significant political trouble at home; it also seems to have had little effect on the Japanese. They already knew that the Nixon administration might well take the position reported, which was sympathetic to the Sato government's needs. But at this stage, the premier wanted more than hints. He needed assurances, and such could hardly be provided by a newspaper account that U.S. officials could write off as incomplete or misleading.

16. The Japanese textile industry was also compensated for the limitations on its exports by large-scale governmental aid.

Due to the asymmetry of power and impact, it has generally been the U.S. side that has been successful in imposing faits accomplis that fundamentally changed the politics of decisionmaking in the other country— most notably through the Nixon shocks of July and August 1971. The opening to Peking undercut the Taiwan-oriented Sato government and led to its replacement a year later by a new LDP mainstream coalition committed to restoring relations with the mainland. The import surcharge and floating of the dollar ended Japanese resistance to revaluation of the yen. And these, together with the September ultimatum threatening unilateral import quotas, helped end Japan's two-and-a-half-year domestic stalemate on textiles by creating a new political climate where it was possible for the new MITI minister, Kakuei Tanaka, to win support for textile concessions.

The effectiveness of such shocks is due in part to the role that the outside intervenor can sometimes play in Japanese politics. Commodore Perry's "black ship," or *kurofune*, has become a symbol of the ostensibly unwanted, but irresistible, external force that can produce policy change in Japan. The stress on consensus in Japan can result in inaction, in stalemate. But if an outside force brings a change in the situation that all Japanese must contend with, a new policy can sometimes be put across domestically as a means of coping with the new outside challenge. A relatively modest example of a *kurofune* was Wilbur Mills's intervention in the textile controversy in early 1971. Because of Mills's pressure— and his threat to move on restrictive legislation by March unless an alternative could be arranged—the fractious Japanese textile industry was able to agree on and proclaim the export restraint program that so angered President Nixon.[17]

This phenomenon suggests why the sorts of tough steps usually opposed by moderates are sometimes effective. But for such actions to bring significant Japanese policy changes, certain preconditions seem

17. Of course, here again the difference between Japanese and other nations' decisionmaking is one of degree. In any government where power is dispersed and opinion and interests diverge, action is easier taken if in response to an external initiative that cannot be ignored. As an extreme example, Pearl Harbor could be characterized as a classic *kurofune* for the United States. For an Anglo-American relations case, see Richard E. Neustadt's account of how, in the Skybolt crisis, each nation's defense chief failed to take preventive action because it would be politically easier for him to win agreement within his government on a substitute strategic weapon for the British if the other took the initiative. (*Alliance Politics* [Columbia University Press, 1970], pp. 45–47, and 106–09.)

necessary. First, the action or threat of action must be unambiguously decisive, believed to be more or less irrevocable, a genuine fait accompli. On textiles, the President's threat to impose quotas on October 15, 1971, unless an agreement were negotiated brought forth the desired Japanese response, whereas his earlier, oft-repeated warnings that Congress would legislate massive trade restrictions did not. Second, within the new set of alternatives that Japanese decisionmakers face, accommodating the outside intervenor must have strong advantages over continued resistance. This criterion was met in the fall of 1971 on both exchange-rate adjustment and textiles, not least because U.S. actions seemed to be threatening the foundations of the postwar economic relationship upon which Japan depended. Third, there must be those within the Japanese system already favorable to accommodation, who are well-placed to use the *kurofune* as a rationale for doing what they wanted done anyway. Thus MITI Minister Tanaka seems to have determined on settling the textile issue on whatever terms he could get before any of the Nixon shocks, though he skillfully concealed this determination and allowed outside pressures to help clear his path. An earlier U.S. threat of unilateral action on textiles might not have brought a bilateral agreement, since Tanaka's predecessor was less ready to make major substantive concessions.

But the broader problem with such shock tactics is that they threaten, in real though hard-to-measure ways, the assumptions of mutual reliability and relative predictability upon which a continuing alliance depends. Their effectiveness rests on their inexorability—they cannot be altered whatever major interests the other country has at stake. But if officials in the target country believe this, they must believe there are times when the country imposing the fait accompli will disregard the alliance. This may then impel them to reduce their stakes in that alliance.

Nor should it be assumed that the effects of such tactics are calculated carefully by those who employ them. No available evidence (except ex post facto rationalizations) indicates any serious advance consideration of the impact of the China shock on Japanese domestic politics or foreign policy; and while elements of the August 15 economic decisions were pointed directly at Japan, those who shaped them did not have detailed knowledge of the politics of the country whose policies they wanted to change. Only the textile shock seems to have been employed in a calculated way, since the inclination of Tanaka to settle was apparently known to Ambassador David Kennedy in advance. The handling of both of the economic shocks, however, reflected a feeling among American policymakers that more diplomatic approaches to these issues had met with continued frustration; there was a widespread belief that the time had come to force the Japanese to yield.

Resolution of Issues

To this point the analysis of initiation and interaction has highlighted the negative effects of signals from one country on decisionmaking in the other, or the accidental nature of much of the impact whatever the results. Why then can the U.S.-Japan relationship still be considered, on balance, a success? Is it simply luck that has prevented domestic and bureaucratic political pressures from moving the two governments in irreconcilable directions?

One force in the success of the postwar relationship was the compatibility of interests as perceived by Japanese and American leaders. For Japanese, unready to face squarely their own security problems, American strategic protection and hegemony were useful if seldom applauded. And if Americans could work out reasonable base arrangements, Japanese rearmament became, in practice, a postponable goal for the United States, the oft-reiterated need for enhanced free world military strength notwithstanding. Similarly, postwar U.S. economic dominance and world leadership meshed nicely with the Japanese need for expanding overseas trade while maintaining protectionist controls at home.

But while these large compatibilities made cooperation far easier, they hardly assured it. Immediately after the occupation, the Dulles-Pentagon emphasis on Japanese rearmament (a product of their global interests and priorities) was both insensitive and unsuited to strengthening alliance-oriented Japanese leaders at home. The softening of this emphasis led to the new security treaty, but that treaty triggered a major crisis in Tokyo (the product of complex political interplay there). While Okinawa, the emerging security problem of the sixties, was wisely foreseen and astutely managed, it was followed by the bitter, prolonged, unforeseen wrangle over textile quotas in which both governments acted as brokers for their textile industries. Before it was settled, there were the major shocks on China and trade policy where the United States acted as if the Japanese alliance hardly existed.

Obviously the relationship has been prone to crises. But there have also been bridges between the two systems that have helped to resolve them. One contributor to maintaining tolerable U.S.-Japanese relations is informal *transnational alliances,* ongoing relationships based on overlapping interests and mutual support that link particular policy actors in Japan and the United States.[18] A second, somewhat intertwined institutional force bringing order to the politics of the relationship is the official negotiating channels which are employed on specific issues.

Transnational Alliances

In their broadest sense, transnational alliances include any relationship in which actors within the U.S. and Japanese systems collaborate to achieve particular policy outcomes desired by both. At minimum, such allies take compatible positions in their respective internal policy struggles and maintain general mutual awareness of these positions; at maximum, they strive consciously to strengthen one another's leverage and credibility at home, and conspire actively to put across particular negotiated solutions in the two systems.

The first important transnational alliance after the occupation developed in the fifties between U.S. officials specializing in Japan, on the one hand, and Gaimushō and LDP leaders on the other. It was rooted in acceptance by these Japanese of the priority of the U.S. relationship, and the Americans' conviction that the benefits of the relationship— Japanese and East Asian security, tolerable U.S. base arrangements

18. The term *transnational* is drawn from the work of Robert O. Keohane and Joseph S. Nye, Jr. In *Transnational Relations and World Politics* (Harvard University Press, 1972), p. xi, they define "transnational relations" as "contacts, coalitions, and interactions across state boundaries that are not controlled by the central foreign policy organs of government." They distinguish between "transnational interactions" involving "nongovernmental actors" and "transgovernmental interactions" which take place "between governmental subunits across state boundaries," but they also use "the broad term transnational relations" to include both (ibid., p. 383). More recently, they have concluded (with particular reference to *organizations*) that this dual usage of "transnational" is "unnecessarily confusing," and have opted to "restrict the term 'transnational' to nongovernmental actors" ("Transgovernmental Relations and International Organizations," *World Politics,* October 1974, p. 41). But to adopt this restriction here would leave us without an adjective to apply to those particular "alliances" which include *both* governmental and private policy actors. These have been particularly important in the cases we examine. Thus we employ the term *transnational* in the original, broader Keohane-Nye sense. Indeed, we have found it useful to broaden the term still further to allow inclusion of political leaders and foreign office officials in particular transnational alliances, as long as they are employing mutually supportive relations with actors in the other country to strengthen themselves in policy debates at home.

—rested on continuing conservative rule in Tokyo. Thus the U.S. ambassador, while pressing the Japanese government for concessions on specific issues, would simultaneously resist what he saw as inappropriate and counterproductive efforts in Washington to force the security relationship into the NATO mold, since these subjected conservative leaders to opposition attack.

The prime accomplishment of this alliance, the security treaty of 1960, reflected both its strengths and its limitations. It won U.S. accession to a unique security relationship, in which the United States made the security commitment Dulles had withheld in 1951 without either a fully reciprocal Japanese commitment or NATO-type rearmament. But because of its relatively narrow membership, the alliance contributed to misinterpretation and underestimation of the domestic controversy that arose in 1960. As opposition to the Eisenhower visit increased, Japanese scholars independent of the government but particularly concerned about American relations sought to win U.S. embassy acceptance of their view that the visit should be postponed.[19] But the ambassador, a victim of his own narrow interpretation of the event, rejected the message and denounced its purveyors. As Reischauer characterized the "broken dialogue" at the time, "almost all Japanese intellectuals who had contact with Americans showed an almost pathetic eagerness to explain the 'true situation' to their American friends."[20] But their official friends, at least, did not seem to be listening.

Since 1960, however, lines of communication and dialogue have been notably strengthened and broadened—though those between Americans and Japanese opposition groups remain weak and thin. In part the strengthening has been the result of conscious efforts to develop a range of conferences and forums, from the cabinet-level ministerial meetings to less august bilateral gatherings of businessmen and scholars. It is even more a result of the rapid rise in economic interaction, spurred by the continuing surge of Japan's economy throughout the sixties. In any case, the increase in the number of public and private Americans and Japanese in contact with one another has created informal networks of concerned individuals with compatible perspectives on security and trade issues. These have formed the basis for the building of transnational alliances

19. See Asahi Shimbun Staff, *Pacific Rivals,* pp. 217–18; and George Packard III, *Protest in Tokyo* (Princeton University Press, 1966), p. 288.

20. Edwin O. Reischauer, "The Broken Dialogue with Japan," *Foreign Affairs,* vol. 39 (October 1960), p. 23.

on issues where the domestic interests of actors in the two countries led them to favor the same general sort of resolution.

Such alliances were in evidence on Okinawa and textiles. In the first case the alliance (a successor to that of the fifties) included a small group of State and Defense officials, and an equally small group of Gaimushō officials and scholars with close ties to the Sato government who were sensitized by the events of 1960 to the potential impact of the opposition on the issue and the security relationship that it threatened. In the second case the primary alliance (which helped produce both the Kendall plan and the unilateral Japanese industry program negotiated by Mills) was between free-trade-oriented politicians and businessmen in the United States and compromise-prone Japanese in the government bureaucracy and the textile industry. The Okinawa alliance usefully broadened and supplemented official channels; the nongovernmental actors basically supported the official positions that were evolving and exerted constructive marginal influence on them. The textile alliance, by contrast, worked against the fundamental Nixon administration negotiating position. In both cases, however, alliance reflected not just a convergence of interests on the particular issue but a commitment to the larger institutional structure of the bilateral relationship. Those who pushed Okinawa reversion saw it as essential to prevent a recurrence of the violent opposition to the 1960 treaty and to build a new basis for the security relationship that could carry it into the seventies and perhaps beyond. The textile alliance reflected not just convergence of specific economic interests, but a commitment to the GATT structure of free trade which quota proposals threatened. This liberal trade order was believed essential if the U.S.-Japan economic relationship were to continue evolving toward increasingly open national economies and mutually beneficial interdependence.

Because parties to such alliances value strong U.S.-Japanese ties, and favor resolving issues on terms that preserve or strengthen these ties, such transnational alliances are generally a positive force giving breadth and strength to the relationship. But this does not mean that their specific impact on the course of a particular issue will always be constructive or useful. The very fact that allied actors are oriented toward the relationship may make them insufficiently sensitive to the strength and aims of other domestic political actors with different orientations. Moreover, actors on one side—visibly exploiting the opportunities that the alliance presents—may not fully recognize or carefully calculate how the interests of their allies in the other government differ from their interests, and how this may affect critical choices. Each partner in an alliance may also accept too readily the other's reading of the domestic political situation in the other's country—a reading inevitably colored by specific interests.

In some cases, alliances can facilitate those signals and arguments by actors in one country that strengthen proponents of a desired settlement in the other. As the informal dialogue between Okinawa reversion advocates in the two governments proceeded, for example, Japanese actors were explicitly signaled that they should emphasize the politics of the issue on Okinawa and in Japan proper. They would better promote the right decisions in the American government, they were told, if they emphasized not direct strategic arguments for reversion, but rather the political case: that unless reversion came soon, unrest would intensify and make it impossible to maintain either U.S. administrative control of the island or the broader bilateral security relationship. And in formulating their argument in this way, Japanese leaders thereby reinforced the case that was being painstakingly built and argued by U.S. officials who favored reversion. But sometimes the political advice offered by allies can be wrong—as when Japanese sympathetic to their textile industry's unilateral restraint plan were apparently told by Mills and those working with him that President Nixon would acquiesce in it if not pressed to make an explicit endorsement.

A detailed look at that episode of early 1971 illustrates several potential pitfalls such alliances face. After two years of inconclusive and difficult textile negotiations, there was broad agreement in both countries that some resolution was essential, involving some form of new Japanese export restraint. Mills and the leaders of Japan's textile industry shared this view. They also needed one another. The congressman needed the export control plan that the industry leaders could adopt and implement; he could then argue that the issue was at least tentatively resolved, and thereby divert a new congressional move to enact the textile import quotas he opposed and feared. For Japan's textile leaders, any export restraints were undesirable, but some form of quotas seemed inevitable, and the broad general restrictions in the industry program were far more palatable than the stringent, item-by-item quotas the Nixon administration was pushing. But they needed Mills's active opposition to statutory quotas (he had gone along with quotas in 1970, and they had passed the House) so that he—in his pivotal position as Ways and Means Committee chairman—could protect them against this threat. And by blocking statutory quotas, Mills would also be undercutting the Nixon administration's ability to use the threat of congressional action as leverage with the Japanese government in pressing for negotiated restrictions in the form the administration wanted. All of these things Mills could give them— plus the outside pressure needed to bring industry unity. All would enhance their leverage within Japan—in selling their proposal to those in the textile industry who opposed any form of restraint; in dealing with Japanese politicians and officials who felt that much more stringent limitations were the only way to solve the crisis.

But neither Mills nor the Japanese industry leaders wanted the plan to trigger a crisis in relations between the Nixon and Sato governments. Still less did other actors who accepted and increasingly supported the plan—Japanese bureaucrats and politicians; the American free trade community and its business and political allies. Yet whether it would trigger such a crisis depended on how the Nixon administration would react, above all on the President's personal response. And because no one believed that Nixon could openly endorse a solution far less restrictive than that he had been insisting on, the best the plan's proponents could hope for was his tacit acceptance, presumably because he too had tired of the issue and would be willing to accept half a loaf as long as it could be blamed on others. Nixon's reaction was difficult to be sure of in advance. But in predicting it, Japanese actors relied on the assurances of their American allies—Mills and the lobbyist-intermediary, Michael P. Daniels—that Nixon would in fact go along. These assurances proved inaccurate, so when the plan was announced it exacerbated the crisis it was intended to resolve.

This outcome reflected mistakes by many actors. The Nixon White House, for example, failed to exploit several opportunities to signal its opposition while the situation was still fluid. But the crisis also resulted, in part, from the divergent interests of the actors involved in the transnational alliance. Both Mills and the Japanese industry could gain something from the plan even if the White House denounced it: it would continue in force and weaken the case for statutory quotas or a more stringent negotiated solution. But for the Sato government and the Gaimushō, the Nixon rejection was a disaster. It was particularly so because Nixon clearly felt betrayed by the plan and by the Japanese government's endorsement thereof, and his bitterness would affect his handling of other issues involving Japan in that fateful year. Yet the

Washington embassy and the Gaimushō—which perceived the potential danger of a negative Nixon reaction—allowed themselves to be reassured by the assessments of others—Mills and Daniels—whose stakes were different, who did not want a Nixon rejection and might indeed have delayed action if they had expected one, but who could nonetheless live with it.[21]

This illuminates, therefore, two broader weaknesses of transnational alliances: the dependence of actors in one country on the assessments of their allies in the other of that country's political scene, and the tendency to underrate the divergence of interests within the alliance, the possibility that political outcomes tolerable to one party can be disastrous to another. Engrossed in a complex, fast-moving, indirect negotiating effort such as the Mills plan became, participants tend to forget how much each actor's assessment of his own political system is affected by his stakes in the issue, and how these stakes are predominantly in terms of his position and relationships within his own nation.

Similar problems can arise when negotiated solutions are sought more conventionally—through official negotiating channels.

The Choice of Channels

The standard way governments bargain on issues is through designated official channels. Ideally, unified national positions are worked out internally, and each government then negotiates through a designated official, team, or agency. Thus each can "speak with one voice" in conveying its official stance, notwithstanding the inevitable flow of information and signals through other channels as well.

The value of having a clear-cut, single negotiating channel is illustrated by what can happen in its absence. At one point in the textile negotiations, each of three Americans was conveying to Japanese leaders a distinct formula for an agreement—each with some claim to President Nixon's endorsement, each apparently inconsistent with the other two. At the same time, during the spring of 1970, Americans faced problems in judging whether to take more seriously the strong Japanese resistance expressed through official channels up to the cabinet level, or the much more responsive attitude conveyed recurrently by Premier Sato. For each government the result was confusion joined with bitterness toward

21. This story is told at much greater length in I. M. Destler, Hideo Sato, and Haruhiro Fukui, "The Textile Wrangle: Conflict in Japanese-American Relations 1969–71" (1976; processed), chap. 12.

officials across the Pacific, since the other government seemed to be offering proposals with one hand and taking them away with the other. Such chaos might well have been avoided had a regular, single channel been used throughout the negotiations.

If the general case for some dominant channel is strong, however, there is less agreement on what it should be, or how—on controversial issues—it can be maintained. In postwar U.S.-Japanese relations four types of channels have been used. One, of course, is *diplomatic channels*— negotiation of issues through the foreign offices and their embassies. A second is *functional channels*, direct dealing on issues between those government officials and agencies with particular competence and responsibility in the substantive problem area involved. A third route for bilateral negotiations is *summit channels*, defined most generally as dealings between heads of government or their senior political aides. Finally, there is the not infrequent resort to *back channels*, operating around or above those who have formal negotiating responsibility.

DIPLOMATIC CHANNELS. Embassy–foreign office channels have been heavily employed in postwar U.S.-Japanese relations, not just on routine matters but on major issues as well. Once the decisions to proceed were made by the respective political leaders, security treaty revision was negotiated by Foreign Minister Aiichiro Fujiyama and Ambassador Douglas MacArthur II, though LDP factional strife over the terms intervened at several points. Okinawa reversion was similarly handled primarily through diplomatic channels until the shape of the agreement had emerged. The frequent ability of these foreign offices to retain operational responsibility reflects the national patterns of foreign policymaking. In Tokyo, Gaimushō influence has reflected the traditional leverage of career ministries in their spheres of recognized competence, the lack of a strong military competitor, and the general convergence of foreign policy views between senior Foreign Ministry bureaucrats and LDP leaders. In the United States, the State Department's leverage on Japan issues was founded upon both the lack of day-to-day presidential involvement in these issues from the late fifties to the late sixties, and the general State–White House agreement on policy during this same period.

Employment of diplomatic channels has had major and obvious benefits in resolving U.S.-Japan issues. Foreign office officials are—on the average—the persons most likely in each government to be sensitive to the political and bureaucratic scene in the other. They are thus most likely to be able to calculate what can be negotiated and how to go about negotiating it. In the textile case, U.S. State Department officials were most aware of the volatility of the issue in Japan; on Okinawa, both foreign offices were able to work for a reversion agreement guided by some sense of the domestic constraints on each other's decisionmakers. This sensitivity inclines foreign office officials to favor stances that will bridge the substantive gap between the two sides. This is true in any bilateral negotiations, but particularly so in U.S.-Japanese relations. In the Gaimushō, the dominant postwar policy orientation has been the maintenance of close, constructive relations with the United States. And State Department people involved in U.S.-Japan issues have generally seen the U.S. interest as building a constructive, mutually beneficial partnership and thus solidifying the alliance.

Yet these advantages—understanding of the other country, willingness to compromise—are not always sufficient to resolve bilateral issues. Giving the textile issue to the foreign offices might have avoided the confusion of multiple channels. But it is unlikely that it would have resolved the dispute because of the limited responsiveness of officials in both agencies to the politics of the issue at home. Indeed, critics of diplomatic channels sometimes argue that the other country's politics and interests are all that their foreign office is interested in. In other parts of the American bureaucracy, State is frequently regarded as the spokesman for foreign interests. In Tokyo, the Gaimushō has been dubbed the "Japan branch of the State Department," or "the State Department's annex at Kasumigaseki."[22]

The fact that diplomats are thus not trusted domestically is partly inevitable—special interests can hardly expect an agency that is pressed with many claims to give regular priority to theirs. But partly it reflects how foreign offices view themselves—not primarily as domestic political arbitrators and consensus builders but as protectors of international from domestic politics. They tend to seek not so much to master and manage domestic political forces to their advantage, as to limit the intrusion of such forces into the domain of international diplomacy. Former Gaimushō Vice Minister Shinsaku Hogen has stated "the consensus of professional Japanese diplomats"[23] that "no good can come of a diplomacy that panders to domestic public opinion."[24]

22. Asahi Shimbun Staff, *Pacific Rivals,* pp. 315–16.
23. Ibid., p. 316.
24. Ibid.; this quotation paraphrases Hogen. George F. Kennan expressed a parallel view in his response to a reporter's argument that he and State had not

One obvious effect of such an attitude in both governments is to limit the utility of foreign office channels for resolving issues where other strong bureaucratic or domestic interests are involved. Another, ironically, is to lessen a major foreign office strength—insight into the politics of the other country. For to the degree that Gaimushō officials, for example, draw their assessments of American domestic politics from conversations with State Department counterparts, they are likely to reflect the same biases, the same relative insensitivity to the particular domestic interests and to domestic opinion generally. Thus, the Japanese foreign office underestimated the strength of the Nixon administration's commitment to a textile agreement in early 1969, despite a number of strong signals. Diplomats sometimes believe too readily that the other foreign office really speaks for its government. Gaimushō officials believed in early 1971 that the two countries' China policies were being coordinated because they were holding regular consultations with State Department counterparts. The Nixon announcement of July 15 showed how wrong such an assumption could be.

And because they are so close to the current officials of the foreign government and their current problems, diplomats have a tendency to exaggerate the long-term cost of being politically and personally unaccommodating to that government's current leaders, or the cost of those leaders departing from power. A rather extreme example of this bias was the U.S. embassy's apparent definition of U.S. interests in Japan in 1960 as not only the continuation of LDP rule, but the preservation of the embattled Kishi cabinet. Despite overwhelming signs that Kishi could not long remain in power, Ambassador MacArthur opposed any U.S. initiative to postpone Eisenhower's visit as likely to "be a mortal blow for Kishi."[25] In fact, the eleventh-hour cancellation of Eisenhower's

---

adequately made the case for the Marshall Plan to Congress: "I pointed out that personally I had entered a profession which I thought had to do with the representation of United States interests vis-à-vis foreign governments; that this was what I had been trained for and what I was prepared to do to the best of my ability; and that I had never understood that part of my profession was to represent the U.S. government vis-à-vis Congress; that my specialty was the defense of U.S. interests against others, not against our own representatives; that I resented the State Department being put in the position of lobbyists before Congress in favor of the U.S. people." *Memoirs*, vol. 1 (Little, Brown, 1967), p. 405n.

25. Cable no. 3824, U.S. Embassy, Tokyo, to Secretary of State, May 25, 1960. In a later cable, MacArthur denied press reports that Eisenhower had decided to go ahead with his visit "to give shot in arm to waning Kishi Administration." They were "not repeat not true." But the reason he urged a strong White House denial of this

invitation and the ensuing resignation of Kishi probably strengthened U.S.-Japanese relations, for they defused Japan's domestic situation and led to another conservative government with stronger domestic support. Kishi's hanging onto power had exacerbated the crisis; his letting go led to its resolution.

To these limits in the capacity of diplomatic channels to take full account of domestic politics must be added a related problem—limits on substantive expertise. Particularly in the economic area, where trade and monetary issues demand special knowledge of domestic and international conditions, the expertise for handling problems is usually concentrated outside of the foreign offices. These issues where such expertise is particularly important become candidates for direct negotiations through functional channels.

FUNCTIONAL CHANNELS. Competing ministries in Japan seem to agree that

diplomacy left entirely to the Foreign Ministry rarely works well. The Finance Ministry shares some of MITI's irritation with the Foreign Ministry. Haruo Nishima, a Finance official who served as minister of the Washington embassy for more than three years, sums up the attitude by noting: "Common nationality is not enough to insure communication. Experts on specific problems, even if they are of different nationality, invariably understand each other better than an expert and a nonexpert of the same nationality." A colleague of his, also with long experience in Washington, agrees: "In negotiating economic matters, discussions between the Japanese Foreign Ministry and the State Department are likely to founder. Since the former is probably being pressured by MITI, anyway, and the latter by the Commerce Department, direct negotiations generally prove far more effective than the roundabout route via the Foreign Ministry and the State Department."[26]

On many U.S.-Japanese issues substantive expertise is clearly greater outside the foreign offices—textiles is one example; monetary relations, agricultural trade, and military technology are others. Economic and military agencies may not be willing to share their expertise with generalists, since it is for the specialists a major source of leverage, a basis for seeking for themselves a central role in influencing and negotiating policy. Moreover, such expertise is usually linked to particular interests

---

report was that it was "damaging both to the President and Kishi." (Cable no. 4028, U.S. Embassy, Tokyo, to Secretary of State, June 6, 1960.) See also Asahi Shimbun Staff, *Pacific Rivals*, p. 217; and A. Merriman Smith, *A President's Odyssey* (Harper, 1961), chap. 17.

26. Asahi Shimbun Staff, *Pacific Rivals*, p. 326.

—whether in or out of government—and its holders do not generally trust the foreign offices to give priority to these interests.

Such expertise is frequently joined with leverage over implementation. In Japan, much of MITI's power over textiles was tied to its indispensable role in developing and monitoring a system of export restraints that would be imposed by the industry itself. Similarly, it is the U.S. military that has day-to-day custody over nuclear weapons, as the controversy of late 1974 once again highlighted. In each case, it would be difficult—close to impossible—for the foreign office to insist on negotiating terms that the implementing party could not live with.

Yet functional channels have sometimes proved too close to domestic interests to permit bilateral agreement. Certainly, MITI and the Commerce Department could more realistically reflect and represent the positions of the textile industries of each country. Moreover, they were better versed in the technicalities of the issue, and would have been unlikely to reach an agreement that could not be implemented. Indeed, the logical extreme of functional negotiations on textiles occurred in the prewar period, when American and Japanese industry representatives met directly and worked out an arrangement in 1937 that placed quantitative limits on Japanese sales in the American market. Unfortunately, by 1969 the positions of the two industries had become virtually irreconcilable. In a series of negotiations that reflected the responsiveness of their agencies to industry positions, Secretary of Commerce Stans and MITI Ministers Ohira and Miyazawa failed to reach agreement. Interestingly, the channel through which a textile agreement was finally negotiated combined a certain functional responsibility for the issue with high-level political interests. A new MITI minister, Kakuei Tanaka, wanted to settle the issue for political reasons and was able to control his domestic situation. His negotiating counterpart, David Kennedy, was committed to winning what the U.S. industry wanted, and as ambassador-at-large was able to mount a closed operation insulated from day-to-day intervention either from hawks in the Commerce Department or doves in the State Department.

A relatively effective use of functional channels was the negotiation on the financial terms of Okinawa reversion, handled mainly by Treasury and Finance in 1969–71. On this issue—and on international monetary and financial matters more generally—the two agencies could exploit their common expertise (and a common interest in dealing directly).

But usually they were free from the directly conflicting constituent pressures that bedevil dealings between MITI and Commerce.

A frequently employed compromise between functional and diplomatic channels is the interagency team—standard practice on trade negotiations. Members of such teams are expected both to contribute their expertise and to uphold their agencies' respective policy concerns. Interagency negotiating groups were employed by both sides in the textile negotiations—but usually for formal, relatively visible conferences rather than serious bargaining sessions. On Okinawa, interagency teams were effectively employed in negotiating the detailed administrative arrangements after the agreement in principle at the 1969 summit.

SUMMIT CHANNELS. Direct contact between the heads of governments and their entourages has been a recurrent feature of Japanese-American relations since the occupation, and a number of important agreements have been negotiated or at least ratified in summit meetings. They played major roles in all three cases highlighted in this study. An Eisenhower-Kishi meeting inaugurated the consultations that led to the security treaty revision negotiations. Sato's meetings with Johnson and Nixon were the major focal points on Okinawa reversion. And Sato's summit talks with Nixon on textiles had very bad consequences for the issue and the relationship.

As the first two cases demonstrate, summit dealings do not always undercut regular diplomatic channels, but can provide diplomats with substantive guidance and support. Negotiations on revising the treaty and returning the Ryūkyūs inevitably rose to the level of heads of government—because they involved important treaties in the sensitive area of territorial jurisdiction and national security; and because they involved powerful bureaucratic and domestic interests, or (in Japan) major domestic political controversy. Resolution of such issues required the engagement of national political leaders; hence summit conferences have proved important—perhaps even indispensable—in achieving breakthroughs on them. Since this is known in the two governments, summits have the effect—once scheduled—of providing action-forcing deadlines for officials who themselves seek progress on such issues (or are pressed by their leaders to achieve it). Thus the drafting of summit communiqués proves an important focal point for bilateral diplomatic negotiations—with Okinawa once again the prime example. And summits play the further role of bringing Japan-related issues to the attention of the American president, who normally gives them little day-to-day attention. And what the president gives his attention to affects what his key subordinates stress as well. Thus, U.S.-Japan summit meetings are likely to raise the perceived importance of U.S.-Japan issues in the American government more generally.

Summit channels also encourage considering particular bilateral issues within the broader context of the overall U.S.-Japan relationship. Bureaucracies would prefer, if possible, to handle each issue on its own terms. But national leaders frequently see their country's relationship with another as an important general concern—particularly if they develop personal ties with a foreign counterpart. Thus escalating the level of attention and responsibility forces consideration of priorities among various policy objectives and raises the possibility that several issues can be brought together in some sort of negotiating package.

Such gains from summit channels in energizing and broadening governmental policymaking have been considerable in U.S.-Japanese relations. There are also public political advantages. Trips by chiefs of government are major press events—in Japan for all American summits, in the United States if it is the American president who does the traveling. Thus, they provide information and publicity about the other country, the relationship, and issues between them. And they may enhance general political support for a friendly bilateral relationship, since they dramatize and personalize it.[27] Yet the textile case illustrates that summitry can create major problems—particularly if national leaders view it as an alternative to other channels rather than as a complement and stimulus to them.

One problem in that case was inadequate substantive preparation. As Fred Iklé has noted, summit decisions generally are risky because they may be taken "with the advice of people who had to master the detailed issues in as hurried a fashion as the President himself."[28] Particularly on the American side, summit conferences tend to bring into the decision process presidential aides and advisers who are more responsive to the president's own domestic needs than they are knowledgeable in the substantive questions at stake. This was clearly the case in the Sato-Nixon textile discussions of November 1969 and October 1970. In 1969, presummit preparations on the issue seem to have been handled mainly

27. The other side of the coin, of course, is that summits provide a target for critics of the relationship—1960 is the obvious case.

28. Fred Charles Iklé, *How Nations Negotiate* (Harper and Row, 1964), pp. 127–28.

by two persons—Henry Kissinger and a Sato emissary—whose expertise
on the substance and politics of the issue was grossly inadequate. The
result was a basis for agreement that proved politically unviable. In
1970, presummit communications were again carried on through limited, White House–Kantei channels, leading to Sato's endorsement of a
formula that once again was not checked out at home for its soundness
or its acceptability.

Yet the leaders clearly expected more positive results. And this seems
to reflect a more general problem—that because summit meetings can
often be a vehicle for promoting major negotiating breakthroughs, leaders are tempted to see them as sufficient for fully achieving such breakthroughs. Summits become not useful vehicles for moving issues forward, but the definitive forum for their resolution whether or not the
way is prepared. But this assumes a power that neither chief of government possesses, especially the Japanese premier. Nixon seems to have
felt that because he was agreeing to Okinawa reversion, Sato could yield
on a politically very different issue—textiles—and that Sato's personal
assent would be decisive in bringing about the outcome—restraint of
Japanese textile exports—that Nixon desired. This, of course, turned out
to be very mistaken.[29] For such trade-offs look much easier from the
summit standpoint than they prove to be in real life. Issues with strong
domestic political implications just are not that manipulable; textiles-
for-Okinawa-type exchanges are appealing to leaders—and to partisans
who win their objectives thereby—but they do not resolve the problem
of winning domestic consensus on the issue where one's nation does
the bulk of the conceding.[30] And this is related to a larger criticism frequently made of Nixon-Kissinger diplomacy—that it exaggerated the
maneuvering room, the flexibility, the actual power of choice that national leaders possess in the economically complex, politically alert advanced democratic industrial societies.

Finally, the textile case suggests several problems that can arise from
the reliance on a personal political relationship between leaders. The
most obvious is that failures are taken personally too—Nixon found Sato

29. It is interesting to note that the major summit successes in U.S.-Japanese relations involved issues where the primary decision required came from the president;
the main fiasco, textiles, was where comparable decisiveness was expected from a
premier.

30. Nor was this problem reciprocal in this case; a U.S. consensus on Okinawa
had largely been achieved before the 1969 summit; on textiles, the achievement of
Japanese consensus was left to afterwards.

wanting as a politician for failing to help him after he had given the premier what he needed. Thus an economic dispute of secondary importance was converted into a crisis of personal confidence.[31] In construing his relationship with Sato as one requiring reciprocal political support, moreover, Nixon took no apparent account of the fact that while postwar American leaders had consistently sought to help keep Sato's party in power, the Japanese had no reciprocal preference for Nixon's Republicans.[32] And the significance of textiles to Nixon was almost purely electoral.

And reliance on a personal relationship between a Japanese and an American politician brings the problems inherent in communicating through an interpreter to the fore. Each leader, speaking and listening in his own language, does what his political career has rewarded him for doing—he thinks and acts in terms of the political matrix of his own culture. The danger of misunderstandings based on personal styles and nuances is multiplied, therefore, unless the leaders are supported by the checks against such misunderstanding that established institutions can supply, such as cross-cultural expertise, prior analysis and clarification of the issues at stake, and careful preparation of proposed agreements.

BACK CHANNELS. High officials sometimes resort to secret communications routes hidden from many of the people and offices formally responsible for an issue in their respective governments. Essentially a back-channel negotiation is one that occurs parallel to, but separate from, the regular, formal negotiation on an issue. It is carried on between officials —or semiofficials—who operate with direct authority from the president or premier. Often an intermediary is used in these negotiations.[33] Back

31. Again relevant here is Neustadt's characterization of how personal relationships between national leaders can deteriorate, with "muddled perceptions" and "stifled communications" leading to "disappointed expectations" and "paranoid reactions." (See p. 90, above.)

32. When a leading Japanese official in the textile negotiations was asked whether a political obligation to Nixon could have been stressed, in Japanese domestic discussions, as an argument for further Japanese concessions, he replied that the response would have been incredulous laughter—"We want to keep *that* man in office?!"

33. For an extensive discussion of the use of back channels in recent U.S.-Soviet relations, see John Newhouse, *Cold Dawn: The Story of SALT* (Holt, Rinehart and Winston, 1973). For a more general discussion of types of intergovernmental contacts and the roles and functions of unofficial "contact-makers," see Masashi Nishihara, "Kokkakan kōshō ni okeru 'hi-seishiki sesshokusha' no kinō: Nihon to Amerika no taigai-kōshō o chūshin ni" [The function of 'unofficial contacts' in international negotiations: Special focus on external negotiations of Japan and the United States], *Kokusai seiji*, vol. 50 (1973), pp. 66–87.

channels are thus employed, by definition, when at least one of the other types of channel is already in operation. Their use is a special case in the broader area of secret diplomacy, involving keeping information not just from the public but also from large portions of the governments involved. Back channels were employed at critical points in the Okinawa and textile negotiations. Their use has also been reported in the prewar and peace treaty negotiations.

Back channels are used for two overlapping purposes—to convey and obtain information, and to work out the actual terms of bilateral agreements on particular issues. An example of the first occurred midway in the textile negotiations, at a time when they were deadlocked. The parties with assigned responsibility in each government were Minister of International Trade and Industry Kiichi Miyazawa and Secretary of Commerce Maurice Stans. Neither knew the other personally. Each felt the need to get a better feel for the other's position and for whether there might be a basis for agreement between them. Hence, they found it useful to communicate through an intermediary, an American who had gotten to know Miyazawa during the postwar occupation and Stans during the Eisenhower administration. Similarly, Premier Sato in 1967, wishing to make substantive progress on Okinawa reversion, sent an emissary to the Johnson White House to communicate how important the issue was to him, and to learn what Johnson's price might be.

Yet another back-channel effort of a sort was the Ikeda mission of May 1950. Premier Yoshida wished to sound out Washington on a particular formula for future U.S.-Japanese relations—trading U.S. base rights on the Japanese mainland for American military protection and economic concessions. But as Langdon describes it, "the trip would have been disallowed by General Douglas MacArthur's staff for its real purpose." So "it was represented as an inspection tour for the Finance Minister to familiarize himself with the latest techniques abroad."[34] With this as his cover, Ikeda was able to take his trip and help lay the substantive foundations for the peace and security treaties negotiated by John Foster Dulles in the succeeding fifteen months.

In these cases, back channels offered a way for a responsible actor on

---

34. Frank C. Langdon, *Japan's Foreign Policy* (Vancouver: University of British Columbia Press, 1973), pp. 8–9; Langdon's source is Kiichi Miyazawa, *Tokyo-Washinton no mitsudan* [Tokyo-Washington secret talks] (Tokyo: Jitsugyo no Nihon Shu, 1956), pp. 47–52. On this episode, see also Frank Gibney, *Japan: The Fragile Superpower* (Norton, 1975), pp. 47–49.

one side to get through more or less directly to a key actor on the other side and learn what his interests and stands were on an issue, and what he thought his government would ultimately require. Communicating through regular channels usually means that an official has many audiences inside his own government. This is likely to discourage frankness about what he might really be willing and able to concede. By limiting his audience to a counterpart with comparable responsibility, he may be able to communicate with greater frankness. And if he uses an intermediary, the communications can be more tentative and exploratory than direct encounters with his counterpart might allow.

Communicating in this way is not, however, simple and trouble-free. Particularly if a new intermediary is being introduced, his technical expertise in dealing with the subject may prove shaky, or his personal relations with one of the parties may not be sufficiently close and dependable for him to speak reliably for that party. If these problems can be overcome, however, significant benefits can result. Sato seems to have been quite successful in communicating with Johnson through an agent in 1967, even though the immediate result fell short of the premier's maximum goal. A much more qualified success was the Ikawa-Iwakuro mission of early 1941; it conveyed Premier Konoye's interest in peace negotiations sufficiently to help get such negotiations inaugurated, but the talks themselves proved frustrating and unproductive.[35]

The use of back channels becomes more complicated when the aim becomes actual negotiation of specific terms for resolving an issue. Here the potential political benefits of employing such channels can also be substantial. They give the officials thus dealing directly and secretly a temporary freedom from political and bureaucratic struggles, and from cumbersome interagency clearance procedures that are often a part of

---

35. Two Catholic priests visiting Japan in November 1940, Bishop James E. Walsh and Father Drought, first proposed the idea of opening U.S.-Japanese talks for avoiding a war to Tadao Ikawa, who was a director of the Central Agricultural and Forestry Bank. Ikawa conveyed this idea to Premier Fumimaro Konoye, and the latter basically favored it. Instead of formally bringing it up at a cabinet meeting or at a liaison conference with the military, Konoye privately instructed Ikawa and Colonel Hideo Iwakuro to follow through on the idea in January 1941. This eventually led to the opening of negotiations between Secretary of State Cordell Hull and Ambassador Kichisaburō Nomura in Washington in April. For details, see R. J. C. Butow, *The John Doe Associates: Backdoor Diplomacy for Peace, 1941* (Stanford University Press, 1974); and Gaimushō Hyakunenshi Hensan Iinkai [Japanese Foreign Ministry], *Gaimushō no hyakunen* [A one-hundred year history of the Japanese Foreign Ministry], vol. 2 (Hara Shobo, 1969), pp. 541 ff.

such struggles. And if back-channel negotiations do lead to a basis for agreement, the existence of such an accord becomes something that can be used to mobilize the domestic support in the two countries that is required to make the agreement effective. This is a special case of the political argument for secret diplomacy: "Once the agreement is signed, it tends to act as a *fait accompli*, weakening dissent and mobilizing interest groups in support of it. Thus the requisite domestic consent may be obtained in the end, whereas the individual concessions would have been opposed."[36]

In the textile case, the advantages of using secret channels must have seemed obvious to officials employing them. With both governments pressed by strong textile industry spokesmen with close governmental ties, alert to the significance of every technical detail, and with these industries taking sharply divergent—in fact, irreconcilable—substantive positions, an escape from the need for each government to clear its position with domestic interests virtually day by day seemed a prerequisite for a solution. Yet to placate these domestic interests while the dispute continued, visible initiatives (or rebuffs of initiatives) were called for— hence the need to have a formal negotiation also. But the fact that a back channel seemed necessary did not make this approach sufficient. For on textiles, back channels did not eliminate the problems of achieving support domestically; they just changed the character of these problems, and not always in a beneficial way.

First of all, officials excluded from the action did not develop any commitment to agreement formulas negotiated in back channels, such as might have followed from their involvement. Moreover, they resented the exclusion, giving them a double motivation for resisting the secretly developed accord. After Premier Sato acceded to Nixon's textile wishes at the November 1969 summit, he returned home to encounter noncooperation from his MITI minister, who was unwilling to take much heat for sponsoring concessions made without his knowledge. Sato also met strong resistance from Japan's textile industry leaders, fueled by their conclusion that the premier was deceiving them, going around them, acting without the consultation and consideration of their interests that were the norm in consensus-style decisionmaking.

Such opposition was especially potent because the textile industry, and the allied MITI bureaucracy, had to play a key role in implementing

36. Iklé, *How Nations Negotiate,* pp. 134–35.

the export controls. There was no precedent for handling such export limitations without industry acquiescence and constructive cooperation. Efforts to win concessions by working with MITI and the industry had not been effective, and this was why the back channel was resorted to. As Henry Kissinger wrote (prophetically) in 1968 about American decisionmaking, an "unpopular" negotiating stance would have been—and repeatedly was—"fought by brutal means, such as leaks to the press." Hence back-channel negotiations: "the only way secrecy can be kept is to exclude from the making of the decision those who are theoretically charged with carrying it out."[37] But if those "theoretically charged with carrying it out" in fact have close to a hammerlock on the instruments of implementation, then the strategy is likely to backfire—and it did on textiles.

Yet another problem in that case was the emergence of the back channel itself as a major source of controversy in domestic politics. Premier Sato never exploited the potential leverage of an already-existing accord because he was unwilling to risk admitting that he had concluded one. He was reluctant to invite denunciation of a "textiles-for-Okinawa deal" (a "secret deal" has a particularly "dirty" connotation in Japan), fearing that this might force him to resign under fire and threaten those close Japanese-American ties that he felt were essential to Japan's welfare. Thus, an effort was made to transform the Sato-Nixon accord into a final formal agreement while concealing the existence of the accord from most participants in these formal negotiations. Predictably, it proved impossible to get the Japanese government, under heavy pressure from the industry, to arrive at the substantive position demanded by a Nixon administration determined to satisfy the American domestic industry, just as it had before the summit. For to Japanese officials, nothing fundamental had changed.

All of these problems in the use of back channels are, of course, part of a larger limitation applying also to summitry. If the power of the official at the other end of the back channel is limited, or if his role in the general decisionmaking system is constrained, then getting agreement with him is of limited value, for he will not be able to deliver. This proved true not just of the Nixon-Sato channel, but also of the Stans-

37. "Bureaucracy and Policy Making: The Effect of Insiders and Outsiders on the Policy Process," in Henry A. Kissinger and Bernard Brodie, eds., *Bureaucracy, Politics and Strategy,* Security Studies Paper 17 (University of California at Los Angeles, 1968), p. 5.

Miyazawa channel when the commerce secretary sought to pin down a basis for agreement through it.

This would be true even if both key actors were of the same mind as to what they had agreed to, and what the status of their agreement was. But it is anything but clear that they will be under such circumstances, and it remained uncertain in the textile case. One problem is expertise—limiting the direct action to generalist senior officials multiplies the possibilities for technical errors, or for agreements whose substantive and political implications are badly assessed by at least one of the negotiating parties. Both were recurrent problems in back-channel textile dealings. Kissinger did not understand the substance and thus seems to have taken, at times, positions inconsistent with his purposes. Sato, the evidence suggests, did not realize how restrictive was the agreement to which he had acceded.

Nor is it clear whether what was agreed to was conceived of in the same way on both sides. Both leaders did apparently see Sato's 1969 promise as a definite commitment to negotiate a textile restraint agreement, as Nixon desired. But did Sato, like Nixon, feel committed to the substantive details, to the particularly restrictive formula developed in the back channel? Or did Sato see it a bit differently, feeling that it left him some substantive room for maneuver? The latter seems more likely. For there may be significant differences between the ways that American and Japanese officials view the role of intermediaries, or go-betweens. And contrary to the assumptions of some American officials who seem to believe that intermediaries are the best way to negotiate with Japanese, it may be that such channels are generally considered more definitive, more final, by Americans than by Japanese.

Back-channel agents or intermediaries are frequently employed in Japan, probably more so than in the United States. In a society where individuals go to great lengths to avoid direct confrontations, go-betweens provide a vehicle for sounding out the real intentions of another party, encouraging franker communication than would be likely face to face.[38] But because of the strong bureaucratic tradition and the consensus decisionmaking style, official or "front" channels are generally the authoritative ones in Tokyo. Tacit understandings reached through behind-the-scenes bargaining are not considered final until they have

38. On this point, see Edwin O. Reischauer, "Introduction: An Overview," in Priscilla Clapp and Morton H. Halperin, eds., *United States-Japanese Relations: The 1970's* (Harvard University Press, 1974), p. 11.

been approved by the official decisionmaking body, such as the cabinet. Behind-the-scenes bargaining, then, becomes a step or an instrument toward creation of consensus among the parties concerned. Toland in describing a prewar episode comments that the use of go-betweens "was common in critical times, since telephones might be tapped; moreover, ideas could be expressed through a middle-man which would have been difficult to bring up face-to-face; and *if things didn't go well, the go-between could simply be repudiated.*"[39]

For Richard Nixon and Henry Kissinger, by contrast, back channels were unambiguously the place where the serious business of foreign policy negotiation normally took place. Similarly, Stans—in contact with Miyazawa via their intermediary in May and June of 1970—would likely have discounted the information appearing daily in the Japanese press portraying stances and proposals Miyazawa was putting forward that were inconsistent with Stans's minimum requirements. For he would have given more credit to the private signals he was getting, the basis for agreement he felt was emerging through the back channel. But after three days of Washington talks between the two men that ended in

---

39. John Toland, *The Rising Sun: The Decline and Fall of the Japanese Empire, 1936–1945* (Bantam, 1971), p. 130. Emphasis added. Nishihara also emphasizes the frequent resort to intermediaries by Japanese. He argues that employment of back channels is a product of a "diffuse" system of decisionmaking responsibility, which he compares with the "specific" system in the United States, where decision responsibility is more clearly focused. ("Kokkakan kōshō ni okeru 'hi-seishiki sessho-kusha' no kinō," pp. 82–83.) This is certainly true in the sense that consensus policy-making leads, in practice, to shared responsibility, though such diffusion would seem to make it harder—not easier—for intermediaries to operate effectively. But Nishihara's argument does not take account of the particular importance in Japan of responsibilities and procedures based on formal organizational roles and processes. On textiles, for example, the MITI minister was almost always the central policy figure in Tokyo, whereas President Nixon could and did shift responsibility for the negotiations among several officials with varying responsibilities. It may sometimes be more difficult in the Japanese system to attribute a particular decision to a particular individual, but Japanese nonetheless are more likely than Americans to follow established institutional patterns, at least in a formal sense. Back-channel agreements become authoritative only when accepted within the formal system. When working at its best, the system thus combines respect for formal prerogatives with flexible communication through intermediaries with personal ties to leaders.

In *The John Doe Associates*, Butow concludes that despite their apparent success in initiating negotiations in 1941, the overall impact of intermediaries Drought, Ikawa, and Iwakaro was "pernicious," misleading each government (especially Tokyo) as to the other's position, making the Hull-Nomura conversations "more muddled and ineffective than they would otherwise have been," and generally undercutting—despite noble intentions—whatever prospects for peace remained (pp. 315 ff.).

impasse, it became clear that the position Miyazawa was taking vis à vis other Japanese actors in his broader domestic policy process was a more reliable indicator of his ultimate stand.

Finally, there may have been mistakes or misinterpretations made by one or more of these intermediaries. Such a person may be so motivated to press a basis for agreement that he exaggerates the commitment of one principal or the other; he may misinterpret what is said; he may have ambitions or interests or values of his own that color his judgment or his action. Indeed, to play such a role in an error-free way, a person must have a formidable list of talents—political savvy, inside connections, intercultural sensitivity, substantive grasp, and personal self-effacement. Principals are, of course, not entirely at the mercy of a go-between—they can develop ways of checking or testing the information he conveys. But as long as they are conducting a concealed operation, their means of double-checking are necessarily constrained.

All of these considerations suggest that, in recent U.S.-Japanese relations, the advantages of back channels for serious negotiations have usually been more than outweighed by the risks. This does not mean they are not occasionally useful as a tool. It does mean that officials in both countries, frustrated by the constraints of domestic politics on bilateral issues needing resolution, need to guard against the temptation to overuse them. As a route to political intelligence, back channels have clearly proved helpful. As a device for resolving politically volatile issues, they need to be sparingly employed. At the very least, there needs to be clear reason to believe that dealing in secret will lead to resolution, not exacerbation, of the domestic political controversy that made the back-channel approach tempting in the first place.

Conclusions

The Okinawa reversion negotiations attest to the fruitfulness of reliance on regular diplomatic channels. But the three other types of channels were effectively employed in these negotiations as well. Progress was made through the summit of 1967, and agreement was reached and announced by Nixon and Sato in November 1969. Back channels played a key role in political intelligence. And while the weakness of the Japanese military ruled out the use of functional channels on issues related to the military bases, they were successfully employed in negotiating the financial arrangements of reversion after the 1969 agreement to proceed in principle.

Okinawa was also the most successful achievement of the transnational alliance between Americans and Japanese in and out of government who were concerned with protecting and strengthening the political foundations of the security relationship. Actors in both countries moved with increasing coordination and sophistication in pushing both governments to the solution they felt soundest on policy grounds—and salable on political grounds. The precursor of this alliance was important also in paving the way for security treaty revision in 1960, particularly in bringing American demands for Japanese military activity down to domestically realistic levels. Its failure was that it was too narrow, insufficiently sensitive to the power of the opposition to challenge the new treaty and the government that negotiated it. The Okinawa coalition was also limited, by and large, to members of the establishment in Japan, but it included nongovernment academics who were aware of broader intellectual opinion. And all of its main actors had the 1960 experience before them as a lesson in what to avoid.

On textiles, by contrast, the major transnational alliance was unsuccessful—partly because of misreading of decisionmaking in both countries, but even more because it was in competition with the established negotiating channel, and in direct opposition to the interest group the U.S. president was determined to satisfy. In textiles, every type of channel was also used, but often in conflict one with another, and with notably counterproductive results. Negotiators at the bureaucratic and even the ministerial level operated—especially in Japan—in ignorance of the summit-level understanding. Diplomatic channels were intermittently employed, but never firmly based domestically. Back channels and intermediaries were given burdens greater than the politics of the problem would bear. By contrast, the use of other channels in Okinawa was, in general, both substantively and operationally consistent with what the diplomats were seeking, and subject to their influence if not always their control.

For these and other reasons, Okinawa was also handled on both sides with unusual sensitivity to the impact of their actions on the politics of the problem in both countries. One important factor in Japan was Sato's political style—the very caution and indecision that so muddied the waters on textiles. The premier became committed to the Okinawa issue quite early, but he successfully avoided making his demands so urgent, so immediate, that he needed U.S. action faster than the American government could be expected to move. Sato's "indecisive" style also allowed enough internal debate in Japan to clarify what terms would be viable in Tokyo—in contrast to the 1960 crisis where the domestic political parameters became clear only after the treaty's conclusion.

In the United States the political problem was different—premature exposure of State (and Defense civilian) support for reversion ran the risk of triggering strong and immovable military and congressional opposition. Time was needed to negotiate with the military inside bureaucratic walls. The need for secrecy was met partly by the "attention gap" —Japanese calls for reversion did not turn up on the front pages of American newspapers, even when voiced by a premier, whereas U.S. demands for new textile quotas were inevitably prominent in Tokyo. But the Americans' ability to keep the issue a closed one also owed much to the restraint with which Japanese politicians and officials handled the issue. On textiles, American public statements of objectives were not restrained—especially after the mandate passed to Maurice Stans. Thus the Okinawa issue could rise to importance in the U.S. government through the reports of officials especially sympathetic to and oriented toward Japan; textiles reached Japanese political leaders through daily press reports and through complaints from industrialists and nationalists angered by these reports.

In its initiation, the subsequent interaction, and ultimate resolution, then, Okinawa once again demonstrated that a volatile U.S.-Japan issue can be effectively resolved. And textiles once again offers an example of what to avoid.

CHAPTER SIX

Managing Future U.S.-Japanese Relations

"UNTIL THE reversion of Okinawa is accomplished," said Prime Minister Eisaku Sato in 1965, "the 'postwar period' will not end so far as our country is concerned." From our vantage point ten years later, Sato's comment seems prophetic in more ways than he could have known or intended. For as final negotiations were being conducted for the return of Okinawa, the postwar period indeed came to a dramatic end. But the events that punctuated this finale included much more than reversion. From 1969 to 1971 there was the bitter dispute over textile quotas. In July and August 1971 Japan was confronted with the "Nixon shocks": the sharp turn in U.S. policy toward China, and the harsh announcement of unilateral measures to improve the U.S. balance of payments. By the time Okinawa returned formally to Japan in May 1972, Tokyo had responded to the second of the Nixon shocks by revaluing the yen and was lifting the most onerous of its remaining import barriers. The following September a new Japanese premier, capitalizing on the momentum of the sudden American move toward China, moved Japan one step ahead of the United States by normalizing diplomatic relations between Tokyo and Peking. By the close of 1972, therefore, the last major elements of American infringement on Japanese sovereignty had—by one means or another—been removed. Japan had emerged from America's cold war shadow on China policy; it had abandoned, under American pressure, most of that sheltered international economic position that Washington had initially encouraged and long accepted; and it had retrieved full sovereignty over the last of its territory taken over by the United States in 1945. The postwar period had indeed ended.

Our study has dealt mainly with this postwar period, concentrating on bilateral issues that were raised and resolved then. But it has been

animated by concern for the future, and its conclusions and recommendations must be relevant to things not only as they were, but also
as they are and will be. Thus before moving to conclusions drawn from
past experience, we must address two broader questions. (1) Granted
that the alliance relationship was very important to both countries in
the period of cold war confrontation and Japanese economic and political reemergence, does it remain so in an era of American détente policies
and a wider ranging Japanese diplomacy? (2) Assuming its continuing
importance, can an analysis of past bilateral crises yield conclusions
relevant to present and future problems?

The Importance of U.S.-Japanese Relations

Throughout this study, the importance of harmonious U.S.-Japanese
relations has been assumed rather than demonstrated. We asserted the
need in chapter 1; thereafter, it became the objective and the premise
upon which this study was built. This was consistent with our purpose—
to concentrate on the politics and the processes that have affected the
attainment of this goal. And the conclusions reached in this chapter will
also relate primarily to means. But they depend ultimately on the reader's acceptance of the ends to which they are addressed. Therefore, it
seems appropriate at this point to offer a concise statement of why we
believe a strong and cooperative Japanese-American relationship, lasting through the seventies and beyond, is so vital to both countries.

The primary reason why U.S.-Japanese relations are important is that
the countries are important. In terms of gross national product, they are
the world's first- and third-ranking nations, with Japanese output now
above that of any Western European nation. For this reason alone, their
cooperation has a major constructive impact on the international order,
and a serious conflict between them could spell disaster.

The American commitment to Japan's defense responds to no immediate military threat. But it does serve to stabilize a relatively benign pattern of great-power relations in East Asia. Within the current security
framework Japan is able to remain a lightly armed, nonnuclear power
oriented toward the West but increasingly confident in developing its
relations with communist countries. Conversely, the undermining or
abandonment of the U.S. defense commitment could have very serious
consequences. One need not accept the probability of any particular

scenario—a militarily resurgent Japan with advanced nuclear armament arousing deep anxieties throughout East Asia and beyond; a weak and vulnerable Japan buffeted by international threats and domestic turbulence—to conclude that many of the alternatives to the existing arrangement could pose significant new threats to regional and world peace.

We do not mean to suggest that Japanese-American security relations should not continue to evolve to meet changing circumstances, or that they must always be based on the existing mutual security treaty. Other bases for bilateral security cooperation are certainly conceivable. And it is quite possible that one or both governments may one day seek to change the current security arrangement, perhaps in response to domestic pressures or leadership changes (such as the emergence of a coalition government in Tokyo). But were such a renegotiation to take place, a relationship of reciprocal political understanding and mutual credibility would be all the more important—to minimize the danger of a sharp break at a time likely to be punctuated by domestic controversy; to maintain a basis for continued constructive cooperation on security as well as other issues.

The importance of Japanese-American economic relations rests on two simple propositions: that each nation has a large stake in an open, liberal world economic order and that their cooperation is necessary in multilateral efforts to sustain such an order.[1] The fact that the two nations' approaches may diverge on issues such as energy does not refute this basic interest held in common. The Japanese economy, though not so foreign-trade-dominated as sometimes believed, does depend on access both to markets for its products and to commodities for import, particularly raw materials and agricultural products. The United States, while relatively more self-sufficient, nonetheless gains much, both economically and politically, from an open international trading and financial order. It gains particularly from commerce with Japan, its largest overseas trading partner; the recent lifting of Japanese restrictions on product and capital imports increases these gains. Here again the costs of a sharp break would be severe. Current economic interdependence is sufficiently great, particularly for Japan, that a major economic rupture would almost inevitably throw into question U.S.-Japanese relations across the board.

1. For a development of this argument with particular reference to the evolving Japanese economy, see Edward R. Fried and Philip H. Trezise, "Japan's Future Position in the World Economy" (Brookings Institution, 1974; processed).

For all of these reasons, it would be senseless and contrary to the interest of both countries to allow their relationship to unravel through mismanagement, or lack of political support, on either side of the Pacific.

The Relevance of Past Cases to Future Problems

But granted the continuing importance of strong U.S.-Japan ties, what relevance does the practical experience with bilateral crises of the postwar period have to the current, somewhat different situation? Are not emerging problems both different in substance and more multilateral than bilateral—like the energy question? And hasn't the unusual asymmetry of the postwar period been sharply reduced, with Japan both relatively stronger today and less dependent upon the United States?

Certainly the nature of the problems affecting U.S.-Japanese relations has changed in all of these directions, although it is difficult to say exactly how far these changes have gone or how long they will continue. But they do not, we believe, undercut the relevance of our analysis in any fundamental way. Different substantive problems will engage different groupings of actors in each capital, but this is hardly new. And barring major institutional changes these actors will be working within governmental systems very similar to those we have described. The major business of U.S.-Japanese relations has shifted notably in the past several years from bilateral to multilateral issues. But the two nations' cooperation is required to resolve most of these issues, and the development of common or compatible positions within multilateral negotiations will require the same sort of care in U.S.-Japanese dealings, the same effort to make mutual perceptions as accurate as possible. Indeed, it may require greater care. As for asymmetry, it has undeniably diminished at least in the economic area. It may one day disappear. But neither government is yet behaving as though that day is imminent; indeed, the psychological and behavioral tendencies associated with the postwar relationship of dependence remain strong.

Thus, if the episodes we have described will inevitably grow more dated, the larger political patterns and problems emphasized here should remain relevant. In the future as in the past, the issues most likely to endanger U.S.-Japanese relations will be those involving strong and conflicting domestic political values and stakes. And the ultimate course of U.S.-Japanese relations will continue to be shaped not simply by the broad policy conceptions and objectives of national leaders, but importantly by the day-to-day management and mismanagement of specific issues. Thus, although for simplicity of presentation we will frame our conclusions in terms of bilateral negotiations or issues in which agreement between these two governments is the ultimate objective, the conclusions will apply also, we think, to U.S.-Japanese cooperation on issues requiring multilateral resolution.

Explaining Success and Failure

Our concern throughout this study has been the resolution of U.S.-Japanese issues. And our general criterion for judging effectiveness in resolution has been political: the feasibility or sustainability of a bilaterally negotiated outcome (or series of outcomes) in the domestic politics of both countries.

There are, of course, other criteria for measuring the success or failure of bilateral interaction. Instead of concluding that the decision of Okinawa reversion was successful because it met the basic demands of both American and Japanese politics and interests, one could measure it against U.S. base policy worldwide and ask whether the maintenance of a large base like the Okinawa complex is still desirable in the current strategic situation. Instead of criticizing the mutual indisposition to compromise on textiles, one could ask what general pattern of international trade regulation was desirable and evaluate the two countries' positions in terms of their proximity to this pattern. We would not deny the importance of such substantive policy questions; indeed, each of us has particular views on them. But we believe also in the importance of strongly based U.S.-Japanese relations. The cause of bilateral harmony cannot always take precedence over other policy concerns, nor should it. But it is a worthy objective and merits careful analysis of how it can be attained.

This being our purpose, the existence of many other policy objectives and interests in both countries has entered our study not on the assumption that they should or could be eliminated, but as the endemic, enduring characteristic of the politics of U.S.-Japanese dealings which people committed to the relationship ignore at their own peril. We have found that U.S. officials recurrently take actions or make statements that damage or complicate U.S.-Japanese relations because their minds and interests are elsewhere. This applies also, to a somewhat lesser degree, to Japanese politicians and bureaucrats. But these other interests are real and legitimate. They cannot be overcome by exhortations about the overriding importance of U.S.-Japanese relations because to most actors this will *not* be the primary value or interest. Thus for both governments the need is to protect and enhance the relationship by accommodating, modifying, or otherwise coping with these other values and interests in order to move toward common ground on particular issues, ground defensible in both Tokyo and Washington. This requires effective dialogue and mutual understanding between representatives of the two countries, but it requires also effective political management and consensus-building by these representatives at home. And the dialogues both within and between the two countries must proceed more or less simultaneously in the move toward accommodation.

Applying these criteria, and drawing on the analysis of previous chapters, we can arrive at a general explanation of the contrasting experience with Okinawa and textiles that has been highlighted throughout this book.

The underlying reason for success on Okinawa was the unusual degree of reciprocal political sensitivity. Washington policymakers saw the problem, above all, as one of Japanese domestic politics; if reversion were not expeditiously accomplished, opposition groups in Japan could use the issue to mount a strong attack on the overall alliance relationship when the ten-year treaty term expired in 1970. Their Tokyo counterparts were sensitive to U.S. politics because they had to be—they required a substantial, timely U.S. policy change which they lacked the power to force. Thus they needed to relate the form and timing of their initiatives to the needs of those Americans working for reversion within the U.S. government.

But on neither side did sensitivity to the politics of the other country mean a failure to respond to the politics at home. In Washington, military interest in protecting the Okinawa base complex was recognized; civilians and military leaders worked together to assure that reversion could be accomplished on terms consistent with this interest. And in Japan, of course, Prime Minister Sato worked consistently and effectively to avoid the sort of crisis in U.S.-Japanese security relations that confronted his brother and predecessor, Kishi. Once Sato made his decision about the minimum terms his domestic situation required, he went to great lengths to be sure Nixon would grant them. (This included, iron-

Sato being Kishi's brother also heightened analysis of 1960.

ically, the textile promise that caused him so much trouble both with Nixon and within Japan.)

Because of this basic sensitivity on both sides to the politics of both countries, the more specific political requirements for resolving the issue could be met. In both countries the political groundwork could be carefully laid for a consensus on reversion, with key officials in each determined that the two national policy stances would emerge compatible with one another. In both, a relatively small circle of experts could control the issue because they made steady progress in satisfying the needs of major actors in both countries; the incentive for others to fight them or to open up competing channels was minimized. Thus the issue could be negotiated through a mutually reinforcing combination of diplomatic and summit channels; thus moderates in each country were able to strengthen one another. Many of these same strengths were present in the security treaty negotiations in the late fifties, which led effectively to agreement between the governments. But the Japanese opposition and the widespread public anxiety about the treaty had not been brought into the political equation. In 1969, by contrast, the agreement on nuclear-free, home-level reversion was directed explicitly toward meeting broad Japanese domestic concerns. The fact that several of the Japanese and Americans involved on Okinawa had dealt with one another on security treaty revision reinforced their determination to avoid a replay of the 1960 crisis, and their already established personal relationships limited the range of potential misperception as the Okinawa talks proceeded.

In the textile negotiations, such reciprocal political sensitivity was usually absent among those responsible for the issue in both countries. Instead, they took hard-line positions shaped almost entirely by how they construed domestic necessities. Consequently they were frustrated in their efforts to resolve the issue. Other channels then proliferated, and when these too yielded no solution, universal confusion and frustration were the inevitable result. Because moderates who sought compromise were on the defensive in each government, they were not able— as they had done on Okinawa—to deliver specific actions from one capital that would strengthen moderates in the other. On Okinawa, the few important actors outside the two governments who became involved worked with officials who controlled the action within these governments, to common purposes. On textiles, insiders and outsiders were frequently at cross-purposes, and the most remarkable outside initiative

—the alliance of Congressman Mills with the Japanese textile industry—involved designedly limited communication with top Nixon administration leaders and ended up in bitter confrontation with them. Thus Japanese-American interaction on textiles took the form of recurrent polarization, confusion, frustration, and enduring mutual resentment.

It is tempting, then, to attribute success on Okinawa almost entirely to the political sensitivity and skill of those who negotiated it, and to find the roots of the textile crisis in the lack of such sensitivity and skill on the part of those responsible there. But there were other reasons also that Okinawa proved the easier of the two to resolve, factors beyond the control of officials handling one or the other.

On Okinawa, for example, it was Japan that was doing the asking. If international negotiations were simple power contests where the stronger country is likely to prevail, then textiles should have been rather easily settled, whereas Okinawa should have festered unresolved. And between 1955 and 1965 that was what happened; Japanese repeatedly agreed to limit textile exports, while Americans treated Okinawa reversion as out of the question as long as international tensions persisted. But, as the experience of 1965–71 suggests, things can work the other way. Once the wall of U.S. resistance began cracking, the fact that Japan was the initiating country made Okinawa reversion easier for at least two important reasons. One was that the chief executive of the country from which concessions were sought, the American president, had considerable authority and leeway on the issue, much more than his Japanese counterpart had on textiles. A second was that the "attention gap," the relative neglect of Japan issues by the U.S. media, made it possible to avoid a premature Okinawa debate in the United States, which might have hardened military and congressional opposition before inside consensus-building could do its work. The U.S. textile initiative, by contrast, was front-page news in Tokyo, and it triggered a particularly volatile combination of strong Japanese textile industry resistance and broader nationalist resentment both reflected and fueled by the press.

There were also differences in the structure of interests on the two issues that made textiles particularly difficult. In the Japanese government, a strong role was unavoidably played in those negotiations by industry-responsive MITI officials, whereas Tokyo decisionmaking on Okinawa was controlled by politicians and foreign office officials with broader international perspectives. In Washington, the key special interest on reversion—the U.S. military—depended on tolerable U.S.-Japanese relations, and on reasonable tranquillity in Okinawa, in order to maintain viable base operations and thus its overall pattern of force deployment in the Pacific. Moreover, U.S. military leaders operate within a constitutional tradition that predisposes them to accept an unambiguous presidential decision unless it goes very deeply against their values and interests. The U.S. textile industry had no evident stakes in U.S.-Japanese relations that might have encouraged it to moderate its demands. And it was under no comparable presidential authority and discipline, though its leaders might have accepted a more moderate textile agreement without breaking with Nixon if he had confronted them with one and said it was all he could get.

Finally, Okinawa reversion was to most Americans a legitimate goal for the Japanese leadership to be pursuing, whether or not the same Americans felt that they could accommodate it. New textile quotas were, to many Japanese, an illegitimate, unreasonable demand for the U.S. leadership to make. Part of this critical difference involved yet another aspect of the asymmetrical relationship. There was a long tradition of American efforts to accommodate and bolster the conservative Liberal Democratic party leadership, whereas there was no comparable Japanese policy or interest in helping maintain a particular U.S. political party in power. The perceived illegitimacy of textiles stemmed also from the fact that it originated in "low politics"—a deal with a particular industry aimed at votes and money—whereas Okinawa involved the territorial identity of a nation.

Thus in considering why Okinawa was resolved effectively, and textiles was not, we have found part of our answer in how officials perceived the issues and their politics and how they managed national decision-making and bilateral negotiations. But we have also found part of our answer in differences between the issues, differences beyond these officials' control. There will surely be much in future U.S.-Japan issues also that officials will have to accept as given—in how particular domestic actors construe and press their interests, for example, and in the leverage they may be able to exert over the stands their government takes. Thus recommendations for improving the management of such issues should not be represented as a cure-all for future bilateral ills.

Still, Okinawa could easily have become a very serious political crisis without skillful and mutually sensitive diplomacy and political management. Textiles would have been difficult even with such skill, but damage to broader U.S.-Japanese relations could have been much better contained. And the crisis leading to cancellation of Eisenhower's visit in 1960 stands as a pertinent reminder that astute diplomacy within government channels may not be enough, if the broader domestic politics of an issue, in either country, is not effectively addressed.

Skillful and sensitive handling of the politics of U.S.-Japanese relations will remain a necessary, if not sufficient condition for maintaining strong bilateral ties. The remainder of this book considers how this goal can most effectively be advanced. The next two sections address how Americans should deal with Japan.[2] Assuming that influential U.S. actors give high priority to maintaining a strong relationship, how should they handle the difficult political issues that are certain to arise? The final section then deals with the problem of enhancing sensitivity to Japan in Washington. In a government where many others will not have such day-to-day concern, how can the voices of those sensitive to U.S.-Japanese relations be made more influential, or at least more clearly heard?

Japan as a Typical Large Ally

In fundamental respects, Japan is typical of the major countries with whom the United States has developed alliance relationships since World War II. Japan is a large democratic state with a strong bureaucracy and an advanced economy. Like their counterparts in the United States, politicians in Tokyo take varying stands on particular issues with an eye to their present standing and future prospects; officials operate from particular bureaucratic vantage points, with specific interests to defend and roles to play. On important foreign policy issues, influential actors are typically divided not only on ends and objectives to be pursued, but also about the means of pursuing them, and about who should have which responsibility for such means. In all of these respects, foreign policymaking in Japan is comparable to that in European countries with which the United States has close relations—Germany, for example, and the United Kingdom.

Similarly, the postwar Japanese-American alliance has been comparable in its origins and evolution to U.S. alliances with Western European

2. From this point on, we will address our recommendations primarily to the U.S. side, because we write principally for an American audience. In many cases, however, they are applicable to Japanese officials as well.

countries. It was formed under conditions that required dependence on the United States for economic survival, recovery from the war, and military security. It passed through a period during which Japan—like America's European partners—accepted and encouraged a dominant role for the United States, and formulated its own policies in deference to the patron nation. The hard necessities of this dependence limited, for a time, the influence of competing domestic interests and values on policies of the dependent nation's government and leadership, reducing the likelihood of major policy crises. This led many American policy-makers to assume a commonality of interest, a unified approach to international problems that would prevail over any wayward internal tendencies in its client. Moreover, the cold war made the United States subordinate its particular economic interests in the immediate postwar years to the need for alliance solidarity.

But as Japan recovered from abject dependence, strong competing forces inevitably reemerged to influence her policies, and Americans' tendency to underrate such forces contributed to the major, unanticipated bilateral crises that followed—in 1960 over the new security treaty, in 1969–71 on textiles. And the fact that these crises occurred between allies compounded the hurt and the frustration, because political leaders in one allied country expect their interests to be understood and accommodated by their counterparts in another. When this does not happen, their natural reaction is to feel let down personally, even betrayed. Again none of this is unique to U.S. dealings with Japan. Neustadt depicts a similar pattern in the Suez and Skybolt crises, even in an alliance between two nations with the strongest common cultural heritage.[3] And comparable problems resulted from the interplay of American and German politics in the negotiations of the mid-sixties over German balance-of-payments "offsets" for U.S. troop expenses.[4]

Yet despite these basic similarities to U.S. experience with Western European nations, Americans have tended to view Japan through very different lenses. Japanese differ in race, and speak a language very few Americans understand. Their culture appears as exotic and fundamen-

---

3. Richard Neustadt, *Alliance Politics* (Columbia University Press, 1970).
4. See "Offsets and American Force Levels in Germany: 1966, 1967, 1969," based on a case by Gregory F. Treverton, in Graham T. Allison and others, *Adequacy of Current Organization: Defense and Arms Control*, app. K to the Report of the Commission on the Organization of the Government for the Conduct of Foreign Policy (GPO, 1976), pp. 240–51.

tally alien, their modes of communication somehow purposive but hard to fathom. Successful in adopting the technology of the West, in emulating its pattern of industrialization, Japanese have somehow retained their cultural identity. Given this anomalous pattern of achievement, Japan's alternating role in U.S. history as friend and foe, the relative newness of extensive Japanese-American contact and communication, and the tendency of many Americans to fall back on racial stereotypes, it is not surprising that Americans' images of Japan have been fluctuating and simplistic. Thus, economically, Japan has been seen (by some as late as 1969) as an imitative, low-wage country producing shoddy goods for world markets at low prices, or (more recently) as a finely tuned modern industrial machine—Japan, Inc.—marching relentlessly to new economic conquests and threatening ultimately to subdue the world.

These views of Japan have colored concepts of the bilateral relationship and affected how Americans have handled that relationship. Just as the slow-dying "occupation mentality" among Japanese has perpetuated an attitude of dependence, an expectation of being "taken care of" well beyond the period when actual Japanese weakness justified such an attitude, Americans have found the role of patron and tutor all too congenial and hard to shake. As long as Japan behaved cooperatively— and postwar weakness often left her leaders little choice—Americans were friendly and even appreciative, impressed by her devotion to national economic and political reconstruction. American officials argued Japan's interests in international forums; and not merely because these interests were largely compatible with America's own. But the relationship was a somewhat patronizing one, and when Japan became visibly strong once again—this time economically—Americans reacted with concern, even alarm. For those whose cultural arrogance and racism made it inexplicable to them that an Asian country should seem to be beating the West at its own economic game, conspiracy theories became an easy explanation. Among officials, responses were usually more sophisticated, but the feeling was widespread that it was somehow wrong and unappreciative of past favors for Japan not to yield to U.S. needs on textiles once they were forcefully stated. When Japanese did not yield, they were "arrogant." Such expectations would not have been present in a negotiation with Great Britain or Germany. Indeed these countries were major textile exporters to the U.S. market in 1969, but the United States did not even press the issue seriously with them, much less employ the type of insensitive, sometimes brutal, negotiating tactics it employed toward Japan. Not surprisingly, much of the Japanese resentment in that case stemmed from the conviction that this was one more example of Western discrimination against Eastern products and countries. The fact that the U.S. initiative lumped Japan with Korea, Taiwan, and Hong Kong as a "low-wage" textile producer could only reinforce this conviction, and the broader ambivalence toward the United States within Japan.

This tendency to treat Japan as different from other major allies is both outmoded and damaging to U.S.-Japanese relations. Japan is far more like modernized Western countries than the enduring stereotypes suggest, though important political and cultural differences remain. And dealing with Japan as American officials deal with other major allies is likely to be far more productive, to produce considerably fewer misunderstandings and resentments, than treating Japan as a mystery that can be unlocked only with an entirely different sort of key. For whether they make Japan to be a docile partner or a relentless ultimate adversary, simplistic images of a unified, calculating Japan blind Americans to what they need above all to recognize—that Japan is a plural, many-sided country, home to a welter of competing viewpoints and interests, whose government and policies reflect the semiresolved conflicts among these views and interests. America's major postwar problems with Japan have arisen not from her unity but from her disunity—ideological conflict over the revised security treaty, governmental inability to win textile industry agreement to quota concessions, slowness in reaching consensus on measures to correct the trade imbalance.

Thus, the first lesson for American officials dealing with Japan is that she should be thought of like any large allied country. *In analyzing a particular U.S.-Japan political problem and deciding how to handle it, Americans should ask the same sorts of questions, and employ the same sorts of negotiating tactics, as they would when dealing with Britain, Germany, Canada, Italy, or France.* Japan—like these countries—is not a unified entity whose every act is part of a coherent bargaining strategy, but rather a complex political system where issues are being argued out internally even as they are being negotiated externally. In choosing which issues to press and how hard to press them, in selecting which signals to send and how to send them, *American officials need to make explicit, careful calculations about the internal politics of such issues in Tokyo*—about what outcomes seem feasible within this politics, and about which American steps are likely to strengthen the chances for the Japanese decisions and actions the Americans seek. At the same time, they need to be moderate in their expectations (as Neustadt emphasizes in U.S. relations with Britain). The U.S.-Japanese alliance has spawned a large area of overlapping interests, and a considerable range of trans-national alliances and channels, both formal and informal, for handling issues; these suffice for resolving the majority of bilateral issues, or at least averting crises on them. But where domestic interests and stakes in particular issues are high, resolution becomes far more difficult. On such politically sensitive issues, U.S. officials must recognize how strong do-mestic forces inimical to agreement can prove, how hard it often is to calculate the other country's politics correctly and how difficult to con-trol their own government's action, even if they calculate correctly about the "other side." This is true of difficult issues with Britain; it is no less true with Japan.

It follows that, as a general rule, *major issues should be initiated and emphasized only if analysis of the Japanese political scene indicates rea-sonable prospects for a favorable outcome.* Often, such analysis is under-taken too late—an issue is pressed, and Japanese political receptivity is considered only when resistance arises. Sometimes, as in the textile case, American officials seek an international agreement in the hope that Japa-nese cooperativeness will solve their political problems in Washington. Thus Nixon sought to control textile imports through international nego-tiations not because of positive findings abroad but because of negative findings at home. Like Kennedy before him, he did not want to go to Congress for the statutory authority to impose textile quotas unilaterally, fearing Congress would force on him broader trade restrictions that he did not want.

What one would like is the opposite—a presumption against choosing as a major priority objective something for which there is little appar-ent support and strong potential opposition in Japan. And if such an objective is chosen anyway, as in the textile case, it should be pressed with restraint—taking care not to provide a target for critics in Japan; recognizing that the maximum substantive goal may prove unattainable. Japanese initiatives on security treaty revision and Okinawa reversion were better received than the American textile proposal because im-portant American actors saw revision and reversion as important means of protecting and strengthening the security alliance, something the *Americans* valued. Similarly, American pressure for relaxation of Japa-nese import barriers benefited from a growing body of official and business opinion in Tokyo that saw such liberalization as both inevitable and desirable. There was no such support in Japan for textile quotas in 1969.

It is easier, however, to argue the need for such timely political assessments than to prescribe a fool-proof procedure for making them. One important if oft-cited rule is to *keep open a range of information sources* about the politics of an issue in Tokyo, as one should do in any major capital. Foreign office officials are frequently limited in their domestic political sensitivity; actors generally interpret their domestic scene in terms of their particular interests; even the Tokyo allies of American officials will have different stakes that color their perceptions. To avoid overdependence on one information channel, U.S. officials need not only to keep a number of lines open, but also to understand the vantage points, biases, and limitations of them all. Another means of assessing political prospects is *to take advance, "unofficial" soundings* through diplomatic or other bilateral channels, raising an issue tentatively in order to "test the water." Sometimes this can be done by a public statement, though this risks activating opposition once the statement appears in the Japanese press. (If an issue needs to be aired publicly, in fact, it is often better for Japanese actors to launch the trial balloons, since this avoids the connotation of American pressure or an attempt by the "senior partner" to dictate a solution.)

To suggest such general rules is not to imply that U.S. officials with day-to-day responsibility for Japan are typically insensitive to such matters. On Okinawa they were very sensitive, and the actions of particular officials on other specific issues have frequently been animated by a rather sophisticated awareness of the politics of such issues in Tokyo. On occasions where biases and misreadings have plagued U.S. policymaking, the fault has rested not so much with officials specializing in Japan as with political leaders and functional officials who were rejecting their advice. In the 1960 crisis, however, the embassy's readings were wide of the mark, and State Department officials in 1969–70 did underestimate the depth of Japanese textile resistance, though they were sensitive enough to its presence. Even if they do consult many sources and take advance soundings in sophisticated ways, of course, U.S. officials cannot fully judge whether an initiative might win acquiescence in Tokyo if they fail to consider one major influence on Japanese decision-making—how much energy and bargaining leverage U.S. leaders are willing to apply to the issue. But on a case like textiles, a careful advance analysis would have concluded that a very large American effort would be required, and that even such an effort might not prove successful. Such a finding would not, by all evidence, have deterred President Nixon from pressing the issue, given his prior political commitment. But assuming that Nixon had a will to listen to such analysis and take it seriously, he and his advisers might conceivably have selected their means more carefully and been more flexible on terms at critical negotiating junctures.

Once an issue is initiated, the next rule in politically difficult negotiations with allies becomes: *don't expect too much too soon.* Major initiatives are almost always calls for major adjustments of interests within the target country. These almost always take time. It was wrong to hope for quick Japanese adherence to comprehensive textile restraints in 1969 —the Japanese industry saw too great a stake in exploiting rapidly growing markets for manmade fibers; it felt too deep a resentment against the enforcement of existing cotton textile quotas; it was able to mobilize quickly and seize the banner of nationalist resistance to "unreasonable" American demands; there was no strong counterpressure in Tokyo. Since the textile industry not only had strong support on the issue in governmental and political circles, but also controlled the means of implementing an agreement, its acquiescence to any agreement was essential, and it would not be quickly attained. (Nor, conversely, could Sato have won return of Okinawa in 1965 or 1966, no matter how hard he had pressed for it; the adjustment of U.S. military interests could not be accomplished in a day.)

In working toward an objective, *it is often useful to seek limited concrete steps* to create momentum toward a goal. On both security treaty revision and Okinawa reversion, agreement on intermediate goals proved useful—the joint committee to study the security relationship established at the 1957 Eisenhower-Kishi summit; the Johnson-Sato agreement of 1967 on negotiating reversion within "a few" years. And in both cases these steps established a presumption favoring further action that advocates of such action could exploit within their own governments. On textiles, however, the United States (under industry pressure) repeatedly rebuffed proposals for partial restraints to take effect soon, holding out for a "comprehensive" accord covering all textile trade. Americans in charge of the negotiations do not seem to have given much thought to how such a partial accord might have been designed so as to lead to broader coverage later. Of course, one problem was that Japanese negotiators wanted to assure that any partial accord would not lead to broader restrictions, but stand as an alternative to them.

While an issue is being negotiated, *U.S. officials should regularly seek to provide signals that strengthen moderates in Tokyo who are working to bring about agreement.* The aim should be to enhance the latter's ability to serve as brokers between domestic and U.S. interests. This must be done, however, with a good deal of care and finesse. In some cases it may be well to respond positively to proposals by Japanese moderates even if they fall short of what is desired—to encourage further efforts on their part; to make them appear to their colleagues as officials taken seriously in Washington. Unless taken with subtlety, however, such action on the part of American officials may well embarrass the Japanese moderates and discredit them in the eyes of their more nationalistic opponents in the government, mass media, and the general public. In any case, it will almost always be prudent to avoid the opposite—the sweeping denunciations of Japanese "arrogance" and "inflexibility" that Americans sometimes indulged in during the textile negotiations. Not only do these undercut Tokyo moderates by making the Americans with whom they do business appear insensitive and even "anti-Japanese"; they are bound to be picked up in the Tokyo press and to fuel nationalist resistance to concessions. A much more positive and promising line would be to develop arguments in support of U.S. proposals that Japanese actors can pick up and use domestically, arguments that are relevant to the main issues as seen in Tokyo. Still another way to strengthen the hand of Japanese moderates is by granting concessions in the course of particular negotiations that are designed to give them what they need politically at home—like the provision in the 1967 communiqué for gradual adjustment of Okinawan economic and administrative structures to prepare for reunification with Japan. Once again, through these and other actions, U.S. officials should conceive of policy-making in Japan as a typical political process and think about how best to help those who are fighting within that process for actions leading toward bilateral agreement on controversial issues.

Finally, some conclusions common to the handling of all relationships can be drawn about U.S.-Japan summit diplomacy. Like most leaders in parliamentary systems, the Japanese prime minister is limited in his power, so his acquiescence is not equivalent to delivering the Japanese government on an issue. Another postwar lesson, however, is how closely the resolution of major issues has been tied to the current political situation of the reigning premier. The crisis of 1960 reached such a peak because an unpopular treaty was identified with an unpopular premier, Nobusuke Kishi. His brother, Eisaku Sato, failed to move more aggressively on textiles ten years later because of his particular vulnerability to charges he had "tainted" Okinawa reversion by making a textile promise to Nixon.

The basic conclusion that emerges is that *Americans should avoid placing too great a domestic burden on a prime minister in the pursuit of an objective.* If an alliance relationship is to endure, it is important to show reasonable sensitivity to the political constraints within which a counterpart leader must operate. Moreover, *U.S. leaders should normally avoid linking negotiations on politically controversial issues that are essentially separate in substance and involve separate Japanese domestic constituencies.* However attractive—even inevitable—a textiles-for-Okinawa trade may have seemed to Nixon, the two issues were in different political arenas in Tokyo. What Sato gained on Okinawa was not of direct benefit to the industry-related interests most resistant to a textile accord. To them, such a trade-off was all loss and no gain; hence they fought it.[5]

Japan as a Special Case

In all of the ways just cited, Americans can best deal with Japan by behaving very much as they would—or should—toward a major European ally. But dealing with any country requires sensitivity also to its unique features. Japan particularly requires such sensitivity, because the language and cultural gap remains deep, because misunderstandings and misperceptions have been uncommonly frequent.

The ways Japanese policymaking is "different" bear little resemblance to the extreme stereotypes recapitulated earlier in this chapter. The

5. There was also a particularly Japanese reason why this "secret deal" issue proved so volatile in Tokyo. To most Japanese, reversion was an issue of national integrity and honor, an overdue vindication of basic Japanese rights. It was therefore, in a certain sense, illegitimate for the Japanese government to bargain for it, and for the Americans to demand a price for it. For Nixon, holding back on Okinawa to extract textile concessions must have seemed like natural bargaining behavior. But for Japanese the sacred historical event of reversion would be severely tarnished if their government had to make "unreasonable" concessions on an unrelated trade issue in order to bring it about.

Japanese government is not monolithic. Its institutions are neither unusually disciplined nor overridingly purposive. Postwar economic growth policies have been impressive, and relations between officials and industrialists have had a more cooperative, less "adversary" character than in the United States. But there is no "Japan, Inc.," no relentless government-business combine. To the degree that the "special" character of U.S.-Japanese relations has been a product of Americans holding to such erroneous perceptions—and some of it has—their correction can contribute to reducing the degree Americans wrongly treat Japanese as "different," to both nations' benefit. But Japanese policymaking *is* different in that it exhibits, in particularly acute form, the dispersal of influence and decision power found in all modernized democratic societies.

In all modern democratic societies, major policy steps require reasonable political consensus. But in Japan this extends to a belief that all major views and interests relevant to a decision ought somehow to be taken into account, that all those with important stakes in the outcome have a right to a hearing and some influence. Achieving consensus by this broad criterion can take considerable time on controversial issues, if it is attainable at all.

In parliamentary systems generally, the chief of government is a less commanding figure than an American president. But in Japan the constraints on the premier are particularly great—because of consensus values and expectations; because of fragmentation within the ruling party; because of the strength of the permanent bureaucracy; because of the ability of the opposition to exert effective public pressure notwithstanding its permanent minority status.

In every country, the politics of national defense and security has particular features, but in Tokyo the legacy of World War II combines with more general features of Japanese politics to impose constraints unlike those in any other major country.

In many bilateral relationships, there are differences in negotiating styles, but those between the United States and Japan can cause particular trouble unless officials are sensitive to them.

The lessons arising from these differences do not conflict in any fundamental way with our primary injunction—do unto Japanese as you would do unto other important allies. But they do add an important dimension to the relationship, and thus to our conclusions about how it should be handled day by day.

Japan's unusually weak and constrained political leadership reflects the never-ending competition among the Liberal Democratic party's senior members for the premiership. The prime minister's dependence on factional balance within the party limits his authority and shapes the composition of his cabinet. However adept he may be politically, the Japanese prime minister lacks the authority and autonomy of a strong American president in deciding how an issue will be resolved. Moreover, attempts to assert such authority are likely to be resisted as arbitrary or undemocratic. For in Tokyo the premier is expected to move slowly and carefully, articulating the existing consensus on an issue or nurturing gradual changes in it rather than issuing clarion calls for fundamental new policies.

The premier and his cabinet are further constrained by the strong bureaucracy. The major ministries are dominated by elite senior officers who seldom shift between ministries, and are almost never challenged by the kind of in-and-out officials identified with particular U.S. presidents or administrations. Nor is there any layer of politically appointed officials between the cabinet and the bureaucracy. All of this strengthens the ministries as self-confident, elite institutions, and increases the ministers' dependence on them. And it is reflected in conceptions of what is proper for political leaders to do. In Washington it is accepted practice for the president to circumvent the bureaucracy. But in Tokyo the permanent government remains, in many respects, the ultimate, legitimate locus of responsibility.

For Americans dealing with Japan the strength of the bureaucracy can sometimes be helpful; it offers a clear target for communications, a clear locus of responsibility. But when the desired decisions or concessions are not forthcoming, as in the textile case, it produces frustration. Not surprisingly, U.S. leaders then seek to negotiate above or around Japan's bureaucracy. Just as predictably, these efforts usually fail, for there seldom exists an authoritative political counterpart with whom a binding deal can be struck. Acting as further barriers to resolving issues through summit conferences and back channels are the Japanese aversion to "secret deals" and the prevalence of leaks to the Tokyo press.

In general, therefore, *American leaders dealing with Japan should employ summit channels not to substitute for diplomatic or functional channels, but to reinforce them, in careful coordination with them. Americans should confine the use of back channels in U.S.-Japanese relations to the gathering of political intelligence about what agreements may be possible, rather than employing them to negotiate such agreements.* Behind these operational recommendations, however, is a broader conclusion. The concessions sought by Americans will often be politically unattainable, especially if what is asked for is quick Japanese action on contentious issues. *Rather than employing weakly based back channels, or pressing for personal concessions from a prime minister unlikely to be able to deliver his government, Americans dealing with Japan need to lower their expectations about what can be quickly accomplished. The general rule for all alliance relationships—don't expect too much too soon—applies with particular force to Japan.*

Further constraining Japanese political leaders is the ideological split between conservatives and opposition. Though Americans tend to discount the opposition parties because of their extreme ("irresponsible") policy positions, their anti-American stance, and their lack of visible power, the opposition does exercise important inhibiting influence on Japanese foreign policy. In seeking to deny the opposition openings to exploit, conservative governments are moved to caution. Such caution is likely to increase if the conservative Diet majorities diminish further— or disappear. In order to assess accurately the impact of opposition parties on Japanese policymaking, *U.S. officials need to extend their contacts beyond the conservative establishment, probably to a greater extent than they have to date.* The problem of broadening such communications unfortunately is not one resolvable simply by Americans, for part of the difficulty is that opposition figures are often reluctant to be "tainted" by too much contact with U.S. officials. And the fact that American diplomats are accredited to the current government—and must negotiate day-to-day issues with that government—imposes inevitable constraints, of course, on how much they can build relationships with outside groups. A notably encouraging recent development was the successful September 1975 visit to the United States by a delegation of prominent Japan Socialist party members; the fact that the last previous such visit was eighteen years before suggests the gap in communications that remains.

Pressure from the opposition is particularly pervasive on defense and security issues, fueled by ideological opposition to the Self-Defense Forces and the alliance with the United States. Nor is this pressure countered by the kind of institutional strength inside the government that the Pentagon provides. The Japanese military is essentially uninvolved in foreign policy, shies away from strategic discussion, and takes its direction from political leaders and civilians in the Japan Defense Agency. This, plus the enduring popular antimilitary and antinuclear sentiment which is a legacy of World War II, makes Japanese military and security policies far more inhibited than those of any other important nation. Despite American urgings to do more, postwar Japanese governments have consistently avoided major rearmament and military commitments outside Japan's borders. Because of this unique combination of political pressures and because the resulting Japanese security policies are, we believe, generally consistent with U.S. interests, American officials should exercise restraint in pressing Tokyo on defense questions.

The Japanese pattern of decentralized policymaking and the inhibitions on defense issues cause Japanese officials to exercise considerably greater caution in bilateral negotiations than their U.S. counterparts. This Japanese tentativeness, their preference for talking generally about and around a problem, attending first to forms and general principles and leaving the details to a later stage, often comes across to Americans as delaying tactics, and delay may well be its outcome whether intended or not. To Japanese, by contrast, the U.S. push for specifics often seems overhasty, perhaps even rude, and certainly insensitive to the need for time to develop mutual confidence and a general framework for understanding. The Japanese relative lack of verbal assertiveness in communications—particularly in dealing with Americans in English—reinforces this difference in style. And even in the use of go-betweens, a practice particularly attractive to Japanese as a means of facilitating indirect communication, it is the Americans who tend to expect quick and definitive results, while the Japanese consider employment of intermediaries as exploratory and tentative.

Such divergence in negotiating styles is not easy to bridge; nor will greater sensitivity to Japanese negotiating preferences always bring Americans the results they seek. Tentative, informal communication about an issue is certainly useful in its early stages, as officials begin to focus on its substantive and political ramifications. And in initial negotiating sessions, it may well be useful for Americans to follow Japanese preferences and talk about the issues at hand in an exploratory, general, tentative manner. But if they keep doing so, they may contribute to delay rather than resolution; conversely, a clear-cut U.S. stance on specifics is often necessary to move the Japanese government to reach its own specific position. *But while maintaining their preference to push specific issues where possible, American negotiators can pay greater heed to questions of timing—seeking to judge whether a move to specifics is premature or whether the issue has been sufficiently vetted in Japan to make possible a concrete response to a specific initiative. Americans can also give heed to Japanese concern for form by seeking to put their specifics within a framework acceptable to Japanese involved in the issue (as was done on Okinawa), and by understanding that ambiguous Japanese responses do not necessarily have negative connotations.* And in cases where Japanese officials seem personally reticent about pressing policy views that conflict with the Americans', U.S. officials can sometimes move things along if they spend less effort pushing their own positions and more time encouraging the Japanese to articulate theirs. Of course, when the U.S. substantive stance on an issue triggers broad opposition in Japanese domestic politics, delay and more delay is likely to be the ultimate—if not, for all actors, the intended—Japanese response. But where a substantive basis for compromise seems politically attainable, Japanese ambiguity may well reflect a serious feeling out of the domestic and bilateral politics of the issue, and may then be followed by a more specific and constructive substantive reaction.

Yet these recommendations for handling negotiations with Japan differ only slightly from the kind of negotiating practice that would be appropriate toward other countries. And it is particularly important that U.S. officials not allow their awareness of the particular features of Japanese policymaking to move them to treat Japan issues, and Japanese negotiators, in a fundamentally different and perhaps invidious manner. Too often Americans have done that, with unfortunate consequences. For Japanese officials—long sensitive to and resentful of discrimination in the international community—are likely to perceive themselves as being treated differently by Americans, even on the basis of limited evidence. The result can be a clouding of interpersonal dealings that can hinder particular negotiations even though the Americans involved may not be fully aware of what the problem is. Thus, *American officials need to show, in their dealings with Japanese counterparts, the same personal respect, the same avoidance of condescension and cultural arrogance, that they should evidence in dealings with Europeans.* And on substantive issues like trade policy, where Japan is still emerging from a long experience of discrimination against her products, *Americans should avoid both the fact and the appearance of seeking arrangements vis à vis Japan that are inequitable by comparison with parallel arrange-*

ments with European countries. In contrast to the security sphere—where arrangements differing from those in NATO have strong political and substantive justification—Japanese-American economic relations need to be based, to the greatest extent possible, on full reciprocity in benefits and obligations within a larger world economic order founded on the same principles.

Thus, even attention to Japan as a special case yields recommendations similar to what one would urge in U.S. dealings with other allies. American officials should be sensitive to the particular features of Japanese politics, but all countries have unique political configurations which need to be understood and dealt with. The cultural style and language differences are particularly important in this bilateral relationship. But once we focus on how Americans should seek to bridge these differences, we end up saying, in various specific ways, that they should deal with Japanese as they deal (or ought to deal) with representatives of other large countries. The cultural gap does require some extra effort, greater attentiveness so that reciprocal political understanding and communication can be adequate and effective. But it is the same sort of effort that Americans should devote to Anglo-American or German-American relations. Japan remains, of course, special in significant ways, and these need to be recognized. But *Americans dealing with Japan will do so far more effectively, with far fewer mistakes, if they approach Japan and Japanese as a country and people whose government and politics are not all that different, fundamentally, from those of large, modern societies elsewhere in the world.*

Increasing U.S. Government Sensitivity to Japan

All of our recommendations to this point have been based on the assumption that there are U.S. officials who give high priority to U.S.-Japanese relations in their daily work. And clearly there are. Yet only a small minority of American politicians and bureaucrats will be interested in any continuing way in such recommendations. For the rest, concern about Japan is at best rather general and intermittent; their interests, their jobs, their expertise, their institutional and personal stakes involve mainly other things.

How then does one get the U.S. government to act with sensitivity toward Japan and the politics of the relationship? If U.S. government policies toward Japan were clearly separable from other important American objectives and interests, the answer would be obvious—that government decisions with major impact on U.S.-Japanese relations should be made and influenced, insofar as is possible, by those in the U.S. government and society who are expert in the substance and politics of the relationship, and by the overlapping group of those whose jobs make them feel especially responsible for keeping U.S.-Japanese relations on a reasonably even keel.

This is in fact the way things worked on Okinawa. The political case for steps toward reversion was voiced by the dean of America's "Japan experts," Edwin Reischauer, from the beginning of his ambassadorial tenure in 1961. In 1966, after Sato had identified himself personally with the islands' return, the State Department's country director for Japan seized hold of the issue. Working with the new U.S. ambassador U. Alexis Johnson and with civilian and military officials in the Pentagon, he quietly but adroitly built a working-level bureaucratic consensus within which reversion came to be seen as both inevitable and acceptable to U.S. interests.

But the experts' ability to move this issue within the U.S. government did not result from their sensitivity to Japan. From such sensitivity they drew the objective and their determination to press it. But their success arose from their ability to understand the stakes of other key American policy actors on the issue—mainly the military and their potential congressional allies—and to engage them in a dialogue from which a resolution satisfactory to both emerged. Indispensable also was the positive orientation of two presidents—Johnson and Nixon—and the ability of the officials involved to understand and operate within their priorities and constraints. Had there been important presidential political objectives inconsistent with what these officials were doing, or had these officials been perceived as unresponsive to the program interests of the military, they could not have controlled the issue as long as they did. On textiles, where the priorities of key State Department officials were in conflict with the President's (and with those of the commerce secretary and his department), policy determination and management were kept out of their hands.

In the late fifties and early sixties, of course, U.S.-Japan issues did not typically engage competing American political and functional actors in a major way. Bilateral security and economic dealings had little immediate impact on broader U.S. strategic policies or the international economy; Japan was not a focal point for domestic political contention. So in the United States, Japan issues could be left more or less consistently to the country experts at the State Department and its Tokyo embassy. The presence of strong officials in both locations worked also to this end, and the general sympathy and support of senior Kennedy and Johnson administration officials for the alliance was of course essential for the experts to be able to play this role. But this period appears to have ended as the postwar era ended, with Japan's emergence as a front-rank economic power with significant impact on world economic patterns and institutions and growing impact on U.S. domestic markets. And while American political concern about the "Japanese threat" has fallen off since it reached its peak in 1971 and 1972, the pattern of "leaving things to the Japan experts" is unlikely to reemerge. At the very least, these experts on Japan must now share responsibility with other government experts—in monetary and trade matters, for example—whose claims to involvement are no less legitimate than their own. This has become particularly important now that so much bilateral U.S.-Japan interaction is taking place on multilateral issues, and often in multilateral forums.

Thus, if they are to operate effectively within this broader substantive and political arena, *there is a need to strengthen the sensitivity of those expert in and specifically responsible for the U.S.-Japan relationship to other major values, interests, and objectives that affect U.S. national policymaking, thus improving their ability to coordinate the politics of the process and to build internal consensus in support of their policy initiatives.* For good U.S.-Japanese relations cannot be effectively advanced by officials insensitive to other legitimate U.S. policy objectives. Rather, such officials must be knowledgeable and credible mediators between the needs of the relationship and the concerns of other U.S. policy-influencing actors. The U.S.-Japan relationship will be well served if those with responsibility for it are doing the coordinating, but only if they are successful in satisfying, placating, or combating other relevant interests inside their government, as State officials were on Okinawa. And they must also be sensitive enough to the broader political feasibility of a settlement to avoid provoking a crisis domestically with the terms they negotiate, as occurred in Tokyo in 1960.

Yet on many issues the country specialists cannot play a central management role whatever their responsiveness to other interests. They may lack functional expertise or authority. It was Treasury Under Secretary Paul Volcker, not an official of State's Bureau of East Asian Affairs, who coordinated the second dollar devaluation in February 1973 and flew secretly to Tokyo to consult just prior to its implementation. Or the president may view an issue as belonging primarily in a sphere where the Japan specialists' expertise and credibility are limited—electoral politics (textiles), or relations with another country (the July 1971 China shock), or domestic economic policy (the "soybean shock" of U.S. export controls in June 1973). Looking at U.S. foreign policymaking more generally, a State Department skeptic concluded in 1970 that the country director was typically "too far removed from the source of political power to evaluate, reconcile, and arbitrate the U.S. interests involved in any important issue."[6] And if Okinawa is an example to the contrary, it is hard to find very many others.

If those whose principal concerns lie elsewhere are bound to control many issues of major importance to U.S.-Japanese relations, then *those officials not specifically responsible for U.S.-Japanese relations need to be made more sensitive to the politics of the relationship and to how the issues that they help decide will affect Japan and the relationship.* At minimum, the aim would be limitation of damage—officials close to President Nixon and politically credible to him might have argued for a somewhat less demanding stance on textiles, on the ground that it would in fact resolve the issue and could be effectively sold to U.S. industry leaders even if it did not give them everything they wanted. This might have terminated the dispute in December 1970 if not before. More ambitiously, the aim would be to build the needs of U.S.-Japanese relations into broader policy initiatives that a government was pursuing, and into the concepts of international reality that national leaders hold. Again, the examples are negative. The 1971 Nixon shocks reflected no positive concern with Japan ties and Japanese political impact. And the Nixon administration's "five-power world" concept of power centers flexibly adjusting their policies to balance one another does not seem very realistic when set against the politics of a bilateral relationship where (especially in Tokyo) governmental decisionmaking is slow and issues must

---

6. Dissent of Arthur Allen, in U.S. Department of State, *Diplomacy for the Seventies* (1970), p. 357. For a comprehensive assessment of the role of country directors in U.S. foreign policymaking since the position was established in 1966, see William I. Bacchus, *Foreign Policy and the Bureaucratic Process: The State Department's Country Director System* (Princeton University Press, 1974).

be carefully bargained internally before moves can be made externally. Political leaders seldom have the leverage and authority they would need to make such a system work.

A prerequisite for reciprocal sensitivity between Japan experts and other U.S. officials is, of course, continuing intragovernmental communication. Particularly important is a steady, two-way dialogue between the Japan specialists and each administration's political leadership. That communication seems to have been most effective between 1961 and 1969, but under circumstances where the White House gave little day-to-day attention to Japan and tended not to press the priority of other policy values on key issues affecting Japan—a situation not too likely to recur. The nadir of such communication came in 1971, when the Nixon White House—frustrated by the textile case, tending to view Japan experts as Japan apologists—took major actions affecting Tokyo without the experts even being informed, much less involved. There were, of course, particular advantages to the Nixon administration in springing its new China and economic policies on an unexpecting world. But there is no evidence that the costs to U.S.-Japanese relations were seriously addressed, much less the possibility of the United States taking other actions toward Japan to ease or compensate for the shocks.

High American policymaking is peculiarly a product of presidential style, which limits the potential of institutional remedies for this sort of internal noncommunication. *One possibility, however, would be for each president to assign, to one of his senior foreign policy advisers, a "watching brief" for U.S.-Japanese relations, establishing as one of his explicit responsibilities the task of following major U.S.-Japan issues and defending the needs of the relationship both on these issues and on other issues with substantial impact on Tokyo.* This adviser would serve as a natural contact point for Japan desk or embassy officials who needed to raise problems at the presidential level, and also for impressing on these officials the strength of presidential priorities not related to Japan. To be effective in this role, the official assigned this brief would require, at minimum, near-cabinet rank and intermittent access to the oval office.[7]

The future of U.S.-Japanese relations remains anything but assured.

7. We do not mean to suggest that a president apply this prescription uniquely to Japan. A senior official might ideally have several such briefs covering major areas of continuing American policy concern. It might prove desirable, for example, for an official to have such responsibility for a number of major American alliance relationships.

In the era of détente, there is no credible, immediate great-power threat from which the alliance seems to offer shelter; thus the task of its maintenance lacks day-to-day urgency on both sides of the Pacific. This opens the relationship to neglect, even abuse, in the pursuit of other interests domestic and foreign, as the textile dispute and the 1971 Nixon shocks testify. The fact that broader international economic and political relationships were changing in the early seventies fed fears, in Japan, that the United States might be moving to abandon the alliance entirely or at least to reduce it to a formal shell without substance. Time and effort on both sides of the Pacific have repaired much of the damage of 1971, and the alliance has been given renewed priority in Washington. Yet should the future bring crises comparable to those of the early seventies, characterized by misperception, malcommunication, and growing mutual bitterness, a Japanese political leader, incumbent or aspiring, might choose to give voice to such bitterness rather than seek (as did Sato and Tanaka) to dampen it. Or events initiated by other countries could create sharp new difficulties for the U.S.-Japan relationship—war or threat of war in Korea, or a new and perhaps more stringent Arab oil embargo. Either would pose acute domestic and international dilemmas for both countries, taxing their capacity for reciprocal political sensitivity and cooperation.

Whatever the major U.S.-Japan problems of the next decade may be, an approach to avoiding or ameliorating future crises can be found in the roots of past ones. Successful resolution of controversial issues requires effective mediation, in each capital, between the requirements for U.S.-Japanese relations and the claims of actors representing other policy priorities and interests. Those in each country seeking such constructive resolution must be sensitive to the position of their counterparts in the other, and try to shape their official actions so as to strengthen these counterparts. The task is anything but easy. Some degree of misperception and recurrent tension is inevitable between two such large pluralist states. But a constructive long-term relationship requires continuing efforts to contain such tension, and to resolve—gradually sometimes—the issues that produce it.

For Americans dealing with Japan, this means approaching Japan as they would any modern democracy, alert to its particular political features but expecting the sorts of political and bureaucratic divisions, the patterns of recurrent misperceptions and misunderstandings, that they would expect in dealing with other major U.S. allies. And it means following rules of caution and prudence that they would follow toward these allies: assessing the political scene with care; shaping initiatives to be effective in Tokyo but still sustainable in Washington; treating counterparts with sensitivity and respect. The postwar U.S.-Japanese relationship has managed to survive many departures from these rules, but it needed also to survive the two severe crises that resulted. In the future we might not be so lucky.

Bibliography

TWO MAJOR sources for this study were case studies by the authors based on extensive interviews with participants in both national capitals: "Decisionmaking in U.S.-Japanese Relations: Okinawa Reversion," by Priscilla Clapp and Haruhiro Fukui; and "The Textile Wrangle: Conflict in Japanese-American Relations 1969–71," by I. M. Destler, Hideo Sato, and Haruhiro Fukui.

Foreign Policymaking and Organization: General and U.S.

Allison, Graham. *Essence of Decision: Explaining the Cuban Missile Crisis.* Boston: Little, Brown, 1971.

Allison, Graham T., and Morton H. Halperin. "Bureaucratic Politics: A Paradigm and Some Policy Implications," in Richard H. Ullman and Raymond Tanter, eds., *Theory and Policy in International Relations.* Princeton: Princeton University Press, 1972. Brookings Reprint no. 246.

Bacchus, William I. *Foreign Policy and the Bureaucratic Process: The State Department's Country Director System.* Princeton: Princeton University Press, 1974.

de Rivera, Joseph M. *The Psychological Dimension of Foreign Policy.* Columbus, Ohio: Merrill Publishing, 1968.

Destler, I. M. *Presidents, Bureaucrats, and Foreign Policy.* Princeton: Princeton University Press, 1972 and 1974.

Halperin, Morton H., with the assistance of Priscilla Clapp and Arnold Kanter. *Bureaucratic Politics and Foreign Policy.* Washington: Brookings Institution, 1974.

Hilsman, Roger. *The Politics of Policy-Making in Defense and Foreign Affairs.* New York: Harper and Row, 1971.

Hoffmann, Stanley. "The American Style: Our Past and Our Principles," *Foreign Affairs,* vol. 46 (January 1968).

Iklé, Fred Charles. *How Nations Negotiate.* Written under the auspices of the Center for International Affairs, Harvard University. New York: Harper and Row, 1964.

Jervis, Robert. "Hypotheses on Misperception," *World Politics*, vol. 3 (April 1968). Reprinted in Morton H. Halperin and Arnold Kanter, eds., *Readings in American Foreign Policy: A Bureaucratic Perspective*. Boston: Little, Brown, 1973.

Keohane, Robert O., and Joseph S. Nye, Jr., eds. *Transnational Relations and World Politics*. Cambridge: Harvard University Press, 1972.

Neustadt, Richard E. *Alliance Politics*. New York: Columbia University Press, 1970.

Newhouse, John. *Cold Dawn: The Story of SALT*. New York: Holt, Rinehart and Winston, 1973.

Steinbruner, John D. *The Cybernetic Theory of Decision: New Dimensions of Political Analysis*. Princeton: Princeton University Press, 1974.

Japanese-American Relations

Armacost, Michael H. "U.S.-Japanese Relations: Problems and Modalities of Communications," *Department of State Bulletin*, vol. 68 (January 15, 1973).

Asahi Shimbun Staff. *The Pacific Rivals: A Japanese View of Japanese-American Relations*. New York: Weatherhill, 1972; Tokyo: Asahi, 1972.

Clapp, Priscilla A., and Morton H. Halperin. "U.S. Elite Images of Japan: The Postwar Period," in Akira Iriye, ed., *Mutual Images: Essays in American-Japanese Relations*. Cambridge: Harvard University Press, 1975.

————, eds. *United States–Japanese Relations: The 1970's*. Cambridge: Harvard University Press, 1974.

Clough, Ralph N. *East Asia and U.S. Security*. Washington: Brookings Institution, 1975.

Cohen, Jerome B., ed. *Pacific Partnership: United States–Japan Trade*. Lexington, Mass.: Lexington Books, for the Japan Society, 1972.

Destler, I. M. "Country Expertise and U.S. Foreign Policymaking: The Case of Japan," in Morton A. Kaplan and Kinhide Mushakōji, eds., *Japan, America, and the Future World Order*. New York: Free Press, 1976.

Fried, Edward R., and Philip H. Trezise. "Japan's Future Position in the World Economy." Processed. Washington: Brookings Institution, 1974.

Hunsberger, Warren S. *Japan and the United States in World Trade*. New York: Harper and Row, for the Council on Foreign Relations, 1964.

Kitamura, Hiroshi. *Psychological Dimensions of U.S.-Japanese Relations*. Occasional Papers in International Affairs, no. 28. Cambridge: Center for International Affairs, Harvard University, 1971.

Meyer, Armin H. *Assignment: Tokyo*. New York: Bobbs-Merrill, 1974.

Nagai, Yōnosuke. "Dōmei gaikō no kansei" [Trap of alliance diplomacy], *Chūō kōron*, January 1972.

Nishihara, Masashi. "Kokkakan kōshō ni okeru 'hi-seishiki sesshokusha' no kinō: Nihon to Amerika no taigai-kōshō o chūshin ni" [The function of 'unofficial contacts' in international negotiations: Special focus on external negotiations of Japan and the United States], *Kokusai seiji*, vol. 50 (1973).

Reischauer, Edwin O. "The Broken Dialogue with Japan," *Foreign Affairs*, vol. 39 (October 1960).

Rosovsky, Henry, ed. *Discord in the Pacific: Challenges to the Japanese-American Alliance*. Washington: Columbia Books, for the American Assembly, 1972.

Sato, Hideo. "United States–Japanese Relations," *Current History*, vol. 68 (April 1975).

Taylor, Allen, ed. *Perspectives on U.S.-Japanese Economic Relations*. Cambridge, Mass.: Ballinger Publishing, for the U.S.-Japan Trade Council, 1973.

Japanese Decisionmaking and Organization

Campbell, John Creighton. *Contemporary Japanese Budget Politics*. Berkeley and Los Angeles: University of California Press, forthcoming.

Fukui, Haruhiro. "Bureaucratic Power in Japan," in Peter Drysdale and Hironobu Kitaōji, eds., *Japan and Australia: Two Societies and Their Interactions*. Oxford: Oxford University Press, forthcoming.

————. "Foreign Policy-Making in Japan: Case Studies for Empirical Theory." Processed. Paper prepared for delivery at the 1974 annual meeting of the Association for Asian Studies.

————. "Policy-Making in Japan's Foreign Ministry." Processed. Paper prepared for delivery at the Conference on Japan's Foreign Policy, Jan. 14–17, 1974, Kauai, Hawaii.

Hellmann, Donald C. *Japanese Domestic Politics and Foreign Policy: The Peace Agreement with the Soviet Union*. Berkeley: University of California Press, 1969.

Hosoya, Chihiro. "Characteristics of the Foreign Policy Decision-Making System in Japan," *World Politics*, vol. 26 (April 1974).

Johnson, Richard Tanner, and William G. Ōuchi. "Made in America (Under Japanese Management)," *Harvard Business Review*, vol. 52 (September–October 1974).

Kusayanagi, Daizō. "Tsūsanshō: Tamesareru sutā kanchō" [MITI: Star agency on trial], *Bungei shunjū*, August 1974, p. 114.

Matsuyama, Yukio. "Japanese Press and Japan's Foreign Policy," *Journal of International Affairs*, vol. 26, no. 2 (1972).

Misawa, Shigeo. "An Outline of the Policy-Making Process in Japan," in Hiroshi Itoh, ed. and trans., *Japanese Politics, An Inside View: Readings from Japan*. Ithaca: Cornell University Press, 1973.

Oberdorfer, Don. "The Lockjaw of Tokyo Dailies," *Washington Post*, Jan. 4, 1975.

Trezise, Philip H., with the collaboration of Yukio Suzuki. "Politics, Government, and Economic Growth in Japan," in Hugh Patrick and Henry

Rosovsky, eds., *Asia's New Giant: How the Japanese Economy Works.*
Washington: Brookings Institution, 1976.
Vogel, Ezra F., ed. *Modern Japanese Organization and Decision-Making.*
Berkeley and Los Angeles: University of California Press, 1975.

Japanese Politics, Culture, and Foreign Policy

Brzezinski, Zbigniew. *The Fragile Blossom: Crisis and Change in Japan.* New
York: Harper and Row, 1972.
Doi, Takeo. *The Anatomy of Dependence.* Translated by John Bester. Tokyo
and New York: Kodansha International, 1973.
Emmerson, John K. *Arms, Yen and Power: The Japanese Dilemma.* Rutland,
Vermont: Charles E. Tuttle, 1972.
Fukui, Haruhiro. "Factionalism in a Dominant Party System: The Case of
Japan." Processed. Paper prepared for delivery at the 1974 annual meeting
of the American Political Science Association.
————. *Party in Power.* Berkeley and Los Angeles: University of California
Press, 1970.
Gibney, Frank. *Japan: The Fragile Superpower.* New York: W. W. Norton,
1975.
Kaplan, Eugene J. *Japan: The Government-Business Relationship.* U.S. De-
partment of Commerce. Washington: Government Printing Office, 1972.
Langdon, Frank C. *Japan's Foreign Policy.* Vancouver: University of British
Columbia Press, 1973.
Morley, James W., ed. *Forecast for Japan: Security in the 1970's.* Princeton:
Princeton University Press, 1972.
Mushakōji, Kinhide. *Kokusai seiji to Nihon* [International politics and Japan].
Tokyo: Tokyo University Press, 1967.
Nakamura, Hajime. *Ways of Thinking of Eastern Peoples: India-China-Tibet-
Japan.* Honolulu: University Press of Hawaii, 1964.
Nakane, Chie. *Japanese Society.* Berkeley and Los Angeles: University of
California Press, 1970.
Packard, George III. *Protest in Tokyo.* Princeton: Princeton University Press,
1966.
Pempel, T. J. "Japan's Nuclear Allergy," *Current History,* vol. 680 (April
1975).
Reischauer, Edwin O. *Japan: The Story of a Nation.* New York: Alfred A.
Knopf, 1970.
Scalapino, Robert A., and Junnosuke Masumi. *Parties and Politics in Con-
temporary Japan.* Berkeley: University of California Press, 1962.
Thayer, Nathaniel B. *How the Conservatives Rule Japan.* Princeton: Prince-
ton University Press, 1969.
Watanabe, Akio. *The Okinawa Problem.* Melbourne: Melbourne University
Press, 1970.
Watanuki, Jōji. "Japanese Politics: Changes, Continuities, and Unknowns."

Processed. Institute of International Relations for Advanced Studies on Peace and Development in Asia. Tokyo: Sophia University, 1973.

Weinstein, Martin E. *Japan's Postwar Defense Policy, 1947–1968.* New York: Columbia University Press, 1971.

Yanaga, Chitoshi. *Big Business in Japanese Politics.* New Haven: Yale University Press, 1968.

Yukawa, Hideki. "Modern Trend of Western Civilization and Cultural Peculiarities in Japan," in Charles A. Moore, ed., *The Japanese Mind: Essentials of Japanese Philosophy and Culture.* Honolulu: University Press of Hawaii, 1967.

Memoirs and Histories: Pre-1960

Acheson, Dean. *Present at the Creation.* New York: W. W. Norton, 1969.

Allison, John M. *Ambassador from the Prairie: or Allison Wonderland.* Boston: Houghton Mifflin, 1973.

Borg, Dorothy, and Shumpei Okamoto, eds. *Pearl Harbor as History: Japanese-American Relations, 1931–1941.* New York: Columbia University Press, 1973.

Burns, James McGregor. *Roosevelt: The Soldier of Freedom.* New York: Harcourt Brace Jovanovich, 1970.

Butow, Robert J. *Japan's Decision to Surrender.* Stanford: Stanford University Press, 1954.

Coughlin, William J. "The Great *Mokusatsu* Mistake," *Harper's,* March 1953.

Craig, William. *The Fall of Japan.* New York: Dial Press, 1967.

Dunn, Frederick S. *Peace-Making and the Settlement with Japan.* Princeton: Princeton University Press, 1963.

Feis, Herbert. *The Atomic Bomb and the End of World War II.* Princeton: Princeton University Press, 1966.

———. *The Road to Pearl Harbor.* Princeton: Princeton University Press, 1950.

Hoopes, Townsend. *The Devil and John Foster Dulles.* Boston: Little, Brown, 1973.

Iriye, Akira. "The Failure of Military Expansionism," in James William Morley, ed., *Dilemmas of Growth in Prewar Japan.* Princeton: Princeton University Press, 1971.

Kido, Kōichi. *Kido Kōichi nikki* [Kōichi Kido dairy]. Vol. 2. Tokyo: Tokyo University Press, 1966.

Kurzman, Dan. *Kishi and Japan: The Search for the Sun.* New York: Ivan Obolensky, 1960.

Smith, A. Merriman. *A President's Odyssey.* New York: Harper and Brothers, 1961.

Toland, John. *The Rising Sun: The Decline and Fall of the Japanese Empire, 1936–1945.* New York: Bantam Books, 1971.

Yabe, Teiji. *Konoye Fumimaro* [Fumimaro Konoye]. Tokyo: Jiji Press, 1958.

Index

Academic community, effect on government policy, 56–57
Acheson, Dean, 92
Agency for International Development, 83
Agriculture, U.S. Department of, 83
Aichi, Kiichi, 32, 63, 95n
Allen, Arthur, 193n
Allison, Graham T., 3n, 91n, 96n, 136, 177n
Allison, John M., 14n, 15n
All Japan Prefectural and Municipal Workers' Union. *See* Jichirō
Amae, 108–11, 116
Amaya, Naohiro, 81n
Armacost, Michael H., 94n
Army, U.S. Department of, 25, 28
Asahi Shimbun Staff, 15n, 127n, 138n, 144n, 150n, 152n

Bacchus, William I., 193n
Back negotiating channels, 149, 157; advantages of, 158–59; decisionmaking and, 161; problems involving, 159–64; purpose of, 158; recommendations for use of, 186–87
Baerwald, Hans, 163n
Balance of trade, U.S.-Japan, 1–2, 38, 42, 45
Bator, Francis, 105n
Bilateral issues: back channels to resolve, 149, 157–64; balance of interest during negotiations over, 135–38; broadening political arena of, 138–39; criteria for evaluating resolution of, 171–72; declining importance of, 170–71; diplomatic channels to resolve, 149–52; functional channels to resolve, 149, 152–54; indirect communications over, 129, 130; informal direct communications over, 129; Japanese caution in negotiating, 188; management of, 74–76; political reasons for initiating, 126–29; problems in solving, 125–26; recommendations for initiating, 179–81; recommendations for negotiating, 186–90, 192–94; summit channels to resolve, 149, 154–57; transnational alliances on, 143–48. *See also* Interaction, between political systems; Signals; United States-Japanese relations
Bonin Islands, 24, 30, 31
Borg, Dorothy, 50n
Brodie, Bernard, 161n
Bureaucracy: careerists in, 72–73; comparison of Gaimushō and State Department, 69, 73–76; consensus procedures in, 103–04; for foreign policymaking, 50, 70–71, 73; for national security policymaking, 84–86; policy-influencing role of, 71–72; political leaders and, 68, 69, 71, 76–77; size of, 70–71. *See also* Decisionmaking; Interagency relations
Burke, Arleigh, 137, 138
Burns, James MacGregor, 93n, 113n
Business community, 50–51, 53, 54, 59
Butow, Robert J. C., 120n, 159n
Byrnes, James F., 133n

Cabinet Research Office, Japan, 85
Cabinet Secretariat, Japan, 66–67
Campbell, John Creighton, 75n, 78n
Caraway, Paul W., 26
Central Intelligence Agency, 71
China, Nationalist, 11–12, 64
China, People's Republic of, 1, 2, 44, 114

Chūritsu Rōren (Liaison Conference of Neutral Labor Unions), 56
Clapp, Priscilla, 3n, 9n, 77n, 100n, 162n
Clark, Keith C., 67n
Commerce, U.S. Department of, 37, 42, 83, 153
Condon, John C., 101n
Congress, U.S., 25, 63–65
Connally, John, 82, 83
Consensus, 90; broad criterion for, 125n, 185; Japanese emphasis on, 101–08, 140; relation of "form" to, 116
Constitution of 1947, 50, 110
Coughlin, William J., 120n
Council on International Economic Policy, 82, 83
Craig, William, 120n
Crocker, Chester A., 70n
Cultural gap, 2, 90; *amae* and, 108–11; effect on attitude toward consensus, 101–08; effect on attitude toward "form" of agreement, 114–17; effect on decisionmaking, 100–01, 105; effect on textile dispute, 105; effect on U.S.-Japanese relations, 177–78, 190; *haragei* and, 111–13; language barrier and, 119–21, 190; sincerity and, 109–11; U.S. cultural arrogance and, 117–19, 178

Daniels, Michael P., 147, 148
Decisionmaking: back-channel negotiations and, 161; by bureaucrats, 48, 69–70; consensus in, 103–04; decentralization of, 188; effect of cultural differences on, 100–01, 105; imposing faits accomplis to change, 139–41; interaction between national systems for, 125–26; overestimation of negotiating nations' unity in, 91–94; politically based misconceptions in, 90–91, 94–100, 123–24; press and, 59; signals between nations as product of, 131–33
Defense, U.S. Department of, 69, 71
Democratic Socialist party, 54, 56
de Rivera, Joseph, 100n
Destler, I. M., 9n, 67n, 70n, 76n, 77n, 78n, 115n, 120n, 148n
Diet: debate over security treaty revision, 20–21; under imperial constitution, 49; majority LDP in, 50; powers of, 50, 65–66; prime minister and, 62, 63
Dillon, Douglas, 83n
Diplomatic negotiating channels, 149–52
Doi, Takeo, 101n, 109n

Dōmei (Japanese Confederation of Labor), 56
Drysdale, Peter, 70n
Dulles, John Foster, 64; role in peace treaty negotiations, 10, 12; support for Japanese rearmament, 14, 16, 18, 142, 144; on mutual security, 13

Economic issues, 78–84, 169
Economic Policy Board, U.S., 83n
Eisenhower, Dwight D., 2, 18, 20, 21, 22, 23, 86, 89, 97–98, 151–52

Factionalism. *See* Liberal Democratic party
Fait accompli, 139–42, 160
Federation of Economic Organizations. *See* Keidanren
Feis, Herbert, 92n, 113n, 120n
Finance Ministry, Japan, 79
Flanigan, Peter, 41
Ford, Gerald, 2
Foreign Ministry, Japan. *See* Gaimushō
Foreign policy: bureaucracy and, 50, 70–71, 72; effect of domestic politics on, 49, 59–60; effect of political polarization on, 59–60; influence of Diet on, 65–66; influence of intellectuals on, 51, 56–57; influence of press on, 57–59; interagency differences over, 78–84; labor unions and, 56; LDP and, 52; MITI and, 81; role of military in, 49–50; role of opposition parties in, 51, 54–55; secrecy on, 60. *See also* Decisionmaking
Fried, Edward R., 169n
Fujiyama, Aiichiro, 19, 20
Fukuda, Takeo, 51, 63, 120n
Fukui, Haruhiro, 9n, 51n, 70n, 74n, 75n, 78n, 104n, 115n, 120n, 148n
Functional negotiating channels, 149, 152–54

Gaimushō (Foreign Ministry): decentralization of, 75; management of bilateral issues, 74–75; Okinawa reversion and, 27–28, 30, 31, 33, 69, 78; relations with other agencies, 77–78, 79, 80; relations with political leaders, 76–77; relations with U.S. State Department, 150–51; role in foreign policy, 60, 69, 70, 73, 75–76, 149; staff of, 70, 73–74, 75
General Agreement on Tariffs and Trade (GATT), 10, 37

General Council of Japanese Trade Unions. *See* Sohyo
Germany, 177, 178
Gibney, Frank, 158n
Goyō gakusha, 57
Great Britain, 12, 178
Grew, Joseph, 133n

Hagerty, James, 21, 98
Halperin, Morton, 3n, 75n, 77n, 84n, 90n, 91n, 100n, 136n, 162n
Hammond, Paul Y., 104n
Haragei, 111–13, 116
Hatoyama, Ichiro, 112n; peace agreement with Soviet Union, 20, 104; role in security treaty revision, 15, 16, 126–27
Hellman, Donald C., 69–70
Herter, Christian, 98
Hirohito, Emperor, 2
Hoffmann, Stanley, 118n
Hogen, Shinsaku, 150
Hoopes, Townsend, 10n
Hull, Cordell, 109, 113, 159n

Ikawa, Tadeo, 159
Ikeda, Hayato, 24, 25, 26, 62, 107
Iklé, Fred, 155, 160n
Imai, Seiichi, 50n
Imports, U.S., 1, 4, 39, 44, 64
Intellectuals, 51, 56–57
Interaction, between political systems, 125–26, 130–42, 171–72. *See also* Signals
Interagency relations, 77; on economic issues, 78–84; between MITI and Gaimushō, 79–82, 103–04; on security issues, 84–86
Iriye, Akira, 77n
Ishibashi, Tanzan, 17n
Iwakuro, Hideo, 159n

Japan: economic expansion of, 37, 38; dependence on U.S., 177; neutrality in international relations, 14–15; peace agreement with Nationalist China, 11–12, 64; peace agreement with Soviet Union, 20, 69, 70, 104. *See also* United States-Japanese relations
Japan Chamber of Commerce and Industry. *See* Nisshō
Japan Committee for Economic Development. *See* Keizai Dōyūkai
Japan Communist party, 15, 54
Japan Defense Agency, 85, 188

Japanese Confederation of Labor. *See* Dōmei
Japan Federation of Employers' Associations. *See* Nikkeiren
Japan Federation of Textile Workers' Union. *See* Zensen Dōmei
Japan, Inc. concept, 42, 81, 119, 178, 185
Japan Socialist party, 54, 56
Japan Teachers' Union. *See* Nikkyōso
Japan Textile Federation, 42
Jervis, Robert, 91, 96n
Jichirō (All Japan Prefectural and Municipal Workers' Union), 56
Johnson, Lyndon B., 30, 64, 67, 83n, 129
Johnson, Richard Tanner, 102n
Johnson, U. Alexis, 29, 34, 191
Joint Chiefs of Staff, U.S., 28, 31
Jurich, Anthony, 79
Jūshin, 49, 50

Kalb, Bernard, 119n
Kalb, Marvin, 119n
Kantei, 66, 95
Kanter, Arnold, 3n, 91n, 100n
Kaplan, Morton A., 77n
Kashiwagi, Yūsuke, 79
Keidanren (Federation of Economic Organizations), 53
Keizai Dōyūkai (Japan Committee for Economic Development), 53
Kendall, Donald, 101, 137, 138
Kennan, George F., 150n
Kennedy, David, 44, 45, 79, 137, 141, 153
Kennedy, John F., 23, 24–26, 45, 83n
Keohane, Robert O., 143n
Khrushchev, Nikita, 112n
Kido, Kōichi, 92n
Kishi, Nobusuke, 16, 86; Liberal Democratic party and, 17, 18; resignation of, 22, 62, 106, 107, 151–52; role in security treaty revision, 17–21, 27, 46, 62, 87, 99, 103, 104
Kissinger, Henry, 67; on back-channel negotiations, 161, 162, 163; role in textile dispute, 34, 41, 95, 138, 156
Kitamura, Hiroshi, 118n
Kitaōji, Hironobu, 70n
Kōmeitō, 55
Kōno, Ichirō, 15n, 112n
Konoye, Fumimaro, 92n, 112, 159
Korean War, 11, 60
Krisher, Bernard, 112n
Kunihiro, Masao, 112
Kurofune, 140, 141

Kurzman, Dan, 15n, 17n
Kusayanagi, Daizō, 81n
Kyoto conference, 1969, 137

Labor unions, 56
Langdon, Frank C., 158
Language, misperceptions caused by differences in, 119–21, 190
LaRocque, Gene, 55, 58, 60, 127n
LDP. See Liberal Democratic party
Legere, Lawrence J., 67n
Liaison Conference of Neutral Labor Unions. See Chūritsu Rōren
Liberal Democratic party (LDP), 7; big business and, 53, 54; bureaucracy and, 52; declining support for, 53–54; factionalism of, 27, 51, 54, 62, 63, 149; governmental experience of leaders, 68; as majority party, 51; major officials of, 52; on Okinawa reversion, 32; presidential election of 1964, 26; prime minister and, 186; rural support for, 52; on security treaty revision, 19, 46
Long-Term Arrangement on Cotton Textiles, 37

MacArthur, Douglas, II: arrangements for Eisenhower's Japan visit by, 21, 98–99, 107, 151; role in security treaty revision, 19, 20, 22, 149
Management-Labor Advisory Committee on textiles, U.S., 111
Matsuyama, Yukio, 58n
Meyer, Armin H., 33n
Miki, Takeo, 51, 61n
Military bases, U.S., 13; back channels in negotiations over, 158; in Japan, 13; in Okinawa, 25, 28, 29, 31–32, 33, 34, 35
Military, Japan: on Okinawa reversion, 85; postwar decline of, 80, 85; role in defense and security issues, 187–88; role in foreign policy, 49–50, 187. See also Japan Defense Agency; Self-Defense Forces
Military, U.S., interest in Okinawa reversion, 85, 175
Mills, Wilbur, 41–42, 64, 65, 89, 93, 95–96, 140, 146–48
Ministry of International Trade and Industry (MITI), Japan, 37; functions of, 80; line bureaus of, 81; relations with business, 82; relations with Gaimushō, 79; role in foreign policy, 70,

81; in textile dispute, 39, 40, 48, 79, 95n, 97, 106, 111, 153, 160–61
Misawa, Shigeo, 70n
MITI. See Ministry of International Trade and Industry
Miyazawa, Kiichi, 40, 95n, 106, 115–16, 158, 162
Moore, Charles A., 108n
Moose, Richard, 67n
Morgenthau, Henry, 92
Mushakōji, Kinhide, 77n, 108n
Mutual security treaty, 1952, 10–11, 12, 13
Mutual security treaty, 1960 revision, 1, 8; breach of Japanese consensus over, 103, 104, 106–07; debate in Diet on, 20–21; diplomatic negotiating channels for, 149, 151; history of, 12–23; Japanese rationale for, 15; misperceptions over political interests in, 97–100; opposition parties' positions on, 28, 54–55; political implications of, 45–46; provisions of, 20; summit negotiating channels for, 154; transnational alliance working toward, 143–44; U.S. broadening of controversy over, 138–39

Nagai, Yōnosuke, 78n, 81n, 90n
Nakamura, Hajime, 108n
Nakane, Chie, 104n
Nationalism, 43, 81
National Security Council, U.S., 32, 67, 84
National Security Force, Japan, 16
Neustadt, Richard E., 90, 94, 96n, 140n, 157n, 177, 180
Neutrality, Japanese, 14–15
Newhouse, John, 157n
Newspapers, 57–59
Nikkeiren (Japan Federation of Employers' Associations), 53
Nikkyōso (Japan Teachers' Union), 56
Ninyokyoku, Jinjiin, 70n
Nishihara, Masashi, 157n, 163n
Nishima, Haruo, 152
Nisshō (Japan Chamber of Commerce and Industry), 53
Nixon, Richard M.: policy change toward China, 1, 44, 114; position on Okinawa reversion, 32–33, 34; reaction to Mills's plan, 42, 64, 95–96; role in foreign policy, 67; role in textile dispute, 35, 36, 38, 39, 40, 41, 48, 93, 109, 113, 122, 126, 130, 156–57, 161–62

Nixon shocks, *1971*, 1, 2, 44, 140, 141, 167, 193, 195

Nomura, Kichisaburō, 109, 159n

Nuclear weapons: entering Japanese ports, 55, 58; as issue in Okinawa reversion, 31–32, 33, 34, 35, 115, 122–23, 137–38

Nye, Joseph S., Jr., 143n

Oberdorfer, Don, 59n

Ohira, Masayoshi, 63, 97, 110

Oil crisis, *1973*, 3, 6, 63

Okamoto, Shumpei, 50n

Okinawa: Japanese "residual sovereignty" over, 11, 25; U.S. aid to, 25; U.S. bases on, 25, 28, 29, 31, 33, 34, 35

Okinawa reversion, 1, 5, 23, 35; back channels for negotiating, 158; communiqué on, 34; diplomatic channels for negotiating, 149–50; financial arrangements of, 78–79; "form" of agreement for, 114–15; functional channels for negotiating, 153–54; history of, 23–35; indirect communications during negotiations over, 129; Japanese interest versus U.S. apathy over, 134; Japanese position on, 24, 26–28; misperceptions in negotiations over, 122–23; negotiations over, 30–34; nuclear-free, 31–32, 35, 59, 137–38; political implications of, 35, 36, 45–46; reciprocal political sensitivity in negotiations, 172–76, 181, 191; role of Japanese consensus in, 104, 108; secrecy in negotiations, 139; transnational alliance on, 145–46, 165, 166; U.S. and Japanese national security and, 85; U.S. position on, 8–9, 24–26, 28–30

Opposition political parties: on foreign policy issues, 53–55, 59; intellectuals and, 14–15, 57; labor groups and, 56; role in Diet, 62; on security treaty revision, 28

Ōuchi, William G., 102n

Packard, George, III, 17n, 19n, 21n, 117n, 144n

Parsons, J. Graham, 98n, 100n, 107n

Patrick, Hugh, 78n, 94n

Peace treaties, Japanese: with 48 nations, *1951*, 10; with Nationalist China, *1952*, 11–12; with Soviet Union, *1956*, 20, 69, 70, 104, 127

Pempel, T. J., 55n

Polarization, 57, 59–60

Policy affairs research council, Japan, 52

Policymaking. *See* Decisionmaking; Foreign policy

Political parties. *See* Democratic Socialist party; Japan Communist party; Japan Socialist party; Kōmeitō; Liberal Democratic party; Opposition political parties

Political system: under constitution of *1947*, 50; under imperial constitution, 49; interaction between U.S. and Japanese, 125–26; misconceptions in policymaking based on, 90–91, 94–100; polarization in, 57, 59–60

Politics, in U.S.-Japanese relations, 3–4, 9; in Okinawa reversion, 35, 36, 45–46, 48, 126, 128; in security treaty revision, 45–46, 48–49, 126–27; in textile dispute, 9, 36, 46, 48, 126, 127–28

Potsdam Declaration, *1945*, 120, 133n, 136

President, U.S., 62, 63, 67, 95–96

Press, 57–59

Prime minister: Cabinet Secretariat and, 66–67; election of, 61; misperceptions on power of, 95; powers of, 63, 86–88, 183, 186; proposed role in U.S.-Japanese negotiations, 184; relations with cabinet, 61–62; role in Diet, 62, 63; supporting staff, 66, 68

Racism, 118–19, 178

Ransom, Harry Howe, 71n

Rearmament, Japanese: increase in, 15–16; Japanese opposition to, 59, 188; U.S. attitude toward, 11, 14, 45, 142

Reischauer, Edwin O., 23, 28, 129, 144, 162n, 191

Richardson, John, Jr., 101n

Roosevelt, Franklin D., 122, 136; embargo on U.S. oil exports to Japan, 91–92; misperception on Japanese unity, 92–93; proposed summit meeting with Premier Konoye, 112–13

Rosovsky, Henry, 78n, 94n, 112n

Rostow, W. W., 23n

Ryūkyū Islands. *See* Okinawa

Saito, Mitsuko, 101n

Sato, Eisaku: role in Okinawa reversion, 24, 26–27, 28, 30, 31, 32, 34, 63, 88, 108, 126, 128, 158, 167, 172; role in textile dispute, 39, 41, 44, 48, 87, 93, 95, 109, 110–11, 113, 122, 156, 160–62

Sato, Hideo, 9n, 78n, 115n, 120n, 148n
Schilling, Warner R., 104n
Schlesinger, Arthur, Jr., 76n, 77
Security issues: bureaucratic structure for, 84–86; effect on U.S.-Japanese relations, 168–69; role of Japanese military in, 187–88; U.S. and Japanese conceptions of, 118
Security treaty. See Mutual security treaty, 1952; Mutual security treaty, 1960 revision
Self-Defense Forces, 16, 54, 72n, 187
Shigemitsu, Mamoru, 15, 16, 17
Shiina, Etsusaburō, 61n
Shultz, George, 82, 83
Signals, 131; asymmetry of impact of, 134–35, 140; to broaden controversy, 138–39; to change balance of influence, 135–38; counterproductive, 131–33; politics as source of, 131, 133; recommendations for use of, 179, 183
Sincerity, 109–11
Smith, A. Merriman, 23n, 89, 152n
Snyder, Glenn H., 104n
Socialist party, 14–15
Sohyo (General Council of Japanese Trade Unions), 56
Sōka Gakkai Buddhist organization, 55
Soviet Union, 20, 69, 70, 104, 127
Sparkman, John, 23
Special Representative for Trade Negotiations, U.S. Office of, 82
Stans, Maurice, 4; in textile dispute, 40, 95, 110, 119, 130, 131–32, 133, 158, 161–62, 163; trade mission to Europe, 38–39
State, U.S. Department of: management of bilateral issues, 74–76; on Okinawa reversion, 25, 26, 28, 68–69, 78; relations with other agencies, 77–78; relations with political leaders, 76–77; role in foreign policy, 73, 75–76, 149; as spokesman for foreign interests, 150; staff of, 71, 73–74, 75
Steinbruner, John D., 96n
Stimson, Henry, 93, 113, 133n
Summit negotiating channels, 149; advantages of, 154–55; problem of reliance on, 155–57; suggestions for use of, 183–84, 186
Suzuki, Kantarō, 120
Suzuki, Yukio, 78n

Tanaka, Kakuei: downfall of, 54, 58–59, 61; policy on China, 62; press and,

58–59; in textile dispute, 44, 45, 106, 137, 140, 141, 153
Tanter, Raymond, 91n, 136n
Tariff Commission, U.S., 111
Taylor, Maxwell, 137, 138
Textile dispute, 1, 14; absence of reciprocal sensitivity in, 173–76, 181–82; amae and sincerity in, 110–11; back channels used in, 158, 160–61, 162, 163; counterproductive signals in negotiations, 131–32, 133; diplomatic channels used in, 150; effect of language barrier on, 119; factors leading to, 37–38; "form" of agreement in, 115–16; functional negotiating channels used in, 153; haragei in, 111–12; history of, 35–45; indirect communications during, 130; Japanese broadening of controversy in, 138; Japanese interest versus U.S. apathy over, 134; Kendall's failure to mediate, 101, 137, 138; Mills's plan to resolve, 41–42; misperceptions in negotiations over, 97, 123; political implications of, 36, 46; resentment generated by, 43–44; role of Japanese consensus in, 105, 106–07; summit negotiating channels used in, 155–57; transnational alliance on, 145, 146–48, 165; U.S. overestimation of Japanese unity in, 93
Textiles, Japanese: decline in export of, 45; impact on U.S. textile industry, 36; U.S. quotas on, 4, 39, 44, 130; voluntary export limitations on, 36–37, 38, 39, 42, 64
Tōgō, Shigenori, 92
Tōjō, Hideki, 92
Toland, John, 110n, 113n, 120n, 163
Trade Expansion Act of 1962, 37
Transnational alliances: on Okinawa, 145–46, 165, 166; resulting in security treaty, 143–44; on textiles, 145, 146–48, 165; weaknesses of, 146–48
Treasury, U.S. Department of, 79, 82–83
Treaties. See Mutual security treaty, 1952; Mutual security treaty, 1960 revision; Peace treaties, Japanese
Treverton, George F., 177n
Trezise, Philip H., 78n, 94n, 169n
Truman, Harry S., 10, 133n

Uemura, Kogorō, 113n
Ullman, Richard H., 91n, 136n
Unger, Ferdinand, 29
United States: balance of trade, 1–2;

embargo on oil exports to Japan, 91–92; misperceptions over Japanese unity on policymaking, 91–94; negotiations with Germany, 177; relations with China, 1, 2, 44, 114; support for Japanese economic expansion, 37; troops stationed in Japan, 15, 17; views of Japan, 177–79. *See also* United States-Japanese relations

United States-Japanese relations: criteria for measuring success of, 171–72; effect on economic stability, 169; effect on security, 168–69; factors influencing, 3, 89–90, 177–79; reciprocal political sensitivity in, 172–73, 191–94; recommendations for future, 179–84, 186–90, 192–94; shift from bilateral to multilateral issues in, 170–71. *See also* Bilateral issues; Mutual security treaty, 1960 revision; Okinawa reversion; Politics, in U.S.-Japanese relations; Textile dispute

Universalism, of U.S. interests and values, 117–18
Ushiba, Nobuhiko, 106
U-2 incident, 22, 98

Watson, Albert, 26n
Weinstein, Martin E., 13n, 16n, 60
World War II: effect on Japanese attitudes toward defense and security, 185, 188; negotiations prior to, 91–93, 109–10, 112–13, 132, 136, 159

Yen, 44, 45, 140
Yoshida, Shigeru: back channel efforts of, 158; resignation of, 16; role in peace and security treaties, 11–12, 64, 104; secrecy on foreign policy, 60

Zaikai, 50–51
Zengakuren, 57
Zensen Dōmei (Japan Federation of Textile Workers' Union), 56

GEORGE W. BUSH

Cheryl Fisher Phibbs, *Book Editor*

Daniel Leone, *President*
Bonnie Szumski, *Publisher*
Scott Barbour, *Managing Editor*
David M. Haugen, *Series Editor*

GREENHAVEN
PRESS®

THOMSON

GALE

973.931
GEO

San Diego • Detroit • New York • San Francisco • Cleveland
New Haven, Conn. • Waterville, Maine • London • Munich

THOMSON

GALE

LIBRARY OF CONGRESS CATALOGING-IN-PUBLICATION DATA
George W. Bush / Cheryl Fisher Phibbs, book editor.

George W. Bush / Cheryl Fisher Phibbs, book editor.
    p. cm. — (People who made history)
    Includes bibliographical references and index.
    ISBN 0-7377-1847-1 (pbk. : alk. paper) — ISBN 0-7377-1846-3 (lib. : alk. paper)
        1. Bush, George W. (George Walker), 1946– . 2. Presidents—United States—Biography. 3. Presidents—United States—Election—2000. 4. United States—Politics and government—1993–2001. I. Phibbs, Cheryl Fisher. II. Series.
    E903.G46 2004
    973.931'092—dc21   2003040860

Printed in the United States of America

CONTENTS

Foreword   7

George W. Bush: An Appointment with History   9

Chapter 1: Early Influences

1. Midland Influence *by Nicholas D. Kristof*   27
Growing up in Midland, Texas, gave roots to George W.
Bush's personal and political philosophy. Midland provided a common life full of optimism and security. Opportunity and risk were a way of life. These west Texas values
instilled in Bush are essential to understanding who he is
as a person and as president of the United States.

2. Tragedy Binds Mother and Son
by George Lardner Jr. and Lois Romano   35
At the age of seven, George Bush lost his younger sister to
leukemia. Bush's self-proclaimed objective became to
make his mother smile again. It was this event that nurtured a powerful bond between Bush and his mother.

3. Failures in the Oil Business *by Joe Conason*   43
Three years after Bush left Harvard he began his own oil-
drilling venture. Dropping oil prices and rising interest
rates required that Bush be rescued from one business
failure after another.

Chapter 2: The Making of a President

1. Team Player *by Joe Nick Patoski*   52
George W. Bush's first brush with success came when he
joined the management of the Texas Rangers baseball
team. As managing general partner of the ball club, Bush
put a public face on the team and ran an effective business, displaying his organizational and negotiating skills.

2. Running for Governor *by Skip Hollandsworth*   59
Embarking on a grueling personal journey, Bush entered
the governor's race to unseat one of Texas's most popular
governors. Struggling to keep media attention on his issues
rather than his family history, Bush ran a campaign focused on changing crime and education policies.

3. The Republican Front-Runner *by Ramesh Ponnuru* 72
As governor of Texas, Bush held a solid record of being a
moderate conservative who fulfilled his campaign
promises. This successful run as governor helped Bush
emerge as the strongest nominee for president that the Republican National Committee could produce in 2000.

4. Progressive Politics *by Dana Milbank* 79
Bush's political philosophy as governor was untouched by
Republican constituencies and that allowed him to implement his progressive way of thinking in the state government. Bush carried his ideals over into his bid for the presidency. In determining the issues for his campaign, Bush
repeatedly asked, "Is it good for America?"

Chapter 3: The Election of the Century

1. The Presidential Race *by Lee Edwards* 92
A review by political science standards compares how the
2000 presidential candidates George W. Bush and Al Gore
ran their campaigns. With Americans divided over the
proper role of government, neither candidate seemed to
dominate over the issues. As the race narrowed, the candidates spent millions of dollars keeping their messages current, yet in the end the race was not as close as it seemed.

2. The Predicted Tie
by James W. Ceaser and Andrew E. Busch 99
Political scientists had predicted for years that America's
electoral methods made a perfect tie conceivable. Partisan
faithfulness combined with disputes about accuracy of balloting machines and election laws in Florida created a see-
saw political battle that lasted five weeks past the election
date.

3. Victory at Last *by Andrew Phillips* 108
The presidency of George W. Bush began with a cloud of
controversy. Legal battles and ballot recounts in Florida
held up confirmation of the Bush victory. The election
over time challenged the legal system, the public's patience, and even the Constitution. In the end, the U.S.
Supreme Court concluded the drama and George W. Bush
became the forty-third president of the United States.

Chapter 4: The White House

1. The First Foreign Policy Test *by William Schneider* 117
The collision of a U.S. Navy spy plane and a Chinese fighter
jet in April 2001 became the first international policy test
for the Bush administration. China held twenty-four Americans hostage demanding that the United States issue a full
apology to the world. Bush implemented patience and economic pressure to defuse this potentially critical accident.

2. **Fulfilling Education Promises** *by Siobhan Gorman* 120
President Bush sent an early message to Congress that he
wanted a bipartisan education bill hammered out immediately. On just his second full day in office, Bush unveiled
his education blueprint. The policy implemented statewide
accountability systems that would withhold federal monies
if goals were not achieved.

3. **Resurrecting the Economy** *by Richard Cheney* 130
Taking office in the height of an economic recession, Bush
ran on a growth agenda, and then spent the first eighteen
months in office surviving a national emergency, war
abroad, and economic slowdown. Bush placed several
stimulants into the economy to facilitate long-term growth
including the largest tax cut of any U.S. president.

Chapter 5: Terrorism on American Soil

1. Terrorism Changes the Bush Presidency
by Robin Wright 140
The Bush presidency began with legislative and political
plans but became redefined with the terrorist attacks of
September 11, 2001. From this point on, Bush conditioned
Americans and the world for the ensuing war against terrorism. As he rallied a new coalition of support around the
world, global respect for Bush's leadership increased and
gave him a fresh start in foreign policy.

2. Terrorism Gives Bush a New Image
by Jeffrey H. Birnbaum 145
The tragedy that struck in New York and Washington on
September 11, 2001, gave George W. Bush his mission for
America. His ability to command under pressure gave him
new credibility as a leader. He banked on this image to
help him push his domestic policies as well as an international war on terrorism.

3. A Higher Calling *by Tony Carnes* 152
Bush's faith is a vital part of his politics yet, after the terrorist attacks in New York and Washington on September
11, 2001, Bush displayed a spiritual presence that bound
people of all faiths. Bush felt his new mission to eliminate
terrorism was not only a political duty but a divine calling.

Chapter 6: America at War

1. The Decision to Go to War *by Kenneth T. Walsh* 158
Soon after discovering that terrorists were behind the September 11 attacks, George W. Bush drew upon his powers
as the nation's commander in chief. Without hesitation, he
called America to war and began developing a strategy to
eliminate terrorist networks around the world.

2. **Bush's Battle Cry: Drawing on Prayer and a Sense of Personal Mission, W Becomes a War President** *by T. Trent Gegax* 163

After September 11, 2001, the battle against terrorism at home or abroad became the focus of the Bush administration. Bush called twenty-seven men of differing faiths to help him pray for divine help before addressing Congress and the world. Then George Bush defiantly vowed in God's name to lead the civilized world in a campaign against terror.

3. **Bush Commits to the Middle East** *by Michael Duffy* 169

After a year of disengagement with the Middle East, George W. Bush took an about-face and confronted the American risks of becoming involved in the peace process between Israel and the Palestinians. Bush addressed the nation and staked his presidency on helping to secure peace and stability in the Middle East.

4. **The Invasion of Iraq** *by Kenneth T. Walsh* 177

Bush made his case before the United Nations and the American people arguing that Iraq and its leader, Saddam Hussein, were in breech of a 1990 UN resolution to destroy its nuclear and chemical weapons. Bush vowed he would do whatever it took to eliminate these weapons and change Iraq's political regime.

Appendix of Documents 183

Discussion Questions 208

Chronology 211

For Further Research 214

Index 218

FOREWORD

In the vast and colorful pageant of human history, a handful of individuals stand out. They are the men and women who have come variously to be called "great," "leading," "brilliant," "pivotal," or "infamous" because they and their deeds forever changed their own society or the world as a whole. Some were political or military leaders—kings, queens, presidents, generals, and the like—whose policies, conquests, or innovations reshaped the maps and futures of countries and entire continents. Among those falling into this category were the formidable Roman statesman/general Julius Caesar, who extended Rome's power into Gaul (what is now France); Caesar's lover and ally, the notorious Egyptian queen Cleopatra, who challenged the strongest male rulers of her day; and England's stalwart Queen Elizabeth I, whose defeat of the mighty Spanish Armada saved England from subjugation.

Some of history's other movers and shakers were scientists or other thinkers whose ideas and discoveries altered the way people conduct their everyday lives or view themselves and their place in nature. The electric light and other remarkable inventions of Thomas Edison, for example, revolutionized almost every aspect of home-life and the workplace; and the theories of naturalist Charles Darwin lit the way for biologists and other scientists in their ongoing efforts to understand the origins of living things, including human beings.

Still other people who made history were religious leaders and social reformers. The struggles of the Arabic prophet Muhammad more than a thousand years ago led to the establishment of one of the world's great religions—Islam; and the efforts and personal sacrifices of an American reverend named Martin Luther King Jr. brought about major improvements in race relations and the justice system in the United States.

Each anthology in the People Who Made History series begins with an introductory essay that provides a general overview of the individual's life, times, and contributions. The group of essays that follow are chosen for their accessibility to a young adult audience and carefully edited in consideration of the reading and comprehension levels of that audience. Some of the essays are by noted historians, professors, and other experts. Others are excerpts from contemporary writings by or about the pivotal individual in question. To aid the reader in choosing the material of immediate interest or need, an annotated table of contents summarizes the article's main themes and insights.

Each volume also contains extensive research tools, including a collection of excerpts from primary source documents pertaining to the individual under discussion. The volumes are rounded out with an extensive bibliography and a comprehensive index.

Plutarch, the renowned first-century Greek biographer and moralist, crystallized the idea behind Greenhaven's People Who Made History when he said, "To be ignorant of the lives of the most celebrated men of past ages is to continue in a state of childhood all our days." Indeed, since it is people who make history, every modern nation, organization, institution, invention, artifact, and idea is the result of the diligent efforts of one or more individuals, living or dead; and it is therefore impossible to understand how the world we live in came to be without examining the contributions of these individuals.

GEORGE W. BUSH: AN APPOINTMENT WITH HISTORY

George W. Bush has been a strong leader in every aspect of his presidency. He has held history-making presidential approval ratings, healed a grieving nation through one of its darkest hours, led the world in a fight against terrorism, instigated the largest restructuring of government in seventy years, and proved to be a successful campaigner not only in his own election but in helping to garner Republican control of the House of Representatives and the U.S. Senate during his first midterm elections in 2002. For a man who almost did not become president, Bush has proved a powerhouse in office.

GROWING UP A BUSH

Growing up in the shadow of a successful family and spending most of his earlier years struggling to find his way, Bush learned to take advantage of the chances life offered and to approach situations placed before him not only analytically but with a dose of humor. An incredibly accomplished family history put a lot of pressure on Bush to develop within the family context. Although Bush states that his father, George H.W. Bush, never tried to shape him, he had to figure out where he was going and who he was outside of family expectations. Bush's heritage was saturated with Wall Street successes, politics, East Coast prep schools, and the military.

His paternal grandfather, Prescott Bush, was a U.S. senator and served on the boards at Yale, Pan American Airlines, CBS, Prudential Insurance, and Dresser Industries. His paternal grandmother's family developed a national dry goods business and one of the oldest and largest investment houses on Wall Street.

Bush's maternal heritage was in the publishing industry, and his father was a military hero. The elder Bush was successful in the oil business and in the political arena, serving as head of the Republican Party, an ambassador to China,

9

vice president, and the forty-first president of the United States. The weight of the family legacy was always present.

SEIZING OPPORTUNITIES

Bush's life has been shaped not only by high expectations but by personal tragedy as well. Bush's sister, Robin, died of leukemia when he was only seven years old. Her death helped him learn to live his life in chapters and seize opportunities as they came. Bush argues that the source of his personality is more than the scope of one or two events, yet close friends say his sister's death helped mold him and taught him to deal with a world driven by chance.

Bush's philosophy of seizing opportunities as they present themselves is oddly illustrated by a story about the family cat, Ernie. One night, when Bush was fifty-two years old and serving as governor of Texas, he thought his dog Spot had treed a squirrel and Bush went to investigate. According to Bush, in the tree

> was a scrawny, tiny kitty, which had somehow survived the streets of downtown Austin and ended up in a tree in the only backyard for miles, the backyard of the Governor's mansion. The kitty was skittish and afraid at first, but as food was put out the cat gradually warmed up. The kitty has six toes. Its paws look like baseball gloves and the Bush's named it Ernie because Ernest Hemingway had six-toed cats. Ernie became a member of the Bush family. The lesson of Ernie is, no matter what tough circumstances you find yourselves in, never give up. Ernie went from the streets of Austin to the Governor's mansion, all because a dog chased him into a tree.[1]

This philosophy to use every moment, seize opportunities, and make the most of what life offers describes how George W. Bush has tried to live his life.

EDUCATION

Bush's years at prep school and college helped him figure out his own path in life. At the age of fifteen, Bush left his free-spirited life in Texas to attend Phillips Academy, a New England prep school in Andover, Massachusetts. The academy was rigorous, competitive, and elite—quite a scary change for someone who had never left home. Bush, however, was following in his father's and grandfather's footsteps, a pattern he would adopt for much of his early adulthood.

At Phillips Academy, Bush was an average student, and a solid athlete, who played varsity basketball and baseball, but he was never the class star. His friends saw him as a self-assured, larger-than-life Texan and nicknamed him "Lip" because he had an opinion on everything.

When Bush graduated from Phillips Academy in 1964, he headed to Yale. He entered his freshman class as a "legacy," following a long line of Bush alumni. Elsie Walker, one of Bush's closest relatives and friends says he had bitter, uncomfortable moments at Yale. Walker explains, "It was awkward for him, as the son of his father, to be at Yale when there was so much antiwar and so much antiestablishment . . . and he comes from quite an establishment family. He felt real conflict and a real loyalty to his family, and I think it was hard to come from a prominent Republican family."[2] While his classmates were protesting the Vietnam War and the political establishment, Bush took the opposing view. He argued that if the United States was in a war, it should be supported by its citizens.

Bush embraced college, enjoying fraternity parties and football weekends. He was known for his ability to include others in social activities. His friends cite several examples of Bush reaching beyond his social circle to move effortlessly among different college cliques.

MILITARY

As Bush moved closer to graduating from Yale in 1968, his student deferment from military service in Vietnam was about to expire. Distinguished military careers dotted his family history and that of his friends, so twelve days before graduation, at the age of twenty-one, Bush registered with the Texas Air National Guard. During extensive interviews and a battery of tests, Bush told the commander of the 147th Fighter Group that he wanted to be a fighter pilot like his father. There were only ninety-eight officer slots when Bush enlisted, and seventy-two were already assigned. Out of the twenty-six that remained, only five were for pilots. These were assigned based on college degree and the candidate's performance on the written exams. Bush made the cut and headed for training at Moody Air Force Base in Georgia. There, he studied Morse code, aerodynamics, and physiology. In 1969 Bush earned his wings and headed back to Houston to fly night maneuvers as part of the Texas Air National Guard.

When Bush's commitment to the Texas Air National Guard

was completed in the early 1970s, he had not settled on a path in life. With the encouragement of a college friend, Bush applied to Harvard Business School. Bush said completing the application forced him to think about what he had accomplished and what he hoped to achieve. At the time, he was working with an inner-city poverty program known as Project PULL in Houston. Bush recalls,

My job gave me a glimpse of a world I had never seen. It was tragic, heartbreaking, and uplifting, all at the same time. I saw a lot of poverty. I also saw a lot of bad choices: drugs, alcohol abuse, men who had fathered children and walked away, leaving single mothers struggling to raise children on their own. I saw children who could not read and were way behind in school. I also saw good and decent people working to try to help lift these kids out of their terrible circumstances.[3]

When he received his acceptance letter to Harvard, he was not sure he wanted to give up his work at PULL. Bush's partner and mentor at PULL, John White, encouraged him to attend. "If you really care about these kids as much as I think you do, why don't you go and learn more and then you can really help."[4] So, in 1973, George W. Bush entered Harvard Business School to earn his master of business administration degree. Bush describes business school as a turning point.

By the time I arrived, I had had a taste of many different jobs but none of them had ever seemed to fit. I had worked as a management trainee for an agribusiness company in Houston, and worked in a couple of political campaigns. One summer I delivered mail and messages at a law firm; I spent another on the customer service and quote desk for a stockbroker. One summer I worked on a ranch, and another I rough necked on an offshore rig. It was hard, hot work. I unloaded enough of those heavy mud sacks to know that was not what I wanted to do with my life. . . . [Harvard] taught me the principles of capital, how it is accumulated, risked, spent and managed.[5]

In March of his final year at Harvard, Bush went to visit a friend in Midland, Texas. He recalls,

When you step outside in Midland, Texas, your horizons suddenly expand. The sky is huge. The land is flat, with not even the hint of a hill to limit the view. The air is clear and bright. Appropriately, "the sky is the limit" was the slogan in Midland when I arrived. It captured the sense of unlimited possibilities that you could almost feel and taste in the air. You can see as far as you want to see in Midland, and I could see a future. I could smell something happening. This is one of the

few places in the country where you can go without a portfolio and train yourself and become competitive. The barriers
to entry were very low.[6]

Bush was immediately inspired by the energy and entrepre-
neurship of the oil industry.

MIDLAND

Bush began his career in the oil business as a "landman" in
Midland. A landman reads the land records in a county
courthouse to determine who owns the mineral interests
that lie below a piece of property. A landman also determines whether the minerals are available for lease and, in
many cases, negotiates a lease for the rights. Bush states,

> I eventually learned to trade mineral and royalty interests
> with some of the $15,000 left over from an education fund my
> parents had set up. I began to invest in small pieces of drilling
> prospects. The first well I participated in was a dry hole. It
> was disappointing, but I knew the risks and had not gambled
> very much.[7]

As the energy business flourished during the late 1970s,
he built a small, solvent outfit of his own. "I formed my first
company, Arbusto (Spanish for Bush), to hold the mineral
and royalty interests I had begun trading. Eventually, Arbusto would become the general partner of the limited partnerships that I would form as an investment vehicle for
people to participate in the energy business.[8]

MARRIAGE

While Bush was in Midland running his business, Laura
Welch had come to Midland to visit her family. She was
working on a graduate degree in library science in nearby
Austin, Texas. Mutual friends introduced Bush and Welch in
the summer of 1977 at a dinner party. "The next night we all
went to play miniature golf and the next weekend I visited
Laura in Austin. I was scheduled to go to Maine to visit Mom
and Dad; I went and stayed one day, then flew back to Austin
to see Laura. That's when my mother said she knew I was
smitten,"[9] said Bush. Three months later, on November 5,
1977, they were married.

In 1978 Bush campaigned for Congress. "It turned out to
be a wonderful way to spend our first year of marriage. We
were united on a common mission; we spent lots of time together,"[10] Bush recalls. Friends came over to await election

returns. "As soon as the votes from Lubbock came in, I knew that I had lost,"[11] said Bush. Disappointed, he went back to work developing his energy company.

OIL

In 1979, oil prices surged as a result of the Arab oil embargo. Investors like Bush were lured by the high prices. Over the next three years Arbusto invested more than $3 million in U.S. wells. According to Bush, each of the partnerships were returning cash.

In 1982 Bush sold stock in his company to an investor. The capital bought oil and gas leases and enabled him to hire an engineer to oversee drilling operations, several geologists, a vice president of finance, and a landman. Arbusto became a fully operational oil company.

Bush was then introduced to the investors of Spectrum 7. They were "looking to expand with an operating company that could develop prospects and operate wells. I was looking for people who could help raise drilling capital. So the merger that took place in 1983 was a perfect fit."[12] Bush became the chief executive officer, running the business in Midland while the investors raised money and ran their other businesses.

The price of oil plummeted in late 1985 when the Organization of Petroleum Exporting Countries could not maintain discipline among its members and the oversupply of foreign crude made its way to the United States and began to affect oil prices. Midland suffered through its version of the 1929 stock market crash. Bush sought a buyer for his business. The chief investor, Harken Energy, was better able to wait out the crisis, and it wanted Bush's oil and gas reserves. Harken was also a publicly traded company. "We worked out a trade, our assets for Harken stock. This gave the investors in Spectrum 7 a saleable asset. I would serve on Harken's board of directors as a consultant to the company,"[13] Bush recalls. Once his business was sold, Bush took his family and moved to Washington, D.C., to participate in his father's campaign for president.

CAMPAIGNING WITH HIS FATHER

Lee Atwater, a political consultant known as the emerging prince of new politics, was chosen to run George H.W. Bush's campaign. Although Atwater was incredibly talented, he had ties to Bush's rivals for the Republican nomination, and George W. was not sure his father would be favorably served by him. Bush told Atwater, "In our family, if you go to war, we want you completely on our side." Atwater responded with the suggestion that changed young Bush's life: "If you're worried about me, join the team and keep an eye on me."[14] Bush did just that.

He was put in the thick of the campaign, monitoring not just Atwater's activities but also everyone else who worked for his father. "I was a loyalty enforcer and a listening ear,"[15] Bush says, describing his work. He was instrumental in bridging political gaps between the Republican Party and political interest groups. Bush met with everyone from environmentalists to evangelicals and was the liaison for governors, mayors, influential fundraisers, and anyone who needed special attention. He never left a room until everyone was satisfied. Bush was a sounding board, assessor of problems, and a general morale booster. He reminded everyone that their job was to get his father elected, but once his father was in office, he headed back to Texas.

THE RANGERS

When Bush returned to Texas in 1980, he heard about the sale of the Texas Rangers baseball team. "I began reading speculation in the newspapers. Television station owner Ed Gaylord might buy the Texas Rangers; a group of Florida investors was interested. And so was I. If they were selling, I was buying. Of course, I had more determination than money." Bush met with the owner, Eddie Chiles, to convince Chiles to sell him the team if he could come up with the investors. Bush assembled a group of friends that merged with a few Dallas, Texas, businessmen, and a partnership agreement was arranged. "Once all the investors received their original money back, plus a 2 percent return, they would split 85 percent of any profits." One of the partners, Rusty Rose, and Bush were to share in the day-to-day management of the partnership and split the remaining 15 percent of profits,"[16] says Bush. "A lifelong baseball fan, I was about to own a baseball team. I remember thinking, 'This is as good as it gets. Life cannot be better than this.'"[17]

Bush's role as general managing partner of the Texas Rangers became his political springboard. It publicized him, demonstrated that he could manage a complex organization,

and gave him financial independence. Fans sought his autograph as eagerly as they did the players'. Baseball made
Bush a regular guy, not a president's son from Yale or Harvard, but a neighbor cheering on a ball club with his family.

Those who worked with Bush said he had an uncanny
ability to hire the right people and to create consensus and
contentment among peers and subordinates.

His most significant achievement as managing partner of
the Rangers was getting the Arlington taxpayers to agree to
pay for two-thirds of a new stadium for the team. He sold the
stadium to the public by speaking at rallies and on television. Bush helped create a desirable image for the Rangers,
pitching season ticket sales and corporate sponsors and
even winning over the media by building the press boxes at
club level. Bush insisted that the Rangers would not have
good reviews if they did not have great press boxes. His gift
for public relations vastly improved not only the team's image but also its profits.

While his mother was the first lady of the United States,
Bush invited her to attend an evening at the ballpark as his
guest to throw out the first pitch of the game. Barbara Bush
later wrote in her memoirs,

> We started with a reception for the wives of the players, wives
> of the owners and some key women in the management. We
> had pictures taken and everyone was darling. On to the game
> and I was so excited. George knew every living human, al-
> most seemed like all 38,000! He introduced me to the "best
> grounds keeping in the major leagues," the "finest ticket-taker
> in any park," and the "fastest hot dog vendor." He knew them
> all. He had Reading Is Fundamental [RIF] posters everywhere
> and gave tickets to kids participating in the RIF program and
> handed out bookmarks with Texas Rangers on one side and
> RIF on the other to every single person who came. The ball I
> was to throw out had been signed by all the players and by the
> coach. Below their names they put their favorite books.[18]

George W. Bush says, "For five years, Laura and I went to
fifty or sixty home games a year. We'd talk about baseball,
about our girls, about life. It was a time of family and friends.
Our girls grew up at the ballpark."[19] Commenting that baseball was a great training ground for politics and government,
Bush states, "The bottom line in baseball is results: wins and
losses. We succeeded in baseball because we had a vision
and a message. I learned to overlook minor setbacks and focus on the long haul. I would find those skills invaluable in
my campaigns and tenure as Governor of Texas."[20]

GOVERNOR BUSH

At a political rally in 1993, Bush was introducing Kay Bailey Hutchison, a friend who was running for the Senate. As Bush walked onstage, the crowd started hollering, "Run for governor" and "Governor Bush." Worried about how Texas schools were governed, crime—especially juvenile crime—and the state's business climate, Bush was interested in the idea. He said his wife, Laura, knowing how much he enjoyed their life in baseball, was surprised over the course of the next few months "when all I could talk about was how I wanted to change Texas and become its Governor."[21]

Bush turned out to be a tireless and nearly flawless campaigner when he ran for governor of Texas against the popular incumbent, Ann Richards. She derided Bush as "Shrub," claiming he was just running on his father's name, but voters saw Bush as a substantial candidate and elected him with nearly 54 percent of the vote.

As the chief executive in Texas, Bush let political appointees do their jobs and intervened only when he saw a problem. He had a bold education agenda implementing a controversial plan to end social promotion. It required children to pass reading and math tests in fifth grade and reading, math, and writing tests in the eighth grade.

At his urging, legislators toughened educational standards, and the juvenile justice code. Under his guidance, the legislature passed welfare reform and the largest tax cut in Texas history. Employment increased while juvenile crime and welfare rolls decreased. According to November 1996 statistics, while other states were struggling, Texas had a growing economy and Bush's fiscal stewardship as governor had left a billion dollars in surplus funds in the state budget. Bush saw this as a down payment toward a fundamental tax-cut package.

One of the most controversial issues Bush faced as governor was the decision to uphold the death penalty. Many executions took place during his tenure as governor, including the execution of the first woman in more than twenty years. "Some advocates of life will challenge why I oppose abortion yet support the death penalty; to me, it's the difference between innocence and guilt,"[22] Bush says.

During the reelection campaign for his second term as governor, Bush recalls, he "couldn't get on an elevator or walk through the back of a hotel kitchen on the way to make a speech without someone saying, 'Governor, please run for President.' The question had become a distraction, interfering with my attempts to deliver any other message."²³

Bush finished his reelection campaign uncertain of whether he would seek the presidency. "It might have affected some votes, but overall, I think most of my fellow Texans were proud to have their Governor considered a potential president."²⁴ Bush became the first governor elected to two consecutive four-year terms in the history of Texas.

Once reelection was behind Bush, the pressure to make a decision about seeking the presidency mounted as the deadline to enter the race neared. He worried about exposing his family to a national stage. On the other hand he felt the country was at a critical moment in history.

A DEFINING MOMENT

During a private prayer service with the Bush family for his second gubernatorial inauguration, Bush's hesitations about running for president were overcome during a twenty-minute speech by Pastor Mark Craig. Craig spoke on the hunger of people for faithfulness and honesty in government. He retold the biblical story of Moses, who was asked by God to lead his people to a land of milk and honey. Moses had a lot of reasons to shirk the task. As the pastor told it, Moses' basic reaction was, "Sorry, God, I'm busy. I've got a family. I've got sheep to tend. I've got a life. Send some other person. But God did not and Moses ultimately did his bidding."²⁵ Craig added that people were starved for leaders with ethical and moral courage who would do what is right for the right reasons even if it was not easy or convenient. Later Bush's mother told George that the pastor had been talking about him. Bush responded to her that Craig was calling on everyone to use what power they had to do good for the right reason, but he acknowledged that the sermon had spoken directly to his heart. Bush felt that Craig was personally challenging him to do more. With this conviction, Bush began his national campaign to be president:

> I know that I am seeking an awesome responsibility. I know that serving as Governor of Texas is not anywhere near the same as being President. But if Texas were a nation, it would be the eleventh-largest economy in the world. I've had some success, and I've learned to lead. You cannot lead by dividing people. I am a uniter, not a divider. My campaign will be positive, hopeful and inclusive. I want to show that politics, after

a time of tarnished ideals, can be higher and better, I hope to give our country a fresh start after a season of cynicism.[26]

FAITH IS THE MAN

Bush believes that religious faith changes lives, and he credits his faith with teaching him humility and giving him focus and perspective. Realizing that his faith could be misinterpreted in the political process, Bush said that he tries to live out his faith rather than flaunt it.

In 1986, while the Bushes were on summer vacation in Maine, the Reverend Billy Graham visited them. Bush says he knew he was in the presence of a great man because he could see the Lord reflected in Graham's demeanor. Bush credits Graham with leading him to a path of faith. "It was the beginning of a change in my life. I had always been a religious person, but that weekend my faith took on new meaning. It was the beginning of a new walk where I would recommit my heart to Jesus Christ."[27]

According to Bush, his life is built on a foundation of faith that does not shift. This faith also gives him the freedom to fail. "I believe in a divine plan that supersedes all human plans. My faith frees me to put the problem of the moment in proper perspective and frees me to make decisions that others might not like. It frees me to do the right thing."[28]

THE RUN FOR PRESIDENT

In 1999, as Bush began his presidential race, one of the problems he wanted to fix was the glimpse of hopelessness he saw in the national soul:

> We live in the greatest and freest and most prosperous nation in the world, yet too many of our citizens do not believe their lives have meaning or value. The American dream is a distant offer meant for somebody else. Many people do not believe the fundamentally American conviction that you can be what you want to be and achieve what you want to achieve, so long as you are willing to work hard and earn it. This gap of hope is found in the poverty of our inner cities, where neighborhoods have become urban war zones, a world of barred windows and gang violence and failed schools, a world of shattered glass and shattered dreams. We see glimpses of this hopelessness in schoolyards where children inexplicably, tragically, horrifically murder other children.

> I worry that we are being divided into two nations, separate and unequal: one nation with the tools and confidence to

seek the American dream; another nation that is being left behind. We risk becoming two societies; one that reads and one that can't, one that dreams and one that doesn't.[29]

This was the message of Bush's presidential campaign. Bush supported individual accountability, believing that Americans are a single, moral community with obligations to each other, not a society dependent on more government programs as the answer.

Bush ran his presidential race with this conviction and held the lead in the campaign until just before the Democratic National Convention. At the time, opponent Al Gore's lead went up and did not come down until late September when the presidential debates took place. Postdebate polls reported that the American people thought Gore presented a different image of himself at each debate and came across as divisive. This propelled Bush back to the front of the race until the week before the election on November 7, when Gore made a push for the win. The indecision of the American people seemed to strengthen, with neither candidate holding a strong lead. As election day drew closer, more states appeared undecided.

FIVE WEEKS TO VICTORY

Of the dramatic seesaw contest, reporter Jamie Dettmer observed,

> Election day started badly for the Bush campaign. The GOP's [Republicans'] morning exit polls looked ugly and reports of high turnouts in the battleground states of the Northeast and Midwest revived fears about the black vote, (historically strong in the Democratic camp) turning out in droves.

> Midday brought relief, say Bush campaign sources. The exit polls started to swing their way and by mid-afternoon, they believed they were ahead in several of the battleground states. Bush and Gore had insatiable last minute campaign appearances, making calls to radio stations, and urging voters to turn out.[30]

By the end of the day, once the polls had closed and actual results began to be reported, two phone conversations took place between Bush and Gore. The first was placed by Gore to concede the race, but a second call from Gore retracted the concession explaining that the state of Florida was too close to call and there would need to be a recount.

Historically close elections have been defined in several ways: by the difference between the candidates in the national popular vote, by their difference in the electoral vote, and by the difference in popular votes that would actually have changed the election outcome. The 2000 election seemed to challenge all three.

This would be the fourth time in American history when a presidential election entered into a disputed phase after initial ballot counts. The outcomes of the previous contests, however, were not determined by a court of law as in the 2000 election. Gore stayed active in the postelection campaign, pushing the election results to be played out in the judiciary system. The Bush campaign preferred the Florida legislature. It was going to take Florida's electoral votes to swing the election one way or another. Additionally, disputes over election inconsistencies in Florida clouded the vote totals. In the end, after a historical five-week battle through political, state, and federal processes, the U.S. Supreme Court upheld the original Bush victory in Florida, making him the forty-third president of the United States.

BUSH'S FIRST YEAR IN OFFICE

Bush spent much of his first few weeks in office implementing his campaign agenda: courting a Democratic-controlled legislature to advance a $1.6 million tax cut. He introduced his education reform bill and his Patient's Bill of Rights for congressional approval.

Surrounding himself with seasoned staff members and one of the most experienced national security teams in the history of the presidency, Bush faced his first foreign policy crisis just three months after he entered the office. In April 2001 an American surveillance plane and a Chinese fighter collided over China. The American surveillance plane made an emergency landing in China, and the Chinese government refused to release the twenty-four grounded Americans. For ten days China held the hostages and demanded an apology from the United States for the incident and for the death of its fighter pilot. The Bush administration took an uncompromising stance, avoided a concession for the surveillance, apologized for the Chinese pilot's death, and used economic interests to negotiate the return of the hostages. Once the China incident was resolved, Bush went back to managing the national agenda, focusing on his education reform package until terrorist attacks on U.S. soil redefined his presidency.

A WARTIME PRESIDENT

On September 11, 2001, as Bush was reading to a group of kindergartners to promote his education reform package, he received a message that both of the World Trade Center towers in New York had been hit by airplanes. Later that same morning, he would join the nation to hear of two other terrorist attacks involving airplane crashes: one into the Pentagon and one diverted to Pennsylvania that was believed to be headed for the White House. America was in shock and grieved the loss of those killed during the attacks. Overnight, these incidents handed Bush a mission as the leader of the free world in a war against terrorism.

To heal the nation, Bush made a strong presence at the rubble of the World Trade Center and the Pentagon disaster areas. He organized a National Day of Prayer and Remembrance for the victims of the tragedy during which he delivered a moving and healing speech to the nation. He also stood before the nation to accept worldwide condolences to the American people and vowed retaliation for these terrorist attacks. Bush's visibility and leadership during the aftermath of the attacks helped him achieve and maintain the highest presidential approval ratings ever recorded. Writing for *Presidential Studies Quarterly*, Fred Greenstein noted that a Gallup poll completed a day before the terrorist strikes found only "51 percent of the public expressed approval of his presidential performance. Three days after the attacks, Gallup fielded the first of an extended run of polls in which Bush registered approval levels in excess of 85 percent."[51]

A major challenge for Bush after September 11, 2001, was to respond to the urgent need to protect America. He chose to model a new Homeland Security office after the National Security Council. The Security Council was a White House department responsible for coordinating the various operating agencies and getting them to work as a team. Bush put a good friend, Tom Ridge, governor of Pennsylvania, in charge. Creating this office was the largest reorganization of the federal government in seventy years.

Additionally, as a president called into war, Bush made specific demands of Afghanistan. Bush stipulated that terrorist training camps be closed; leaders of al-Qaeda, a religious terrorist group behind the September 11 attacks, be turned over to authorities; and illegally detained foreign nationals be released. When these demands were not met, Bush ordered military campaigns against al-Qaeda terrorist training camps and military installations of the Taliban regime.

Bush argued that his actions were justified in a world in which the moral choice was obvious. "Every nation, in every region, now has a decision to make. Either you are with us or you are with the terrorists,"[52] Bush declared on September 20. Three months later, in December 2001, the Taliban was gone and Afghanistan was stable enough to install an interim form of government in which its 26 million people would have the opportunity to be politically represented.

THE WAR AGAINST IRAQ

One year after the terrorist attacks, Bush addressed the nation and reminded Americans that September 11, 2001, was a milestone passed but that the mission against terrorism would go on. The next day, at the General Assembly of the United Nations (UN), Bush asked the world to unite and end the danger posed by Saddam Hussein of Iraq. As a condition to end the Persian Gulf War in 1991, Iraqi leadership pledged to reveal and destroy all weapons of mass destruction, cease repression of its people, renounce all involvement with terrorism, and prove its compliance through rigorous inspections. Bush claimed that Hussein had broken every aspect of these promises and had shown contempt for the UN by ignoring his previous commitments to the world. Bush further argued that twelve years of defiance by the Iraqi regime to the 1991 UN resolutions was a threat to peace. He asked the UN to require the Iraqi regime to honor its previous commitments as a sign of accountability. "If Iraq's regime defies us again, the world must move deliberately, decisively to hold Iraq to account. . . . The purposes of the United States should not be doubted. The Security Council resolution will be enforced—the just demands of peace and security met— or action will be unavoidable."[53]

Bush also claimed that Iraq was building and hiding weapons that would enable Hussein to dominate the Middle East and intimidate the civilized world, stating further that the safety of America depended on ending Hussein's direct and growing threat. "We must stand up for our security and for the permanent rights and the hopes of mankind. By heritage and by choice, the United States of America will make that stand."[54]

Before the United Nations would honor Bush's request

and vote for a military solution, it decided to give Hussein one final chance to disarm. A new team of inspectors was sent into Iraq to perform weapons inspections and determine Iraq's compliance.

For four and a half months the United States and its allies worked with the Security Council to enforce its twelve-year-old demands. In the interim, while weapons inspectors worked in Iraq, Bush was rallying an international coalition to help disarm the Iraqi regime militarily. Acknowledging Hussein's threat to world security, the U.S. House and Senate authorized President Bush the use of military force in Iraq if it became necessary.

On March 16, 2003, the Security Council extended compliance deadlines for the Iraqi regime. Frustrated with UN inaction, Bush and allied countries held a summit in the Azores as a last resort for a political solution to this conflict. Feeling every measure to avoid war had been taken, Bush gave Hussein forty-eight hours to leave Iraq. Three days later, Bush ordered the coalition forces of forty countries to begin military action in Iraq.

People from around the world argued that this was a historical operation, claiming the United States had never participated in a preemptive attack on another nation. But Bush's presidency had been filled with historical records: a president whose father had also been president, a historical post-election campaign and victory, organizing the most experienced presidential staff ever assembled, implementing the largest tax cut and educational restructuring in American history, survival of the most tragic terrorist attacks on American soil, and the establishment of a Homeland Security Department, and leading his first midterm elections in 2002 to usher in the strongest change in political power in the House of Representatives and the U.S. Senate since the formation of America. Bush continued to seize opportunities and lead America with courage through challenging times during his appointment with history.

NOTES

1. George W. Bush, *A Charge to Keep*. New York: William Morrow, 1999, p. 89.
2. Quoted in Bill Minutaglio, *First Son George W. Bush and the Bush Family Dynasty*. New York: Random House, 1999, pp. 107–108.
3. Bush, *A Charge to Keep*, p. 58.

4. Bush, *A Charge to Keep*, p. 59.
5. Bush, *A Charge to Keep*, p. 60.
6. Bush, *A Charge to Keep*, p. 56.
7. Bush, *A Charge to Keep*, p. 62.
8. Bush, *A Charge to Keep*, p. 62.
9. Bush, *A Charge to Keep*, p. 80.
10. Bush, *A Charge to Keep*, p. 82.
11. Bush, *A Charge to Keep*, p. 82.
12. Bush, *A Charge to Keep*, p. 63.
13. Bush, *A Charge to Keep*, p. 64.
14. Bush, *A Charge to Keep*, p. 179.
15. Bush, *A Charge to Keep*, p. 180.
16. Bush, *A Charge to Keep*, p. 199.
17. Bush, *A Charge to Keep*, p. 198.
18. Barbara Bush, *A Memoir.* New York: Charles Scribner's Sons, 1994, pp. 290–91.
19. Bush, *A Charge to Keep*, p. 206.
20. Bush, *A Charge to Keep*, p. 208.
21. Bush, *A Charge to Keep*, p. 26.
22. Bush, *A Charge to Keep*, p. 147.
23. Bush, *A Charge to Keep*, p. 223.
24. Bush, *A Charge to Keep*, p. 224.
25. Bush, *A Charge to Keep*, p. 8.
26. Bush, *A Charge to Keep*, p. 241.
27. Bush, *A Charge to Keep*, p. 136.
28. Bush, *A Charge to Keep*, p. 6.
29. Bush, *A Charge to Keep*, p. 136.
30. Jamie Dettmer, "A Wild and Crazy Election Night," *Insight on the News*, December 4, 2000.
31. Fred Greenstein, "The Contemporary Presidency: The Changing Leadership of George W. Bush: A Pre- and Post-9/11 Comparison," *Presidential Studies Quarterly*, June 2002.
32. George W. Bush, speech to the nation, September 20, 2001. www.whitehouse.gov.
33. George W. Bush, speech to the United Nations, September 12, 2002. www.whitehouse.gov.
34. Bush, speech to the United Nations.

CHAPTER 1

EARLY INFLUENCES

GEORGE W. BUSH

Midland Influence

Nicholas D. Kristof

Steeped in optimism and embedded with values, the community of Midland, Texas, gave George W. Bush life lessons and a character that brought him to the White House. He has commented that if you want to understand him, you must understand the attitude of Midland. Midland offered Bush a world of right and wrong, dreams, opportunity, respect for tradition, faith, and the acceptance of risk as a way of life. Self-reliance was also a part of the community's character. When the people of Midland needed a theater or hospital they worked hard to raise the funds themselves without governmental help or intrusion. Because of the lifestyle growing up in Midland provided, Bush believes that people can do anything if they work hard enough. Nicholas D. Kristof, a staff writer for the *New York Times*, explores this foundational period and how it shaped George W. Bush in the following article from May 2000.

Many of the roots of Mr. Bush's political philosophy as a presidential candidate . . . seem to go back to his childhood. Midland, a conservative, up-from-the-bootstraps town that has grown from 25,000 when he was a little boy to almost 100,000 today, mirrors Mr. Bush's optimism, his faith in business and his doubts about an activist government. While playing Little League baseball, running for class president, or even sobbing in the principal's office, George W. Bush absorbed West Texas values that many old friends say are central to understanding who he is today.

"I think his political philosophy comes completely from the philosophy of the independent oil man," said Joe O'Neill, a fellow rapscallion in childhood. "His homage to his parents, his respect for his elders, his respect for tradition, his belief in religion, his opposition to abortion—that's the philosophy he grew up with here."

Nicholas D. Kristof, "A Boy from Midland: A Philosophy with Roots in Conservative Texas Soil," *New York Times*, May 21, 2000. Copyright © 2000 by New York Times Company. Reproduced by permission.

Mr. Bush himself, in a long interview about his roots, made a similar point. "I don't know what percentage of me is Midland," he said, "but I would say people, if they want to understand me, need to understand Midland and the attitude of Midland."

It is in the soil of Midland that Mr. Bush has said he would like to be buried when he dies, and it was to Midland that he returned in the 1970's to marry and start a family. It gave him an anchor in real America.

AN ORDINARY UPBRINGING

Mr. Bush has often said that "the biggest difference between me and my father is that he went to Greenwich Country Day and I went to San Jacinto Junior High." That may be an exaggeration of the younger Mr. Bush's populist credentials, because he is also a product of Andover, Yale and Harvard. But there is still something to it.

The father, chauffeured to and from private school in Connecticut in a black sedan, suffered politically because of the perception that he was a blue blood who could not relate to ordinary people. The younger Mr. Bush also has been tainted by the idea that he was born into privilege with a visa to effortless wealth and prominence. Yet George W. Bush actually had a rather ordinary childhood, and his years biking around small-town streets in jeans and a white T-shirt left him with a common touch that is among his greatest assets as a politician.

"He understands Bubba because there is more Bubba in him," Karl Rove, the longtime political adviser to the Bushes, told a reporter in 1992, when Mr. Bush's friends were still carefree enough to say colorful things about him. "He is clearly the wild son—even today. Part of it is rooted in Midland, where he grew up in an ordinary neighborhood, where houses are close together and risk was a way of life.". . .

Midland, impatient with ideas and introspection, was a world of clear rights and wrongs, long on absolutes and devoid of ethical gray shades. It may be the source of some of Mr. Bush's greatest political strengths, the unpretentiousness and mellow bonhomie that warm up voters, and also of his weaknesses, including an image of an intellectual lightweight that is underscored whenever he mixes up the likes of Slovenia and Slovakia. . . .

A CONSERVATIVE TOWN

Oil made Midland a boomtown, attracting ambitious businessmen like the elder Mr. Bush and many other out-of-staters as well. These people made for a conservative town but not a redneck one; Midland had a large proportion of geologists, engineers, lawyers and accountants, and Ivy League college graduates were everywhere.

Mr. Bush recalls it in Norman Rockwell pastels, and so do many other residents. Children bicycled everywhere on their own, crime was almost nonexistent and if anyone suspicious—say, someone with a beard—showed up in town, then-Sheriff Ed Darnell (known as Big Ed) would stop him, escort him to the edge of town, and tell him to "get out."

Yet what no one volunteers is that it was also rigidly segregated in those days, like most places in the South. Black children went to their own school rather than to Sam Houston Elementary with George Bush. The bus station and train station had separate waiting rooms for blacks and whites, and there were separate, dilapidated drinking fountains marked "colored" at the stations and at the courthouse.

The Bushes' first encounter with West Texas racism came when they casually invited a black man, working for the National Association for the Advancement of Colored People, to come by their temporary home in neighboring Odessa. The man had the tact to stay away, but neighbors heard about this and warned the elder George Bush to stop these invitations unless he wanted to be tarred and feathered.

Racial slurs were routine, and young George picked up the words from neighbors. Once when he was about 7 years old he used one in the living room in front of his mother, Barbara.

Michael Proctor, who lived across the street and was playing with George at the time, remembers watching as Mrs. Bush grabbed her son by the ear and dragged him into the bathroom. She washed his mouth out with soap as he spluttered indignantly.

"His family was probably the only one around that didn't use racial slurs," Mr. Proctor said. "I probably didn't realize it was wrong until I saw that."

Alongside the racism directed at blacks, there was a measured respect for the Mexicans who came over the border to work in the oil fields. As a boomtown, Midland needed laborers and welcomed Mexican immigrants, who were regarded as hard-working and thrifty. Some old friends find an echo of that attitude in Mr. Bush's efforts to push the Republican Party to reach out to immigrants.

"We saw these people cross the border and just wanting a good job," recalls Randall Roden, a neighbor boy and best friend. Mr. Roden recalls going out with George and his father to an oil well and spending the night sleeping in the back of the Bushes' station wagon as the crew—Mexicans among them—struggled to get the well going.

"I formed the very strong impression, and I think George has the same one, that these people came for economic opportunity and worked very hard," Mr. Roden said. "If you wanted a Mexican worker to have a new pair of boots, you'd have to buy it for him. Because if you gave him money, he'd send it home."

GAINING A FOOTHOLD IN TEXAS

George W. Bush, though born in 1946 in New Haven, Conn., while his father was still an over-achieving student at Yale, moved to West Texas when he was not quite 2 and grew up in this nurturing environment. These days, as the son of a president and scion of a wealthy family, he is often perceived as a child of privilege, but neighbors in those days insist that in the 1950's that was not the case.

The Bush family in the Northeast had money, but the elder George left all that behind to make his own fortune in West Texas. Equipped with connections but initially without seed money, George and Barbara Bush and little George, their firstborn, settled in a tiny apartment in the hard-driving oil town of Odessa, where they shared a bathroom with a mother-daughter team of prostitutes living next door.

Local people say that you raise hell in Odessa but raise a family in nearby Midland, a much more respectable place. So, after a one-year interlude in California, the Bushes moved to Midland, living in a bright blue 847-square-foot bungalow on a newly built street in which every home was identical—but painted bright colors to make them seem different. It was called Easter Egg Row, because the houses looked like colored eggs.

The family prospered in the oil business and moved into a series of nicer houses in Midland, culminating in one with a swimming pool. But this was not as much of a draw as it might have been. Just down the street lived Peggy Porter, one of the cutest girls in school, and because she had a pool as well, it was in much greater demand than the Bush family's. Occasionally George W.'s grandfather, Senator Prescott S. Bush of Connecticut, would visit and cause a mild stir of interest in the neighborhood. But for the most part, the Bush family was regarded as fairly typical of the out-of-staters. . . .

Young George was not some country hick, and he also learned to fit into the world of his Connecticut grandparents. The family regularly spent part of the summer at the family retreat in Kennebunkport, Me., and in 1954 the father took George and his best friend, Randall Roden, to Washington to see the White House, the United States Capitol and a baseball game with the Washington Senators (whose later incarnation would move to Texas and become the Rangers, owned in part by George W. Bush).

They had lunch at the senator's home in Georgetown, and a thirsty Randall promptly demonstrated the distance from Midland to Georgetown by drinking from his finger bowl.

When they are tracked down, the boys and girls who once played dodgeball at Sam Houston Elementary School, while now scattered around the country, offer recollections that are very similar: Midland was an idyllic place in which to grow up, and George W. Bush was a very typical child. In contrast to other recent presidential candidates, Mr. Bush in childhood is remarkable primarily for his ordinariness. . . .

As a boy, Mr. Bush's ambition was to be another Mickey Mantle.

"All George ever wanted to be was a Major League baseball player," recalled a buddy, Terry Throckmorton. "That's all he ever talked about."

A STUDENT OF BASEBALL

No one has ever accused Mr. Bush of being an intellectual, and the indifference to books started early. Childhood friends recall Mr. Bush reading only two sets of books for pleasure—the Hardy boys and a series of mystery books about baseball. As one asks about his reading habits, there are a few snickers.

"Did we sit around in those days reading books?" asked Mr. McCleskey, smiling broadly. "No."

George and Barbara Bush led a drive to build a school library (the school did not previously have one), but books were not a major part of a boy's childhood in Midland. Erstwhile acquaintances, while deeply admiring of the Bushes' goodness and decency, have trouble recalling early signs of greatness in the son.

"Well, no, I never did think about what he might do in life," said Austine Crosby, his third-grade teacher. "He was just a good, well-rounded young man, and he did his work." And academically? "He was O.K.," Mrs. Crosby said, a bit defensively. "He was O.K."

So was he in the top quarter of his class academically?

"Well, in the upper half, anyway."

Even if he did not distinguish himself as a student, former classmates describe him as smart and blessed with an excellent memory. He had a passion for baseball statistics, a first-rate collection of baseball cards and a reputation as such a shrewd trader that boys were careful not to agree to a trade with George Bush without thinking it over very carefully.

In the mid-1950's, George came up with a scheme that showed remarkable ingenuity and helped make his collection of baseball cards the best around. He began sending baseball cards to famous players, enclosing return postage and a cheery good-luck message, and asking the players to autograph the cards and send them back.

This way, he got autographed cards from Mickey Mantle, Willie Mays and other famous players. Some of those cards are now worth thousands of dollars.

Mr. Bush's lifelong adoration of baseball began when he and other neighborhood boys would go early to school to play ball. Mr. Bizilo, the principal, would take off his jacket, loosen his tie and hit balls for the boys to field.

George was a good ballplayer, friends say, a bit on the small side but making up for it with enthusiasm and aggressiveness. He played catcher for the Cubs, a Little League team, and made it to the town's Little League All-Star team. . . .

BECOMING A TEXAN

"There's an assurance that you have growing up in a place like Midland, a self-confidence and a real genuine interest in connecting with people," said Marge Petty, the other politician in the group (a Democratic state senator in Kansas).

In particular, it was in Midland that Mr. Bush first learned to fit in, even if his parents were Yankees and his grandfather a senator. That ability to adapt and bridge groups has never left him.

Moreover, Midland values were remarkably unshaken by the 1960's. Some Midland alumni say they let their hair grow a bit longer, but—like George W. Bush—they mostly stood with the establishment instead of rejecting it. Very few seem to have protested significantly against the Vietnam War, seriously used drugs, thought of police as "pigs," denounced their parents as oppressors or picked up a copy of [philosopher Karl Marx's] *Das Kapital.*

"It's a town of embedded values," Mr. Bush recalled, adding that it had "a heavy dose of individualism and fairly healthy disrespect for government." Asked if his own skepticism about the role for government is a product of Midland attitudes, Mr. Bush paused and finally nodded, saying: "I think there's a parallel there, I do."

Midland was steeped in optimism, and for many people growing up here in the 1950's, the moral of childhood was that the system worked, that anyone who struggled enough in that baking desert had a good chance of finding oil and striking it rich. The trajectory of the Bush family itself, from the apartment with the shared bathroom to the sprawling house and pool, underscored the point.

"The lesson lasted with George W. for years," said Bill Minutaglio, a Texan who has written a biography of Mr. Bush. "I think he truly believes that people can win the lottery if they work hard, that if they put their nose to the grindstone it'll all work out without government help or intrusion."

The antipathy for government seems a little odd, from afar, because in those days the oil business depended heavily on quirks in the tax code to encourage investments. Still, when the people of Midland sought a theater, a hospital and a new baseball diamond, they did not ask the government but raised money themselves and turned out on the weekends to do much of the work on their own.

When Mr. Bush talks about "compassionate conservatism" or "faith-based initiatives," he evokes what old classmates remember as the spirit of Midland of the 1950's. Asked if that is what he has in mind, Mr. Bush interrupts half-way through the question. "Yeah, absolutely," he said.

Those who know Midland are convinced that Mr. Bush is sincere when he preaches compassion and calls for a "responsibility era." But some also admit that it is fair to question the relevance of lessons from a town where raw capitalism made so many people rich and where community spirit wove such a strong safety net. . . .

Mr. Bush's political debut appears to have come in the seventh grade, although both he and his wife, Laura, (who was in the same seventh grade but barely knew him) say they have no recollection of it. Classmates recall that he ran for seventh-grade class president against Jack Hanks. . . .

George was elected by a narrow margin.

"I voted for George because he was cuter," recalled Peggy Porter Weiss, "and in the seventh grade that's what counted."

Tragedy Binds Mother and Son

George Lardner Jr. and Lois Romano

The death of his younger sister helped deepen a powerful link between Bush and his mother. According to his brother Marvin, Bush was intuitive and spontaneous, yet when his four-year-old sister Robin died of leukemia, it became necessary for Bush to fill life with humor. Bush made it his personal responsibility to make his mother and father smile again, using his outspokenness and wit to heal his grieving parents. In the following essay from 1999, George Lardner Jr. and Lois Romano portray Bush with his father's looks and his mother's spirit. As a mother deeply involved in her son's development, Lardner and Romano describe the powerful influence Barbara Bush had on her eldest son. Both writers are staff writers on the political team for the *Washington Post*.

On a fall day in 1953, George and Barbara Bush drove their green Oldsmobile up the gravel driveway at Sam Houston Elementary School in Midland, Texas, looking for their oldest child. George W. Bush and a friend from second grade were lugging a Victrola from their classroom to the principal's office when he spotted his parents' car. He was sure his little sister was in the back seat.

"He went running back to the teacher and said, 'I've got to go. My mother and father and Robin are here,'" Barbara Bush, the former first lady, recalled in a recent interview.

"I run over to the car," said George W., remembering the same moment, "and there's no Robin."

"That's when we told him," his mother said. "In the car."

Two days earlier, Pauline Robinson Bush—"Robin"—had died in New York of leukemia, two months shy of her fourth birthday. Her big brother had known she was sick but never dreamed she was dying. "Why didn't you tell me?" Bush repeatedly asked his parents, and for years the question would resonate in the Bush family.

INDELIBLE SCARS

At age 7, Bush found himself surrounded by bewildering grief. His parents were not even 30 years old, trying to move past a devastating loss while raising George W. and his baby brother Jeb.

The death left indelible scars on the Bushes. Barbara Bush still has trouble talking about her daughter's death. Her husband would cite the experience when he ran for president and was asked if he had ever known hardship. George W.'s eyes welled with tears when discussing his sister in an interview in May [1999].

A child's death reverberates in a family in unexpected ways. For the Bushes, among other consequences, the loss of Robin helped to establish and deepen an enduring and powerful link between Barbara Bush and her oldest son. It was during his childhood in Midland and Houston, the years he spent at home before going to boarding school at age 15, that George W. in many ways became his mother's son.

When Robin had become sick, it was Bush's father who wore his anguish openly, who had to leave the room at Memorial Sloan-Kettering cancer center each time Robin had another transfusion. And it was Barbara Bush who stayed resolutely at their daughter's side in New York, her strength belied only by her hair, which at age 28 began to turn white.

After the couple returned to Midland, Barbara plunged into despair. Her husband tried his best to cheer her up. But he was pulled away by the demands of building an oil business, working long days and traveling frequently. That left Barbara alone with her two children for long stretches. Of the two boys, only George understood what had happened.

As the gloom began to lift from the Bushes' three-bedroom frame house on West Ohio Street, it was their ebullient cutup of a son who, despite his own pain, helped drive it away—joking, playing, working hard to make his mother smile again. Time helped salve Barbara Bush's pain, but so did "Georgie."

Barbara Bush once said it didn't dawn on her what was

happening until one day when she heard her son tell a friend that he couldn't come out because he had to play with his mother, who was lonely. "I was thinking, 'Well, I'm being there for him,'" she recalled. "But the truth was he was being there for me."

Elsie Walker, a Bush cousin who lost one of her own sisters, put it this way: "You look around and see your parents suffering so deeply and try to be cheerful and funny, and you end up becoming a bit of a clown."

As part of a family famously allergic to engaging in public introspection, Bush is reluctant to talk about the forces that shaped him. He acknowledges, of course, that his sister's death was profoundly sad for him and his parents, but he also sees the sources of his personality as "more complex than one or two events." Few would argue with that assessment.

Yet some close to the Bushes do see the death of his sister as a singular event in George W.'s childhood, helping to define him and how he would deal with the world. Life would be full of humor and driven by chance. And it would be something approached with a certain fatalism. Even as an adolescent, Bush would tell his friends, "You think your life is so good and everything is perfect; then something like this happens and nothing is the same," recalls John Kidde, a high school classmate.

This attitude would ultimately liberate Bush to live his life in the present, "in chapters" as his brother Marvin would say, seizing opportunities as they came without fretting about what tomorrow might bring.

THE SPIRIT OF BARBARA BUSH

From his mother he would pick up a verve that echoes in the traits that have made Bush a more lively and comfortable politician than his father. His large-sized personality, his blunt outspokenness, his irreverence and readiness with a joke drew friends and allies to him long before he sought office, then became an important source of success once he entered politics.

From the time he was a boy, the intuitive, spontaneous son seemed very different from his guarded, dignified, overachieving father. When members of the extended Bush family gathered in Maine in the summers of George W.'s youth, the physical resemblance they noticed was to George, but the spirit was all Bar, headstrong and quick-witted. Mother and son, as one relative put it, were "always in your face."

"I don't think George W. would ever be sassy or sarcastic with his father and if he was, it would be within the foul lines," said cousin John Ellis. "But Bar will say to George W. something like, 'Oh, don't be ridiculous,' and they're off to the races."

Nor have George W. and his mother ever gotten out of each other's faces. Even when her son was married and in his forties and on the cusp of his political career, Barbara did not hesitate to let him know what she thought.

Bush spent hours thinking and talking about running for governor of Texas in 1990, encouraged by the enthusiasm of his friends. Barbara Bush thought he should stick to running the Texas Rangers, the baseball team he had just bought with a group of other investors. "When you make a major commitment like that, I think maybe you won't be running for governor," she told a group of reporters at the White House in 1989, who lost no time relaying her remarks to her son.

As he fielded calls from the reporters, Bush tried to make light of his mother's remarks. But he was privately irked, according to a source who saw him that day. As it happened, it would be four years before he ran for governor.

A relationship of affectionate tension and banter, it has its origins in the Texas of the 1950s, when George W. was a boy coming of age and Barbara a young mother coping with the unexpected trials of early adulthood. . . .

Nightmares and Tragedy

It was just a few weeks after Jeb was born in February 1953 that the Bushes began to realize something was wrong with Robin. She had been strangely exhausted, telling her mother one morning she couldn't decide what to do that day—lie down and read or lie down and watch cars go by outside. Blood tests showed she had advanced leukemia—a disease that today might well be curable.

Leaving their sons with friends, the Bushes immediately took Robin to New York, where an uncle, John Walker, was a renowned surgeon and president of Memorial Sloan-Kettering cancer hospital.

The ensuing months were a blur of cross-country trips and sadness. George W.'s father flew back and forth to New York on weekends while working long hours at Zapata [Petroleum Corp.]. Barbara Bush remained in New York.

By October, Robin was dead.

Even after all these years, Barbara Bush still questions the decision not to tell her son that Robin was dying. "I don't know if that was right or wrong. I mean, I really don't, but I know he said to me several times, 'You know, why didn't you tell me?'" she said. "Well, it wouldn't have made a difference."

She and her husband feared that the young boy might inadvertently let Robin know she was gravely ill, but mostly, she said, they didn't want to burden him. "We thought he was too young to cope with it," she said.

After Robin's death, the pain that hung over the house was often unspoken, according to Randall Roden, a childhood friend of George W. Once, while Roden was spending the night, Bush had a bad dream and his mother rushed in to comfort him.

"I knew what it was about—he had nightmares for some period of time," said Roden. "It was one of the most realistic experiences I have ever had about death and I am certain it had a profound effect on him because it had a profound effect on me."

It bothered Barbara Bush that friends never mentioned Robin, no doubt because they wanted to spare her and her husband's feelings. But the silence rankled. Finally, as she tells the story, George W. helped break the ice, when one day at a football game he told his father that he wished he were Robin.

Friends who were sitting with Bush and his father froze in embarrassment, and his father asked him why he said it. "I bet she can see the game better from up there than we can here," his son replied.

BARBARA BUSH SETS THE RULES

Even as a young man, George W.'s father had an exalted place in his family. Graced with good looks, athletic ability and proper ambition, "Poppy" Bush—a nickname bestowed because his grandfather George Herbert Walker was called "Pop"—was held up as a role model. Barbara Bush treated her husband with similar deference, insulating the first man she had ever kissed from the nagging and tiresome issues that naturally consume a growing family. Two more sons were born—Neil in 1955 and Marvin in 1956—and finally, in 1959, Dorothy, filling a void left by the daughter her husband so deeply missed.

It was Barbara Bush who set the rules and became the authority figure, while her husband was held up as a much-revered statesman-like figure among the children. It was Barbara who drove the car pools, supervised the homework and piled five kids in a car with a housekeeper for the grueling cross-country trips to Kennebunkport for summer vacation. It was a time when fathers had relatively little to do with raising their children, so George W.'s father was hardly conspicuous among the other Midland oilmen by his frequent travel and hard work. Joe O'Neill, a boyhood friend, recalls that some weekends George W.'s father, the former Yale baseball captain, would help coach the neighborhood boys, impressing them mightily by leaning forward to catch fly balls with his glove behind his back.

But, said Mike Proctor, another childhood friend, "The one who was always there was Barbara Bush.". . .

THE ENFORCER

In 1959, the Bushes finally pulled up stakes from Midland and moved to Houston. George W. had just finished the seventh grade at San Jacinto Junior High, where he played quarterback, ran for class president—and won. Bush has often invoked the school as proof of his Texas pedigree, compared to that of his father. "He went to Greenwich Country Day and I went to San Jacinto Junior High," Bush likes to say. What he doesn't say is that he spent just one year at the school—his last year in public education.

The Bushes enrolled their oldest son at the Kinkaid School, a private academy in one of the nation's wealthiest suburbs, an exclusive Houston enclave called Piney Point Village. The newly arrived eighth-grader made an easy transition. He was quickly elected a class officer and made the school football team. One classmate remembers him as a "classic good old boy type"—easygoing and swaggering, with a gift for making friends.

Even though Bush would live in Houston full time for only two years, he managed to amass a large group of friends who would carry him through holidays and summers. Sundays were the big socializing day, when the Bushes would open their home to neighborhood families for hamburgers and hot dogs and endless backyard softball games.

Barbara Bush always had a jigsaw puzzle going at the end of the living room, which she brilliantly used to rope her children—and the children of others—into conversation. "Come on down here, and help work on this," she would say to an awkward teenager who stumbled into the house.

"Before you knew it," a family friend recalled, "you were working on the puzzle, then talking about the puzzle and then telling her all your problems."

But she was also "the enforcer," as her children described it, the parent most concerned with discipline and rules. Barbara Bush never subscribed to the "wait till your father gets home" school. "I don't think that's any good," she said. "I don't think your husband comes home, exhausted from work, and you say, 'Well, go sock Marvin.'"

More often than not it was her oldest son who was the offender. "I think one of the things I'm most grateful to George for is that he certainly blazed the path for those of us who followed," said his brother Marvin.

Obnoxious behavior on Bush's part drew swift retribution, according to Douglas Hannah, an old friend. When the three of them played a round of golf one summer in high school, Barbara Bush admonished her son to stop swearing—and then banished him from the game after he ignored her warnings. Hannah and Barbara Bush played out 16 holes while Bush cooled his heels in the car.

Bush's friends recall his father being present mostly on weekends, frequently running the grill. But as his father's career became all-consuming, the oldest son—only 20 years younger than his parents—came to function as a third adult in the household, and something of a young uncle to the other children. . . .

On the Edge

To his much younger brothers and sister Bush seemed his own force of nature, an exciting, unpredictable hurricane who could make any family gathering an event. "We all idolized him," said sister Doro Bush Koch. "He was always such fun and wild, you always wanted to be with him because he was always daring. . . . He was on the edge."

"We'd go out in the boat at night [in Kennebunkport] and that was always an adventure. Now, if we went out in the boat at night with Neil, you know that was fine because he's a boatsman, my brother Neil, and he knew everything about it—and still does. George, on the other hand, it was more of a kind of a wild risky thing because we're not sure that he, you know, could manage the boat as well."

As the handsome son of a rising business and civic figure in Houston, George W. was always on the list for holiday balls and the social rituals of what was essentially a traditional southern town. But those who remember him from his early teen years recall a young man devoid of polish and pretense, spurning "snobs," sneering at anything that resembled ostentation.

"It was almost a reverse snobbery," recalled Lacey Neuhaus Dorn, Bush's neighbor in the early '60s. "He just hated the glitz. . . . If someone had a fancy car, he'd make a comment that it was too fancy for his blood."

But as George Herbert Walker Bush's first-born, there were some privileges that he could not turn down. Ninth grade would be his last year at Kinkaid. His parents decided that in the fall of 1961 he should continue his education at Phillips Academy in Andover, Mass., one of the nation's most exclusive and rigorous prep schools and his father's alma mater.

For the first time, Bush would feel the full weight of his father's illustrious past.

Failures in the Oil Business

Joe Conason

Growing up close to money and political power, George W. Bush used both to start his own oil-drilling venture only three years after receiving his Harvard MBA. In the 1980s, oil prices were down and interest rates were skyrocketing. Bush needed one financial savior after another to rescue him from a multitude of business failures until 1988, when he organized a partnership to purchase the Texas Rangers baseball team. In this February 2000 article, Joe Conason details Bush's difficult history in the oil business, outlining the successes and failures that haunt Bush's past. Conason writes for *Harper's Magazine*.

From the outset of his career, George W. Bush exhibited an impatience that would have embarrassed his father, who underwent a long apprenticeship in the oil business. In 1978, only three years after graduating from Harvard Business School and returning home to Midland, Texas, he incorporated his own oil-drilling venture.

Almost simultaneously, he made an even more startling announcement. Again unlike his father and grandfather, who established their fortunes and reputations before running for public office, George W. declared his candidacy for Congress in 1978 from the district that included Midland. His name was his only political credential, aside from a year as president of the Delta Kappa Epsilon fraternity at Yale.

His candidacy seemed almost plausible, however, when he defeated a far more seasoned opponent in the Republican primary. He went on to lose badly in the general election to a Democrat who had mocked Bush's pretentious description of himself as an independent oilman. Actually, Bush didn't commence any operations of his oil firm, Arbusto Energy, until early in 1979.

Joe Conason, "Notes on a Native Son," *Harper's Magazine*, February 2000. Copyright © 2000 by Joe Conason. Reproduced by permission.

43

SAVED BY INVESTORS

With assistance from his uncle Jonathan Bush, a personable Wall Street financier, George W. assembled a limited partnership of two dozen investors. The Arbusto partners included George W.'s grandmother Dorothy Bush; Rite Aid drugstores chairman Lewis Lehrman, then a rising force in New York Republican politics; William Draper III, a corporate executive and family friend who was later appointed to head the Export-Import Bank; and James Bath, a mysterious Houston aircraft broker who appears to have been fronting for several Saudi Arabian sheiks.

About $3 million poured into Arbusto, producing little oil and no profits but expansive tax shelters. In 1982, George W. changed his company's infelicitous name to Bush Exploration Oil Co. His father by this time was vice president of the United States, but the new company name didn't improve the son's luck or alter the fact that petroleum prices were sinking while interest rates were rising. More than once, Bush's venture was near ruin when wealthy benefactors suddenly appeared with fresh cash. The most generous was Philip Uzielli, an old Princeton buddy of James Baker III, the family friend then serving as chief of staff in the Reagan White House. For the sum of $1 million, Uzielli bought 10 percent of the company at a time in 1982 when the entire enterprise was valued at less than $400,000.

Soon Uzielli's million was gone, too. But just as his company was heading toward failure, George W. met William DeWitt and Mercer Reynolds, a pair of Ohio investors with their own small oil firm, called Spectrum 7. DeWitt, who had graduated from Yale a few years earlier than Bush, happened to be the son of the former owner of the Cincinnati Reds, and he shared Bush's passion for baseball. After a quick courtship the Spectrum 7 partners agreed to merge with Bush Exploration, naming George W. as chairman and CEO and awarding him a substantial share of stock. Although the vice president's son helped Spectrum 7 to raise additional money, catastrophic losses continued. During a six-month period in 1986, Spectrum 7 lost $400,000, and the partners feared creditors would foreclose their remaining assets.

Once more George W. attracted a financial savior. That September, Spectrum 7 was acquired by Harken Energy Corporation, a medium-sized, diversified company. After Bush joined Harken, the largest stock position and a seat on its board were acquired by Harvard Management Company, the private firm that invests the university's endowment. The Harken board gave Bush $600,000 worth of the company's publicly traded stock, plus a seat on its board of directors and a consultancy that paid him up to $120,000 a year. His partners understood perfectly what had happened. As Spectrum 7's former president, Paul Rea, recalled later, the Harken directors "believed having George's name there would be a big help to them."

Thus ending his years as an oilman with a substantial income and minimal corporate duties, George W. in the spring of 1987 moved his family from Texas to Washington, where he served as "senior adviser" in his father's presidential campaign. Intense and sometimes volatile, he made appearances at fund-raisers and rallies, acted as an emissary to major campaign donors and leaders of the religious right, and occasionally bullied reporters whose publications he disliked. Those confrontations injured his own reputation, but his father rolled to victory over Democrat Michael Dukakis in one of the nastiest elections in decades.

TEXAS RANGERS

Toward the end of the 1988 campaign, George W. heard from his former Spectrum 7 partner Bill DeWitt that the Texas Rangers were on the market. To make a successful bid, DeWitt would need Texas backers, and the son of the incoming president was perfectly situated to find them. George W. also had a powerful advantage in dealing with the team's owner, an aging Midland oil millionaire named Eddie Chiles, who had been a Bush friend since the 1950s.

For George W., an ardent lifelong fan with no real job, DeWitt's proposal was a providential opportunity. His duties as a director of Harken Energy, though undemanding, offered little chance to improve his resume. His hopes of running for governor in 1990 had been squelched by incredulous party insiders, who complained that he had never "done anything." To acquire the Rangers and thus keep the franchise in Texas would be to do something of profound significance to Texans.

Baseball commissioner Peter Ueberroth was eager to help the son of the new president, but he was not so eager when George W. said the biggest investors in the proposed Rangers syndicate were his old Yale frat brother Roland Betts and

Tom Bernstein, Betts's partner in a film-investment concern. Betts and Bernstein were from New York, not Texas.

The indispensable local money came from Richard Rainwater, formerly the chief financial adviser to the Bass brothers of Fort Worth. Little known to the general public, Rainwater was famous on Wall Street for growing the Bass inheritance from around $50 million in 1970 to more than $4 billion by the time he left in 1986 to manage his own investments.

Both Bush and Ueberroth met with Rainwater in early 1989 to persuade him to join the Rangers syndicate. Rainwater then took effective control of the deal, bringing along Edward "Rusty" Rose, a well-known Dallas investor, to oversee the franchise. Under an agreement worked out by Betts and Rainwater, the title of "managing partner" would be shared between Rusty Rose and George W.—but the president's son would operate under a tight rein. He would function as the new ownership's friendly public face while Rose ran the business.

Bush's stake in the team, just under 2 percent, was among the smallest. He purchased his shares with a $500,000 loan from a Midland bank of which he had been a director and eventually scraped together another $106,000 to buy out two other limited partners. Rainwater, Rose, and their associates put up $14.2 million, while Betts and Bernstein invested about $6 million; the balance came from smaller investors, loans, and the equity of minority partners in the old Chiles partnership.

Two months after his father's inauguration, George W. Bush called a press conference in Arlington to announce that the Rangers sale had been successfully completed for a price that was later reported to be $86 million. Proclaiming that the new owners would share a "civic dividend" with Texas, he began to promote himself along with the team. While Rainwater, Rose, and all the other partners remained in the background, George W. behaved as if he were "the owner" of the Rangers. He attended every home game and even printed "baseball cards" bearing his own picture to hand out from his box.

Meanwhile, George W. maintained a financial interest in Harken Energy. He had been granted enough additional stock options, at a generous discount, to increase his holdings by more than half. By 1989, however, those shares were falling in value. A series of questionable decisions by chairman Alan Quasha had jeopardized the company's future, and its losses reached $40 million in 1990. Even the company's CEO admitted that its financial statements were "a mess."

BAHRAIN

Once more, however, the Bush name seems to have provided sudden deliverance—this time in the form of a contract with the emirate of Bahrain. Until 1989 the Bahraini oil minister had been negotiating an agreement for offshore drilling with Amoco, a huge energy conglomerate with decades of worldwide experience. Those talks were abruptly broken off, supposably because the Bahrainis had decided that a smaller firm would give their project more attention. The Bahraini officials were put in touch with Harken through a former Mobil Oil executive named Michael Ameen. At the same time, Ameen also happened to be working as a consultant to the U.S. State Department, which had assigned him to brief Charles Hostler, the newly confirmed American ambassador to Bahrain (a San Diego real estate investor who had given $100,000 to the Republican Party for the 1988 election).

These several events culminated in a January 1990 announcement that astonished oil-industry analysts: the government of Bahrain had awarded exclusive offshore drilling rights to Harken. "It was a surprise," one top analyst told *Time* magazine with dry understatement. Quite apart from Harken's shaky financial condition, the company had never drilled a well anywhere but Texas, Louisiana, and Oklahoma, and had never drilled undersea at all. So depleted of cash and so deeply in debt was Harken that the company was forced to bring in the more experienced and solvent Bass brothers as equity partners, so that construction on the $25 million project could begin.

Only the presence of President Bush's oldest son could explain Bahrain's extraordinary decision. There was no question that the rulers of Bahrain were aware of his role. In addition to his Harken directorship, George W. sat on the company's "exploration advisory board," which meant that his name had been mentioned at least twice during initial discussions with Bahraini officials. "They were clearly aware he was the president's son," said Monte Swetnam, a former Harken executive who conducted the talks with the emirate's oil ministry.

George W. flatly denied any part in Harken's bid. "Ask the Bahrainis," he replied flippantly when journalists asked whether they had been enticed by his name. Harken has said that Bush was not involved in the Bahrain deal. Later, Bush claimed he had opposed the project because Harken was not "prepared."

However it was procured, the Bahrain contract pushed up the price of Harken stock from $4.50 to $5.50 in a matter of weeks. And on June 22, 1990, six months after the contract was announced, George W. quietly sold off 212,140 shares, or two thirds of his interest, which grossed him $848,560. He used most of the proceeds to pay off the bank loan he had taken a year earlier to finance his portion of the Texas Rangers deal. A few weeks later, in early August, Iraqi dictator Saddam Hussein invaded Kuwait. Saddam's aggression drove down the share prices of every oil company doing business in the Gulf, including Harken, whose shares fell to $3.12.

SELLING HARKEN STOCK

By the time George W. unloaded his Harken stock in late June, diplomatic alarms had been sounding in the Bush White House about Saddam's aggressive intentions. Although there is no evidence that the president's son was tipped off about the impending Gulf crisis, he certainly had reason to know that Harken was still in trouble. He served on the company's three-member audit committee and also on a special "fairness committee" appointed that spring to consider how a corporate restructuring would affect the value of the company's outstanding shares. Two months after Bush sold the bulk of his Harken holdings, the company posted losses for the second quarter of well over $20 million and its shares fell another 24 percent; by year-end Harken was trading at $1.25.

When Bush's stock dumping was first reported by the *Houston Post* in October 1990, there were no accusations of insider trading. Then in April 1991 the *Wall Street Journal* revealed that the Securities and Exchange Commission had not been notified of his timely trade until eight months after the legal deadline. The regulatory agency commenced an investigation that concluded in 1991 with no action against George W. It was hardly a surprise. The SEC chairman at the time, Richard Breeden, was an especially ardent Bush loyalist, and the agency's general counsel was the same Texas attorney who had handled the sale of the Rangers baseball team for George W. and his partners in 1989. Bush has insisted that he didn't know about the firm's mounting losses and that his stock sell-off had been approved by Harken's general counsel.

Although no wrongdoing was proved, the suspicions surrounding Harken Energy and other dubious enterprises associated with the president's sons—particularly Neil Bush's directorship of a crooked Colorado savings-and-loan—caused the family severe embarrassment during the 1992 election. George W. described the twelve months he spent on the futile Bush-Quayle reelection effort as "the most miserable year of my life."

BUILDING A BALLPARK

But that unhappy interlude scarcely stalled his own quest for success. Soon after buying the Rangers, he and his partners realized that the franchise would never make money unless they replaced the team's old ballpark, badly outmoded in an era of luxury skyboxes. With the backing of billionaire Rainwater they could have built a new stadium themselves, of course, but that would have violated an important tenet of major league economics. The construction costs of new sporting facilities are provided by taxpayers, not club owners. But because few municipalities accept such fiscal burdens without coercion, Rangers management began to hint unsubtly that unless the city government of Arlington provided land and financing on favorable terms, they would have to move the team to nearby Dallas or Fort Worth.

Major league baseball's negotiating advantage almost invariably leads to "public-private" deals, in which public funds subsidize private profit with the justification that the presence of the team will stimulate wider economic activity. Even by those standards, however, the capitulation of Arlington mayor Richard Greene was uniquely abject. In October 1990, Mayor Greene signed a contract that guaranteed $135 million toward the stadium's estimated price of $190 million. The Rangers put up no cash but financed their share through a ticket surcharge. From the team's operating revenues, the city would earn a maximum of $5 million annually in rent, no matter how much the Rangers reaped from ticket sales and television (a sum that rose to $100 million a year). The most remarkable provision, however, permitted the franchise to buy the stadium after the accumulated rental payments reached a mere $60 million. The property acquired so cheaply by the Rangers included not just a fancy new stadium with a seating capacity of 49,000 but an additional 270 acres of suddenly valuable land.

This scheme predictably generated local opposition to "corporate welfare." But together with Mayor Greene, George W. convinced an overwhelming majority of Arlington voters to approve a sales-tax hike that would back the stadium bonds in January 1991. The referendum must have left an impression on Governor Ann Richards, who quickly signed legislation creating the Arlington Sports Facilities Development Authority—with power to issue bonds and exercise eminent domain over any obstinate landowners.

Never before had a municipal authority in Texas been given license to seize the property of a private citizen for the benefit of other private citizens. That is exactly what happened to a recalcitrant Arlington family that refused to sell a 13-acre parcel near the stadium site for half its appraised value. Their land was condemned and handed over to the Rangers. The ensuing lawsuit revealed that well before any of the enabling legislation had passed, the Rangers management had planned to wield condemnation as a weapon to drive down the price, and an outraged jury awarded more than $4 million to the Arlington family whose land had been expropriated.

Long before that verdict came down, however, the shiny new structure George W. had christened The Ballpark in Arlington was finished. It may have been no accident that the arena's outer walls were clad in reddish brick and pink granite that subtly echoed the appearance of the beautiful old state capitol in Austin. On November 8, 1993, with the stadium being readied to open the following spring, Bush announced that he would be running for governor. He didn't blush when he proclaimed that his campaign theme would demand self-reliance and personal responsibility rather than dependence on government.

CHAPTER 2

THE MAKING OF
A PRESIDENT

PEOPLE
WHO MADE
HISTORY

GEORGE W. BUSH

Team Player

Joe Nick Patoski

George W. Bush was managing general partner of the Texas Rangers baseball team for five years. It was during this time that Bush managed to build a reputation. The management skills he exhibited and fine-tuned with the Rangers enabled Bush to become a successful businessman. While in the public eye, he used creative financing, exceptional negotiating skills, and political finesse to make the Rangers one of the most successful clubs in the league. Besides winning him friends and supporters, his success also guaranteed him and his partners a positive return on their investment.

In the following 1999 article, Joe Nick Patoski reviews Bush's career with the Rangers and the successes that eventually enabled him to secure the job of governor of Texas. Patoski is a senior editor for *Texas Monthly* magazine.

The Ballpark is the legacy of Bush's five-year stint as managing general partner of the Rangers, a time in which he built up both the franchise's bottom line and his own, along the way honing many of the skills he draws upon in politics. Fundraiser Bush shook out $46 million from various investors during the depths of Texas' last economic bust in the run-up to buying the team. Consensus-builder Bush got the Ballpark referendum passed in Arlington when similar measures were being nixed by voters elsewhere. Manager Bush ran a business efficiently in the glare of the public eye. People-person Bush nourished the egos of the famous and the anonymous, from Juan Gonzalez to the groundskeepers, always addressing them by name. After all that, running the free world might seem like T-ball.

Privilege, pedigree, and personal relationships were the reasons Bush hooked up with the Rangers in the first place.

Joe Nick Patoski, "Team Player: George Bush's Career Running the Texas Rangers," *Texas Monthly*, vol. 27, June 1999, p. 113. Copyright © 1999 by *Texas Monthly*. Reproduced by permission.

His name surfaced as a possible major league owner in the
weeks after his father was elected president. "George had
spent most of 1988 campaigning and then on the transition
team, but he decided he didn't want to be in Washington—
he wanted to go back to Texas," says one of his fraternity
brothers, Roland W. Betts, a movie financier who'd been
looking for a pro sports team to buy. "In December he called
me and said the Rangers were in play. The Macks [a vener-
able baseball family] wanted to buy the team from Eddie
Chiles, but there was growing concern that they wanted to
move the team to Florida."

FINDING INVESTORS

Chiles, the Fort Worth oilman who achieved notoriety with his
"I'm Mad" radio spots, had known George W. as a kid. A friend
of the Bush family, he flew George's sister Robin to hospitals
in his private plane when she was diagnosed with leukemia.
He'd bought the Rangers in 1980, but at age 78 he was ready
to call it quits—a fact Bush was made aware of by William De-
Witt, Jr., his oil-business partner in Midland in the eighties.
DeWitt, whose father had owned the St. Louis Browns and the
Cincinnati Reds, wanted a piece of a team himself.

Bush got cash commitments from several sources. Betts
signed on, but only after receiving assurances that his friend
wasn't going to run for office anytime soon. Also ponying up
were Connecticut real estate whiz Craig Stapleton, Bush
cousin through marriage; former Marriott Corporation executive Fred Malek, who had been a member of Richard
Nixon's inner circle; and three Cincinnati investors: produce
wholesaler Bob Castellini, oilman Mercer Reynolds, and
broadcasting executive Dudley Taft. Chiles was so impressed
that he signed a letter of agreement with the Bush group.

But baseball commissioner Peter Ueberroth wasn't satisfied. Although he wanted Chiles to find a buyer who would
keep the Rangers in Texas, a top ten media market, he
thought Bush's investors didn't have enough local ties. At
Ueberroth's urging, Bush went to see Fort Worth financier
Richard Rainwater, the money man behind the Bass family.
Subsequently, Rainwater met with Bush, Betts, and Stapleton at the Highland Park home of Edward "Rusty" Rose, a financier known as the Mortician for his ability to squeeze
profits from falling companies acquired through leveraged
buyouts. "We talked about the possibility of owning the team

together," Betts recalls. "At the end of the day Rainwater said if he was going to do it, he wanted Rose as general partner because he liked and trusted him. I said the same thing about George. Rose and George met, and after a few lunches they agreed to run the team together." The publicity-shy Rose made one stipulation: Bush would be the managing general partner, meaning he'd deal with the media and the public, while Rose would serve as chairman of the board.

Rose threw in $3.2 million and raised another $9 million from other investors, including Rainwater and cable television mogul Jeff Marcus. Bush rounded up $14 million, contributing $606,000 of his own—the smallest amount of any major investor. All told, seventy investors representing 39 limited partnerships bought a piece of the team. Betts and fellow film financier Tom Bernstein paid the most money ($7 million) and received the largest share (18 percent).

Once those initial arrangements were hammered out, Bush approached several other investors. Among them were Schieffer, a former state representative from Fort Worth, and Comer Cottrell, the CEO of a Dallas hair products firm. Edward Gaylord, the Oklahoma City media magnate, reduced the one-third piece of the team he'd bought from Chiles in 1986 to 10 percent. Other small shareholders from the Chiles era, including Arlington realtor Mike Reilly, held on to a total of 4 percent.

The Bush-Rose group was formally incorporated as BR Rangers. No decision would be made without the approval of the two general partners. "Neither of us has the responsibility to make any decision without consulting with the other," Bush would later explain. "On a certain task, he may lead on it or I may take the lead. The buck stops on our desks." For his efforts, Bush was paid an annual salary of $200,000; Rose's company would reportedly receive a retainer of $120,000. In addition, once all the investors were repaid with accrued interest, both Bush and Rose were to be compensated for putting the deal together with a bonus, or promote fee, of 10 percent and 5 percent, respectively. The $86 million deal was officially approved by baseball's executive committee in April 1989. But the real work had only just begun.

LEARNING THE BUSINESS

To put it kindly, the Rangers were a beaten-down franchise. Since relocating to the Dallas–Fort Worth area from Washington, D.C., in 1972, they had consistently performed poorly on the field and at the ticket office. They were finally drawing fans (they passed the 1.5 million mark in attendance in 1986, 1987, and 1988) and cultivating talent (pitcher Nolan Ryan, a bona fide star; Ruben Sierra, an outfielder with Hall of Fame potential) but they were playing in a jerry-built stadium that was originally intended for minor league competition. "The first time I went down there, I was just shocked," says Betts, and he wasn't alone in his assessment. "At our first meeting, that was the mantra: To turn this thing around and add value to our investment, we were going to build a new stadium."

Most of the 1989 season was devoted to learning the business of baseball. Quickly adapting to his role as the public face of the owners' consortium, Bush was as much of a fixture at the old Arlington Stadium as John "Zonk" Lanzillo, Jr., the drum-beating superfan. He was always in his seat next to the dugout, boots up on the railing, munching peanuts, watching the game, signing more autographs than most of the players. His parents got involved too. In 1989 their springer spaniel Millie gave birth to Spot Fletcher, who was named in honor of Rangers shortstop Scott Fletcher. Two years later the president broke tradition and threw out the first pitch of the season in Arlington instead of Baltimore, the closest city to Washington with a major league club.

Behind the scenes, George W. set to mending fences, improving the team's image, and winning over critics like Jim Reeves of the *Fort Worth Star-Telegram*, who covered the sale of the Rangers and had few kind words for the Bush group. "I had an early built-in grudge against George in particular," says Reeves. "I thought he was a failed politician and obviously a guy who was playing off his dad's name because he wasn't putting much money in." Bush went out of his way to win over Reeves, even inviting him to play a round of golf, and the reporter gradually came around. "I found him to be a very personable, direct, very informed general partner. The more we were around him, the better the team's relationship with the press would be. You could believe what he told you."

He was good at other things as well: He was instrumental in neutralizing the agendas of various personnel, marketing Ryan aggressively, and broadening the team's appeal by instituting Spanish-language broadcasts. Baseball details, however, were left to the baseball people. "They went out of their way to let us know they weren't going to be hands-on owners," said Tom Grieve, then the Rangers' general manager. "They made it clear from the start they did not buy the team because they wanted to brag to their friends that they owned a baseball team. They told me, 'We're business people and expect to be profitable, and we expect our baseball people to be accountable.' But never did they come in and say, 'When are you gonna get rid of this guy?'"

By the end of the first year the initial plan that had been in the back of everyone's mind was formalized. If the Rangers were going to make the transition from a have-not franchise to one of the haves and maximize their value, they would have to play in a new stadium—ideally, a state-of-the-art facility that looked old and traditional but had all the requisite sky boxes and other modern bells and whistles. The partners looked around for someone who could manage a large public project, considering both Tom Luce and Bush himself at one point before designating Schieffer the stadium czar in July 1990. He was charged with selecting a site, developing a strategy, and getting the project under way despite a seemingly impossible obstacle: The partners didn't want to have to pay for the new park themselves.

BUILDING THE BALLPARK

Schieffer looked around the Metroplex for a few months before concluding that Arlington was the best site and that a halfcent local sales tax was the best way to pay for it. He then got busy winning over voters to raise the $135 million in bonds it would take to build a new home for the home team. Tarrant County judge Tom Vandergriff, who was instrumental in luring the Rangers from Washington, and Arlington mayor Richard Greene were enlisted to spearhead the three-month effort. Both Schieffer and Bush were actively involved. At one point both men spoke from the pulpit of the Mount Olive Baptist Church in Arlington, with Bush declaring, "A vote for the tax would be a vote for contracts for African American businesses."

With minimal opposition—Arlington's economy is based on tourism and entertainment, and a large percentage of its sales taxes are paid by out-of-towners—the bond issue passed in January 1991 by a two-to-one margin. Nearly 34,000 voters went to the ballot box—more than in any election in Arlington's history. Under their agreement with the city, the Rangers would chip in $30 million from revenues of ticket sales, surcharges, and luxury-box leases, and pay for any additional costs, which added up to another $26 million. The team would assume full ownership of the stadium when the bonds were paid off. "This eventually will give us the ability to compete on a payroll level that will put us with a whole new echelon of ballclubs," Bush said after the referendum passed. "We'll be able to pay the market price to keep our talent and, at the same time, keep ticket prices down." Following the vote, Schieffer shifted his focus to the Texas Legislature, which passed a bill that would ratify the arrangement, then he took the lead in getting the park built, soliciting designs from architects—nineteen submitted bids—before hiring David Schwartz of Washington, D.C., a Bass family favorite.

Back home, two flaps surfaced around the construction of the stadium. The first involved the condemnation of thirteen acres of land owned by the Curtis Mathes family, for which the city offered $1.375 million and the Matheses wanted $2.1 million. A state district court eventually declared the condemnation illegal and ordered that the Mathes group be paid the full amount they asked for, plus damages, which ultimately came to more than $11 a square foot, far higher than the $2.67 per square foot maximum that the city paid for any other single parcel during the land acquisition. The Rangers eventually worked out a payment plan to pay off the difference. The second snag was the awarding of minority contracts. The Rangers were criticized by the Arlington chapters of the NAACP and LULAC, the Arlington Hispanic Advisory Council, and even one of their own partners, Comer Cotrell, for not throwing enough business to black and Hispanic firms.

In the end, of course, the problems got resolved and the Ballpark got built. Much of the credit went—correctly—to Schieffer, who demonstrated he could orchestrate and delegate and was rewarded by being named the team's president. But Bush's behind-the-scenes involvement—in managing Schieffer, troubleshooting, and going public when necessary—was crucial, people familiar with the situation say. "The bond election, the ballpark, the financing technique, that was all George's deal," says Mike Reilly. "He quarterbacked the whole thing, but he never took the credit."

LEAVING THE TEAM

Bush took a leave of absence from the team before the 1994 season to run for governor, missing much of the Ballpark's inaugural season. The venue's classic lines and distinctively Texan look—from the native granite and red brick to the Longhorns in the facade—were an instant hit, drawing almost 3 million fans. A museum, sports bar and restaurant, luxury boxes, and a four-story office building outside the outfield fence bumped up the final cost to $191 million, but those additional revenue streams led *Financial World* magazine to rate it as the most profitable facility in baseball.

During the election, [governor of Texas] Ann Richards tried to make the public-private arrangement for financing the stadium an issue in the governor's race, a means of showing Bush as a beneficiary of corporate welfare, but it didn't take. After he won, Bush put his assets—including his share of the Rangers—in a blind trust and resigned as managing general partner. (His timing couldn't have been better: A players' strike cut short the 1994 season, caused the World Series to be canceled, and alienated many fans.)

Bush's official parting with the team came four years later, in June 1998, when buyout king Tom Hicks snapped it up for $250 million. By the time of sale, Bush's 1.8 percent share of the ownership had ballooned to 11.3 percent, and he pocketed almost $15 million: $2.7 million as a return on his investment and a $12.2 million "general partner interest"—his 10 percent "promote fee" for putting the ownership group together back in 1989. Not surprisingly, he was widely criticized by the usual suspects—the *Texas Observer* among them—for earning so much while seemingly doing so little, but his fellow owners sprang to his defense. "To me and to everyone in the partnership," Schieffer says, "it was not unusual to get a percentage on the back end like that for putting the deal together."

In any case, what Bush really got out of the deal was something more important than money: After years as Junior, he finally became his own man. "Before the Rangers, I told him he needed to do something to step out of his father's shadow," says Roland Butts. "Baseball was it. He became our local celebrity. He knew every usher. He signed autographs. He talked to fans. His presence meant everything. His eyes were on politics the whole time, but even when he was speaking at Republican functions, he was always talking about the Rangers."

Running for Governor

Skip Hollandsworth

Bush's success in running the Texas Rangers ball-club helped boost him into the governor's mansion. Bush's big struggle during the gubernatorial campaign was how voters perceived him. Separating himself from his family history and focusing on his own achievements was a constant battle. Bush ran on the platform that he had the guts to shake things up and make changes for the good of Texas. Sincere in his concerns about the deteriorating state of education and the widespread fear of crime in the state, Bush ran an issues-oriented, energetic campaign to put him into the governor's seat. In this May 1994 article, Skip Hollandsworth, executive editor for *Texas Monthly* magazine, captures Bush the campaigner and reviews his successful unseating of a popular incumbent. Hollandsworth is the winner of the 1998 Texas Institute of Letters O'Henry Award for Journalism and the 1996 Charles E. Green Journalism Award.

Bush is keenly aware that a lot of people, even those who swear allegiance to him, don't know a thing about him as a politician except that he is the former president's boy. George the Younger, he's called. The First Son. The Shrub. Regardless of how much George W. Bush wants to talk about issues, the decisive factors in many voters' minds are likely to be how they perceive him to be like his father and how they perceive him to be different—whether they believe he has his father's strengths or his weaknesses.

[Incumbent Texas governor] Ann Richards' most piercing attack against Bush is that he has done nothing to prove himself as a leader. Yes, he ran an oil company and then helped put together the group of investors that bought the Texas Rangers baseball team, of which he is the managing general partner. But until his gubernatorial announcement, he had only taken a cursory interest in politics: an impulsive 1978 run for Congress and work in his father's presidential campaigns. Bush's critics claim he is little more than an untested candidate who hides his ignorance of government behind a wall of self-confidence—and behind his last name. "If his name was George Smith," snorts a Richards aide, "no one would take him seriously."

CAMPAIGNING FOR GOVERNOR

Bush's friends and supporters, however, portray him as an articulate, quick-witted leader, a far better debater than his father, and surprisingly, a savvier politician. Nor is he timid about matching his personality against that of the legendary wisecracking Richards. "Don't underestimate this guy," says Fred McClure, a former senior legislative aide to President Bush in Washington and now a Dallas financier and neighbor of the younger Bush. "He's no doubt the biggest political animal in the family—and clearly more competitive than his father."

Demonstrating that he has indeed learned from the mistakes of his father, Bush is trying to paint Richards exactly as Bill Clinton painted the elder Bush during the 1992 presidential campaign: as a likable but ineffectual incumbent, a defender of the status quo. Bush has already positioned himself as the candidate of change in this campaign. He has introduced proposals to overhaul the state's public education, welfare, and juvenile justice programs. He uses phrases— "the landscape for change," "a startling new vision"—that surpass normal Republican lingo. "Believe me," says Bush, "I'm not afraid to shake things up. Otherwise, we're stuck with more of the same problems no one has ever had the guts to fix."

In his office, Bush sighs again. He knows he is embarking on a grueling personal journey to step out of the shadow of his beloved old man. "All that I ask," he says, giving me another glare, "is that for once you guys stop seeing me as the son of George Bush. This campaign is about me, no one else."

"If the election was held on Southwest Airlines," Bush tells me, "I'd win in a heartbeat." We are on a morning flight from Dallas to Midland for a campaign appearance, and he has already signed half a dozen autographs on cocktail napkins for other passengers. On a Southwest flight a few days earlier, sixteen people sitting in the eight rows behind him handed him a sheet of paper that they had signed, promising to vote for him. Before boarding a flight on another day, he ran into Roger Staubach, a former Dallas Cowboys quarterback and avid Republican who is rumored to be a future political candidate himself. . . .

Like his father, Bush gets an adrenaline rush when he's out campaigning, shaking hands with strangers, saying "Nice-ta-mee-cha," and cheerfully telling them, if they are unsure of how to reply, that they should come out to watch the Rangers play in their new stadium. He also has his father's gift for remembering names. Often he travels with only one young aide, Israel Hernandez, who gives him a schedule of the day's events and hands him breath mints— about a dozen a day. "Hand me a mint there, Israel," Bush says when he shows up at a campaign stop, then he's out of the car with jackrabbit speed, jaw-boning with everybody. There is no one whispering into his ear the names of his bigger supporters. Bush knows them.

Casual Style

Unlike his father—who startled voters with his inane asides . . . —George W. has the ability to win over strangers. On the Midland flight, he sees a boy wearing a Rangers hat and says, tongue in cheek, "Listen, kid, work hard at baseball and you too can get a $45 million contract like Juan Gonzalez." Pause. "But if you can't hit the curve, please try to make a nice income when you grow up so you can buy lots of Rangers tickets." The passengers chortle and hand him more napkins to sign.

While the elder Bush has always been known as an unfailingly polite man, George W. takes pride in his own irreverence. He loves to needle his friends. He can cuss like a sailor. And he tells stories with great good humor, even the embarrassing ones about himself. If his dad, as the *Washington Post* once wrote, really is a slight bore, like "every woman's first husband," then George W. is the wild boyfriend every woman dated in her youth. His closest pals, who all say he can act brash and cocky, have nicknamed him the Bombastic Bushkin. . . .

Bush does have a casual style that's rarely seen in his patrician parents. When he strides into his office in Dallas, he throws his inexpensive Haggar sport jacket on the floor—he has no coatrack—and eats from a bag of popcorn as he answers phone calls and shouts at his secretary through the always open door. His office is decorated like a dorm room. Baseball gloves and baseball bats and replicas of Bowie knives are scattered about. A Texas flag lies on top of a counter, half buried under some books. A personalized Texas license plate—reading BUSH—is on another table. The Baseball Encyclopedia is near his chair. . . .

Something Bush has inherited from his father is a kind of manic energy. He ran a marathon in Houston after the 1992 presidential race (finishing in a respectable 3 hours and 44 minutes). He prefers to spend his lunch hour running and sometimes lifting weights at Dallas' tony Cooper Aerobics Center. At the end of the day, in his comfortable one-story North Dallas home, Bush sits at his desk in an office just to the right of the front door, simultaneously talking on the phone, flipping through television channels with his remote control, and helping his daughters, who attend Hockaday, the most exclusive private girls' school in Dallas, with their homework. Sometimes he leaps up and heads out to the front yard with his springer spaniel, Spot (a daughter of the former first dog, Millie), and throws a tennis ball for her to chase. . . .

Laura initially felt reluctant about Bush's entering the governor's race. "She wanted to be sure I was running for all the right reasons," Bush tells me, "and that I wasn't running because I felt I had something to prove." It is a striking admission, for it suggests that even those closest to Bush have wondered about his need to become governor. Ambition, of course, is a tricky matter: All politicians are motivated to run for office through some mixture of private needs and public desires. But because Bush is the son of a famous man, and especially because he is trying to prove he can succeed at his father's profession, his drive to become governor is perhaps a little more perplexing. Is this campaign his grand attempt to win his father's approval? Is George W., the loyal son, running out of spite against Ann Richards, who has never hesitated to take potshots at the Bush family, as in her famous 1988 Democratic Convention speech, when she said that the elder Bush was born with a silver foot in his mouth? Or is it because he has a plan, as he says in every campaign speech he gives, to turn Texas into "a beacon state, a place where other people say, That's what I want my state to be"?

Bush makes a point to tell me, over and over, that he has

never had long-range political ambitions. "I've never been a long-term planner about anything," he says. "I have lived my life with more of a short-term focus—on the theory that other interesting things would come up for me to do." If there is a theme that runs through Bush's adult life, it's that of a man who quickly, sometimes impulsively, seizes the opportunities that are put before him. He admits he never considered becoming an oilman until the day he stopped in Midland for a brief visit in 1975 and decided to stay there. He says he never planned to buy a major league baseball team until a friend gave him a tip in late 1988 that the Rangers were for sale. And he swears he didn't make up his mind to run for governor until June 1993, "when everything began to feel right and when everything that Ann Richards was doing, or not doing, began to feel so wrong."

SINCERE CONCERNS

All of his friends say in interviews that Bush is sincere in his concerns about the deteriorating state of education and the widespread fear of crime in Texas. But, they add, to understand the candidacy of Bush, it is important to understand what it means to be a Bush in Texas, a member of Texas' most famous political family. Congenial and closeknit, the Bushes are far from a tortured clan like the Kennedys, with their scandals and their obsessive drive toward power. The Bushes obviously feel imbued, however, with an invincible sense of self-confidence, a kind of family faith, a conviction that they are the right people to lead. . . .

George W. Bush has often joked that the key difference between him and his father is that "my dad went to Greenwich Country Day School in Connecticut and I went to San Jacinto Junior High in Midland." The elder Bush was raised in a home with three maids and a chauffeur. He went to tea dances. At home, he had to wear a coat and tie to the dinner table. George W. grew up in a nice but unpretentious neighborhood with a bunch of brash, rough-and-tumble oilmen's sons—and he fit right in. Early photographs of George W. show a boy with a rakish gleam in his eye, an amused look on his face—"A wonderful, incorrigible child," says Barbara, "who spent many afternoons sitting in his room, waiting for his father to come home to speak to him about his latest transgression."

Perhaps because the elder Bush felt it so difficult to shake loose from the influence of his own stern father, U.S. senator Prescott Bush, he never played the role of the fierce disciplinarian with his own children. "I can't exaggerate to you what wonderful parents George and Barbara Bush were," George W. says. "They were liberating people. There was never that oppressiveness you see with other parents, never the idea that their way was the only way. My dad went out of his way to make sure that I felt accepted by him.". . .

When Bush talks about "the family as the backbone of Texas" and "Texas as a wonderful way of life" in his gubernatorial campaign speeches, what he's referring to is his own Midland childhood. This is not the Midland that Clayton Williams, the last Republican gubernatorial candidate, described during his 1990 campaign. Williams' Midland was a world of flamboyant wildcatters and cowboys. Bush's Midland, however, was a world full of people like his parents, Ivy Leaguers who had come to West Texas to make their fortunes. The families got together for golf at the country club. They had backyard barbecues in their neighborhood—a neighborhood no different, really, than any upscale neighborhood in Houston or Dallas. They went to First Presbyterian and joined the board of the United Way and sent their kids off to private schools back East. Although the younger Bush saw his parents mingle with poor people, theirs was a world devoid of hardship. . . .

GOING POLITICAL

[Bush] shocked his friends—and, of course, his parents, who once again had no idea of his plans—with his announcement that he was entering the 1978 race for the House of Representatives in a West Texas district that stretched from Midland-Odessa past Lubbock. After 34 years, the incumbent Democratic officeholder, George Mahon, had decided to retire, and Bush, after just two years in Midland, saw another opportunity. If his father's political ambition was shaped by the idea of noblesse oblige, the obligation of public service among those born in high places, George W.'s was shaped by the idea of carpe diem: Seize the day. Close the deal. Make something happen. . . .

"George did sort of leap into it," says Laura, "but even back then he was smart enough to know that a lot of politics was simply timing. You know, there are a lot of would-be governors of Texas sitting around today who never took the opportunity to get into a race when the time was right. If George is good at anything, it's timing."

In what seemed to be a largely amateur effort, Bush

"HE IS GOOD, THIS BOY OF OURS"

George H.W. Bush included a letter in his memoirs describing George W. Bush on election day in 1998 when young George was running for governor. In the letter to friend Hugh Sidey, the elder Bush speaks of his son's popularity and charisma and says with pride that George had the right reasons for wanting to serve.

Yesterday we attended George's final Houston rally. He was the rock star—Mr. Charisma. The rest of the ticket and some congressmen were all on stage when George entered. Then came Laura and Jenna, then Bar[bara] and me. The rest of the ticket became mere strap hangers. George was in command.

He is good, this boy of ours. He's uptight at times, feisty at other times—but who wouldn't be after months of grueling campaigning.

He includes people. He has no sharp edges on issues. He is no ideologue, no divider. He brings people together and he knows how to get things done. He has principles to which he adheres but he knows how to give a little to get a lot. He doesn't hog the credit. He's low on ego, high on drive.

All the talk about his wild youth days is pure nuts. His character will pass muster with flying colors.

Yesterday I told him—"George, on November 4th things will be very different." He knew exactly what I meant. And, Hugh, it will be different. Though the national press has already focused on his potential and though the polls look good he will be in a different league come tomorrow. He is strong though—tough enough, too, to withstand the pressure. . . .

Tomorrow I might well be the Dad of the Governors of the second and fourth largest states in the union. But there will be no feeling of personal vindication, no feeling of anything other than pride in two honest boys who, for the right reasons, want to serve—who fought the good fight and won.

People will call to congratulate us, but they will never begin to know the true depth of my feeling towards my sons. It will be what life is really all about for me right now.

Six years ago I was president of the United States of America. Tonight, maybe, the father of two governors. How great it is!

But then tomorrow a whole new life begins.

George H.W. Bush, *All the Best, George Bush: My Life in Letters and Other Writings.* New York: Scribner, 1999.

recruited his buddies, all political novices, to act as his campaign advisers. He never asked his father for help (although his mother did send out a letter to the people on her Christmas card list, asking them to contribute to the campaign).

Bush's opponent in the Republican primary called him a carpetbagger, a Connecticut Yankee, and a member of the Rockefeller-controlled Trilateral Commission which, according to the opponent, was trying to take over the world. "I didn't even know what the Trilateral Commission was," says Bush, who won the primary anyway. He then lost 53 percent to 47 percent in the general election to the popular Democratic state senator Kent Hance of Lubbock. Near the end of the campaign, the easygoing Bush lost votes when he was accused of loose morals because he had served beer at a meet-the-candidate party for Texas Tech students.

Bush's strong showing gave him his first taste of the power of the Bush name in Texas. But for the next decade, he barely mentioned politics again. It was as if his congressional campaign had been just another one of his impulsive ventures. . . .

Bush did consider running for governor in 1990, but he decided the timing wasn't right while his father was still president. (Another story has it that the White House vetoed a George W. race because it would be too embarrassing to the father if the son lost.) But the political bug had returned. In late 1991 the elder Bush asked George W. to visit Washington to interview members of the Cabinet about the upcoming 1992 campaign. George W. got the message that White House chief of staff John Sununu needed to go. After talking to his father, George W. spent the night at the White House and the next morning walked into Sununu's office and came out with his resignation. Some White House staff members were stunned that the coup de grace was administered by such an outsider. But George W. was proving himself to be a savvy political player, the type who would confront people and take stands in a way his father wouldn't.

Political Lessons

In retrospect, George W. says he learned two lessons from his father's 1992 defeat: Baby boomers were looking for a generational change in leadership, and if you campaign on the status quo, you lose. "People don't care what you did for them last year," says Bush. "They want to know what next year is like. Richards is telling people that we're all getting better because the level of crime has gone down a few percentage points. No one cares about that. Everyone is still scared to leave their homes."

He also recognizes that Richards, despite her national stardom, is vulnerable simply because Texas is increasingly becoming a Republican state. Republican leaders still believe the only reason Richards won in 1990 was because Clayton Williams turned out to be such a stereotypical good old boy who infuriated many Republican women. . . . "George W. Bush is too smart to screw up like that," says state Republican chairman Fred Meyer. "If you look at results of the 1990 Williams-Richards race [in which Williams lost by less than 100,000 votes], all George has to do is get back the upscale Republican female voters from Houston and Dallas who abandoned us last time—and he wins." It's a hopeful analysis: In the past four years, Richards has probably won back her share of Democrats who crossed over to vote for Clayton Williams, and she still has a great following among women, Republican and Democrat.

Nevertheless, George W. Bush, the master of timing, sees the 1994 gubernatorial election as his greatest opportunity of all. He has bought four new suits from the Culwell and Son men's store in Dallas. He has paid visits to many older GOP [Republican Party] fat cats, former supporters of his father's, some of whom have been skeptical of his candidacy. A few privately say they aren't sure they appreciate the idea of a Kennedy-like dynasty emerging among Republicans. But supremely confident that "they'll like me if they just get a whiff of me," Bush has persuaded the old fat cats to come through. Of the first twenty donors who gave $20,000 or more to the Bush campaign, seventeen were contributors to his father's presidential campaign.

Most importantly, he has made it to the general election without a primary. . . . Without a primary opponent, Bush had time to develop his platform, which was nonexistent. He also spared himself a bruising fight with an opponent who could have forced him to debate such social issues as abortion or gun control, which might have isolated Republicans on the far right or given Richards more fodder to use against him in the general election. As Bush began delivering his first campaign speeches in November, he told audiences that he was not running because he was the son of George and

Barbara Bush; he was running because he was concerned for the future of his own children. It was a great line. The only problem was that his brother Jeb was also using it in his own Florida gubernatorial campaign. George W. Bush was proving himself to be a terrific campaigner, but a critical listener couldn't help but wonder if, deep down, Bush was truly prepared for this race.

It's a morning meeting of criminal justice officials in the northeast Texas town of Sherman, and Bush has arrived to pass on his vision of Texas: a state where everyone is, to use one of his favorite words, "accountable." A state where people alone are responsible for making their lives better. A state with a drastically reduced welfare program, in which benefits are cut off after two years and the recipients forced to go to work. There will be no guilt-ridden Yalies in Bush's Texas. . . . The kind of government Bush says he prefers is one that creates "negative reinforcement" to make people change their behavior. "A governor can't pass a law to make you love," he says. "But he can pass a law to protect the innocent, law-abiding citizens from thugs."

BUSH AND CRIME

To that end, he is sharing with these Sherman officials his seventeen-point plan to stop juvenile crime, which includes sending especially violent juvenile criminals, even those as young as fourteen, to adult prisons (though segregated from the adult population) for mandatory sentences. "It's always been normal, when a child turns into a criminal, to say that it's our fault—society's fault," Bush says. "Well, under George W. Bush, it's your fault. You're going to get locked up, because we aren't going to have any more guilt-ridden thought that says that we are somehow responsible."

A juvenile probation officer challenges him. "We need more juvenile detention facilities," she says. "We need more rehabilitation for these kids to help them change."

"Wait a minute," says Bush, his temper rising—he does not respond well to criticism—"In order to win the war, we've got to make these criminals realize we mean punishment. They'll start changing once they realize they're going to get punished every time they screw up."

While Governor Richards . . . proposes that juveniles undergo more counseling, including heavy counseling for drug addiction, which she calls the major root of crime, Bush wants quick results. He doesn't think much about the roots of crime. He also doesn't put much stock in open-ended rehabilitation programs. At Richards' urging, the Legislature initiated a policy establishing drug treatment in prison—a program that criminal justice experts almost unanimously agree is long overdue in Texas—but Bush will have none of it. He proposes to take $25 million from drug-treatment programs in the adult prison system to build more local detention centers for juveniles. "The first priority is building more prisons and getting these criminals off the streets," he says.

Bush's approach to crime is indicative of his strengths and weaknesses as a politician. On the stump, his lock-'em-up attitude has great appeal to voters, but it's naive for him to think the high recidivism rates for criminals will ever drop significantly unless there are strong rehabilitation programs for prisoners used to a life of crime.

As a political newcomer who has spent little time studying government policy, Bush is having to learn as he runs. During a tour of a boot camp in Austin one afternoon, a boot camp official was giving an in-depth report on the variety of vocational classes offered to the young inmates. "Hey," interrupted a curious Bush, firing a question out of left field, "what happens when one of these fellows decides he wants to punch you?"

Depending on your point of view, it is either refreshing or a little unnerving that a man who might be governor in November is still working out his ideas about what a governor should do. In a meeting earlier this year, he told his group of education advisers . . . that he wanted to hear some proposals that would completely undermine the top-heavy Texas Education Agency (TEA) that controls local school districts. The advisers met among themselves a few times, then came back to Bush. After a one-hour meeting, Bush pulled the trigger and chose the most radical option presented to him: a "home rule" plan that would allow a locality's voters to declare the locality completely independent from the TEA and set up its own school system, using whatever teaching methods and curricula it chooses. . . .

EDUCATION

Bush envisions schools being run by local school boards that care about education, but it's at least equally likely that the home-rule plan could lead to endless debate among newly autonomous local school boards over whether to include sex education and school prayer in the classroom. Bush doesn't seem to have thought much about this. He says he threw out the idea, in part, to get voters to begin thinking more deeply about various ways to reinvigorate public education. In a frank confession, he also tells me he went public with such a plan early in the campaign "because I knew I needed to show myself to be something other than what people project me to be, which is a nice and decent person but maybe not too substantive, maybe a guy who just floated through Yale as opposed to being a leading-edge intellectual." He adds, "I wanted people to know I cared about ideas and that I was willing to think differently."

Bush does not deny that there are still gaps in his policies. He talks about increasing the share of state spending for education—thereby shrinking the inequitable funding through local property taxes—but he cannot exactly say where that funding will come from. (The cost of raising the state's share of education spending from the current 45 percent to, say, 50 percent, would send state spending soaring from $7 billion a year to $8 billion a year.) He says he wants to use his personal persuasive skills as governor to encourage localities to build "tough love" academies for unruly school kids and start mentoring programs for disadvantaged youngsters—but he doesn't say exactly how he can talk financially overburdened city councils into spending more of their own money without receiving assistance from the state. He vows to overturn a federal court's infamous Ruiz ruling that has made the cost of operating prisons excessively high—but he doesn't know yet what his arguments in court would be. . . .

On March 2, Texas Independence Day, the former president made a rare appearance for his son. He and Barbara were featured guests at a private $1,000-a-person fundraising dinner at Dallas' Loews Anatole Hotel. It was a glorious evening to be a Republican from Texas. Around the tables, the crowd was giddy from U.S. senator Kay Bailey Hutchison's recent acquittal. They talked about how strong she and Bush would look at the top of the Republican ticket in November. The ballroom was filled with polished, professional-looking women in their thirties and forties, exactly the kind of supporters Bush needs to beat Richards. . . .

"This race is really not about me. It is about the desire of everyone in this room to see to it our children can live in prosperity. I'm just the messenger," [said Bush].

But George W. wanted to make sure this audience knew this race was really all about him. When he got to the line in his prepared text that read, "As sure as I'm standing here, I know we're going to win," he said instead, "As sure as I'm standing here, I know I'm going to win." Even at that moment, he was still fighting to be his own man, someone other than his father's son.

The Republican Front-Runner

Ramesh Ponnuru

As governor of Texas, George W. Bush fulfilled campaign promises in his first one hundred days in office. He promoted adoption and parental rights, signed legislation recognizing Texans' right to carry concealed weapons, and reformed the legal and juvenile justice system lowering crime rates.

One of Bush's most successful efforts of involving faith-based institutions in welfare provisions drew rave reviews. His first priority, education, was reformed when Bush passed sweeping school legislation.

In this 1997 article, Ramesh Ponnuru, a reporter for the *National Review*, takes a look at Bush's history as governor of Texas. Noting Bush's need to find a strong agenda, Ponnuru claims the governor's discipline, personal charm, moderate temperament, and conservative record would give him the best odds of winning the Republican presidential nomination in 2000.

He [Texas governor, George W. Bush] is the latest in a long line of establishment candidates who have been conservative enough to succeed in a Republican Party that was moving right. So, for instance, Gov. Bush seems more conservative than Bob Dole, who ran a more conservative campaign in 1996 than Bush's father did in 1988. And the elder Bush [President George H.W. Bush] was to the right of Jerry Ford. . . .

For all the similarities, one thing Gov. Bush isn't is a clone of his father. For one thing, nobody doubts that he's a Texan. He used to own a controlling interest in the Texas Rangers, and, as he often says, he went to San Jacinto Junior High.

Nor is his famous name what's causing national Republicans to take notice. When Bush ran for governor in 1994, there were those who considered him a lightweight trading on his father's name. He had had a wild frat-boy reputation, and a wholly justified one, as he freely admits in speeches. And he's still irreverent, given to needling and a talented mimic. Writes *Texas Monthly*'s Paul Burka: "His enthusiasm for his job is that of a child who has just been let loose in the greatest playground in the world."

But he has also discovered discipline. He married librarian Laura Welch and they had twin girls, now teens. Laura reportedly got him reading the Bible and attending a Methodist church.... [Texas] Republican State Senator David Sibley remarks, "He's maniacal about exercise. He used to drink and he just quit. When he latches on to something, he's like a pit bull."

INTENSIVE FOCUS

As his predecessor, Democrat Ann Richards, learned too late. Gov. Richards had achieved national stature in 1988, when she ridiculed Republican presidential nominee George Bush for having been "born with a silver foot in his mouth." On the face of it, she was in a strong position to win re-election in 1994. As former Democratic consultant Mark McKinnon recalls, "In '94 the economy was in great shape, the incumbent governor was one of the most popular in state history, every Democrat on the ticket won that year—except Richards. Despite everything, George Bush beat her like a red-headed stepchild."

He did it by sticking like rubber cement to a short agenda: tort reform, juvenile justice, education, welfare. He never took the bait when she attacked him. While he talked about the next term, she defended the last one.... Says McKinnon, "He tipped his hat to the lady and said, You've done a terrific job, but I'm a conservative Republican alternative. He had a strategy and stuck to it. In old political-consultant parlance, this guy gets it. He really gets it."

He has kept the same focus as governor. The official powers of the governor are quite limited: Lieutenant Governor Bob Bullock and Comptroller John Sharp arguably wield more power, and both are Democrats. But Bush has deftly used his weak office to become a political powerhouse. He's insanely popular in Texas. According to the Harte-Hanks poll, 71 per cent of Texans think he deserves re-election;

even in the Democratic stronghold of El Paso, he has 92 per cent approval. He has no gender gap. (One adviser half-jokingly remarks that female voters must like the idea of a former wild man domesticated by a good woman.)

Democrats spent the summer debating whether even to field a candidate against him: doing so could raise turnout and endanger Democrats lower on the ticket. National Democrats, on the other hand, want to raise his negatives. That's because they fear him as a presidential candidate. If the polls are right, Bush would narrowly beat [Democratic front-runner] Al Gore if the election were held tomorrow.

ON THE ISSUES

Bush can face the voters with a solid, if uninspiring, record of moderate conservatism. He has promoted adoption and parental rights. He has signed legislation recognizing Texans' right to carry concealed weapons. He delivered on his promises on tort reform and juvenile justice; and, under Bush, Texas performs a third of the nation's executions. Gov. Bush can take credit for the fact that the decline in crime rates that began under Gov. Richards has continued.

On welfare, Bush's performance has lacked luster. Texas's welfare caseload is falling, but no faster than the rest of the country's. Bush might have had more success had he won his public fight with the Clinton Administration over his proposal to privatize the system.

But conservative welfare expert Robert Rector is skeptical: "Why privatizing the administration of the liberals' welfare system is a big deal is something I've never understood at all. The problem with welfare is not that it's administered badly. It's that it rewards idleness and illegitimacy." Indeed, the governor's idea of creating centers where those on welfare could do "one-stop shopping" for state services could expand the reach of that system.

Similarly, though the governor's efforts to involve faith-based institutions in welfare provision have drawn raves from religious conservatives, it is not clear whether their main effect will be to reform welfare or to corrupt those institutions. States like Wisconsin, where welfare rolls have fallen at twice the rate of Texas, have instead focused on work requirements. Texas doesn't have serious sanctions for shirkers, and as a result it failed to meet the federal requirement that 75 per cent of two-parent households on welfare work.

Gov. Bush can claim more success on education, his "number one priority." He has passed sweeping charter-school legislation. Respected education guru Chester Finn says he's "pretty impressed" by the governor: "He seems to believe in what I believe in." On standards, he says, "most states are in so much worse shape that Texas gets a B."

Bush's limited voucher program, however, has been a failure, with few parents aware of it and fewer public schools cooperating. Bush's rhetoric on standards has been conservative: he focused public attention on the need for all third-graders to be literate before President Clinton adopted the theme, and lately he has taken to touting the advantages of phonics. But critics complain about his lack of follow-through: conservatives on the state board of education have been fighting other Republicans—including the Bush-appointed heads of the Texas Education Agency and board of education—on behalf of higher standards, and consequently taking abuse from the press for being Christian fanatics, with nary a peep from the governor. . . .

School finance led Bush to his biggest political defeat—and, worse yet, on taxes, which are still the glue that holds the Republican coalition together. In 1989, the state Supreme Court held the state's school-funding system, based on local property taxes, unconstitutionally inequitable. The legislature's solution was to redistribute tax revenues from rich districts to poor ones. Suburban Republicans saw their tax bills skyrocket under the "Robin Hood" system. So when Gov. Bush saw the prospect of a $1-billion surplus, he jumped at the chance to solve the problem.

He proposed to use the surplus to cut property taxes. But he also proposed a tax reform: a shift from property taxes, which he called "a tax on the American dream of home ownership," to an array of consumption taxes and business taxes.

The substantive objection to the plan was that it would, over time, change the political landscape in a way that would make conservative policy goals harder to achieve. The proposal that the state provide the majority of school funding could only weaken local accountability. It's no accident that the states with high-achieving schools, like New Hampshire, rely on local funding. Yet Bush, in his 1997 State of the State speech, endorsed the key finding of the Supreme Court: that "relying too much on local property taxes . . . is inherently unequal and unfair." He thus conceded the framing of the issue as how to spend "everybody's" money on "everybody's" children.

A similar structural defect beset his tax policy. The highly visible, and therefore hard-to-raise, property tax would be cut; an array of less visible, and thus easy-to-raise, taxes would pick up the slack. Anti-tax activist Grover Norquist, who ran $120,000 worth of radio ads attacking the plan, says that though it was a net tax cut, using "a political dynamic analysis, taxes would have been higher in ten years."

The Democrat-run State House promptly hijacked Bush's plan; Norquist's Americans for Tax Reform itemized 75 different tax hikes in the resulting bill. Gov. Bush lobbied for its passage anyway, arguing that the State Senate would fix it. The Senate tried, but no compromise was reached. So the governor settled for a straight property-tax cut of $1 billion, which works out to about $150 per household. That surplus could have been spent instead, and so Gov. Bush effectively blocked any resumption of his predecessor's spending spree. Not a bad final result—if it is final; Bush let the tax-reform genie out of the bottle, and Democrats may have more than three wishes in the next legislative session. . . .

Conservatives have had other disappointments. Bush's administration has been the loudest in claiming a right to tax any commercial transaction on the Internet that has some connection to the state. He supported the creation of the "Texas Healthy Kids Corporation," which will probably receive federal funds under the Hatch-Kennedy kidcare bill. Like his father, Bush eschews partisanship: Republicans have complained about some high-profile Democrats he has appointed, and conservatives about the "movement types" he hasn't. . . .

READY FOR THE NATIONAL STAGE?

Some of Bush's fans wonder whether he's ready for the national stage. Oratory doesn't seem to run in the family, and the younger Bush reportedly tends to mispronounce words. His last two appearances in the national spotlight cast him in an unflattering light. The audience at the Midwest Republican conference in Indianapolis in August was underwhelmed by Bush's speech. And at the dedication of the Bush presidential library in November, the governor's remarks about how his father had "brought dignity and character and honor to the White House" were taken as an ill-timed rebuke to the man who beat his father. Bush's communications director, Karen Hughes, denies any such intent—an explanation that at least suggests a tone-deafness toward the media. Which raises another issue: Gov. Bush doesn't have to deal in Texas with a press as liberal or as nasty as that in Washington, or indeed with as entrenched a liberal culture. How would he handle it in a national campaign, or in national office?

And how would he deal with his father's legacy? Norquist wants Republicans to hold the line on taxes: "Bush's son cannot be a national figure until he has repudiated his father's tax increase, and demonstrated to the world that he has zero intention of doing anything so stupid and destructive." But by the next primary season, almost ten years will have passed since that tax increase. Memories may have faded. On the other hand, if Gov. Bush wastes time trying to rehabilitate his father's Administration, control of the past would become an independent reason for conservatives to oppose him. . . .

If Bush decides to run for President, though, perhaps his biggest challenge will be to explain why he wants the job. So far, he has no signature issues. His self-description as a "compassionate conservative" is the same as that of his potential rival Rep. John Kasich (R., Ohio)—and in Bush's case, it inevitably recalls his father's much-mocked promise of a "kinder, gentler" nation. Anything else? Bush often speaks of a "cultural crisis" and says, "We need a spiritual renewal in America.". . .

Bush is pro-life, with the standard exceptions for rape, incest, and the life of the mother. He failed in his effort to get a parental-notification bill through the legislature, but he succeeded in blocking a pro-euthanasia bill. Yet he wouldn't divide Republicans: Ann Stone of Republicans for Choice calls him "a bridge-builder" and takes comfort from his feud with [chairman of the Texas Republican Party Tom] Pauken, "who was the great Satan to a lot of moderates."

If he won the nomination, Bush would be a strong candidate in the general election. His personal charm is not to be underestimated. . . . Republican strategists also think that Bush's support for welfare for legal immigrants and the public education of the children of illegal immigrants, and his opposition to official-English laws would make it harder to tag him with the anti-Hispanic label.

Indeed, Gov. Bush is probably the strongest, and most conservative, candidate the Republican establishment is likely to produce. As such, how conservatives evaluate Bush in 2000 will depend on the extent to which they believe their movement has been absorbed by the Republican establishment. If they think it has largely been ensconced, many of them will go with Bush. What the country needs now, they will conclude, is the implementation of an existing center-right consensus rather than the creation of a new, more conservative one. In that case, they will find the combination of substantive conservatism and temperamental moderation quite attractive.

Progressive Politics

Dana Milbank

Dana Milbank paints a clearer picture of what
George W. Bush stands for in the areas of economics,
taxation, and international affairs. Leaning toward
private sector solutions, Bush prefers a limited role
for government and welcomes church and state cooperation on contending with social ills such as
drugs and crime. As a governor untouched by Republican constituencies, Bush also gravitated toward
progressive thinking on taxes, prescription drugs,
poverty, and education. Many commentators have
likened Bush's "concern for the underclass" rhetoric
to ideals traditionally espoused by liberals. Milbank's
1999 article focuses on the ideology of Bush as the
governor of Texas and highlights the themes and political agenda Bush would later bring to his bid for
the presidency. Milbank is a writer for *New Republic*
magazine and has authored books on politics.

To get a clearer idea of what Bush is about, one must leave
the governor's mansion and drive 20 minutes north to the
improbably named Austin suburb of Jollyville. There you
will find Mrs. Gutierrez's second-grade class in the middle
of its weekly character-building lesson. A boy named Tray
raises his hand to compliment Philip for "trying not to hurt
people's feelings." Pint-sized Jessie pipes up to compliment
Pamela because "when I had no friends at recess she came
over and played with me." But then a boy complains about
some naughty behavior. "Is that responsible?" Mrs. Gutierrez asks. "No!" the class says in unison. "Is that compassionate?" "No!" "What should we be doing at all times?" the
teacher asks. "Personal best," the tots respond. Thus do the
happy children of Jollyville, under a public school program
championed by Governor Bush, learn how to become "good
citizens for Texas." In December, they studied perseverance;

Dana Milbank, "What 'W' Stands For," *New Republic*, vol. 220, April 26, 1999, p. 66.

in March, self-reliance. Those with exemplary character get a seat at the "VIP Honor Table" in the lunchroom.

Still don't grasp George W.'s philosophy? Then drive north for another hour to Waco, the town David Koresh and his radically anti-government Branch Davidian sect put on the map. Here, in another public school program backed by Bush, a Baptist seminary student named Brandon Barnard is warning a group of sixth-graders at Midway Intermediate School about genital warts "the size of my fist." Such warts are tough to remove, he adds. "You do what you want," Barnard says, as the children squirm. "I don't want anybody cutting, burning, or freezing that part of my body." Barnard flashes a slide on the screen listing the consequences of pre-marital sex: cancer, AIDS, death, pain, emotional scars, infertility. Then he shows a slide listing the consequences of abstinence: self-control, self-respect, self-discipline. "Virginity is a gift," Barnard declares, holding up a package in purple wrapping paper. "I'm proud to be a virgin."

The two scenes, and hundreds like them playing out across Texas, encapsulate the Bush ideology. It is, at first glance, a conservative message, based on the notion that traditional values will help prevent poverty and other ills. But, deeper down, Bush's approach, warts and all, should sound familiar—and possibly comfortable—to some liberals. He assumes that government can be a force for good and that it has a responsibility to help the weak. Bush's stances so far on national issues such as Kosovo and abortion have been full of ambiguity and obfuscation, seemingly dictated more by tactic than by principle. Still, beneath Bush's mush is some evidence that he's trying to introduce a government-friendly conservatism to a party often hijacked by harsh and selfish ideology.

Bush's own label for his philosophy, "compassionate conservatism," is a tired phrase and easy to ridicule. Bob Dole used it to great effect in his 1988 presidential campaign. But, in Bush's case, it appears to imply a more activist style of conservative governance. Instead of demanding anti-abortion laws, he seeks alternatives, such as abstinence and adoption programs, which will reduce abortions. Instead of the usual Republican lock-'em-up-and-throw-away-the-key line on criminal justice, he has fostered a faith-based rehabilitation program for prisoners. He has demanded increases in education funding and opposed anti-immigration measures. Instead of a flat tax, he talks of modest cuts and reducing regressivity. "What he understands about conservatism that many conservatives don't is that, at its core, it's caring about the poor, the underclass," says Al Hubbard, an old business-school classmate of Bush's who has helped him line up advisers. "The biggest problem facing our country is the underclass and the lack of opportunity for the underclass." And the answer, says Hubbard, "is not about saying, 'Lower taxes, reduce regulation, and everybody will be fine.'" It is, rather, about a host of government interventions that Bush and his advisers have proposed: mentoring programs, literacy programs, welfare-to-work programs in which church volunteers offer both skills training and Bible study, cuts in sales taxes that disproportionately affect the poor, tax incentives to aid poor neighborhoods, and substantial increases in public education spending.

These ideas may sound more Jesse Jackson than Ronald Reagan, but they are common in Bush circles. Typical is Mark McKinnon, who worked for Democrats . . . before agreeing to be Bush's media strategist. "He's willing to step out on issues that have long been contrary to the interests of the Republican Party," McKinnon says. "He's figured out a way for Republicans to actually be for something." Several conservative Democrats in the Texas legislature, likewise, backed Bush's reelection. Even Texas Democratic Party spokeswoman Liz Chadderdon admits: "When you look at Bush's agenda, you could plug in Clinton's name and it would be the same."

NEW COALITION

More of such words from Democrats would make Bush a formidable challenger to Vice President [Al] Gore. On the other hand, the very things that make Democrats embrace Bush will irk the GOP's conservative primary voters. The Bush strategy appears to be a calculation that the hard right of the Republican Party, after two presidential defeats, may be willing to take half a loaf—much as liberal Democrats accepted the more centrist Clinton in 1992 after twelve years in the wilderness. Bush may also be gambling on support from independents, who can vote in Republican primaries in some states. It's a plausible strategy, particularly because so many Republican candidates are already vying for the far right's backing.

But, while Bush's philosophy may have a ring of familiarity to some Democrats, they would be mistaken to think he is one of them. "It sounds like liberalism because there's concern for the poor, but it doesn't come out of liberalism," says Marvin Olasky, a University of Texas professor who advises Bush. "He's a throwback to one of the conservative strains of the nineteenth century." Bush doesn't come from the economic conservative/social Darwinist school but neither does he side with the fundamentalists/moralists.

So what is Bush? Some conservatives have argued that he is reunifying the Reagan coalition of fiscal conservatives and the religious right that fell apart under Bush's father. But those wishful thinkers will be disappointed. First, Bush isn't fleeing from his old man. Many of young Bush's top advisers—Larry Lindsey, Michael Boskin, John Taylor, Martin Feldstein, Al Hubbard, Paul Wolfowitz, Condoleezza Rice, Bob Kimmitt, and Josh Bolten—also served in or gave advice to his father's administration.

More significantly, the coalition Bush is assembling is in some ways the opposite of Reaganism. Reagan's alliance was in large part libertarian, and young Bush's is communitarian. The communitarian movement, known also by its "civil society," "social capital," and "quality of life" buzzwords, is vaguely defined, but it's based on the idea that too much Hobbesian individualism has created an atomized, selfish, and disconnected society. Government, by encouraging private and nonprofit efforts to restore community, and by tempering individual rights with responsibility to society, can help to restore the purpose. But, in truth, the philosophy's roots go much further back, to Aristotle, who believed that government could help to engineer an ideal society. It's the kind of conservatism championed by Edmund Burke, and it claims such historic figures as Disraeli and Bismarck, who were pioneers of the welfare state. A few modern conservatives, including Olasky and columnist George Will (whose 1983 book *Statecraft as Soulcraft* was an anti-individualist tract), have taken this view, but they were oddballs until now.

"It's a new coalition," Olasky says. "That's why some people on the right are so uncomfortable" with Bush. In Bush's way of thinking, the individual-rights champions on both sides—the civil libertarians on the left and the anti-government, leave-us-alone right-wingers—are on the outside. They'll be replaced by a mixture of incentive-based conservatives and good-government liberals. "He could bring a lot of communitarian Democrats with him," Olasky says. If liberals were willing to give up some federal control, Bush and likeminded conservatives would be content to spend more money on the poor and other government pursuits. "Let's throw away the budget cutters," Olasky says. "I see that coming with Bush. I see that as part of a governing alliance."

Some still suspect that Bush is a moderate, establishment Republican in his father's image. But they, too, are mistaken. President Bush, with a sense of noblesse oblige, saw himself as a duty-bound steward with little ideological passion. But his son, a baby-boomer and a product of the 1960s, is more activist than caretaker.

In this sense, his outlook is somewhat like Al Gore's, and the two are largely vying for the same governing coalition. Gore's "livability" agenda, proposals to rescue communities from urban sprawl, are part of the same quality-of-life genre that inspires Bush. Young Bush and Gore, of course, are both scions of powerful political fathers, educated in prep schools and the Ivy League. Both men are correspondingly cautious and tend to favor small initiatives to sweeping change. Gore also grasps the "limited government" philosophy that is a pillar of Governor Bush's thought. In fact, Bill Bradley, taking a more traditional Democratic view, contrasts himself from Gore by promising to "cultivate ten strong oaks rather than sprinkling water on a thousand house plants." Former Clinton official Lanny Davis, a fraternity brother of Bush's at Yale (and a Gore backer), says: "Among all the Republicans running, [Bush] comes closest to the centrist Democratic philosophy." Bush, says Davis, is "as close to Bill Clinton and Al Gore as he could be politically. George Bush is on the forty-seven yard line in one direction, and Al Gore is on the forty-seven yard line in the other direction."

Bush aides, not surprisingly, bristle at the Clinton-Gore comparison, which they see as an attempt to make their candidate appear too liberal to Republican primary voters. "Sorry, Lanny," says Karen Hughes, Bush's press secretary. "Governor Bush is not on the same field. The Democrats are trying to make comparisons that will hurt him in the Republican primary. It's ridiculous, and they know it's not true." Hughes, for her part, calls her boss an "activist conservative." "He's not anti-government," she says. "He believes there is a role for government, but it should be limited."

EMERGING PHILOSOPHY

Hughes, in many respects, is correct. Though their coalitions overlap and their philosophies intersect, there will still be plenty to separate Bush and Gore. Bush leans toward private-sector solutions, while Gore errs on the side of government intervention. Bush backed legislation allowing Texans to carry concealed firearms; Gore is a strong gun-control advocate. Gore is famously green, while Bush, backed by business and oil men, has been advised by the Competitive Enterprise Institute's Fred Smith, who wants public land privatized and says that the "EPA is a massive mistake." Their differences on abortion and organized labor are equally stark. The two men also will be forced to placate the hardcore interest groups in their parties: Gore and labor, Bush and fundamentalists. If they are nominated, the choice for many voters may come down not to the men but to their fellow travelers: Bush's Bob Barr or Gore's Ted Kennedy?

Virtually none of this Bush philosophy has emerged yet, and that's just fine with the governor's advisers. "He gains in the polls every week by doing nothing," says one. Even Bush has been marveling at his good fortune. "I held a press conference on the drought, and it rained the next day," he told the Texas Daily Newspaper Association at a recent luncheon. "Now my mother's calling up for tips on the lottery." The reception for Bush is, as always, adoring. The governor, after a round of handshakes, gets a fawning introduction and a standing ovation from the newspaper executives. His speech is full of progressive-sounding themes—research and development tax credits and references to his sales tax cut for diapers and over-the-counter medicines. He calls education "by far the most important thing a state does," vowing to hold schools accountable, a favorite theme of New Democrats.

PIONEERING A VISION

After the session, the Texas press tries to trap Bush into stating positions. They pepper him with abortion questions ("I'm pro-life, and I've had a consistent position"), gay rights ("I believe we should never discriminate against anybody"), and hate-crime legislation ("All crime is hate"). Three times, Bush falls into a reporter's trap and begins to elaborate on his philosophy but then catches himself. "I've stated my position," he says. Then he returns to his preferred subjects:

limited government, local control, strong families, personal responsibility. The governor chats with the reporters about his latest fishing trip in his familiar, locker-room manner. His banter is friendly. . . . The reporters are charmed. And, when they return to their typewriters, they will find, once again, that deft Governor Bush has told them nothing new.

But, while Bush continues to be cleverly opaque in public, he has been meeting in Austin with a steady procession of policy advisers. Bush is far from devising a specific agenda, but his advisers paint a surprisingly unified vision of the philosophy he would adopt as president.

The Russian kitsch industry specializes in matryoshka, hollow wooden figures of the country's leaders. Inside a Yeltsin shell is a Gorbachev egg, which surrounds a Brezhnev egg right down to a solid Lenin core. If one were building such a toy to explain Bush's domestic policy, the first layer inside the Bush shell would be Indianapolis Mayor Steve Goldsmith. Inside Goldsmith would be Harvard Professor Robert Putnam.

Goldsmith, a Republican, is Bush's chief domestic policy adviser. He is by necessity a pragmatist, and he has been a pioneer in the civil-society movement also championed by the likes of New York Mayor Rudolph Giuliani. His idiosyncratic policies in Indianapolis have a streak of concern for social justice running through them—and Bush's will, too. "I think the governor is articulating a new vision for the Republican Party," Goldsmith says. "You can't miss the idea that the marketplace operates unevenly. . . . Prosperity ought to have a purpose. We're talking about the poor in a very serious way." Among the proposals that civil-society conservatives favor is a large charity tax credit for those who volunteer to help the poor. "I do think he's seriously conservative," Goldsmith says of Bush, but he doesn't think conservatism should be "an excuse to ignore people who are without opportunity."

Goldsmith's website lists a profusion of good-government proposals: reinventing government, more police, fatherhood initiatives, high-tech incentives, neighborhood empowerment, worker retraining. That agenda may well turn out to be Bush's, but it also happens to summarize Al Gore's. "A legitimate observation," Goldsmith says with a chuckle. To be sure, the similarity is more in nomenclature than in policy. But, Goldsmith adds, "As the New Democrats have moved to the center to some extent and as the Republicans recognize the need to be compassionate to the poor, the distinction narrows." The mayor lists among the civil-society thinkers who influence him Harvard's Putnam, a left-leaning thinker who worked in the Carter administration.

Putnam, whose "bowling alone" theory seeped into national political discourse, sees promise for the left in the direction Bush and Goldsmith are taking. "Civic reengagement is a fundamental prerequisite for a new progressive era," he says. Though Goldsmith and Putnam disagree on the role of government in such efforts, Goldsmith's community programs are just the kind Putnam favors. "That's what worries the far right about Bush," he says.

PROGRESSIVE POPULIST

Bush often seems to be torn between progressive instincts and Republican constituencies. In other words, he waffles. This year, for example, the Texas legislature has been debating a federally authorized expansion of health care to children living at 150 percent of the poverty line, or even 200 percent. In February, Bush said, "If you get up to one hundred and fifty percent, we are going to be covering a lot of children that aren't covered today," according to the *Austin American-Statesman*. But two weeks later he softened, and the same paper quoted him as saying, "I'll take a definite position at the appropriate time." On affirmative action, similarly, both opponents and supporters have claimed him. He says he's for "goals" but against "quotas," a vague distinction further complicated by his support for "affirmative access" (the awarding of spots in state universities to high school students who finish in the top ten percent of their graduating classes). Some say that's affirmative action by another name—or that it's little different from Clinton's "mend it, don't end it" fudge.

On policies at the core of his civil-society philosophy, though, Bush hasn't been ambiguous. He admires such programs as "Turn Around Texas," in which local residents and police harass drug dealers in their neighborhoods. Like Giuliani, he's a tough law-and-order guy who has presided over expanded police powers. And he welcomes church-state cooperation. When a faith-based drug rehab group got into trouble with a state agency, Bush called off the regulatory dogs, saving the program. "The state has been our advocate, our boosters," says Gerry Phelps, a Methodist minister who founded a welfare-to-work program that offers job training, life-skills lessons, and Bible study.

Bush's economic policy, like his social policy, has a peculiar preoccupation with the poor and working class. Some of his friends and advisers hear echoes of Jack Kemp. "In a funny way, you can almost call him a populist," says James Langdon, a Democratic lawyer and an old friend of Bush's. When the two men discussed foreign policy, Langdon recalls that Bush declared: "I want to know how it's going to affect American workers." Thought Langdon: "That's a strange thing for a Republican to say."

Bush's economics chief, Larry Lindsey, a former Fed governor, has strong supply-side credentials. But Lindsey says times have changed. "The country doesn't need another revolution," he told me. "In my view, we need to refine. One group that particularly needs conservative help are those with low and moderate income." That sounds like the old liberal complaint about income inequality. Lindsey, who has described himself as a populist, would cut taxes but keep the charitable-contribution and mortgage-interest deductions and the capital gains tax. To offset tax cuts that favor the wealthy, he would cut regressive taxes like the telephone excise tax or offer a higher percentage cut to those in lower brackets.

Missing from Bushian thinking is the voodoo-economics idea (as Dad put it) that tax cuts pay for themselves. "The governor would think that's silly," says Glenn Hubbard, a Columbia University economist who is advising Bush on taxes, budget, and health care. "I don't think he's ideological at all," says Hubbard. "He has strong principles, but they're at the big-picture level. He wants market solutions wherever possible, but he also recognizes a role for government in helping markets work." Bush's record in Texas, a boom-time combination of modest tax cuts and small spending increases, confirms this. His latest budget includes a $2 billion property tax cut, $1.5 billion more for teachers and schools, and plans to cut sales taxes on diapers and medication.

The anti-tax Republicans, already suspicious because of President Bush's tax-raising budget deal in 1990, seem to be acquiescing to the son, but not without some difficulty. Grover Norquist's Americans for Tax Reform spent $120,000 on radio ads protesting a tax shift Governor Bush proposed early in his administration. Bush wanted to relieve the tax burden by shifting it in part onto small businesses. Conservatives were sure that the creation of new taxes would eventually make taxes higher. Bush retreated in favor of a straight cut. "He sinned in thought but not in action," Norquist says. Norquist, who has made the pilgrimage to Austin, says Bush backs his view on all major issues: school choice, tort reform, and a supermajority for raising taxes. He's not a purist, of course. "He will be a creature of what's around him," Norquist says. Still, unlike purists such as Forbes, Bush can win. "There are ideologues, icebreakers who open new paths," Norquist says. "But you get your head beaten in when you do that."

INTERNATIONAL AFFAIRS

In international affairs, Bush comes closer to being his father's son. This shouldn't be surprising. He is a typical governor, meaning he hasn't had to worry about foreign events. And he grew up with a foreign-policy-obsessed father, so something was bound to rub off. Young Bush doesn't care as deeply about the international scene as his father, who served as CIA chief and ambassador to the United Nations and China. He would, advisers say, follow the Clinton model of a domestic policy presidency.

Bush is surrounding himself with a hawkish crowd: Wolfowitz, of the Johns Hopkins School of Advanced International Studies (and a sometime contributor to the *New Republic* magazine), Stanford Provost Rice, and Dick Cheney. Others include Donald Rumsfeld, Kimmitt, and Richard Perle, committed internationalists who have no patience for [ultraconservative Pat] Buchanan's protectionist line. His foreign policy advisers say Bush would be determined to project a more muscular presence overseas and pursue an aggressive missile defense system at home. He is determined that GOP "rivals won't out-tough him," as one adviser puts it. "He strikes me as tougher-minded in some ways than his father," says Perle. And, says Perle, Bush is likely to take the internationalism displayed by Clinton and Gore even further: "There will be sharp differences on almost every foreign and security issue."

So far, however, there's been precious little evidence of this. For instance, while his rival John McCain has taken a detailed and forceful stance on the unfolding Kosovo crisis [in the former Yugoslavia]—stating that, if he were president, he would "intensify the bombing campaign to a very significant degree" and that, in contrast to Clinton, he would "consider the option . . . of ground troops"—Bush has shied away from offering any opinions at all. "As governor of Texas, I do not have access to all the information and military intelligence available to the commander-in-chief," he explained to reporters at a March 25 press conference—one of the few times he's actually commented on Kosovo. Having thus excused himself from coming up with any answers of his own, Bush contented himself with asking questions instead. "Will the [NATO air strikes] lead to the goal of ending the conflict and bringing peace and stability to the region? I fervently hope so, although, I share the concerns and misgivings of many Texans and Americans.". . .

On matters of international economics, Bush is an ardent free-trader, his advisers say, even less inclined than Clinton to engage in trade wars. George Shultz, the former Reagan secretary of state who has been coaching Bush, sees him developing a trade-based foreign policy emphasizing overtures to Mexico and a stronger emphasis on our own hemisphere. Other than his free-trading inclinations, Shultz doesn't believe Bush has an overarching worldview. "Obviously we need to have a sense of strategy, but we need to realize things we do along the way add up," he says.

But, as in the Clinton White House, Bush's aggressive foreign policy could at times conflict with his free-trade stance. The GOP, for example, plans to hammer Gore over the Chinese security issue, arguing that the administration's engagement policy has given away too much to China. But this won't work well for Bush, because his father had much the same policy and because he may have a weak spot of his own for a troublesome foreign country, if his overtures to Mexico as governor are any indication. Like China, Mexico is a country where the U.S.'s interest in fostering trade often conflicts with its other interests—for example, in fighting the drug trade and supporting efforts to clean up the corrupt and anti-democratic tendencies of the Mexican government. The question then is whether Mexico could be to Bush fils what China was to Bush pere. And, notes one adviser, "it would be a tricky dance for Bush" to try to tar Clinton with the China-appeasing brush.

In his talks with advisers, Bush has confessed his ignorance of foreign policy details. But, at the same time, he seems almost cocky. A couple of months back, at a meeting on the defense budget, Bush cut off his advisers who were reciting the minutiae of Pentagon budgeting. "Shouldn't we back up?" he asked, requesting a discussion on military strategy. "If you get that right, the budget will take care of itself." At another meeting, Bush started the discussion with a bold assertion. "I'm going to be the next president of the United States," he said. "I need your help, not to become president—I'll take care of that—but to be a good president."

CHAPTER 3

THE ELECTION
OF THE CENTURY

GEORGE W. BUSH

The Presidential Race

Lee Edwards

Thirty days after the 2000 election George W. Bush finally accrued the 271 electoral votes need to secure the U.S. presidency. Lee Edwards, senior editor at the *World & I*, claims that the election was not as close as it seemed. Bush won twenty-nine out of fifty states and three-fourths of the counties in America. Bush also carried small towns and rural areas with 60 percent of the vote. Edwards evaluates the 2000 presidential race using five areas of a campaign: funding, organization, issues, the media, and the candidates as campaigners to determine the strengths and weaknesses of Bush and his political rival, Democrat Al Gore. According to Edwards's analysis, Bush clearly matched or bested Gore in all of these key areas of the 2000 campaign.

A presidential election is usually a referendum on continuity or change, but in 2000 the American people seemed to vote for continuity and change.

The public's desire for change frustrated Vice President Al Gore, who should have been able to win the presidency by promising to continue the unquestioned peace and prosperity of the Clinton-Gore years. But President Bill Clinton was so personally unwelcome in the living rooms of most Americans that Gore kept Clinton at arm's length throughout the campaign, insisting again and again, "I am my own man." Gore strove to negate the wish for change by emphasizing the "dangerous" nature of his opponent's reforms, such as tax cuts for the "rich" and partial privatization of Social Security.

The desire for continuity hampered Gov. George W. Bush, who had to be careful not to criticize too harshly the popular record of the Clinton-Gore administration. He instead promised to solve the problems that had not been addressed by Clinton and Gore while using nonthreatening rhetoric such as "compassionate conservatism." Bush was unable to use the character issue as much as he had planned after Gore successfully decoupled himself from Clinton at the Democratic convention.

CLOSEST CONTEST SINCE 1960

The ambivalent mood of the electorate produced the closest presidential contest since 1960 when John Kennedy defeated Richard Nixon by only two-tenths of one percent of the popular vote—about the same margin by which Gore apparently topped Bush in 2000. But Kennedy won both the popular and electoral contests, while Gore narrowly won only the popular vote on November 7. Bush won the electoral vote and therefore the presidency, accruing 271 electoral votes (one more than needed) to Gore's 267. Or did he?

Bush was preparing to announce some of the more prominent members of his cabinet (Colin Powell as secretary of state, etc.) when Florida with its 25 electoral votes suddenly became too close to call. The nation was plunged into a protracted political and legal battle over whether a majority of Florida's voters had voted for Bush or Gore that ended more than one month later.

And yet, depending upon your measuring stick, the election was not close. Bush carried 29 out of 50 states and over three-fourths of the counties in America. The disparity is even greater when you note that the Bush counties covered some 2.4 million square miles of the country, the Gore counties only about 580,000 square miles.

On the other hand, according to *National Review*'s Kate O'Beirne, Gore carried voters in the largest cities by a three-to-one margin. In cities with populations between 50,000 and 500,000, Gore's margin was three to two. The suburbs split evenly between the candidates, and Bush carried smaller towns and rural areas with 60 percent of the vote.

This geographic divide, says O'Beirne, "reflects a cultural split over the role of government." Federal subsidies and mediation are valued in the cities, but in less densely populated areas government and its benefits are "best kept at arm's length."

From the viewpoint of political science, the 2000 presidential race was amazingly close because the two aspirants were so evenly matched in the five essential areas of a campaign: money, organization, the candidates as campaigners, issues, and the media.

MONEY

A shrewd and successful politician once remarked, "Money is the mother's milk of politics." In our modern media society, a political campaign cannot survive without it. And because the stakes were high (control of the White House and the Congress) and the economy was booming, the 2000 federal elections were the most expensive in U.S. history, with analysts estimating that as much as $3 billion was raised and spent on the presidential and congressional races.

The two major presidential candidates each received $67.6 million in public funds. But that funding was easily exceeded by the soft money [private donations] the two parties spent to promote their presidential contenders—an estimated $236 million. Another $300 million was spent by various groups, including single-issue organizations, trade unions, and corporations, on issue ads on behalf of all federal candidates, with most of the advertising appearing on television.

Although Republicans raised more money than Democrats as usual—an estimated $505.5 million to $371.6 million—the gap between the two parties was not as wide as in the past, and liberal groups held their own with conservative groups in political fund-raising. In the crucial area of money in the 2000 race, therefore, Bush had an advantage over Gore by a surprisingly small margin.

ORGANIZATION

Democrats have always depended on the trade unions to deliver the vote on Election Day. The AFL-CIO delivered "big time" in 2000, with union households accounting for 26 percent of all votes, up from 19 percent in 1992. In Michigan, one of the battleground states that Gore carried, union members provided 43 percent of the votes as auto workers got Election Day off.

Black voters, another key Democratic voting bloc, were also a prime objective of organized labor and groups like the NAACP. Although the national black voter turnout was the same in 2000 as four years ago, the turnout by blacks in pivotal states such as Florida and Illinois increased dramatically. Gore benefited enormously: 93 percent of Florida's black voters backed the vice president, compared with 86 percent for President Clinton four years ago.

The Christian Coalition is the Republicans' equivalent of the Democrats' AFL-CIO. The coalition distributed 70 million voter guides last November, up from 40 million in 1996, but it had nothing like the unions' voter delivery system on Election Day. Members of the pro-business National Federation of Independent Business were contacted by phone and mail six million times, up from three million times four years ago. But the federation has no organized plan to get voters to the polls.

In all, the Republican Victory 2000 drive spent an estimated $100 million on automated phone-mail messages, a paid and a volunteer phone-bank operation, a massive direct-mail drive, and an Internet and E-mail operation. The Democrats' Election Day drive cost about $30 million and fielded 50,000 volunteers. Although Republicans outspent Democrats several-fold, they did not outorganize their rivals because of the highly efficient and experienced AFL-CIO effort.

In the area of organization, then, Gore had a slight but decisive advantage over Bush.

THE CANDIDATES AS CAMPAIGNERS

With his ready smile and easy way with people, George W. Bush reminded people of Ronald Reagan; Bush was what the polls call a "natural" on the hustings. The governor even strolled back to the press section of his campaign plane to banter with reporters. In the minds of some observers, Al Gore, always prepared, ever-striving, resembled another former but less attractive president: Jimmy Carter. Gore compensated for his admitted lack of charm with a ferocious tenacity—he was still phoning the news media and urging Democrats to turn out the vote late in the afternoon of Election Day.

The early line on Bush was that he was not smart enough to be president, but after his steady performance in the three presidential debates, most Americans agreed that the Texas governor could handle the programmatic and intellectual demands of the presidency. Gore was overly aggressive in the debates—at one point he came so close to his opponent that Barbara Bush later said she feared the vice president would punch her son in the nose. Gore was eager to portray himself as a fighter, while Bush portrayed himself as the healer. TV viewers seemed to prefer healing to fighting.

Bush is a delegator, who approves a strategy and then lets aides implement it. He is enormously disciplined. He stuck to a basic message of tax cuts, Social Security reform, a stronger military, and school choice wherever he went. Gore is an 18-

hours-a-day, hands-on, check-every-nuance administrator. During the campaign, Gore seemed to offer almost as many themes as there are states in the Union, finally settling on a classic Democratic argument—he was the man of the people fighting the evil corporate interests.

The candidates understood that personality matters: they appeared more often on The Tonight Show With Jay Leno than Meet the Press. In the final weekend before election day, both nominees taped self-deprecating cameos for the satirical Saturday Night Live. But the affable Bush topped the uptight Gore in almost every poll. "Gore is smarter, more articulate, more experienced," explained pollster John Zogby, "and yet he's not blowing this election away." Because, said Zogby, "he's just a less likable character than George Bush."

In the category of candidate-campaigner, therefore, George Bush clearly bested Al Gore. Bush's only serious flaw was a tendency to coast when ahead: he took a Sunday off just one week before the election and never stumped as energetically (one could say frenetically) as Gore.

ISSUES

Candidates distill the issues in the closing days of a campaign, and Bush and Gore followed this traditional pattern in late October and early November 2000. Before conservative crowds, Governor Bush stressed cutting taxes, strengthening the military, and promoting school choice (i.e., vouchers). To swing voters, he promised prescription drugs for seniors, Social Security reform, and tax cuts for the middle class and working poor. "My opponent," Bush invariably said, "thinks the surplus is the government's money. I believe the surplus is the people's money."

Before Democratic audiences, Vice President Gore portrayed himself as a Harry Truman–like populist who advocated equal pay for women, housing protection for gays, and an increase in the minimum wage. He consistently attacked his opponent as beholden to millionaires and special interests. He dismissed Bush's tax cut plan as "a massive redistribution of wealth from the middle class to the wealthiest few" and his proposed partial privatization of Social Security as "dangerous." In contrast, Gore offered targeted tax cuts aimed mostly at lower- and middle-income taxpayers and increased federal spending of at least $2.5 trillion over 10 years.

In other words, George Bush campaigned as a slightly to

the right, limited-government Republican while Al Gore campaigned as a slightly to the left, activist-government Democrat. In the 2000 presidential race, Bush was no Reagan revolutionary, Gore no Clinton New Democrat.

Because Americans are divided in their feelings about the role of government—exit polls revealed an electorate wary about Washington's entanglement in their lives but still desirous of federal entitlements—neither candidate was able to dominate in the area of issues.

THE MEDIA

There are two kinds of media in a political campaign— "free" media (what television, radio, newspapers, magazines, and other media report about a candidate and his campaign) and paid media (what the candidates say about themselves in advertisements run mostly on television).

In 2000, both major candidates showed they had studied and absorbed the lessons of the successful Reagan and Clinton campaigns. Bush and Gore usually spoke before enthusiastic crowds with a bank of American flags behind them and a field of placards before them. Their stump speeches were a litany of short, punchy sentences, crafted for sound bites. They wore blue suits and red ties for the TV debates but switched to open-necked shirts at partisan rallies.

Although most Washington journalists lean to the left politically, they did not regard Vice President Gore with the same fondness as they had President Clinton. They conceded Gore his brainpower but mocked his constantly shifting search on the campaign trail for the right-colored suit and the right facial expression.

In contrast, many national reporters personally liked Governor Bush, although they doubted his capacity to be president. They welcomed Bush's relaxed manner, his sense of humor, his willingness to talk informally with them outside staged events. They even came to admit that he was not as dumb as they had suggested he was at the beginning of the campaign.

But when the race narrowed in the last week, many in the media revealed a political bias. On the final weekend, Gore asked churchgoers at a prayer breakfast to support him, saying, "Good overcomes evil if we choose that outcome." And responding to Bush's promise to appoint "strict constructionists" to the Supreme Court, Gore recalled "the strictly constructed meaning" applied to the Constitution when it was written—"how some people [i.e., slaves] were considered three-fifths of a human being." The networks barely mentioned the vice president's highly charged remarks.

In contrast, they went into a frenzy over a 24-year-old story of young George W. Bush being arrested for driving under the influence of alcohol in Maine. ABC's Nightline devoted an entire program to the incident, NBC's Today much of its morning show.

In the area of paid media, Gore and Bush spent millions of dollars a day to keep their campaign messages running and up to date in key markets across the country. Many ads presented a smiling, energetic, concerned candidate, explaining how he would solve the problems of the day. Others—so-called attack ads—critically analyzed his opponent's positions, often by omitting essential facts. A GOP [Republican Party] ad, for example, derided Gore for claiming he invented the Internet, although the vice president admitted he had exaggerated in taking credit.

The TV networks' most egregious and public error came on election night when they declared, just before 8:00 P.M., that Gore had carried Florida, signaling that Bush had probably lost the presidential race, only to reverse themselves six hours later to say that Bush had won the state and therefore the presidency, only to retract that assertion 90 minutes later and admit the state was too close to call. "This syndrome of rushing to judgment," wrote veteran correspondent Georgie Anne Geyer, "has, step by foolish step, been institutionalized into television news."

In the fifth and final area of a presidential campaign, the media, Bush and Gore once again were almost tied, with neither candidate having a clear advantage.

The 2000 presidential election reflected American politics in all its high drama (the presidential debates) and low comedy (butterfly ballots and hanging chads). But Americans did not worry needlessly about the outcome. They knew there would be no military coup, no UN peacekeeping force, no new election. They knew, rather, that in time there would be a winner, a transition, and an inauguration. And they were encouraged by the spirit of bipartisanship that emerged in Washington, led by the man who offered himself as a unifier and not a divider during the campaign—George W. Bush, the forty-third president of the United States of America.

The Predicted Tie

James W. Ceaser and Andrew E. Busch

In the following 2001 article James W. Ceaser and Andrew E. Busch examine the political climate of the United States that culminated in the closest and most controversial election in a century. Ceaser and Busch note that Republican and Democratic voters had reached parity in numbers during the 2000 election, leaving little doubt that a race between George W. Bush and Al Gore would be close. The authors then trace the events of election night in which a see-saw contest for electoral votes left neither candidate a clear winner. James W. Ceaser is professor of government and foreign affairs at the University of Virginia. He is the author of several books on American politics and American political thought. Coauthor Andrew E. Busch teaches American government at the University of Denver where he is an associate professor. He has also authored several books on American politics.

Compared to the results of other general elections in American history, the contest in 2000 ended with the closest possible division of seats between the parties in the Senate (50 senators from each party), the fourth closest division of seats (by percentage) in the House, and the second closest presidential race by the electoral vote. . . . It is by far the closest election in American history. . . .

Trouble began on election night with the collapse of the television network's vote projection system, which is relied on today, informally, to declare presidential winners. Trouble spread next to disputes about the accuracy and reliability of election and balloting machinery in Florida, and by implication in the nation as a whole. It then finally moved on to confusion over Florida's election laws and, more ominously, to controversy over the rightful powers of state judicial and political institutions.

James W. Ceaser and Andrew E. Busch, *The Perfect Tie: The True Story of the 2000 Presidential Election*. Lanham, MD: Rowman & Littlefield Publishers, Inc., 2001. Copyright © 2001 by Rowman & Littlefield Publishers, Inc. Reproduced by permission.

In the end, the nation's political system held up. Or at least it held up in the sense that a president of the United States, George W. Bush, was finally chosen, albeit more than five weeks after election day. . . . It took a highly controversial decision by the U.S. Supreme Court (determined by a five to four vote) overruling a highly controversial decision by the Florida Supreme Court (determined by a four to three vote) to issue George Bush his election. Bush assumed the presidency with the formal blessings of almost everyone in the political class, and with general support from the American people. . . .

The last disputed presidential election [was] the Hayes-Tilden contest of 1876, when a close national election result led to a revisiting of the votes in a few of the reconstruction governments in the southern states, including Florida. . . . [In the 2000 election] it was the exceptional way the vote was distributed around the country, coupled with an unexpected technical challenge that by chance occurred in the state of Florida, where the difference in vote totals between the two main candidates was smaller than the margin of error that the electoral mechanisms could handle. . . .

PREDICTING THE TIE

Could the improbable results of the election of 2000 have been foreseen? . . .

Political scientists in the middle of the last decade began to suggest that the general electoral condition of our era made a perfect tie conceivable. Even to think in such terms, it must be said, required a conceptual breakthrough in the study of elections. Historical patterns had led analysts to conclude that "normal" electoral alignments consisted of one party gaining a clear long-term advantage over the other, as the Democrats had managed to do for the two or three decades following the elections of 1932 and 1936. Electoral observers in the 1990s were therefore on the lookout for one of the parties to establish clear dominance. . . . Repeated observations in the middle 1990s [showed, however,] that Democratic and Republican partisans were fairly evenly balanced in the electorate. . . . According to a well-known political scientist, Paul Allen Beck, Democrats . . . are about a third of the electorate (perhaps a bit more) and Republicans also about a third. The large remaining slice of the modern electoral pie contains the grouping of non-partisan voters, also roughly a third of the electorate, therefore equal to each of the two partisan slices.

This segment floats between the two parties and is easily attracted to independent candidates and third parties. Modern elections accordingly display a good deal of volatility from one contest to the next. . . .

Successful presidential candidates have been those who have found a way to maintain the enthusiasm and support of their core supporters, while managing to appeal to a larger portion of this floating vote.

Now imagine an election in which almost all of the partisans stick by the candidate of their own party and in which the short-term factors pressure the floating voters equally in different and ultimately offsetting directions. Given the basic shape of the modern electorate, the result would approach parity. This is just about what happened in 2000. Party adherents voted overwhelmingly for "their" candidates, a result that probably had less to do with any extraordinary appeal of Gore and Bush among the candidates' own supporters than with their inability to generate much cross-partisan interest. Whatever the cause, partisan faithfulness in 2000 reached the highest level for any modern election and netted each candidate a roughly equal number of votes by partisans. Next, the net effect of short-term forces split the nonpartisan or floating voters about down the middle. In some instances these forces pressured different groups of voters in opposite directions, though in approximately equal amounts. In other instances these forces pulled and tugged the same people in different directions, causing cross-pressured voters, by far the greatest number of whom were women, to swing greatly back and forth between the candidates. . . .

There are two basic ways of measuring relative party strength, one . . . that looks at how people respond in *surveys* to the question of which party they identify with (Democratic, Republican, or Independent), and the other that looks at which party's candidates people actually vote for in real *elections*. By this last measure, as we have seen, the results in 2000 show the two parties at near parity for each of the national institutions. It is also important, of course, to consider how people vote for the three major political offices at the state level: governor, the state Senate, and the state House. The results here are striking. For the state legislative chambers, Democrats in 2000 control 25 state Houses to 24 for the Republicans, while Republicans control 24 state Senates to 21 for the Democrats. Four Senates are tied between the two parties. There is, however, one office today where one of the parties holds a clear advantage. Among the governors, 29 are Republican and 19 are Democrats. And therein lies a tale. It is surely no accident that the president, George Bush, not only came from the ranks of the Republican governors, but also was nominated with their support and campaigned for the presidency, conspicuously, with their help.

These figures make clear that an important change in relative party strength has taken place over the past decade. At the beginning of the decade, the Republican Party was predominantly a presidential party. Republicans held the presidency (as they had since 1980), but both houses of Congress were in the hands of the Democrats. In the states, the Democrats had the edge in governors (30D-20R) and the decided advantage among state Senates (38-11) and state Houses (40-9). By 1994 the contours of partisan control had begun to change. Democrats now held the presidency, while Republicans captured the House and Senate. Republicans in 1994 gained their large advantage among governors (30R-19D), and had pulled almost even among state Senates (25D-24R) and close among state Houses (26D-22R). The elections of the 1990s therefore did indeed realign American politics. But they did so not by placing a single party in control, but by bringing one of the parties (the Republicans) from an overall minority status into a position of parity. . . .

As the [2000] campaign entered late October, forecasters with help from the hot new instrument of daily tracking polls became even more deeply impressed with the sustained closeness of this race, constantly calling it a "dead heat." And what a peculiar kind of dead heat it was—not just close, but oscillating. The Gallup tracking poll showed the lead changing no fewer than nine times over the course of the fall campaign. Although similar data are not available from past elections, the best guess is that previous close races have tended to follow the pattern of a horse race or marathon, in which one candidate is consistently in the lead, and at the very end the trailing candidate makes a single upward bid, either managing to pull ahead or ending up just short. But the 2000 race continually moved back and forth in September and October, with George W. Bush generally maintaining an ever so slight lead in the final week or so of the campaign. At the last possible moment in early November, however, the polls began to close with momentum swinging in the direction of Al Gore.

Final results of four of the most respected polling firms were as follows: Zogby/MSNBC (Gore plus 2), Gallup (Bush plus 2), Washington Post (Bush plus 1), CBS (Gore plus 1). All of these results, of course, were well within the margin of error that allowed victory for either candidate. And averaged together, they just happen to make a Perfect Tie. . . .

ELECTION NIGHT 2000

[On election night in 2000,] the television commentators, who were privy to the early returns of the national exit polls, let it be known at 7 P.M. that this election was going to be close—very, very close. And to eliminate any suspicions that this claim was just media hype or feigned impartiality, some took the unusual step of saying that they really meant it. If this was disappointing news for Bush supporters, things shortly would return much worse. Just before 8 P.M. the networks declared Al Gore to be the winner in Florida. Within the next hour and a half, Gore was also awarded Pennsylvania and Michigan. Bush had thus lost all three of the big battleground states. Almost every scenario for a Bush victory depended on his carrying at least one of them. What hope remained now for Bush was the slim prospect of winning almost all of the remaining states where the outcome had been considered doubtful. That, or else the miracle that only George Bush himself had predicted: winning California. . . .

Under these circumstances, a good many sensible citizens, with jobs to attend the next morning and with children to awaken for school, took the cue and went off to bed. . . .

[But George Bush] questioned the networks' call of Florida. His sources on the ground, he insisted, were reporting something very different. Viewers no doubt regarded this statement as understandable spin, designed to buoy supporters in the West, where voting was still going on. The networks, as the anchors assured viewers, make calls only when they are certain. As [CBS news anchor] Dan Rather put it, "If we call a state, you can take it to the bank. Book it!" But to everyone's astonishment, Bush's claim, not Dan Rather's, proved correct. The networks soon discovered that they had miscalled Florida, based, so it was later explained, on important errors and miscalculations made from their combined pool source of information, the Voter News Service. Shortly before 10 P.M. EST the networks pulled Florida from Gore's column and placed it back among the undecideds.

Viewers were now witnessing a near television equivalent of the famous media debacle of 1948, when major newspapers declared Dewey the victor over Truman. Only this time there were real consequences to the error. A wrong call had been made not only before voters in other states had voted, but also—contrary to general network policy—while some of Florida's own polls were still open. The western part of the Florida panhandle lies in the central, not the eastern, time zone. Were some Florida voters discouraged from turning out at the last moment in areas of the state that strongly favored George W. Bush? . . . Bush now actually ahead in the vote count in Florida, CBS News anchor Dan Rather commented at 10:06, "It's beginning to look increasingly like the advantage is going to George W. Bush." By 10:10 he had Gore "hanging, hanging by a thread." Still, after what had just happened no one was ready to call Florida again. . . .

Along with the change in status of Florida from Gore to undecided, over the next few hours Bush either won or remained in the running in enough of the states to keep alive the possibility of his winning an electoral victory without carrying Florida. This possibility, greater than most had earlier expected, surged and then faded as more states were called. At one point, indeed, NBC's Tim Russert, who had abandoned high-technology graphics for makeshift calculations with a Magic Marker, sketched a highly plausible scenario under which each candidate would win 269 electoral votes, a tie that would throw the election into the House of Representatives. But by about 1 A.M., the possibility of Bush winning without capturing Florida ended, as Gore closed in on the contested states of Iowa, Minnesota, and Wisconsin. Everything finally narrowed down to just Florida. Like the classic drama, in which all of the subplots must first be resolved before turning back to the central story line, whoever now carried Florida would pass the threshold of 270 electoral votes and become the 43rd president of the United States.

In the actual vote count in Florida, George Bush now held a modest lead, although commentators noted that some of the Democratic-leaning areas in large southern Florida counties had not yet reported. Bush's lead began to dwindle, but so too did the number of precincts outstanding. It was a race between Bush's vote margin (his distance ahead) and the precincts remaining (the distance to the finish line). Would Bush be able to hold on? His lead, once 130,000 votes, shrank to 30,000. Then, just after 2 A.M., his lead ballooned again to 59,000, a seemingly insurmountable advantage. One network after another announced Florida for George W. Bush, making him the 43rd president of the United States. . . .

PREMATURE CONCESSION

But this drama was nowhere near being over.

Having watched the network's declaration of Bush's victory, Vice President Gore called Governor Bush and graciously offered his congratulations in what was reported as a brief, but correct and pleasant, conversation. Gore said that he would be making his way shortly from his hotel to the Legislative Plaza, where he would offer his public concession. Governor Bush began to go over his victory comments.

As Vice President Gore's motorcade made its way to the plaza, the television anchors proceeded with their soothing narrative. They were now clearly more relaxed with everything in the studio once again under control, even as they felt compelled, with a great deal of relief, to mention the turbulence earlier in the evening. As the various pundits, commentators, and anchors continued on, Bush's vote margin in Florida, displayed on the boards behind the anchor desks, began to shrink dramatically. Some took note of this fact in passing, as if it were a small curiosity. It was inconceivable that their system for calling elections could fail a second time. But suddenly, when the margin fell beneath 6,000 votes, the actual vote totals could not be ignored.

Meanwhile back in the real world, frantic calls were placed from Gore supporters in Florida to his headquarters, and then from his headquarters to the motorcade, trying to get the message through to the vice president not to go ahead with a public concession. On arriving at the plaza and learning of the closeness of the vote, a decision was made to wait. Shortly thereafter, the vice president made a second call to Governor Bush [retracting his concession]. . . .

For the second time that night, the networks now had to retract their Florida call. . . . George Bush was ahead in the counting of the ballots in Florida, and this result was—and would have to be—the most important material fact. But with a lead this narrow, nobody could have expected the vice president to forgo the automatic recount to which he was entitled under Florida law, and no one would have expected that he should concede until that recount had taken place. The only "real" story, then, was that no definitive result had yet occurred. The networks' call helped to set in motion a different story, where one candidate (Gore) now seemed to have to go further to change a "result," while the other (Bush) was pushed into an awkward position of groveling for the office that had been "awarded" to him.

At just about this point, as if to relieve momentarily the gathering tension, another singular event, unrelated to the main drama, intruded itself. All night long, George Bush had been ahead in the national popular vote, even as he trailed at times in the electoral vote. This result corresponded to a scenario that had been widely discussed before the election: a race that would be close enough to enable Al Gore to win the electoral vote while losing the popular. Gore, in fact, had been queried on this matter in a number of television interviews. Very few thought that the race could ever turn out the other way, with Bush losing the popular vote but winning the presidency. Yet now, with the returns from California coming in, Al Gore for the first time pulled ahead in the national popular vote, and it was a safe bet that he would remain so. If Bush were to win the presidency, he would be the one, strangely enough, to be the "minority" president. Commentators took note of this striking fact, important politically because the Democrats would by the next day begin to use it to Gore's advantage. But its significance for the moment paled next to the outcome of the real drama.

Having now "unconceded," Al Gore returned to his hotel room reportedly to go to sleep. The emotional swings of what remained of the two crowds were on the surface a near reversal of what had taken place a couple of hours earlier: in Gore's camp, renewed hope and chants of "recount, recount"; in Bush's camp, frustration. Probably a fairer description of the scenes was that partisans on both sides were more dazed than energized. There had been one twist of fortune too many. Instead of the vice president arriving to deliver his concession, it was William Daley, Gore's campaign chairman, who appeared before the crowd. Daley made clear that the election was not over, and that "until the results, the recount, is concluded and the results of Florida become official, our campaign continues." An hour later Donald L. Evans briefly addressed the few remaining Bush supporters. "We hope and believe we have elected the next president of the United States."

What had begun was another phase of the 2000 race, a postelection campaign that would last five more weeks and that would be filled with as many ups and downs as the melodrama of election eve.

Victory at Last

Andrew Phillips

After thirty-five days of post-election campaigning in U.S. courts, President George W. Bush turned immediately to his two political priorities: people and policy. Whatever doubts surrounded his election, Bush's priority would be to reconcile the nation after year-long campaign rancor and to facilitate a spirit of cooperation with the Democrats.

In this December 2000 article, Andrew Phillips reports on the victory of George W. Bush in the highly contested presidential election and discusses how the questionable legitimacy of the presidency, a divided Congress, and a slowing economy were the best things President Bush had going for him. Phillips covers Washington for Rogers Media.

Expect to hear a lot over the next few weeks about Bob Bullock, a legendary Texas Democrat who plays a key role in the George W. Bush Official Mythology. When Bush was first running to be governor in 1994, Bullock was the state's powerful lieutenant-governor and the key power broker in its legislature. Bush knew he could get little done without Bullock's cooperation, so three weeks before the election he went to the older man's home and told him: "I'm here to tell you that I want to work with you." After Bush won, the Republican governor and the Democratic lawmaker did forge a successful partnership—one that allowed Bush to take credit for a string of reforms that he used to demonstrate his readiness for the White House.

The story is dear to Bush supporters, who use it as proof that their man has what it takes to unite bitter rivals and heal old wounds. Bush himself invoked the name of Bullock (who died in 1999) . . . as he stood in the chamber of the Democratic-controlled Texas House of Representatives to address Americans for the first time as their president-elect.

Exactly an hour earlier, Vice-President Al Gore had finally bowed to the inevitable and gracefully conceded defeat. Now, Bush implicitly promised, he would do for the United States what he did for Texas—reach out to his opponents. Five weeks of recounting and recrimination would give way to reconciliation and renewal. "I was not elected to serve one party," he pledged, "but to serve one nation."

A DIVIDED NATION

Good luck. The Bullock story, like so many others in Bush's improbable rise to power, conceals as much as it reveals. Gov. Bush had to deal with a state legislature that meets only every two years for a session limited to 140 days, and a Democratic party dominated by old-style conservatives (like Bullock) who would be well to the right of Republicans in many parts of the country. President Bush will take office at noon on Jan. 20 on the steps of a Congress divided and riven by round-the-clock ideological warfare. The Democrats he will face are decidedly not the get-along, cut-a-deal types he so successfully charmed back home.

Just as bad, right-wingers in his own party may quickly become impatient if Bush does stick to the middle. The politics of personal persuasion, he may quickly find, don't go all that far in a capital better known for tear-out-the-throat attack politics. "The Democrats are going to be like sharks," warns Allan Lichtman, an expert on the presidency at American University in Washington. "They're going to be swimming silently for a while, but as soon as there's any blood from Bush in the water, there will be a feeding frenzy."

Still, soothing words about unity and cooperation were clearly what Americans wanted to hear after a year-long election campaign—plus the rancorous fight over ballots triggered by the photo finish in Florida. The back-to-back speeches by Gore and Bush capped an extraordinary six days that saw Gore's hopes momentarily revived by one Supreme Court (the one in Florida), then finally dashed by another (the one in Washington). The man who had hoped to arrive in the White House as a healing "uniter, not a divider," promising to "change the tone in Washington," instead found himself winning only after a legal donnybrook far more divisive than the lacklustre campaign.

The omens are not good, although Gore did his part to repair the breach. After taking a night to digest the Supreme

Court's confusing but ultimately devastating ruling, he made his decision. The presidency, the job for which he had been groomed from childhood by his senator father, for which he had worked all his adult life, would not be his. . . .

Gore managed to strike a tone that was both self-deprecating and dignified, a combination he never seemed to find during the campaign itself. He acknowledged Bush's right to claim the White House and promised his support despite the bitterness of losing the presidency through a decision by a Supreme Court split cleanly along ideological lines. "While I strongly disagree with the Supreme Court's decision," said Gore, "I accept it. I accept the finality of the outcome. What remains of partisan rancour must now be put aside."

A Tough Job Ahead

But nothing could hide the fact that Bush will always be "President Asterisk"—the man who won the office on a technicality, whose victory hangs on the slenderest of threads. The validity of his court-mandated victory in Florida will be questioned for years to come; he won the electoral college by a single vote more than the bare majority needed; and he lost the nationwide popular vote by 337,576 votes. Only three other men won the presidency while losing the overall vote —and historians have been quick to recall that all three served a single, troubled term in office. The first of them, John Quincy Adams in 1824, was also the only other son of a president to win the office himself.

Bush, clearly, must beat the odds—a tall order for a man who turned seriously to politics only six years ago and who must battle the perception that he is an empty suit, propped up by Republican heavyweights and his father's old lieutenants. The road to his eventual victory only made a tough job more difficult. The campaign itself, though inevitably partisan, was not particularly divisive. The candidates were uninspiring; few but the most partisan voters found much to fight about. Instead, it was the unprecedented 35-day recount circus in Florida that inflamed passions. And the final scene of the play, with the U.S. Supreme Court first intervening in dramatic style to stop another effort to count disputed ballots, and then finally crushing Gore's remaining chance at victory, left a bitter taste.

There were few hopes that the high court would allow a

recount when it met on Dec. 11 to hear 90 minutes of oral arguments in Bush v. Gore, Case No. 00-949. Two days earlier, the court had split 5 to 4, between its conservative majority and its moderate-to-liberal minority, and ordered an immediate halt to a recount authorized by the more liberal Florida Supreme Court. The complex arguments came down to an essential choice: would the federal court decide that manual recounts amounted to an illegal change in the rules of the election after the votes were cast (as the Bush team argued), or would it rule that a recount could be done to make sure that all votes were tallied (as Gore's lawyers contended)?

In the end, the court split again along its ideological fault line. Anyone who had hoped that the Supreme Court might be able to resolve an issue that had already ensnarled state courts and the Florida legislature and threatened to spill over into Congress was sure to be disappointed. The five most conservative judges—Chief Justice William Rehnquist, along with justices Antonin Scalia, Anthony Kennedy, Sandra Day O'Connor and Clarence Thomas—ruled on Dec. 12 against any further recounting of the contested Florida ballots. It came down, they said, to the fact that there was no clear standard for deciding when a voter had marked a punch card for Gore or for Bush—and that would violate the clause in the Constitution guaranteeing "equal protection" to all citizens.

Further, they ruled, prolonging the count beyond Dec. 12 would throw doubt on the validity of the presidential electors selected by Florida because of a federal law protecting electors from challenge if they are chosen by that day. As a result, the five judges wrote, "it is obvious that the count cannot be conducted in compliance with the requirement of equal protection and due process." The bottom line: no more recounts. Bush would be the victor in Florida by a margin of just 537 votes out of six million statewide.

Gore supporters were outraged—and they needed to look no further for ammunition than the series of blistering dissenting opinions issued by the four judges who found themselves in the minority. Ironically, it was the liberal minority that ended up lecturing the conservative majority for failing to respect the authority of a state court—a traditional conservative position. Justice John Paul Stevens, appointed in 1975 by President Gerald Ford, accused the five-member majority of effectively disenfranchising voters whose choices were not registered during machine counts of the ballots. And, he wrote, the court showed no confidence in the state judges who would be called on to oversee any new recount: "Although we may never know with complete certainty the identity of the winner of this year's presidential election, the identity of the loser is perfectly clear. It is the nation's confidence in the judge as an impartial guardian of the rule of law."

Justice David Souter, another liberal, appointed in 1990 by the new president-elect's father, underlined the paradox involved in the court's first halting the recount—and then ruling that it could not continue because time had run out: "If this court had allowed the state to follow the course indi-

---

POST-ELECTION EVENTS

The post-election campaign encompassed five weeks of battling in the state and U.S. federal courts. Election analysts James W. Ceaser and Andrew E. Busch show by date the unfolding of events that ultimately gave George W. Bush the White House victory.

- Nov. 8th: The morning after: Bush leads by 926 votes; automatic machine recount begins.
- Nov. 9th: Gore requests hand counts in Broward, Miami-Dade, Palm Beach, and Volusia counties.
- Nov. 10th: The machine recount is completed; Bush's lead slips to 327 votes.
- Nov. 12th: Palm Beach and Volusia counties begin their hand recount.
- Nov. 15th: Katherine Harris collects the final votes from all Florida counties.
- Nov. 17th: The Florida Supreme Court issues an injunction, blocking certification of a final vote tally.
- Nov. 18th: Overseas absentee ballots are counted; Bush's lead is back up to 930 votes.
- Nov. 20th: The Florida Supreme Court holds its hearing on Gore's motion to include late hand-recount totals in the official vote certification.
- Nov. 21st: The Florida Supreme Court hands down ruling, extending the certification deadline five days.
- Nov. 24th: The U.S. Supreme Court announces it will hear Bush's appeal of the Florida Supreme Court decision.
- Nov. 25th: The "Brooks Brothers Revolution" erupts, and Miami-Dade County stops its hand recount.

cated by the opinions of its own Supreme Court, it is entirely possible that there would ultimately have been no issue requiring our review, and political tension could have worked itself out in Congress."

The ruling may have shattered any illusion that the top court is above the partisan fray. Critics of the conservative majority found even more to fuel their concerns in reports that one of Scalia's sons works for the Washington law firm that argued Bush's case before the Supreme Court, while Thomas's wife is at a right-wing think-tank in the capital, helping to recruit prospective members of a new Bush administration. It all looked too convenient, though Thomas told high-school students the morning after the momentous

---

- Nov. 26th: Katherine Harris certifies the vote, giving Bush a 537-vote victory.
- Nov. 27th: Gore contests the certification.
- Nov. 30th: The Florida legislature announces a special session to debate naming Florida's electors themselves.
- Dec. 1st: The U.S. Supreme Court hears oral arguments on the Florida Supreme Court recount deadline extension decision.
- Dec. 4th: Judge N. Sanders Sauls rejects Gore's contestation of the certified results, and the U.S. Supreme Court vacates and remands the Florida Supreme Court's certification deadline extension decision.
- Dec. 8th: The Florida Supreme Court orders manual recounts of all counties with significant numbers of undervotes.
- Dec. 9th: The U.S. Supreme Court halts the manual recounts and schedules oral arguments on Bush's appeal of the Florida Supreme Court order.
- Dec. 11th: The U.S. Supreme Court holds oral arguments in *Bush v. Gore.*
- Dec. 12th: The U.S. Supreme Court rules for Bush, effectively ending the hand recounts.
- Dec. 13th: Gore concedes defeat, and Bush accepts victory.
- Dec. 18th: Individual state electors make official Bush's 271-to-266-vote victory in the Electoral College.
- Jan. 6th: A joint session of Congress opens and agrees to the electoral votes submitted by the states.
- Jan. 20th: Bush is sworn in as the president of the United States.

James W. Ceaser and Andrew E. Busch, *The Perfect Tie: The True Story of the 2000 Presidential Election.* Lanham, MD: Rowman & Littlefield, 2001.

ruling that he has never heard his fellow judges discuss partisan politics. "Don't try to apply the rules of the political world to this institution," he said. "They do not apply."

BUSH'S IMMEDIATE PRIORITIES

Whatever the doubts surrounding his election, the newly anointed president-elect had to turn immediately to two priorities: people and policy. A new administration must fill some 6,000 jobs, including several hundred senior positions that must be confirmed by the Senate. Doubts over the outcome in Florida made it awkward for Bush to publicly announce top appointments—and impossible to begin the lengthy background and security checks needed to get a new administration in place by Jan. 20 [2001]. But that changed quickly with the naming of retired general Colin Powell as secretary of state, four days after the Supreme Court decision. Condoleezza Rice, a foreign policy veteran of the previous Bush administration, . . . [was] named national security adviser. They would be the most senior African-Americans appointed to any U.S. cabinet—a move that might help Bush among black voters, who opposed him on election day by a whopping nine to one. . . .

Bush will have to decide how to best use his small stock of political capital. Right-wingers in his own party are champing at the bit. Tom DeLay, the ultraconservative Republican whip in the House of Representatives, said recently that he had been waiting his whole life to have his party control the White House as well as both houses of Congress (Republicans have a very slight edge in the House, and the tie in the Senate can be broken by the vice-president). "The things we have been dreaming about we can now do unfettered," he said.

But Bush's advisers have made clear that they know they will be anything but unfettered. Instead, Bush said . . . he will start off by proposing action on education reform and lowering prescription drug prices for seniors—areas where he may be able to find allies among Democrats. And rather than push ahead with a massive tax cut, as he proposed during the campaign, he is more likely to start with something more modest, such as doing away with the federal inheritance tax.

Expectations could hardly be lower—questionable legitimacy, a divided Congress, even a slowing economy. Of course, low expectations may be the best thing Bush has going for him. He likes to remind people that he has always been underestimated, even by his parents, who earlier put their White House hopes on his smarter, more telegenic brother, Jeb, now governor of Florida. In the best of circumstances, George W. Bush was unlikely to be a great president. Now, with so many obvious handicaps, even modest achievements may be greeted as major triumphs.

CHAPTER 4

THE WHITE HOUSE

PEOPLE
WHO MADE
HISTORY

GEORGE W. BUSH

The First Foreign Policy Test

William Schneider

Chicago Tribune writer William Schneider evaluates President Bush's handling of his first foreign policy challenge in office. In April 2001, a U.S. Navy spy plane collided with a Chinese fighter pilot over China. The U.S. plane was forced to land inside the Communist nation with twenty-four Americans on board. China demanded that the American government apologize for the incident. Schneider states that Bush's discipline and deal-making were responsible for getting the hostages returned without acquiescing to the Chinese. For ten days, Bush relied heavily on his team of experienced advisers to find the formula that would satisfy the Chinese government. The Bush administration released tapes showing the incident was the fault of the Chinese pilot and that China had a policy of harassing U.S. reconnaissance planes. Once the incident was resolved, Bush also avoided political pressure to make the Chinese pay for the incident.

As a result of the 11-day standoff between the United States and China, we learned something about President Bush and something about the American people.

We learned that President Bush is not a confrontation-seeker. He's a deal-maker. Bush was serious when he said in debating Al Gore last October: "If we're an arrogant nation, they'll resent us. If we're a humble nation but strong, they'll welcome us." Or at least, go along with us.

What we learned about the American people is the same thing. Americans, too, prefer a deal to a showdown. Like their President, the American people show no excess devotion to abstract principles. . . . The rule in this case was, "Get

William Schneider, "Bush Wins 'Let's Make a Deal,'" *National Journal*, vol. 33, April 21, 2001, p. 1194. Copyright © 2001 by National Journal Group, Inc. Reproduced by permission.

the crew." They're back. We won. Let's move on.

By that standard, Bush passed his first test in an international crisis. He demonstrated resolve by resisting pressure to do something rash that might have endangered American lives. "Our approach has been to keep this accident from becoming an international incident," the President said at the outset. The China standoff ended just in time. It was in danger of turning into a full-fledged hostage situation, with debilitating consequences for Bush. The U.S. government could have ended up being held hostage by the crisis, as the Carter Administration was during the Iranian ordeal: "America Held Hostage" became the media drumbeat.

In this case, the Bush Administration had to spend 10 days publicly searching for a formula that would satisfy the Chinese. "Sorry" wouldn't do. We had to be "very sorry" for the loss of the Chinese pilot. Were we also "very sorry" that our pilot entered their air space without permission? Not particularly. "For that, we are very sorry," Secretary of State Colin L. Powell said, "but glad he did it."

Former U.S. Ambassador James Lilley noted: "The Chinese insist upon sincerity. I notice that 'sincere regret' was put in there. That must have given them a blush of pleasure." But it certainly did not give Americans a blush of pride.

PUBLIC OPINION

A week into the crisis, the Gallup Poll asked Americans whether the U.S. should apologize to the Chinese. The answer was no, by 54 percent to 41 percent. That's a "No," but it's not a "Hell, no."

To hear "Hell, no," you had to ask men. Men opposed an apology by 64 percent to 31 percent. Being a man, apparently, means never having to say you're sorry. On the other hand, women favored an apology by 51 percent to 44 percent: "Well, maybe, yes, if it will get our crew back."

Conservatives were certainly not happy with the U.S. loss of face. The *Weekly Standard* declared: "President Bush has revealed weakness. And he has revealed fear: fear of the political, strategic, and economic consequences of meeting a Chinese challenge." For the most part, however, conservatives were willing to cut Bush some slack. Imagine what would have happened if Bill Clinton had been the President who made those concessions to China. Conservatives would be howling for his blood.

The Chinese extorted concessions from the United States. Embarrassing? Yes, but Americans put saving lives over saving face. Once the lives of the crew were saved, Bush felt some pressure to regain face. So he took a harder line: "China's decision to prevent the return of our crew for 11 days is inconsistent with the kind of relationship we have both said we wish to have."

The Administration also released information showing that the accident was the fault of the Chinese pilot and that the Chinese had a policy of deliberately harassing U.S. reconnaissance planes. Moreover, US. officials claim the crew destroyed all vital security information before surrendering to the Chinese.

THE QUESTION OF RETALIATION

Beyond those face-saving revelations, there doesn't seem to be a lot of political pressure to make the Chinese pay. Impose trade sanctions? U.S. business interests would strongly resist that. Sell advanced weapons to Taiwan? The Chinese warn that such a step could be dangerous and provocative. Keep China from hosting the 2008 Olympics? That invites an unflattering comparison to Carter's "punishment" of the Soviet Union for its 1979 invasion of Afghanistan.

Why so little pressure for retaliation? Because Americans don't care that much about foreign policy these days, as long as American lives and interests are not threatened.

Bush provided the one element necessary for diplomatic success: patience. As Condoleezza Rice, his national security adviser, acknowledged: "From time to time, he would buck us up a little bit and say, 'You know, diplomacy takes time.'"

Bush shunned confrontation with China, just as he shunned confrontation with the Senate over his budget. When the Senate slashed Bush's tax cut by a quarter, the President's response was to declare victory and move on. Both actions were perfectly consistent with the American public's mood.

Fulfilling Education Promises

Siobhan Gorman

Postponed by tax cuts and terrorist attacks in the United States, President Bush declared a new era in public education in America by signing a federal education bill into law in 2002. Expanding on the current education package, the Bush administration put statewide accountability systems in place. The new system implements rigid testing requirements, exemplifying Bush's tough-love approach to education reform. But according to Siobhan Gorman, who covers education for the *National Journal*, Bush's real impact on education will be the accountability of his administration to enforce this expanded education bill and all its requirements in the public school system. Gorman states that even with a troubled economy and continuing worries about terrorism, education remains a primary concern for the American people and Bush's presidency.

Amid a throng of cheering teenagers in the Hamilton High School gymnasium, President Bush declared victory. "Today begins a new era, a new time in public education in our country," he intoned confidently into the microphone. "As of this hour, America's schools will be on a new path of reform, and a new path of results." With that, he signed into law the bill that reflected much of his education agenda. This Ohio school was the first stop of the two day tour the president and his merry band of liberal and conservative lawmakers took in January [2002] to celebrate the president's first true bipartisan triumph.

But the party's a bit premature. To be sure, the president gets credit for forging a consensus after years of ideological and political gridlock. And the law does make some signifi-

Siobhan Gorman, "Bipartisan Schoolmates: President Bush Deserves Credit for Forging a Consensus on Federal Education Policy. But It Will All Be for Naught If the Law Is Not Enforced," *Education Next*, vol. 2, Summer 2002, p. 36. Copyright © 2002 by *Education Next*. Reproduced by permission.

cant changes in federal education policy. Nevertheless, the reauthorized Elementary and Secondary Education Act (ESEA) hardly represents a new era. Instead, it builds on at least a decade's worth of federal reform efforts. Where the Bush administration could make its mark is in its enforcement of the law, an area in which few, if any, previous administrations have found the political will to play rough with the states.

The law calls for annual tests in reading and math for children in grades 3 through 8, plus a science test in three different grade levels by the 2007–08 school year. (States were already required to test students once in high school.) States must also establish a definition of a failing school that meets federal guidelines. Schools labeled failing for two or more years face increasingly stringent penalties, which states must impose. The law also leaves a host of issues unresolved, giving the states and the federal Department of Education plenty of wiggle room. Thus the quality of implementation may vary widely. . . .

Lawmakers in both parties hope that this time a combination of tough federal sanctions, more public reporting of student performance, and an aggressive White House will be enough to prompt change in the schoolhouse. "This bill delivers the goals and the tools to achieve them," says Congressman George Miller, D-California, one of the four top congressional negotiators on the bill. Still, he says, "The bill is not a silver bullet."

BUILDING ON PAST PROPOSALS

President Clinton kicked off the ESEA debate in May 1999, when he submitted his proposal to reauthorize the law, which was due to expire that year. But Congress continued arguing about the proposal into 2000, and it was shelved in the din of the presidential election. With the two candidates [Bush and Democrat Al Gore] running even in the polls, neither party wanted to risk passing a bill when there was a good chance that they could send a bill that was more to their guy's liking the next year. Furthermore, education would be a less potent issue on the campaign trail if Congress passed a major education reform bill.

Once elected, President Bush sent the early message that he wanted an education bill, and he wanted it to be a bipartisan one. Before his inauguration, Bush held a bipartisan education meeting in Austin, and among the hand-picked Democrats attending was Sen. Evan Bayh, D-Ind. Bayh and Sen. Joseph I. Lieberman, D-Conn., had put forth an education reform bill in early 2000 called the Three R's, aimed at bridging the partisan divide in education.

Borrowing liberally from Lieberman and Bayh's reform package, Bush said that the 54 federal elementary and secondary education programs should be consolidated into five categories reflecting federal priorities: 1) educating disadvantaged students; 2) teacher quality; 3) English fluency; 4) school choice; and 5) school safety. Bush also proposed that states begin testing children in grades 3 through 8. He wanted to allow children in schools that failed to close the achievement gap for three straight years to use federal money to attend private schools. On his second full day in office, Bush unveiled an education "blueprint" that was essentially the same as his campaign proposal. The White House immediately began negotiating with the 10 centrist Democrats cosponsoring the Lieberman-Bayh bill, which they reintroduced the day Bush unveiled his proposal, in an effort to cut a deal quickly.

VOUCHERS AND BLOCK GRANTS

However, when it became clear by the spring that Bush's tax cut would pass with the help of a few centrist Democrats, the Lieberman-Bayh group became leery of ditching their party a second time. The White House had also begun negotiating with Sen. Edward M. Kennedy, D-Mass., and the centrist Democrats feared that the White House would play the centrist and liberal Democrats against one another. For instance, the White House got Kennedy to agree to a limited voucher to pay for tutoring services. It then took that agreement to the New Democrats, who had been holding out on a voucher compromise, to try to get the New Democrats to incorporate the tutoring proposal into the deal they were negotiating separately with the White House. To avoid this, Lieberman decided that future negotiations would have to include Kennedy.

A new negotiating group formed, this time including the White House, Republicans, New Democrats, and Kennedy sympathizers. After a month of negotiations, the group reached agreement on the two most controversial issues: vouchers and block grants. They went with Kennedy's voucher compromise, which allowed students in failing schools to use federal money for private tutoring. They also agreed to a scaled-back block-grant proposal that would have allowed 7 states and 25 school districts to sign a performance contract with the federal government that would free them of most federal education regulations in exchange for a promise to improve student performance. They thought they had a bill ready to send to the Senate floor.

But at a late-night meeting in mid-April, one congressional aide announced that 80 to 90 percent of the schools in states like Texas and North Carolina, both of which had seen rising achievement scores through the 1990s, would be deemed "failing" under the bill's definition. The bill required states to set performance goals for every demographic group of students. The problem was that if a school didn't meet that goal for any one group in any grade level in any one year, it would be labeled failing.

Two weeks later, the senators settled on a complicated formula that required states to calculate an overall performance grade for a school based on several factors, including improving test scores for poor and minority children. But no longer could a school receive a failing grade solely because its poor and minority students didn't see their test scores rise. By the time this definition was devised, it was early May. The Senate began debate, but it dragged on for six weeks as the Senate juggled campaign finance reform and turned over to Democratic control.

On the House side, the bill moved more quickly. A series of bipartisan negotiations between Reps. Miller and John Boehner, R-Ohio, chairman of the House Committee on Education and the Workforce, produced a bill that was similar to the Senate's, but without the block-grant provisions. The Republican leadership and a handful of rank-and-file conservatives protested. But President Bush weighed in on Boehner and Miller's side, and the House passed the bill on May 23. The Senate passed its version a few weeks later.

SQUABBLING TOWARD COMPROMISE

Still, little was settled on the accountability front. The Senate's rejiggered formula was widely seen as too complicated for parents to understand, and the House's formula would run into the same reality-check problems that the Senate's had before it was revised. The conference committee charged with resolving differences between the House and Senate versions of the bill began meeting in late July, but the bill languished in committee as the members squabbled over details small and large.

In the meantime, fears over the shrinking surplus were beginning to dominate debate on Capitol Hill. Democrats charged that Bush's tax cut made it impossible to fund education adequately. Interest groups concerned with some of the testing and accountability requirements began circling.

"There weren't a lot of bipartisan feelings," remembers Bush education adviser Sandy Kress. "[Bush] was concerned. . . . The momentum clearly had slowed. He was aware of the mood and the difficulties when we came back from the August recess. We were supposed to be farther along."

Then September 11 intervened. When he first heard of the terrorist attacks on the World Trade Center and the Pentagon, Bush was visiting a Florida elementary school to publicly prod Congress to send him a final bill. Perversely enough, the attacks probably helped get the process back on track by ending the political bickering, congressional aides said. The negotiations were kicked up to the conference's top four members: Reps. Miller and Boehner and Sens. Kennedy and Judd Gregg, R-N.H. The thorniest issue—the definition of a failing school—was resolved by the Big Four by late September.

Under the new definition, states must design a plan to raise the children in several demographic groups—black, white, Hispanic, poor, and disabled—to a "proficient" level of achievement on state tests within 12 years. States determine what a proficient score will be and choose an initial goal for the percentage of students in each group that will attain a proficient grade that year. They must raise that bar over time, so that each state reaches 100 percent proficiency 12 years later. If a school does not meet the performance goal for one demographic group, but reduces the number of children who are not proficient by 10 percent, the school will avoid federal penalties. Schools that don't meet either goal will be labeled failing.

While congressional negotiators had agreed to this compromise in September, they didn't announce it until the final conference bill was set in order to avoid opening it up to too much criticism from interest groups and others (as had happened in August) and jeopardizing other negotiations in progress. "We kept it quiet for a long time," said one lawmaker involved in the negotiations process. "It was the most sensitive part of the bill."

THE FINAL BILL

The new testing requirement exemplifies Bush's tough-love approach to education reform. "I understand taking tests aren't [sic] fun," the self-proclaimed C student at Yale University told the crowd at Hamilton High. "Too bad." One of the least debated provisions, the requirement for annual testing, is probably the biggest change in the 2002 law. Though the numbers vary depending on how you read the new law, 15 states currently meet the annual testing requirement in math, 17 in reading, and 24 have established a science test, according to the Education Commission of the States.

This is not, however, a sea change in federal policy. Annual testing builds on the efforts initiated by the Clinton administration in 1994, which in turn built on ideas put forth by President George H.W. Bush when he convened the state governors at the first National Education Summit in 1989. "It's a continuation of an era," said John F. "Jack" Jennings, director of the Center on Education Policy and a longtime Democratic aide on the House education committee.

In 1994, Congress began requiring states to establish academic standards in each grade and to create tests to assess whether children have learned the material. Those tests had to be administered to all poor children at least once in grades 3 through 5, 6 through 9, and 10 through 12. Clinton's 1999 proposal would have expanded that testing to all students. The new law mandates that all students take tests that measure their progress against state standards every year in grades 3 through 8.

The bill Bush signed also requires that the National Assessment of Educational Progress (NAEP) be given in every state every other year in math and reading, but the results cannot influence whether a school is designated as failing. Initially, Bush had proposed that NAEP be administered every year as a national barometer for the state tests. Currently, NAEP is administered in those subjects every four years in about 40 states, a number that fluctuates from test to test depending on which states decline to participate.

The 1994 legislation only suggested penalties for schools that failed to improve student test scores, but Clinton's 1999 proposal, which never made it into law, would have required that states intervene in perpetually failing schools. "The Bush administration took the Clinton administration's ideas and ran with them," said one bemused Democratic congressional aide who worked at the Department of Education under Clinton.

The new law sets out a timeline of increasingly severe sanctions to nudge recalcitrant schools along. If a school fails to meet annual state test-score goals for two years, students can transfer to another public school in the district. The failing school also receives extra money to revamp academic programs. After three years of failure, the district must use 5 percent of the money it receives for poor children under the federal Title I program's "Basic Grants" section to pay for outside tutoring services. After four failing years, a school must make significant structural changes, such as revamping the curriculum or firing staff, and may be eligible for a state takeover the following year. At no point does a state or school lose money if it continues producing poor results, although districts eventually have to divert federal money to pay for tutoring services.

Building on the work of one's predecessors can produce success stories. That's just what Bush did as governor of Texas. His reforms expanded those of former governor Ann Richards, whose reforms built on those in places like Dallas and previous statewide efforts led by, of all people, Ross Perot. Dallas, it happens, is where then–school board president Sandy Kress initiated accountability—using standardized tests to reward and sanction schools. "This is our theme," Kress said. "We may not know a lot of music in Texas, but we can sing the song we know well."

A Difficult Road Ahead

The Bush administration tried to set a new tone the night after the president signed the education bill, when Secretary of Education Rod Paige invited 30 state education chiefs to Mount Vernon to discuss the new law and his expectations for the states. After dining on pork and pumpkin mousse, Paige made his pitch: The old days of waivers and delays and closing our eyes to enforcement problems are over.

Analysts say the tough-love message is a good one, but that backing it up will be difficult. "Everybody jumps on this wagon and says we're really going to be tough," said Marshall S. Smith, the acting deputy secretary of education in the Clinton administration. "That's macho talk. That's not going to work in the real world of kids and schools."

So far, only 16 states have complied with the requirements of the 1994 law. The Bush administration's first task will be to get the other 34 states into compliance. Then, they'll have to review the new statewide plans for getting every child in every demographic group to a "proficient" level of achievement within 12 years. After the states have set their yearly performance goals, the Department of Education will have to monitor the performance of the nation's 92,000 public schools to see whether each demographic group in each grade being tested is meeting the state performance goals.

The law also leaves open a number of questions, mostly surrounding the quality of the reforms states undertake. One of the most significant ambiguities is whether states can develop an annual testing system by piecing together state and district tests given in different grade levels. Some critics worry that states will create systems where a student's results on a district test one year cannot be compared with results on a state test the next year. "There's going to be a lot of discussion about that," Kress said. "There's no easy answer right now."

Others worry that with 50 different statewide tests, the federal government will lack a meaningful tool with which to compare test scores across state lines. "What happened was you had a whole bunch of folks who wanted standards but not standardization," said Arnold Fege, president of Public Advocacy for Kids, a nonprofit public education advocacy group. "As a result, we've got 49 different states with 49 different standards and 49 different testing systems. The question is what does it all mean? You can't compare the states." (The number is only 49 because Iowa declined to create statewide academic standards per the 1994 law's requirements.)

For many of the testing quality issues, the federal government is taking a hands-off approach. "Our job will not be to pass judgment on the quality of state standards or the quality of the assessments based on those standards," said Undersecretary Eugene Hickok, the Department of Education's point person on enforcement.

ENFORCEMENT

The department's approach to enforcement is largely preventative. Hickok is setting up an implementation team in Washington that will be bolstered by staff members in the department's regional offices. The team will assemble an analysis of where states are in the reform process, and it will be updated as states make additional changes. Meanwhile, top department officials will reach out to state officials to encourage them to comply. "Our goal is to respond as quickly as possible, and not just to say yes or no, but to help them achieve it," Hickok said.

Some states and schools are likely to test how serious the administration is about enforcement. "There are going to be a lot of schools that take a wait and see attitude with compliance," said David Shreve, senior committee director for the National Conference of State Legislatures. "I think there will be a great number of states and systems that will say, 'Let's do as much as we can without breaking our backs,' knowing full well that the bill will be up for a new reauthorization before any of these really bad consequences kick in."

States are also now facing budget deficits—at least in the near term. Some liberal members of Congress, like Sens. Paul Wellstone, D-Minn., and James M. Jeffords, I-Vt., even voted against the bill because they view the funding level as insufficient to help the reforms really take hold. Jeffords called the bill "counterproductive, if not destructive." Even Miller, who advocated accountability before it was cool, worries about states being able to pay to fix the problems the test scores highlight. "It comes in a down economy, and we worry the states are going to be forced to make cuts that will challenge the success of this bill," he said. Just a month after Bush signed the education bill, with Miller and Kennedy at his side, the two Democrats held a press conference to denounce Bush's 2003 education budget, which they say falls way short of what's needed to fulfill the mandates of the new education law.

To a large degree, says Hickok, the key to enforcement will be parents. He hopes that parents of children in failing schools, armed with information about how their schools and children are doing, will force schools to offer them the options that are laid out in the federal law. Having been there and done that in Washington, Marshall Smith agrees. "The only way you're really going to get accountability—accountability at the point where politicians really feel the pressure—is bad press," he said. But, he says, the statistics the federal government is requiring schools to report offer parents no useful information about what their children do and don't know.

The first test of the Bush administration's enforcement chops will come in handling the schools that are already on the Department of Education's list of failing schools. Students in schools that have been on the list for three or more years, estimated to be at least 3,000, should now be entitled to tutoring services, and students in at least 6,500 should earn the option to transfer to another public school.

Once the statewide accountability systems are in place, enforcement will get increasingly difficult as states are required to raise the goals for student achievement no less than every three years. As more and more schools face sanctions, how will the administration handle the inevitable logistical and political quicksand? What happens if all the high-performing schools in a district are full and can't take the children who were granted public school choice because their own school failed two years in a row? "We've had a lot of discussion about it," Hickok said. "The law does not impose the Department of Education into the state to make sure they're doing public school choice the way we want to or supplemental services the way we want to." In fact, Hickok isn't even sure what the federal government can do if students in a failing school can't transfer to another public school in the district because there's no room at the better schools.

Sustaining the momentum on enforcement may be the administration's biggest challenge. "Paige is saying he won't give any waivers. Now we shall see. I hope that he can keep the pressure on," says Jack Jennings of the Center on Education Policy. "Elections come up. Is Bush going to deny [New York] Gov. [George] Pataki federal aid when he's running for reelection, if the state has not met its testing requirements?" (Money can be withheld from a state for not complying with the requirements of the law, but not for poor results.)

Even with a troubled economy and continuing worries about terrorism, education remains a high-level concern among voters. Bush's education record will no doubt play an important role in the next election. That means the person who will ultimately be held most accountable in the eyes of the public for reforming the schools is President Bush.

Resurrecting the Economy

Richard Cheney

George W. Bush and Vice President Richard Cheney took office in the height of an economic recession. In the following speech made in August 2002, Vice President Cheney discusses economic revival under the Bush administration. In spite of a terrorist attack at home, war abroad, and economic slow down, Cheney highlights conditions set in place by Bush to stimulate the economy and formulate long-term growth. Cheney states that lengthening unemployment benefits, providing tax incentives for business, issuing $11 million in tax rebate checks, and signing a corporate integrity bill to renew confidence in American business practices are all tools Bush has used to propel the nation's sluggish economy.

In the past eighteen months, the United States has gone through a serious economic slowdown, a great national emergency, a war abroad, and a series of scandals in corporate America. Yet there is no doubt about our nation's strength. This is a tribute, above all, to the American worker and entrepreneur. Worker productivity in the last four quarters has been impressive. Higher productivity leads to wage increases, greater investment, and even more jobs down the line. In the month of June, personal income rose at the fastest pace in two years. Also in June, sales of new homes reached an all-time high. The number of unemployment claims has remained below the 400,000 mark for most of the last nine weeks. Industrial production has been rising since January, after 17 months of almost steady decline. Mortgage interest rates stand at near 30-year lows. Inflation remains firmly under control.

We have the most productive, creative, and promising eco-

Richard Cheney, "Vice President Discusses the President's Economic Security Agenda," www.whitehouse.gov, August 7, 2002.

nomic system the world has ever seen. In America we value freedom of movement, competition, private property rights, the rule of law, and limited government—and all these have made our country the best place to work and invest. We lead the world in technological progress, and scientific and medical breakthroughs. We have by far the most skilled and productive work force. Our companies and universities attract the greatest talent from every continent. The energy and innovativeness of American business, especially in the high-tech industries, have made the economy much more flexible and better able to absorb the kinds of shocks we've experienced in recent months.

All of these conditions create a platform for long-term growth and prosperity. . . . If we continue in the positive direction President Bush has set for the nation—with solid, pro-growth, pro-job reforms—Americans will enjoy even greater prosperity in the years ahead. We will not be satisfied until every sector of this economy—from agriculture to high-tech—is vigorous and growing. We will not rest until every person who wants to work can find a job.

The primary objective of this administration's economic policy is faster growth that leads to new jobs. Here the federal government's responsibility is plain. Outside its own limited functions, government doesn't build plants or create jobs. Our responsibility is to create an environment in which private-sector employers want to expand and hire more people. That is the way to lift wages and the standard of living across the country. That is the way for companies to innovate, and grow, and produce value that attracts investors.

A growing economy brings the added benefit of higher revenues for the government—revenues that permit us to balance the budget, meet key priorities, and protect Social Security and Medicare, without ever resorting to ruinous tax increases on the American people.

Recession

The President and I ran for office on a growth agenda, starting with an across-the-board rate reduction for every income taxpayer in the nation. Our goal was to ensure long-term prosperity by increasing the incentives to produce, save, and invest—and by limiting the total amount of our national wealth controlled by the federal government. Bipartisan majorities in both Houses of Congress agreed with us.

Under the 2001 tax cut we reduced the tax bills of more than a hundred million individuals, families, and sole proprietorships—the largest reduction in a generation. We made those reductions retroactive to the first of January, 2001, in order to give the economy an immediate boost.

January of 2001 was also the month that brought a change in administrations. It is now clear from the data that when President Bush and I took office, the nation had slid into a full-blown economic recession. The first sign of a slowdown had appeared around the summer of 2000. Among the contributing factors were high and unpredictable energy prices, a steadily rising tax burden, and high interest rates. By inauguration day, business investment growth had halted—and the nation had already lost nearly a third of a million manufacturing jobs in a year's time. The slide continued, with the economy contracting throughout the first, second, and third quarters of 2001.

In the third quarter, of course, we had the terrorists attacks [on September 11, or 9/11], which themselves caused a massive disruption of economic activity throughout the country. Every foreign and domestic flight was cancelled for days, some of them for weeks or even months. For a time, many hotels, shopping malls, and restaurants went practically empty. Stock trading was halted for nearly a week. Hundreds of thousands of Americans were laid off, some of them still looking for work to this day. Overall, the attacks cost the economy about 120 billion dollars in the last few months of 2001 alone.

Even so, the worst period for the economy last year was actually the second quarter, prior to the attacks. By September 11, millions of tax rebate checks had already arrived in American homes, and had begun to strengthen the economy. The Bush tax cut came just in time. Together with the great flexibility of this economy, and the extraordinary resilience of the American people, tax relief helped us to climb out of the recession, and to weather the terrible financial effects of 9/11.

The nation gained as well from the President's economic stimulus package, enacted last March. We lengthened unemployment benefits for those who lost jobs in the recession or in the aftermath of 9/11. We provided tax incentives for companies to expand by investing in plant and equipment. The stimulus also extended net operating loss rules, granted some alternative minimum tax relief, and provided more than five billion dollars in tax relief to assist in the economic recovery of lower Manhattan. Following passage of the stimulus, business investment in equipment and software went up by 2.9 percent in the second quarter, the first gain in a year and a half.

All of these steps—the rebate checks, the additional rate reductions on tax day, and the stimulus package—have helped turn three quarters of decline into three quarters of positive growth. By leaving more money in the hands that earned it, we trusted the American people—and the American people have produced this recovery.

ECONOMIC GROWTH

So far this year, the economy has grown at an annual rate of about three percent. This is significantly better than those nine months of recession in 2001. Many private sector forecasters anticipate that we'll stay at a solid three percent growth rate for the balance of the year. Just as the President's tax cuts put a floor under the recession, Federal Reserve policy has been critical to our progress. Eleven consecutive cuts in interest rates have reduced deflationary pressures and helped stabilize prices. We believe the economy is poised for sustained growth without inflation—so long as we hold to the right policies.

Going forward, our Administration will continue the work of strengthening the free enterprise system and reducing the barriers to further growth. We will keep the federal government squarely on the side of growth, business starts, and new jobs.

I am not here today to analyze the stock market. Yet we're all aware that just as the first signs of recession became visible in 2000, the equity markets began a major adjustment in the spring of that year. Some of the more recent declines are at least partly explained by a loss of confidence in the corporate sector.

The President has acted firmly on the matter of corporate integrity, because it goes to the heart of our economic system. That system rests on confidence—the basic belief that corporate officials are truthful, numbers are real, audits are thorough and independent, and investors are protected by law from fraud and deception.

All of us recognize that the vast majority of men and women in the business community are honest and above-board. They run solid companies, providing the goods and services that enhance our quality of life—and, for some of us, even save our lives. At the same time they provide jobs for their workers and real value for investors. Acts of fraud and theft are outside the norm in corporate America. But when those acts do occur—where corporate greed and malfeasance causes honest people to lose their jobs, life savings, and pensions, the people's confidence in the system is undermined—and the wrongdoers must be held to account.

We are pleased that Congress came together to pass the President's corporate integrity proposals, and last week he signed the most far-reaching reforms of American business practice since Franklin Roosevelt lived in the White House. Under this law, financial disclosures will be broader and better for the sake of shareholders and investors. Corporate officials will be held to higher standards of accountability for the statements they make and the papers they sign. For the first time ever, the accounting profession will be regulated by an independent board, which sets clear standards to uphold the integrity of public audits.

These reforms will bring out the best in the free enterprise system, answering abusive practices with stricter enforcement and higher ethical standards. When there is corporate fraud, the American people can be certain that the government will fully investigate, arrest, and prosecute those responsible.

We intend to do even more to protect the interests of the small investor and pension holder. More than 84 million Americans own stock, either as individuals or through their retirement plans. This level of participation in the market is unprecedented, and it is good for the country.

Investing in the stock market gives individuals the opportunity to build wealth over the long term—a real chance to enjoy a level of security and independence in retirement that was out of reach to earlier generations. This is precisely the kind of responsible investing we should promote in America. And one of the best ways to encourage stock ownership is to make sure that pension plans give workers better information, and treat them fairly.

Some workers today are locked into pension plans that hold stock in a single company, which is sometimes an unwise risk. Workers should be able to sell company stock and diversify into other investments after three years in their own company's plan. They should receive updates on their retirement savings every three months. And they should have access to sound investment advice. President Bush has proposed these and other reforms to protect Americans and their pensions. The House has passed this legislation. It remains only for the Senate to act, and we call on them to do so as soon as possible.

We are also asking Congress to take the next crucial step to reduce the tax burden on the nation's families and entrepreneurs.

Under present law the reductions we worked so hard to enact are scheduled to expire in 2011. The return of higher marginal tax rates, a restoration of the marriage penalty, a cut in the child credit—all these would almost certainly cause an economic reversal. Even the expectation of these events will put downward pressure on the economy's ability to grow, as families and firms prepare for an approaching tax increase. We should prevent that increase, and make the President's income tax reductions permanent. The House has already voted for permanent tax relief—and here again, we call on the Senate to do the same.

The death tax is also scheduled to return nine years from now. That would spell trouble for farmers, small business owners, and employees across America. A farm or a family business should be a legacy for your children, not a target for the tax collector.

We need to pass terrorism risk insurance. The latest figures show a decline in construction spending. The fact is that billions of dollars in projects are on hold today because the developers can't obtain coverage against the risk of terrorism. This problem also affects the transportation industry. With terrorism risk insurance, the federal government would step in and cover losses above a certain level of claim. Coverage would therefore become both accessible and affordable to employers across the country. Congress should enact this reform without delay—and without offering a windfall to trial lawyers.

Bush's Budget

We in Washington must also keep federal spending under control. A period of war and recession-induced deficits imposes the need for extra care in our spending priorities, and discipline that fits the times. The President's budget commits most new spending to national security and homeland defense, and seeks to hold the rest of government to an increase of two percent.

We will meet these and other priorities, but we must not permit spending to grow without restraint. This would divert more billions from families and entrepreneurs, limiting the economy's ability to expand in the future. President Bush is going to insist on spending discipline in Washington, and use his veto power if necessary.

Another fundamental condition of long-term growth is a reliable and affordable supply of energy. If we are to avoid regular price spikes and chronic shortages, we must continue our progress in energy efficiency and conservation, and increase energy production here at home. The Congress should pass the President's energy plan to strengthen our economy and reduce our dependence on foreign oil.

Our administration is committed to a broad agenda to promote small business. To buy or start a small business is to stake one's livelihood on the American Dream—believing that good ideas, hard work, and fair dealing will pay off in the end. Because so many have put forth that effort, smaller firms today create three out of every four new jobs, and account for half the private-sector output of the entire economy. The small business sector has become an especially promising avenue of opportunity for women. Over the last five years, the number of women-owned businesses has increased by 14 percent nationwide, twice the rate of firms overall. This economy can thrive only if our small businesses thrive—and we want to see a lot more small businesses in all parts of the country.

One way to make that occur is to continue holding the line on federal regulations, which so often cause wasted effort, lost jobs, and higher costs to the consumer. The annual cost of federal regulations now stands at some 8,000 dollars per household. I'm pleased to note that the year 2001 brought an actual decrease in the number of new regulations coming out of Washington. That's a positive trend we hope to continue.

Small business also stands at the center of America's trade policy. Fully ninety-six percent of America's exporters are firms with fewer than 500 employees. The nation's farmers and ranchers receive a quarter of their income from sales abroad, and one out of every three acres is producing goods for export. For the farms and ranches and manufacturers who trade with the world, the prospects have grown even brighter with the passage of trade promotion authority. It's been more than eight years since a president had that tool. Last week Congress, on a bipartisan basis, granted this authority to the President. Yesterday he signed it into law. He will use it to enter into favorable trade agreements wherever possible, giving people around the world many more opportunities to buy American.

GLOBAL TRADE

America strongly supports a new round of global trade negotiations. We're also working with nations in Central and South America to establish a Free Trade Area of the Americas by January of 2005. We will move quickly to build free trade relationships with individual nations such as Chile, Singapore, and Morocco. Such agreements, and others we intend to pursue, will create jobs in America and hope around the world.

Every advance for global trade is an opportunity to expand our economy, and include more of our people in the nation's prosperity. America is also the engine of economic growth for the rest of the world. Just as we stand to gain from wider trade, so do our trading partners—especially the less developed nations. For them, the stakes are even higher. Short-term grants and foreign aid can only go so far. In the long term, open trade and investment can bring their first real hope for material uplift all the more when economic reforms are joined with political freedom. And we must provide it.

Many nations on the path of democracy and open economies look to the United States as an example, and an ally. They rely on our support, our encouragement, and our leadership in the world—and we must always provide it.

Our future security, and the hopes of the civilized world, also depend upon America's continued leadership in the war on terror. Even with a very full agenda for this fall and beyond, never for a moment do the President and I forget the most important responsibility we have: To protect this nation against further attack, and win the war that began on September 11.

We still face an enemy determined to kill Americans by any means, on any scale, and on our own soil. We're dealing with a terror network that has cells in more than 60 countries. Such a group cannot be held back by deterrence nor reasoned with by diplomats. For this reason, the war against terror will not end in a treaty. There will be no summit meeting or negotiations with the terrorists. This conflict can end only in their complete and utter destruction.

In this challenge to our freedom we have already asked a great deal of the men and women who wear our country's uniform. And as a former Secretary of Defense, I've never been more proud of our military. For missions that lie ahead, we are investing in our military so we can deploy swift and agile forces—anyplace and anytime they're needed. We are building precision weapons that can spare the lives of American soldiers in combat, and innocent civilians in foreign lands. We will multiply every advantage in order to prevail over any enemy. . . .

President Bush has made very clear, the government of the United States will not look the other way as threats accumulate against us. . . . The President and I are mindful of the tremendous responsibilities that have been placed in our hands. And we are grateful to you, our fellow citizens, for giving us the opportunity to serve the greatest nation on the face of the earth.

CHAPTER 5

TERRORISM ON AMERICAN SOIL

PEOPLE
WHO MADE
HISTORY

GEORGE W. BUSH

Terrorism Changes the Bush Presidency

Robin Wright

In the following article, *Los Angeles Times* journalist Robin Wright analyzes President Bush's strides in worldwide diplomacy following the terrorist attacks in America on September 11, 2001. Wright credits Bush's embrace of a global solution to the war on terrorism for his increase in international respect.

According to Wright, Bush created a new coalition to move beyond retaliation for America's attacks. The new multinational agenda focused on eliminating terrorism in the name of global security.

Six weeks ago, George W. Bush was still the new kid on the global block, widely perceived by his peers as a good-old-boy Texan grappling, and sometimes fumbling, with the sophisticated nuances of foreign policy.

He was under fire for his controversial missile defense plan, resented for his go-it-alone approach and challenged for doing too little or nothing on the Middle East conflict, nuclear testing, climate change, land mines, creation of an international criminal court, chemical weapons and children's rights.

Today, presidents, prime ministers, sultans, sheiks and kings defer to him. He has redefined the global agenda. And everyone wants to see him.

The shift has been the most striking part of the Asia-Pacific Economic Cooperation. . . . Chinese President Jiang Zemin . . . hosted . . . [a] summit of 21 member economies [to] highlight his nation's leadership and transformation. . . .

But the summit decidedly was Bush's show.

In a telling episode, Japanese Prime Minister Junichiro Koizumi, whose country is one of America's closest allies and the world's second-largest economy, kept apologizing

Robin Wright, "Response to Terror: The Presidency—News Analysis," *Los Angeles Times*, October 22, 2001. Copyright © 2001 by The Times Mirror Company. Reproduced by permission.

for taking up Bush's time Saturday during their one-hour bilateral meeting.

"I appreciate your strong leadership to fight terrorism. Your determination and patience, I appreciate," the prime minister said during a photo opportunity.

Koizumi also presented Bush with a decorative arrow used by Japanese warriors dating to the 6th century that, when shot, produces a sharp whistle signaling the onset of battle. On the wooden box containing the arrow, Koizumi personally inscribed, in calligraphy, "to defeat evil and bring peace on Earth."

A FRESH START

One of the unexpected consequences of the Sept. 11 tragedy is that it has given the new American president a fresh start on foreign policy. It's a sort of second honeymoon with the world to revive a marriage that, U.S. officials concede, wasn't going all that well.

"At earlier meetings, he either had to overcome misconceptions or face the implication that people were going to teach him something about how the world works," said a senior U.S. official who has worked with both Republican and Democratic administrations. "He came to this meeting having stood up and established himself on the issue, where he's demonstrating U.S. leadership to a world that is looking for it."

The global challenge of terrorism has helped. The United States is a relative newcomer in dealing with terrorism on its own turf, though it has been a long-standing problem for many countries.

"The issue makes it easier to empathize with our objectives. Unlike missile defense, where we appear to be doing something to protect ourselves, this is something where other countries feel a broad common interest," said James Steinberg, deputy national security advisor in the Clinton administration and now director of foreign policy studies at the Brookings Institution in Washington.

NEW RESPECT

Bush is winning new respect in large part because of his reaction, which was to not go it alone. At least on terrorism, his approach has embraced the era and ideas of globalization.

"The people in this administration have gone from being

serious unilateralists to being active multilateralists," said
Moises Naim, editor of Foreign Policy magazine. "Everyone
sees that both Bush and [Secretary of State Colin L.] Powell
are on the phone constantly, consulting with other countries
that are playing important roles in the new coalition."

The fact that one of the first things the Bush administration did after the Sept. 11 attacks was to make a long-delayed
payment of dues to the United Nations helped prove its intent, Steinberg added.

Substantively, Bush also has scored points by not acting
precipitously and devising a deliberate longer-term strategy
to deal with terrorism, U.S. analysts and officials agree.

"The initial concept of response was that we were going
to do what we did in the past—blow some holes in something and maybe get some U.N. resolutions that these criminals had to be brought to justice," said a senior State De-

DEFINING MOMENT

*John Hughes describes how Americans rallied behind
Bush following the September 11, 2001, terrorist attacks
and discusses two defining moments where Bush showed his capabilities as a world leader.*

In two defining moments during the crisis over terrorism,
George W. Bush crossed the dramatic threshold from amiable
domestic politician to confident world leader.

The first moment was in the early minutes after the attack
on New York. Air Force One, with President Bush on board,
was soaring away from Florida at 40,000 feet, shepherded by
an escort of F-16s. Vice President Cheney, secure in a bomb-
proof shelter in the White House basement, warned the air-
borne president that the threat to Washington by additional hijacked jets was real. In the seconds available for decision, Mr.
Bush had to issue one of the most chilling instructions a president could make. It was to shoot down any airliner that imper-
iled Washington, even though it might be crowded with captive passengers.

The second moment came during Bush's speech to a joint
session of Congress and the nation. Tight-jawed, with an expression of righteous menace, he seemed to look through the
camera lens, and over the jagged mountains of Afghanistan
into the very eyes of Osama bin Laden, to promise: "Whether
we bring our enemies to justice, or bring justice to our enemies, justice will be done."

partment official who asked to remain anonymous.

"But Bush said those things may have stopped a particular type of terrorism or changed the behavior of certain countries, but they didn't stop terrorism or make us any safer," the official added. "So he said we have to take this to the next level—to move beyond retaliation to a long-term struggle to eliminate terrorism. And that meant getting everybody to do something, like choke off safe havens or close down financial networks, not just military actions."

For a man sometimes perceived as insensitive to other nations' concerns, Bush also publicly demonstrated sensitivity to an array of background issues, Steinberg said.

After initially bumbling by referring to the global effort against Islamic extremists as a "crusade," he subsequently stressed that the U.S. is not at war with Islam. He went to the Islamic Center of Washington on Sept. 17 to meet with Mus-

---

Thus was completed Bush's presidential coming of age, suddenly burdened with the most awesome responsibilities of that office, but at ease with deploying the weapons of diplomacy and military power he can project around the world.

A couple of years ago on the campaign trail, a mischievous reported sand-bagged Bush because the presidential candidate wasn't entirely sure who was the new leader of Pakistan. Today, Bush has co-opted a now-familiar Pakistani president (Gen. Pervez Musharraf) in the campaign against terrorism, engaged in near-daily conversations with President Putin as he ensures Russia's cooperation, rekindled the Anglo-American alliance, and and established a Rolodex of world leaders whom he has persuaded to stand on his side of the line he has drawn in the sand. . . .

Americans seem rallied behind their president, ready to pay the price for defending these freedoms. They give blood to the Red Cross. They volunteer. They donate money in the millions for disaster relief and to aid the families of those killed. They're putting up good-naturedly with cumbersome new security restrictions. . . .

Some Americans may know as little about geopolitics and the president of Pakistan as George Bush did a couple of years ago.

But they sure can identify with their president when he tells them: "Freedom and fear, justice and cruelty, have always been at war, and we know that God is not neutral between them."

John Hughes, "Bush's Coming of Age," *Christian Science Monitor,* September 26, 2001.

lim leaders. And he included Muslims in official remembrances, speeches and public events.

To avoid the kind of political fallout that accompanied the Persian Gulf War against Iraq, the administration also began dropping bombs and food in Afghanistan at the same time, Steinberg noted.

MAINTAINING INTERNATIONAL SUPPORT

Honeymoons always end, however, and the international support Bush is receiving is unlikely to be as cohesive or widespread indefinitely.

"It won't easily be sustained unless our strategy takes others' interests into account," said Les Gelb, president of the Council on Foreign Relations in New York.

Most of the world is generally in sync about the Sept. 11 attacks, which offers the U.S. cover for the first phase of its war against Osama bin Laden, his al Qaeda terrorism network and their Afghan hosts. But cooperation within the loosely knit coalition and support for the war on terrorism could face hurdles if or when the U.S. moves beyond Afghanistan.

"That's when we face a real hard trade-off between what we need to do to get their support for our [war on] terrorism and our values regarding other countries' treatment of political opposition," Gelb said.

Many countries have signed on to the coalition partly because of their own domestic problems. Russia's most serious security challenge is from Muslim guerrillas in its republic of Chechnya, while China faces Uighur Muslim militants in the western province of Xinjiang. Though Washington concedes that some Chechens and Uighurs have engaged in terrorism, the U.S. also has traditionally viewed both problems as political issues that grew out of repression of minorities and human rights violations.

Bush's legacy almost certainly will be determined by how his war turns out, analysts predict. But the verdict may not be in until long after he leaves office.

Terrorism Gives Bush a New Image

Jeffrey H. Birnbaum

The mission of a war on terrorism in the aftermath of September 11, 2001, helped George W. Bush find his identity as president of the United States. As commander in chief during this crisis, his approval ratings soared. He coordinated police actions around the world to round up terrorists, assembled a coalition of nations to fight terrorism, froze millions in financial assets owned by terrorist groups, and organized a successful military campaign in Afghanistan.

In this 2001 article, Jeffrey H. Birnbaum examines how the leadership role of Bush grew under the pressure of the terrorist crisis. According to Birnbaum, Bush's ability to command under pressure and to stir the American people with his words were two traits of the new president that were unseen before the terrorists attacks in New York and Washington, D.C. His newfound presidential image has also helped Bush press his domestic policies, and it is on these issues that the success of Bush's presidency may ultimately rest.

Birnbaum is the Washington bureau chief of *Fortune* magazine and a contributor to the Fox News Channel.

Seven months into the new administration in Washington, D.C., George W. Bush was still an enigma. Everyone wanted to know: Was he a conservative ideologue or the compromiser-in-chief? One minute he was eager to drill in the fragile Alaskan wilderness, the next he was cutting deals with [renown Democrat] Ted Kennedy to spend more money on education. Europeans didn't like him much and Americans were split. Nobody knew what to make of the United States' new president.

Jeffrey H. Birnbaum, "Bush's Growth Spurt: George W. Has Found His Presidential Authority and Voice Since September 11th," *The International Economy*, November/December 2001. Copyright © 2001 by *The International Economy*. Reproduced by permission.

Then tragedy struck. The September 11th attacks gave Bush, indeed his entire Baby Boom generation, its mission and, as Bush told us, its "moment." It is said that great presidents can emerge only at times of great struggle. Well, Bush now faces such a crisis. The question is: Is he up to the task? . . . He clearly seemed to be. He was moving methodically, effectively, and, yes, impressively against an intractable foe. He had assembled an expansive coalition of nations willing to help militarily and otherwise to defeat the terrorism of al-Qaeda, the Taliban, and Osama bin Laden. Coordinated police actions throughout the world had rounded up hundreds of suspected terrorists. Millions of dollars in assets tied to the plotters had been frozen. Military strikes were underway and hitting their targets in Afghanistan.

By all accounts, Bush, with his astronomically high job-approval ratings in the polls, had gone from goat to hero in Americans' minds, and in the minds of civilized people around the world. But as any student of management will attest, that's a superficial and probably fleeting assessment. The war won't last forever, at least not at its initial, fevered pitch. So qualities beyond that extraordinary circumstance will be the ultimate measure of the man. This article takes that broader view.

NOT MERELY A FIGUREHEAD

Bush's ability to command under pressure and to stir the American people with his words were two traits not apparent prior to the attacks on New York and Washington. But clearly he possesses both. We also now know that he is willing, actually, eager, to delegate as long as he has competent appointees. And his appointees have turned out to be first rate.

Bush all but turned over centralized control of the emergency on September 11th to his chief lieutenant, Vice President Dick Cheney. It was Cheney who ordered the evacuation of congressional leaders as well as the hopscotch trek across the country of the President himself aboard Air Force One on that fateful day. In addition, the able team of Secretary of State Colin Powell and Defense Secretary Donald Rumsfeld pieced together the international coalition.

Bush has taken this delegation of authority so far that we can now say that for the first time in decades, true Cabinet government has been restored. For years, the White House staff had been preeminent in policy matters, and the cabinet was mostly a mouthpiece. No longer. Cabinet members are true players, not public relations purveyors, in Washington. At the same time, Bush makes the final decisions on strategic matters. He isn't a figurehead CEO.

DETERMINATION

Bush is also as determined as any president in memory to get what he wants on the domestic front, even when facing war abroad. His behavior on domestic issues, in fact, can shed some insight into his overall presidential style. To wit: Bush swaggers and promises a lot, never expecting to get everything. And in that way he accomplishes more of what he wishes than anyone might have anticipated.

This cowboy demeanor is partly a Texas tendency, one that annoys many Europeans. But it is also a calculated strategy. Bush likes to promise the moon, as he did when he pledged to eradicate global terrorism. But that is mostly an expression of resolve, meant both to inspire and provoke. He will always accept less, when he has to.

There are many examples of this. When Nick Calio, the President's top congressional lobbyist, first visited the then-President-elect in Texas in January, Bush told him, "We're not going to negotiate with ourselves." The modus operandi of his White House, Bush explained, will be to talk tough for as long as possible, but mostly as a bargaining tool. Referring specifically to tax cuts, a top priority at the time, Bush described the strategy this way: "We're not going to negotiate with ourselves on taxes. We'll say, '$1.6 trillion over ten years,' and they'll move toward us. We won't get everything we want but we'll get a tax bill." In other words, Bush never expects to win what he wants. But he intends to state loudly and clearly his fondest wish for as long as he can as a way to make the other side compromise more. A similar tack was used against the Taliban when Bush announced jauntily that he wanted bin Laden "dead or alive."

The danger is that Bush often overpromises, as Calio soon found out. The grousing on Capitol Hill about the size of the tax reduction rapidly grew shrill in early 2001. And when Calio went to Bush to seek guidance, Bush wouldn't bend. He reminded Calio of the game plan. "Don't wobble," Bush urged. Calio did what he was told. And lo and behold, the stubbornness paid off. In May, Bush managed to get most of what he desired. Congress passed and he signed into law

$1.35 trillion in tax relief over eleven years. The wisdom of his tactic became manifest. And a pattern of his presidency became clear.

Here's what you need to know: Bush can't be seen in a snap shot. He's a moving target. He begins with a firm position, almost always on the political right, and moves leftward only when he has to. He will issue veto threats, as he did once with the so-called Patients' Bill of Rights (health care reform), and he will swear support for proposals, such as education vouchers, that he knows have no chance. He will strut and bluster (to the pleasure of Republican stalwarts) until he gets as much as he can. Then he'll relent, declare victory, and move on. And that's the key. "The goal," Calio says, "is to get things done." Bush believes he'll be judged by results, not process. His administration's daily press briefings detailing progress on the war front (bombings, numbers of people arrested, etc.) all fit with the philosophy.

Too Much Swagger?

This tactic may work in the long run, but in the short run it is exceedingly messy. On domestic issues, middle-of-the-road and left-of-center American voters, as well as plenty of foreigners, will see him as too conservative. Indeed, to watch the President at the beginning of any debate, you'd never know that he won the White House after losing the popular vote. He operates with the confidence of a landslide victor. He acts as if he has a mandate from the electorate to govern as far to the political right as he can reach.

In fact, he has no such mandate. So by pushing so hard for so long to the right, he not only angers the left but also gives false hope to his conservative loyalists. When he's through with a legislative debate, and he compromises leftward as he almost always must, his credibility with congressional allies (read: conservatives and Republicans) will often be in shambles. They will see him as too liberal and too willing to accommodate. Over time, he will be stranded alone, with little more than his swagger. His fellow Republicans will be especially disappointed.

Before Bush got his tax cut, for instance, his aides had to meet somber-faced Republican leaders in a Capitol hideaway to implore them to accept more tax breaks for low-income parents than they had planned. The lawmakers shook their heads but acceded. Prior to that, angry Republicans, including House Majority Leader Dick Armey and House Whip Tom DeLay, had to be brought to an Oval Office showdown with the President before they accepted a hugely expensive education bill. This will also be part of the Bush pattern: carnage on the political right after lengthy despair on the left.

Much of this division has been hidden for the sake of the war effort. Bush is slightly more willing to compromise with the Democrats to display unity as far as is possible. His tough posture, however, carries risks. If he presses Arab allies too hard, he could ignite dissension that could topple their regimes. Bin Laden could become more of an icon than he already is. Bush also might prove unable to topple terrorism, and this could create a backlash that would undermine his standing both at home and abroad.

One bulwark against such calamities is the fact that his White House is exceptionally well run. George W., a Harvard MBA, insists on complete loyalty and organizational discipline among his underlings. The Bush I [George H.W. Bush] White House wasn't nearly as collegial; its aides always feuded, and George W. saw that and hated the situation. Bush II staffers, by contrast, get along well, perhaps because they have to. War will do that.

Nevertheless an inevitable question remains: How long will Bush's own party continue to back him if he keeps tugging it to the center? The answer is: probably forever. "The right is as house broken as the President's dog," says Marshall Wittmann, a Republican analyst at the Hudson Institute. The reason: Republicans prefer having their own guy in the White House and they realize that the best way to keep him there is to hold their nose and vote for watered-down legislation. More important, war requires more solidarity than is usual, and Bush will certainly get it from Republicans and Democrats.

STANDING FIRM

Bush also benefits from being underestimated. For example, Republican insiders worried prior to his speech on federal stem cell research over the summer [of 2001] that Bush had chosen an obscure, no-win topic for his first nationally televised address. But Bush knew better. He understood that bioethics is a political frontier that Presidents will have to cross in the new century. He also was willing to risk a display of courage. Sometimes that backfires. But not this time. Bush came out a winner. He delivered a thoughtful and eloquent explanation for his preference for allowing limited research by the federal government. He worked hard at showing how thoroughly he had studied the complex issues. . . . And in so doing, he effectively undercut the raps against him that he is camera shy and slow-witted. In truth, he is neither and his enemies merely fall into his trap if they try to sell the story, so popular in Europe, that he is a buffoon or a naif.

He is, in fact, a fellow amply clever enough to change his mind if he is forced to. And also to express unflinching determination when he must. His top White House counselor, Karl Rove, who is considered the reigning political genius of the Republican Party these days, aids him when he needs to know when to do which. A better helpmate would be hard to find.

Before the terror events, Bush was flexible to a fault. Every time you looked up, you saw a new George W. Whether he was endorsing a form of energy-price controls after decrying them, stumping against global warming after downplaying it, or ending bombing on Vieques Island, Puerto Rico, after permitting it, the President was forever changing course. Such flips have happened so frequently that the White House devised a euphemism to describe them: mid-course corrections. In truth, they were reversals made in response to international pressure or voter opinion, making Bush, early on, the U-turn President.

Yet when war came, he showed that he could stand firm as well. He refused to negotiate with the Taliban, for instance. He also remained nimble enough not to press the coalition into doing things that could cause strife within the partners' own borders. When Saudi Arabia and Egypt expressed concern that public support might undermine their own power to control the mob, Bush reportedly accepted private assurances and deals under-the-table, the details of which we aren't likely to know for years. In addition, Bush balanced our guns with butter by delivering humanitarian aid packages along with military salvos to the people of Afghanistan. Unlike his predecessor Bill Clinton, Bush doesn't pander at the drop of a poll. He isn't oblivious to his popularity, but he also doesn't make a fetish of finding his policy positions at a focus group. Bush can't be counted on to do things just because they gain him votes. At the same time, a more complete picture of Bush must include the following:

Bush understands that, at times, he will have to adapt to forces beyond his control, such as a diverse international partnership against terrorism and a U.S. Senate controlled by the opposition party.

Take the situation at home. After Democrats took control of the Senate in June [2001], the Patients' Bill of Rights and an increase in the minimum wage moved to the top of the legislative calendar. Both are popular with voters but weren't what Bush wanted to tackle right away. Yet Bush embraced both and has tried to put his stamp on each. He also wanted to wait on the next Democratic agenda item, a new prescription-drug benefit for Medicare. But here, too, he will accept the inevitable, probably next year, and try to mold the finished product.

Over the long haul, reviving the economy will be as large a challenge for Bush as winning his war against terrorism. The attacks pushed the U.S. economy into a recession. As a result, there simply isn't as much money to pay for the many items that once topped his wish list, such as energy tax credits. Other propositions, like his multibillion-dollar missile defense, seem like unnecessary and anachronistic extravagances. In addition, his plan to invest in the stock market some payroll taxes that now go exclusively into the so-called Social Security Trust Fund has faded with the Dow Jones Industrial Average.

But don't count on Bush's presidency sinking with the GDP [Gross Domestic Product]. What had looked like the Bush Recession prior to September 11th is now and forever the bin Laden Recession. Besides, voters don't seem to give as much credit or blame to politicians as they once did for the state of the economy. And that can only help Bush.

A Higher Calling

Tony Carnes

The devastation from the terrorist attacks on September 11, 2001, would challenge the nation to cope with its grief and outrage. President Bush's spiritual and moral convictions helped him emerge as a strong political leader in that time of crisis. Tony Carnes, a writer for *Christian Reader*, describes President Bush's example of coping as a powerful tonic to the national mood. By calling the nation to prayer and establishing a national day of remembrance, Bush's example of faith and trust in God sustained the country during one of its darkest times in history. Bush felt he was not only a political leader with a high profile, but a servant of God called to help lead America during this time.

President Bush, from the day of the attacks on the World Trade Center (WTC) last September [2001], has led the nation with a deft spiritual presence that radiates solidarity with people of all faiths. "Bush's stature as a leader rose right before your very eyes," says Richard Cizik, vice president of the National Association of Evangelicals. The nation seemed to agree. A *Newsweek* poll taken a week after the WTC catastrophe found that 83 percent of Americans thought that the President appeared to be a strong leader. Bush administration aide Timothy Goeglein said he agrees with the widespread view that the terrorist catastrophe is "absolutely a spiritually defining moment for the country and its leader."

After the September 11, 2001, attack, Bush displayed great skill at expressing his spiritual and moral convictions. His development as a political leader took enormous strides forward as he spoke at the National Cathedral, at Ground Zero of the collapsed World Trade Center, at the White House, at a joint session of Congress, and on national television.

Tony Carnes, "Bush's Defining Moment," *Christian Reader*, vol. 40, March 2002, p. 29.

BUSH'S MISSION FOR RELIGIOUS LEADERS

A few hours before his address to Congress on September 20, President Bush met at the White House with a broad spectrum of religion leaders. Twenty-seven leaders, including 13 evangelicals, attended. The group included evangelists Luis Palau and Franklin Graham, pastors Max Lucado, Bill Hybels, T.D. Jakes, and Charles Blake, and Edward Cardinal Egan of New York. Buddhist, Hindu, Sikh, and Mormon leaders also attended the meeting.

In the Roosevelt Room, the President got to the point. "I am not Pollyannish, imagining things are great," he declared. "I feel at peace, but a lot of that is due to the prayers of the American people. This is a major wake-up call for America. . . . Now, I need your help as spiritual leaders to be truthful with the American people without creating panic."

Bush then outlined what his speech to Congress and the nation would cover. He told the group that only religious leaders could give the comfort and handle the spiritual questions.

"Government will do some things, but you need to be praying and be prepared for questions," Bush told them.

Palau, who took notes at the meeting, said Bush drew a comparison between himself and the country. Bush told the gathering, "I was a sinner in need of redemption and I found it." The President was referring to the difficult time earlier in life when he was a heavy drinker and lacked a sense of purpose. But the gospel became clear to him through a conversation with evangelist Billy Graham.

Bush told the group that the nation was staggering and needed to get back on its feet. He said the devastation in New York challenged the nation to look deep into its heart. "I think this is part of a spiritual awakening in America," the President said.

Others who have talked with Bush said the President's disciplines of Bible reading and prayer sustain him.

Bush's faith is a vital part of his politics. "I don't think the President would consider himself an evangelical leader," says a prominent evangelical who knows Bush well. "He sees himself as a political leader and a man of faith."

HIGH PROFILE, HIGHER CALLING

At the White House prayer session, Bush referred to his Christian faith indirectly. It was "a candid, natural way of talking about the Lord and his faith," one participant said.

"He was very cautious and respectful in talking with the Muslims present, and he let them talk."

One purpose of the September 20 meeting was to "get Christian leaders around non-Christians ones so that [non-Christians] would feel welcomed," says Pastor Tim Keller of Redeemer Presbyterian Church in New York City.

The embrace was welcomed. Bush managed to be true to his personal evangelical testimony, while also creating a tolerant and inclusive meeting.

Gerald Kieschnick, president of the Lutheran Church-Missouri Synod, read aloud from Romans 13 and told Bush that he has a divine calling in this crisis: "Mr. President, I have just come from the World Trade Center site in Lower Manhattan, I stood where you stood. I saw what you saw. And I smelled what you smelled," Kieschnick said. "You not only have a civil calling, but a divine calling. . . . You are not just a civil servant; you are a servant of God called for such a time like this."

"I accept the responsibility," Bush said, nodding.

The President came close to tears only when he described his first thoughts after hearing that the fourth hijacked airliner may have been headed for the White House. "The White House is an old building made of plaster and brick," Bush said. "If it had been struck, it would have collapsed and many people would have been killed, including my wife."

The President paused for a long moment, squinching the side of his face as he does when he wants to hold back his emotions. "Those fellows who gave their lives—they gave their lives for freedom," Bush said. After squinching a bit more, the President said, "We need to keep people praying."

Franklin Graham and four other religious leaders were invited into the Oval Office to pray with the President. Bush pointed out a portrait of Abraham Lincoln and said it was a reminder of his own calling to extend freedom and bring the nation together.

The fusion of personal piety and civic responsibility comes from Bush's deep sense of vocation. Bush says he sensed a higher call during his second inauguration as governor of Texas. He called a friend in Fort Worth, telling him, "I believe God wants me to run for President." The President now tells friends he understands God's call with greater clarity.

"Bush believes that the Lord prepares you for whatever he

gives us," says one friend who visits the White House regularly. "The President really feels that this is his mission."

WITH GOD AT HIS SIDE

Since the terrorist attacks and the subsequent military action, the change in national mood was unmistakable. Praying and going to a religious service seemed a natural, normal thing to do. As *Wall Street Journal* columnist Peggy Noonan, put it, "God is back."

Bush's example of coping has been a powerful tonic to the national mood. Political observers say the President seems genuine, not calculated or manipulative. Ari Fleisher, press spokesman for Bush, watched the President interact with grieving families of the missing New York firefighters and police officers three days after the attack.

"He spent time listening and talking with everybody, just one on one, hearing their individual stories of their family members. It was gut-wrenching," Fleisher says. "Watching the President throughout all of this, there was a real transformation."

At the National Cathedral service, the President revealed how carefully he selected his words to fit the nation's mood. "We are here in the middle hour of our grief," he began. "We come before God to pray for the missing and the dead, and for those who loved them."

Bush said the providence of God may not be what we expect, but we can count on the grace of God. "God's signs are not always the one we look for," he told the congregation. "We learn in tragedy that His purposes are not always our own."

Since September 11, Bush's speeches have married his informal, choppy syntax with his newly forceful vision for the country. Michael Gerson, Bush's chief speechwriter and a graduate of Wheaton College, shares similar religious convictions with Bush. Gerson crafted this elegant sentence in Bush's September 20 national address: "Freedom and fear, justice and cruelty, have always been at war, and we know that God is not neutral between them."

The Bush speech was widely praised. One political columnist wrote a favorable comparison of Bush and President Lincoln. "The yardstick on how to judge a President will always be Lincoln," says Allen Guelzo, Lincoln scholar at Eastern College near Philadelphia.

Bush has "projected an image as a determined, farsighted

leader," Guelzo says, but his pieties "are still bland and conventional" compared to those of Lincoln, who was tried by the fires of the American Civil War. "Whether Bush's growth and impact lasts will depend on his resolve" as he meets further tragedies.

During White House meetings, Bush frequently shows visitors a painting inspired by the hymn "A Charge to Keep." His autobiography, released during the 2000 campaign, bears the same title as the hymn. "I still have a charge to keep," Bush tells his visitors.

Indeed, a verse from the hymn seems to fit Bush's convictions: "To serve the present age, my calling to fulfill/Oh may it all my powers engage, to do my Master's will."

CHAPTER 6

AMERICA AT WAR

PEOPLE
WHO MADE
HISTORY

GEORGE W. BUSH

The Decision to Go to War

Kenneth T. Walsh

Minutes after hearing a second plane had hit the World Trade Center, Bush told his traveling staff the United States was at war. Bush ordered his senior advisers to develop a "grand strategy" to bring down terrorist networks around the world. The radical al-Qaeda group was immediately identified as a prime suspect in the attacks. Bush and the joint chiefs of staff held meetings to set the course for military operations, vowing justice would be done.

Condemning Iraq, North Korea, and Iran as countries that encourage and harbor terrorists, Bush declared them an "axis of evil" and structured the war on terrorism to include them as well as al-Qaeda. He stated America would strike hard to destroy terrorist activity and even fight to change the political regimes of those nations that sheltered or supported terrorists.

In the following article, Kenneth T. Walsh examines Bush's actions following the September 11, 2001, terrorist attacks against the United States and the subsequent formation of his philosophies on terrorism. Walsh is the chief White House correspondent for *U.S. News & World Report;* he has taught courses on media and history at the American University and has authored several books on politics and the media.

As commander in chief, George W. Bush lives by a simple code. The military needs hardware? Send it to them. U.S. allies are hesitant to engage? Go it alone. Iraq, Iran, and North Korea are rogue nations encouraging terrorism? Condemn them as an "axis of evil." "He sees the world almost in theo-

Kenneth T. Walsh, "W, as in War," *U.S. News & World Report,* vol. 132, February 25, 2002, p. 42. Copyright © 2002 by *U.S. News & World Report.* Reproduced by permission.

logical terms," says Rutgers political scientist Ross Baker. "He is making a very stark distinction between the benevolent forces in the world and the forces that want to do people harm. . . . His willingness to simplify, at the risk of oversimplification, has given him a remarkable ability to be in touch with the American people. They feel that way, too."

In fact, Bush's good-vs.-evil construct is the principle on which all of his wartime decisions have been based. Most important, it is the core of an emerging "Bush Doctrine" that was cobbled together by the president and his senior advisers in the minutes and days following the September 11 attacks. That doctrine, which holds that the United States needs to exert itself more forcefully in the world, could turn out to be the most sweeping change in foreign policy since Ronald Reagan declared the Soviet Union an "evil empire."

From now on, Bush says, America will search out and destroy terrorist networks, strike equally hard at nations that harbor terrorists, and act pre-emptively if necessary to change "evil" regimes in Iran, Iraq, and North Korea if they continue to back terrorists or develop weapons of mass destruction. So far, his approach is working, which is not surprising to scholars such as Baker. They say that one of the most important attributes of any commander in chief is clarity of purpose, and Bush has demonstrated more of it than perhaps any wartime president since Franklin Roosevelt.

Even his former critics are impressed with his leadership. "No. 1," says Sandy Berger, national security adviser to President Clinton, "the president has to create the right environment for his team. He sets the tone. And the tone is either agitation and frenzy—or the tone is steadiness and calm." Berger also praises Bush for patiently waiting several weeks before launching military strikes. This gave the Pentagon enough time to properly prepare for the war in Afghanistan.

QUICK RESPONSE

Bush's moral absolutism was clear almost from the first moments of the crisis. News of the first attack came shortly before 9 A.M., when White House Counselor Karl Rove took Bush aside in the corridor of a Florida elementary school, where he was about to speak. A plane had crashed into the World Trade Center in New York, Rove said, and the cause was unclear. "What a horrible accident!" Bush replied, and he wondered if the pilot had suffered a heart attack.

A few minutes later, White House Chief of Staff Andrew Card whispered in the president's ear as he was about to address the schoolchildren, all in full view of television cameras. "A second plane hit the second tower," Card said. "America is under attack." Bush blanched and grimly pressed his lips into a thin line. He announced he would have more to say later and left the room.

He immediately got on the phone with Condoleezza Rice, his national security adviser, and others in Washington. A few minutes later, he told his traveling staff, "We're at war."

"When he went into that classroom," Card told *U.S. News*, "he was the president of the United States, talking domestic issues. He walked out of that room as the commander in chief, where he had the absolute authority to make something happen." En route from Florida to Barksdale Air Force Base in Louisiana, a secure location where Bush could consider his next moves and where Air Force One could refuel, Bush and his shocked staff watched television footage of the planes crashing into the World Trade towers. At one point,

---

AMERICA'S MILITARY

In this excerpt from his autobiography, George W. Bush discusses his belief that the nation should maintain a well-trained, well-equipped military. Arguing that America should always be prepared for conflict, he also notes that the country should only send troops into battle when all other diplomatic options have failed.

My time in the [National] Guard taught me the importance of a well-trained and well-equipped military. It gave me respect for the chain of command. It showed me, firsthand, that given proper training and adequate personnel, the military can accomplish its mission. After all, the military took a novice like me and trained me to be a skilled pilot of high-performance jets. I also learned the lesson of Vietnam. Our nation should be slow to engage troops. But when we do so, we must do so with ferocity. We must not go into a conflict unless we go in committed to win. We can never again ask the military to fight a political war. If America's strategic interests are at stake, if diplomacy fails, if no other option will accomplish the objective, the Commander in Chief must define the mission and allow the military to achieve it.

George W. Bush, *A Charge to Keep*. New York: William Morrow, 1999.

Bush calmly told Vice President Dick Cheney by secure phone that he approved of shooting down civilian aircraft if they posed another imminent threat. "You have my full authorization," Bush said.

THE GRAND STRATEGY

Since taking office, Bush had been extensively briefed by the CIA and others on "asymmetrical threats" including the al Qaeda terrorist network, and took them all seriously. In the spring of 2001, he told his senior advisers he would no longer tolerate small measures. "I'm really tired of swatting flies," he said. Bush ordered them to develop a grand strategy for "bringing down" the terrorist networks around the world, but the plan was still under development at the time of the September 11 attacks. Still, he immediately identified members of al Qaeda as the prime suspects.

Cheney told *U.S. News:* "Lots of time you don't have all the information you'd like, but that's life and you've still got to make a decision and get on with it and not agonize over it. He doesn't look back and lay awake at night, I don't think, in terms of worrying about whether or not he got it right." For his part, Bush tells friends he has not regretted a single decision he has made since September 11.

At key meetings with his war council at Camp David and at the White House over that first weekend after the attacks, he set a bold course. He chose the most extensive list of military options presented to him by the CIA and the Joint Chiefs of Staff. And he wanted his speech to a joint session of Congress that week to flesh it all out. A battery of advisers weighed in, but Bush knew just what he wanted to say. As the hour of the speech approached, aides Karen Hughes, Michael Gerson, and Dan Bartlett were working on the text in the West Wing and wondered if the Bush-approved final draft leaned too heavily toward reassuring the country. Perhaps, they told themselves, there should be more explicit warnings about the dangers ahead. Bartlett went to the East Wing to consult one last time with the president, who greeted him as he was buttoning up his dress shirt. "What do you want?" Bush said curtly. Bartlett dutifully raised the question about the speech's main theme, but Bush cut him off. "I already made that decision. Final!" the president said, and walked off. He told Congress that America's mission would be accomplished no matter what. "Whether we bring our enemies to justice or bring justice to our enemies," he said, "justice will be done."

Card says that since Bush believed there were no shades of gray, it was only natural that he devised "a doctrine that you are either with us or against us. If you harbor, protect, defend, feed, comfort, house—you're them." In his State of the Union address January 29, he condemned Iran, Iraq, and North Korea as an axis of evil because they were potentially helping the terrorists or developing weapons of mass destruction, even though some State Department experts cringed at the characterization as extreme.

When an aide recently asked Bush whether the crisis had changed him, the president said absolutely not. "Presidents either come to the Oval Office equipped and ready to deal with crises or they don't," he replied, adding: "If you're strong and firm, people follow." Rice told *U.S. News:* "He wasn't born somebody else on September 11." The question is whether his bipolar view of the world—so valuable in wartime—will provide the nuanced long-term strategy that may be needed to secure the peace.

Bush's Battle Cry: Drawing on Prayer and a Sense of Personal Mission, W Becomes a War President

T. Trent Gegax

As the death toll mounted and the economic damage became evident from the terrorist attacks in New York and Washington on September 11, 2001, President Bush called the world to war. With a military mission focused at ending terror, leaders from around the world were compelled to pledge allegiance to America's new cause. The American people seemed determined to meet the new challenges facing the nation by embracing both Bush's leadership and mission.

T. Trent Gegax spent seventeen months covering George W. Bush's 2000 presidential campaign. As a writer covering Washington for *Newsweek* magazine, Gegax outlines in this October 1, 2001, article how after the World Trade Center and Pentagon attacks, Bush drew on prayer and a sense of personal mission to become a war president.

Before he spoke his words of war for the world to hear, George W. Bush wanted to pray in private with the ordained of all faiths. It was hours before the most fateful speech of his life. Twenty-seven clergymen had been invited to meet with him. The chairs in the Roosevelt Room of the White House were arranged in a circle, prayer-meeting style. But when he walked into the room and took a seat, no one dared sit beside him for fear of seeming presumptuous. "Move in here next to me," said Bush, motioning to empty chairs on either side of him. "I feel lonely." Two men complied—Cardinal Bernard Law of Boston and Archbishop Demetrios Trakatellis of New York. For the next half hour, as he steeled himself to launch the country on a lengthy, perilous mission to purge terrorism from the world, Bush shared his burdens and hopes.

"You understand what I am facing," he said. "I have to alert the American people to the ongoing dangers without creating alarm and irrational fear. How do I walk that line?" Worry was justified. "Another crisis could hit us, more terrible than this one," he said, according to notes and recollections of several clergy. "It could be more terrible—biological, chemical or plutonium. I don't have direct evidence," he said, "but I have enough evidence." (A White House spokesman later said that Bush was speaking in general of possible threats.)

Bush said he could identify all too well with the public's fears: the White House itself had been an intended target. "It's a very old structure of plaster and brick," he said. "A lot of people could have been killed . . . including my wife." The answer, Bush had concluded, was to fight for peace and justice—and to pray. "Pray for patience, pray it will not happen again," he said. As for him, he was healthy and rested, focused and feeling "confident without being Pollyannaish." But he needed divine help, too. "Pray for wisdom, strength, clear thinking," he said, and joined hands with the circle as they did so.

In the new world of war, God matters—to both sides. Unblinkingly resolute before a cheering Congress, George Bush defiantly vowed in God's name to lead an anxious nation and the civilized world in a decisive campaign against the forces of terror. The fight would focus initially, he said, on Islamic extremist Osama bin Laden and his al-Qaeda network in the mountains of Afghanistan. As the president spoke, American warplanes, ships and troops were speeding bin Laden's way—and the dictatorial clerics who rule the country prepared for what they later called a "showdown of might" in an Islamic "holy war."

As dangerous as that conflict may be, Bush portrayed it as just the start of a decades-long struggle—a choosing of sides based not on territorial claims or clashing theories of government, but on the goal of ending terror as an instrument of human affairs. "Every nation in every region now has a decision to make," he declared. "From this day forward, any nation that continues to harbor or support terrorism will be regarded by the United States as a hostile regime." Besides allies, Bush said, America would need—and receive—assistance from Above. "Freedom and fear, justice and cruelty, have always been at war," he said, "and we know that God is not neutral between them."

Flawlessly delivering a speech that he and his aides had labored on all week, Bush appeared in the well of the House at a time of peril as severe as any since Pearl Harbor. Around the world, leaders pledged allegiance to America's new cause. But except for Britain's Tony Blair (who flew to Washington for briefings and to sit in the Gallery beside Laura Bush), it wasn't clear which countries would answer an American call for men, materiel and diplomatic muscle. Saudi Arabia, the economic and religious linchpin of the region, is allowing the use of its military bases. But it and other moderate Islamic states, facing their own threats from militants, were wary of aiding the United States too openly.

At home, the shock of the plane-bomb attacks on the World Trade Center and the Pentagon gave way to a mounting toll of death, economic damage and anxiety about the long-term impact on psyches and civil liberties. As the estimates for the missing grew to some 6,000, New York Mayor Rudolph Giuliani cautioned that the numbers could go down as various reports were coordinated. But the region was still forced to endure a procession of funerals and camera-toting visitors flocking to the jagged ruins of ground zero.

The full dimension of economic devastation was becoming apparent. The stock markets reopened but reeled, losing $1.4 trillion in book value as shares plummeted faster than they had since the depths of the Depression. The airline industry was crippled, suffering a staggering 80,000 layoffs and facing numerous bankruptcies—a crisis that prompted Bush and Congress to enact a $15 billion bailout. Federal Reserve chairman Alan Greenspan told congressional leaders in a somber private meeting that the $10 trillion-a-year economy would recover—but not any time soon. "The outlook is uncertain at best," one leader quoted him as saying.

The threat to the country's social fabric was less quantifiable but no less real, as officials and average citizens sought to find a new balance between security and privacy, antiterrorism measures and open-mindedness. A package of tough new law-enforcement measures, put forward by Attorney General John Ashcroft, sparked debate in Congress and brought assurances of compromise from the White House. Bush announced a new Office of Homeland Security to oversee border patrols, immigration, public-health threats and water supplies, and named Pennsylvania Gov. Tom Ridge to head it. Responding to scattered incidents of violence and widespread concern, the president pleaded for tolerance, especially for the nation's 6 million Muslim citizens. "We are in a fight for our principles," he declared to Congress, "and our first responsibility is to live by them."

The challenges were daunting, but the country seemed determined to meet them—and eager to embrace the disciplined and confident leadership Bush displayed in his 36-minute address. Americans share a faith of the Founders: that democratic destiny will furnish leaders the times require. Thus far, Bush has more than met the challenge of that belief. In the *Newsweek* Poll, conducted before and after the speech, voters, by an 86-10 percent margin, approved of the way he was handling his job. Asked specifically about his stewardship in the aftermath of the terrorist attacks, voters approved by an 87-7 percent margin before the speech, by a 90-7 percent margin afterward.

The president was a man on a mission—aware, aides said, that his every move was freighted with significance for the country and the free world. The Bush watchword was "focus." The battle against terrorism, at home and abroad, now would "be the focus of our administration," he told the cabinet (and probably, one top adviser said later, "of administrations to come"). "I've never seem him so focused," said another adviser. After Jacques Chirac met with Bush, the French president privately expressed astonishment to aides at the American's sure grasp of the nuances of the situation. At a staff meeting last Friday, Bush moved swiftly through a long agenda of complex items, practically barking out orders as he went. To some he seemed a bit lonely. "He's in the loneliest job in the world," observed Karl Rove, his old friend and top political adviser. Yet the president seemed comfortable with his fate. "Things have a way of being the way they are supposed to be," he told Rove with a shrug. "This is my responsibility."

To meet his responsibilities, Bush has always demanded game plans—or at least the outlines of them. The one he announced last week was devised in momentous day-long meetings a week ago Saturday at Camp David. Bush and his circle of commanders agreed on a two-pronged approach, at once sweeping (to give them latitude and time) and specific (to provide "focus" and at least one clear goal). The administration would call on all nations to join in the antiterrorism campaign, or risk becoming a foe—the Bush doctrine. Meanwhile, they would marshal military, diplomatic and economic force for the tough but unavoidable goal of destroying bin Laden and, perhaps, the Taliban.

As usual, Bush delegated the implementation. Vice President Dick Cheney, in effect, was appointed war minister— the Mr. Inside who would stay largely out of sight and oversee the campaign. Ridge, whom Bush has known since 1980, would take control of the new homeland effort. Josh Bolten, a former investment banker and White House aide known for his policy mastery and meticulous sense of organization, would chair the Domestic Consequences Group—a blandly worded euphemism for the economic-crisis-management team.

That left the president with one enormous and indispensable job: to explain the mission. His vehicle would be a meticulously crafted, carefully worded speech. There would be no freelancing of the kind that had led him to describe the task at hand as a "crusade"—a word with an unfortunately specific historical and theological meaning that had outraged Muslims when he used it. On the Sunday Bush offhandedly uttered the term, there had been no morning "message meeting." Thereafter, no day would be complete without one—and national-security adviser Condoleezza Rice would always be in them.

Bush began planning for the speech last Monday morning, days before aides would ask Hill leaders to invite the president to speak to a joint session of Congress. Bush didn't want to commit to the momentous venue unless he had a speech to match it. He asked for a draft by close of business that day. "Mr. President, I think that will be difficult, if not impossible," counselor Karen Hughes told him. His reply: "By 7." A team of speechwriters worked on the document, aiming for the blunt simplicity and muted expressions of faith he favors.

There were 19 drafts, many pencil-edited by Bush, and repeated practices before the Teleprompter in the family theater. Bush rejected suggestions for an extended discussion of the economy; he wanted the text streamlined—and didn't want to pre-empt congressional leaders, who would have their own ideas about "stimulus" measures. Bush agreed with Hughes that he should take time for plain explanation: Who was bin Laden? What was the Taliban?

But the president, who views the world in personal terms, wanted to conclude with his own witness, his own declaration of purpose. Hughes suggested that he dramatize it by showing the world the brass badge given to him by the grieving mother of a cop who had died at the World Trade Center. Bush agreed. "This is my reminder of lives that ended," he said, holding the badge aloft at a pivot point of history, "and a task that does not end."

In the Oval Office the next morning, he reminded his aides of his message. "We have to be patient," he told one. "This is going to take a long time." The atmosphere in the White House had changed since Black Tuesday—aides learned about evacuation plans, sought counseling, surfed antiterror Web sites. But the president himself was determined to return to a life that was, as he said in his speech, "almost normal." He was jogging outside again. As usual, he talked to his dad. The president asked one of his oldest friends, Commerce Secretary Donald Evans, to join him at Camp David for the weekend. They could talk about the economy. Then again, it was Evans who, long ago in west Texas, introduced Bush to Bible study. There might be time for that, too.

Bush Commits to the Middle East

Michael Duffy

Although President Bush tried to separate his administration from conflict in the Middle East, continued fighting between Israel and Palestinians was something that the United States could not ignore. In April 2002, Israeli troops invaded the West Bank region of Palestine, anti-American demonstrations were taking place all over the Middle East, oil prices soared, and the U.S. stock market plunged. Violence in the Middle East was seemingly out of control. After meeting for several days with top advisers, President Bush endorsed Palestinian statehood, but asked leader Yasser Arafat to stop terrorism and make peace with Israel. Bush also pressed Israeli prime minister Ariel Sharon to withdraw troops from the West Bank region and treat the Palestinians with compassion rather than with military force. The absolutes between good and evil that Bush had declared in the war on terrorism were now being compromised to help reshape the shakey Middle East, where terror was a weapon used by both sides.

Michael Duffy examines the factors that brought the Bush administration into the diplomatic process and some of the dangers this decision brings with it. Duffy covers Washington for *Time* magazine.

Consider the situation in the White House Situation Room last Thursday morning: Israeli troops and armor had invaded almost every city in the West Bank and surrounded about 200 Palestinian fighters barricaded inside Bethlehem's sacred Church of the Nativity. Anti-American demonstrations in Cairo, Beirut, Amman and other Middle Eastern capitals were making it impossible for Washington's Arab allies to stay on the fence. Egypt cut some ties with Israel and warned the White House that the rest could be in jeopardy. Oil prices spiked to $28 a barrel, and the stock market plunged. Anti-Semites vandalized synagogues in France and Belgium. American embassies cabled Washington that they might be the next targets. And White House officials were poring over satellite pictures from the region: Syria was moving its troops in the Bekaa Valley of Lebanon in anticipation of Israeli strikes across the border. The situation, a senior White House official concedes, was "getting out of control."

Talk about grabbing George W. Bush's attention: the President finally saw that he had gone down the wrong road, and he pulled a quick U-turn. When he stepped up to the Rose Garden podium Thursday morning, Bush ended more than a year of stubborn disengagement from the Middle East peace process, sending Secretary of State Colin Powell to the region to seek a solution to the Israeli-Palestinian conflict. Bush's speech was tough and elegant. "The storms of violence cannot go on," he said. "Enough is enough."

The meetings that produced the speech were even more extraordinary. For several days, the most powerful people in the Administration had served as speechwriters. Bush, Powell, Vice President Dick Cheney, Defense Secretary Donald Rumsfeld, National Security Adviser Condoleezza Rice and CIA Director George Tenet had all called or crowded into the Situation Room and worked on the speech line by line—a measure of how troubled and critical this moment really was. The team added a great deal of moral embroidery and made sure that the speech demanded something from everyone. In the Rose Garden, Bush reached out to Yasser Arafat, endorsing Palestinian statehood and giving the leader another chance to stop the terrorists and make peace—but making it clear this chance would be his last. Bush pressed Israeli Prime Minister Ariel Sharon to pull his troops and tanks from the West Bank cities and insisted that Israel begin treating the Palestinians with "compassion." Bush called on moderate Arab countries to stop wringing their hands and start helping the Palestinians build their new nation—but also warned Iraq, Iran and Syria not to undo the deal by supporting terror. During the speechwriting sessions, Administration sources told *Time*, the dependably hard-line Rumsfeld had pushed most fiercely to include tough language aimed at any nation that might try to "fish in troubled waters," as one aide put it. And these sources noticed during the several days of drafting that Cheney was particularly active, more willing than before to wager American prestige in a game with so many risks—and keen to sharpen language that warned rogue nations to stay out of the fight.

This is how a crucial policy is reborn in the Bush White House. In a single day, George W. Bush moved from keeping his distance from a region in flames to all but staking his presidency on its peace and security. He also went a long way toward diluting the simple moral code embedded in the recently hatched Bush Doctrine—the doctrine that divides the world neatly into two camps, one good and one evil. Since last September, Bush has said over and over that the nations of the world have a choice: "You're either with us, or you're with the terrorists." But by taking a chance for peace that depends on Arafat, the President is acknowledging that the moral absolutism that has worked so well in the war against terror doesn't apply to every feud. The inside story of how Bush decided to wade waist-deep into the Middle East quicksand is the story of a President who is learning that there are few simple choices in foreign policy. So it is with Arafat. "He is a liar and completely untrustworthy," says an Administration official, "but for the moment, he is the man."

POWELL WINS THE ROUND

For the past 11 or so presidents, it has been a truism that American leaders ignore the Middle East at their peril. So why did Bush think he could get away with paying so little attention to the place? As with so many questions about the Middle East, there is an answer to fit every neighborhood. Many Democrats and Republicans believe that Bush checked out of the story early in his presidency in part because he came to Washington with a reflexive desire to do the opposite of whatever his predecessor did. It is true that Bill Clinton had his hands deep in the Middle East mess from his first year in office until the final days of his presidency in a way that the Bush team found inappropriate and even dangerous, given that a taste for high-stakes summitry, in its view, led to dashed hopes and renewed violence. "It wasn't all that long ago where a summit was called and nothing happened," Bush told a television interviewer Friday in a not-so-veiled criticism of Clinton, "and as a result we had significant *intifadeh* in the area."

Bush has been unlucky in his potential partners. Last year

Israeli voters replaced Ehud Barak, who wanted peace, with Sharon, who doesn't want it very badly. Bush may have figured early on that neither Arafat nor Sharon was likely to step into the role of peacemaker anytime soon, so why bother trying to convert either? And so Bush spent the first two-thirds of 2001 worrying less about foreign policy than domestic matters. When he did look overseas, first it was Russia and China that tested him. Then it was Osama bin Laden.

But the central obstacle to engagement in the region has been Bush's senior foreign-policy advisers, led by Cheney and Rumsfeld. They are staunchly pro-Israel and have shown little regard for the peace process in the past. Concentrated at the Pentagon but salted all around the White House, the hardliners have regular access to Bush. They take a dim view of the land-for-peace swap on which every peace proposal has been based for more than a decade. Every time the Administration's moderates, led by Powell, pushed Bush for a serious peace initiative in 2001, Cheney and Rumsfeld fought them to a standstill. After a while, Powell stopped pushing. Following two trips to the region last year to try to quell the rising violence between Palestinians and Israelis, he gave up. "Colin got tired," says a veteran diplomat who knows all the players, "of going over there with nothing in his briefcase."

At the center of the hard-line ethic is a strong belief that all conflicts can fit neatly into the war between Us and Them, freedom and tyranny, good and evil. The hard-liners believe that U.S. foreign policy proceeds from straightforward choices between absolutes: trust the nations that work with you; treat everyone else as a potential adversary. The hard-liners' hero is Ronald Reagan, who labeled the former Soviet Union the "evil empire." Reagan, however, rarely let his rhetoric get in the way of pragmatic foreign policy. And Bush is now showing signs of similar flexibility.

In 1989 the first President Bush carefully weeded many of the Reagan holdovers and foreign-policy hard-liners from his Administration. Last year the second President Bush invited them back and allowed them to flourish. In this Bush Administration, it is moderates like Powell who have struggled for influence and who sometimes win only when the hard-line position fails. The two rival teams put their differences aside after Sept. 11. The Pentagon had a strange new war on its hands, and Powell had a multinational coalition against al-Qaeda to plant and nurture. But as the ground war cooled, the hard-liners got busy again. They turned their attention to Iraq, and the back-room tug-of-war began all over again. In January, while Powell was out of the country on a diplomatic mission, Cheney and Rumsfeld teamed up to persuade Bush to cut all ties with Arafat.

SADDAM ON THE BACK BURNER

That gambit fizzled when Powell found out about it, but the hawks moved again a month later, pressing Bush for a broad military action against Iraq's Saddam Hussein, America's latest target of "evil" in the region. They believed Bush should seize his chance while his postwar popularity was high. Powell and the moderates disputed the timing and tactics, if not the goal itself. But Bush agreed to send Cheney to the region last month to drum up Arab support, or at least acquiescence, for an eventual military operation against Baghdad.

Some allies didn't wait to be asked. In an effort to head off Cheney, Egyptian President Hosni Mubarak flew to Washington in early March to tell the President himself that this was no time to make war in the region. Mubarak had been a staunch supporter of Bush's father's war 11 years ago, but he drew the line now that Israel and the Palestinians were skirmishing daily. Mubarak repeated his warning to a small group of private citizens at Blair House in Washington on March 6. As long as the Middle East is in turmoil, he told his guests, there is "no support" in the region for a war on Iraq.

If all that weren't tricky enough, Sharon made things worse by invading Palestinian towns in the West Bank on the eve of Cheney's departure. The U.S. rushed its peace envoy, retired Marine General Anthony Zinni, back to the region to provide cover for Cheney's trip. And instead of talking about Iraq, Cheney had to spend 10 days hopscotching around the Middle East and listening to leaders say the road to Baghdad runs through Jerusalem. One head of state warned that if Bush proceeded with the campaign against Iraq, he would find every Muslim nation allied against him. Almost overnight the air went out of a quick campaign against Saddam; when it will reinflate is anybody's guess. Cheney returned from the trip in late March, says a U.S. official, in an altered state. The man who had dismissed the step-by-step peace process only weeks before was now offering himself up as a go-between with Arafat.

SWITCHING SIGNALS ON ARAFAT

Bush was aching to get out of Washington for Easter. He hadn't visited his ranch in three months, the longest time he has been away from Texas since becoming President. So he went to Crawford, but as the deadly suicide bombings continued, he stayed out of sight, saying nothing for the first 48 hours. His silence amounted to a green light to Israel to counterattack—which in turn triggered more suicide bombings. One reason for Bush's silence was that his aides were again fighting about what to say. The President said he didn't want to "show-boat," appearing for the cameras but not offering much. Powell argued, sources tell *Time*, that it was the moment to intervene and take a more evenhanded approach. But Rumsfeld and the hard-liners balked, arguing that terror was terror, no matter who was behind it. Other advisers wondered what Bush could conceivably do about the Holy Land's widening gyre. British Prime Minister Tony Blair weighed in, contending that making peace requires negotiating with the parties as you find them. And so, little by little, the Administration began to split the difference. On Saturday morning the U.S. voted with a near unanimous majority in the U.N. for a resolution calling on Israel to pull out of the Palestinian cities.

But that afternoon, when he finally made a statement, Bush seemed unaware of what his Administration had been up to. And he was working without a net: none of his top aides had followed him to Texas. "Everyone was on vacation," says a chagrined White House official, "and they pretty much stayed on vacation." Staffing the President was a junior press aide normally assigned to Homeland Security chief Tom Ridge, and it showed. "I can understand why the Israeli government takes the actions they take," Bush said. "Their country is under attack." Given the U.N. vote that very morning, the message was incoherent. And the imagery and atmospherics were all wrong: wearing an open-collar shirt and rocking back and forth in his chair, Bush looked like his pre–Sept. 11 self, a little bit scared and a little bit scary. A top official said later, "It was a mistake."

By the time Bush returned to Washington on Sunday, the White House knew it had a problem. Senators from both parties were calling for Bush to get more involved. Presidential counselor Karen Hughes' morning communications meeting began with an aide who complained, "We're getting killed in the media!" Hughes and Rice joined forces and went to Bush to propose that he make a clarifying statement about the region sometime during the week. This time, to the moderates' surprise, the idea had the support of Cheney, who told Bush it was time to change gears and move toward more active intervention. "He was very realistic this week," says an official in the moderate camp. "Cheney was clearly influenced by his trip." Bush agreed on Monday night but told his aides about his decision Tuesday morning.

When Bush threw himself into the Middle East peace blender, his aides knew his neat and simple foreign-policy doctrine was going to be pureed. That meant Bush's right wing would feel betrayed. Early in the week the neoconservative opinion makers William Bennett and William Kristol tell Bush to stick to his guns and show Arafat no quarter. Bennett and Kristol seemed to have an ally in Rumsfeld, who took an almost strident antiterrorist line in public one week, even as White House officials spread the word quietly that everyone actually agreed in private. Rumsfeld's remarks may have been just for show, designed to modify those Bush was about to throw over the side. If so, it worked: Kristol's criticism of Bush in the *Weekly Standard* magazine on Friday was surprisingly mild.

THE DANGERS AHEAD

Bush's opening statement wasn't exactly a beacon of clarity, since he had to carefully and judiciously slap just about everyone in the Middle East. But it may have been the beginning of a realistic policy. The main problem now is that no one knows what happens next. Arafat quickly accepted the President's proposal "without condition" as his spokesman said, but few believe he can control all the suicide bombers. Sharon pledged to withdraw from the Palestinian cities, but he seemed in a bigger hurry to mop up every potential terrorist and perhaps dismantle what was left of the civilian Palestinian Authority in the West Bank. The death toll for the week rose to more than 100, with Israeli soldiers tightening their grip around Manger Square, where Palestinian gunmen and a huddle of civilians and priests were besieged in the Church of the Nativity complex. Israeli warplanes and artillery struck targets in southern Lebanon on Saturday after Israeli posts in Israel proper and the Golan Heights were shelled by Hizballah, raising familiar fears that a widening conflict could squelch yet another peace mission before it has a chance to take root. And Bush toughened his message to Sharon and called on Israel to pull back from the West Bank cities "without delay." On Saturday, in a telephone conversation with Bush, Sharon said he would expedite the campaign. Bush officials expect both Israeli and Palestinian positions to harden before they crack. That may explain why so many experts now believe the U.S. should come up with an ultimatum—a solution imposed from on high with new rules, sweeteners for every camp and unbearable penalties if they balk. It's an approach favored in one form or another by such old hands as Zbigniew Brzezinski, National Security Adviser in the Carter Administration, and Robert Malley, a former Clinton peace negotiator. Israeli Foreign Minister Shimon Peres thinks the U.S. should at least impose terms for a cease-fire, because "the alternative is another bazaar that will waste time and opportunities." Says Brzezinski: "The U.S. has to face the fact that the parties to the conflict are incapable of reaching a comprehensive peace on their own." But Dennis Ross, a former Bush and Clinton Middle East expert, says an ultimatum won't work. "You're not going to get them to compromise on Jerusalem now, you're not going to get them to compromise on refugees now, and you're not even going to get them to compromise on borders now," he says. "What you will produce is both sides focusing on the issues that give them the hardest line." Watching events unfold from the West Wing last week, one U.S. official sighed and said, "Better late than never." When it comes to the Middle East, that qualifies as optimism.

The Invasion of Iraq

Kenneth T. Walsh

Although it was the second U.S. invasion in twelve years, Bush's orders to begin war with Iraq in March 2003 was a historical first for the United States. After months of political negotiations through the United Nations, Bush gave Iraq's Saddam Hussein forty-eight hours to leave Baghdad or be forced out. Hours before the deadline, Bush met with advisers who had received information regarding where Hussein could be found. After a four-hour meeting with top advisers, Bush gave the word that launched the historical, preemptive attack. Despite Bush's confidence of the win, occupation and reconstruction of Iraq could take years and the war had damaged U.S. relationships with France, Germany, Russia, and other nations that opposed the rogue use of force. According to Kenneth T. Walsh, the plan was for Bush to use the success of the war with Iraq to heighten his political clout and push his domestic policies forward.

Walsh is the chief White House correspondent for *U.S. News & World Report*. He has taught courses on media and history at the American University and has authored several books on politics.

American presidents often try to remake the world. In 1823, James Monroe declared the Western Hemisphere off limits to European intervention in what became known as the Monroe Doctrine. In the 1940s, Harry Truman poured money into a shattered Europe to forestall communist takeovers after World War II as the centerpiece of the Truman Doctrine. In the 1980s, Ronald Reagan established the doctrine of rolling back, not just containing, communism. Twelve years ago, George H.W. Bush tried, with limited success, to organize a "New World Order" based on the allied victory in the first Persian Gulf War.

Kenneth T. Walsh, "Command Presence," *U.S. News & World Report*, vol. 134, March 31, 2003, pp. 30–32. Copyright © 2003 by *U.S. News & World Report*. Reproduced by permission.

Today, George W. Bush is thinking in bigger terms than most of his predecessors. His doctrine of pre-emptive war is one of the most far-reaching White House initiatives in U.S. history. "It's not a war about the past," says historian Robert Dallek. "It's a war about the future. If it goes quickly, smoothly, and comfortably, there will be more inducement for these preventive wars from now on." Iran and, conceivably, even nuclear-armed North Korea could be next, with potentially dangerous consequences: Pre-emptive war could become a model for other nations.

BUSH'S CERTAINTY

Not that such perils have caused any second-guessing by the commander in chief. George W. Bush seems to reside in more of a doubt-free zone than ever. This was certainly true on the Monday [March 17, 2003] he began the final run-up to war by ending diplomatic efforts and giving Saddam Hussein 48 hours to leave Iraq. White House aides, borrowing a phrase from gunslinger folklore, called it the "get out of Dodge" speech. Bush's patience, clearly, had run out.

Then there was a bit of serendipity. Just hours before the 48-hour deadline was scheduled to elapse, U.S. officials received a tip that Saddam and his senior advisers were gathered in a fortified bunker in southern Baghdad. Bush spent nearly four hours discussing his options in the Oval Office with George Tenet, director of central intelligence, Vice President Dick Cheney, Defense Secretary Donald Rumsfeld, National Security Adviser Condoleezza Rice, White House Chief of Staff Andrew Card, and other senior U.S. officials. They became the "action officers," sifting through the intelligence, weighing the use of different weapons, and assessing whether a " decapitation" strike would change the intricately detailed war plans. Several times, *U.S. News* has learned, Bush's advisers called military commanders in the field—and possibly had others contact the source of the original tip—to get more information.

A TWO-EDGED SWORD

At 7:12 P.M. [March 20], Bush gave the order to strike. "Let's go," he said with typical brevity. Bush also accepted his advisers' recommendation that Tomahawk cruise missiles wouldn't be enough to destroy a deeply buried bunker and that F-117 Stealth aircraft should also drop 2,000-pound "bunkerbuster" bombs on the site. Despite all of that, U.S. officials weren't sure if Saddam had been killed or wounded, or if he had escaped unharmed.

By Thursday, the day after he ordered the invasion, Bush's determination was clear at his cabinet meeting. "It was the absolute right decision to commit troops," he said. "It was the correct decision for peace and security. We tried everything possible to solve this through peace."

But Bush's certainty about the need for muscular American leadership may be a two-edged sword, some experts say. "What you have," says historian Dallek, "is sort of secular evangelism: 'I know I'm right. I know what to do.' It's very comforting when you are putting lives on the line and you are putting your administration at risk, and the public doesn't want someone that's Hamlet-like." On the other hand, Bush's certainty has alienated much of the world, evidenced by the massive antiwar demonstrations . . . in Athens, Paris, Tokyo, Great Britain, much of the Arab world, and across the United States. "There's a biblical certainty to the way he expresses himself," says Rutgers political scientist Ross K. Baker. "His self-assertiveness gets under the skin of Europeans. Rather than confident, he appears to them to be dogmatic. Rather than fortitude, he appears to be showing obduracy." Adds Baker: "The doctrine is, in effect, 'We are the world's policeman.' It may seem swaggering, or it may be the reality of the world. But when the drunken cowpokes are tearing up the saloon, who's going to settle things down? Who else is going to come through the swinging doors and put these guys in the hoosegow?"

Senior U.S. officials argue that the terrorist attacks of September 11 radicalized the president's ideas about national security. During the 2000 campaign, he criticized the Clinton administration for "nation building" and stretching the American military too thin. Now the threat of terrorism has made him more willing to take military action around the world, even unilaterally, to protect Americans from another attack. Strikes by America's enemies have become so potentially devastating in an era of weapons of mass destruction, the president believes, that the nation simply cannot afford to await the first blow.

Despite his confidence, Bush's immediate future is filled with risk. Not only does the war have to be won, but there's also the matter of the occupation and reconstruction of Iraq,

MESSAGE TO THE IRAQI PEOPLE

Shortly after America launched its invasion of Iraq, President Bush delivered the following message in a radio address to inform the Iraqi people of the intentions of U.S. military presence.

This is George W. Bush, the President of the United States. At this moment, the regime of Saddam Hussein is being removed from power, and a long era of fear and cruelty is ending. American and coalition forces are now operating inside Baghdad—and we will not stop until Saddam's corrupt gang is gone. The government of Iraq, and the future of your country, will soon belong to you.

The goals of our coalition are clear and limited. We will end a brutal regime, whose aggression and weapons of mass destruction make it a unique threat to the world. Coalition forces will help maintain law and order, so that Iraqis can live in security. We will respect your great religious traditions, whose principles of equality and compassion are essential to Iraq's future. We will help you build a peaceful and representative government that protects the rights of all citizens. And then our military forces will leave. Iraq will go forward as a unified, independent and sovereign nation that has regained a respected place in the world.

The United States and its coalition partners respect the people of Iraq. We are taking unprecedented measures to spare the lives of innocent Iraqi citizens, and are beginning to deliver food, water and medicine to those in need. Our only enemy is Saddam's brutal regime—and that regime is your enemy as well.

In the new era that is coming to Iraq, your country will no longer be held captive to the will of a cruel dictator. You will be free to build a better life, instead of building more palaces for Saddam and his sons, free to pursue economic prosperity without the hardship of economic sanctions, free to travel and speak your mind, free to join in the political affairs of Iraq. And all the people who make up your country—Kurds, Shi'a, Turkomans, Sunnis, and others—will be free of the terrible persecution that so many have endured.

The nightmare that Saddam Hussein has brought to your nation will soon be over. You are a good and gifted people—the heirs of a great civilisation that contributes to all humanity. You deserve better than tyranny and corruption and torture chambers. You deserve to live as free people. And I assure every citizen of Iraq: your nation will soon be free.

George W. Bush, President's Message to the Iraqi People, April 10, 2003.

rebuilding relationships with France, Germany, and Russia, and a host of other concerns. Says a former senior adviser to Ronald Reagan: "The next three months will be the most perilous time for the Bush presidency. We'll see if he's up to the job. And it's not just the war and its aftermath. It's the economy; it's terrorism. It's his leadership in Congress. It's North Korea. It's the price of oil and gasoline."

Administration officials are confident. Some are already discussing ways to build on what they predict will be a quick and decisive victory and say privately that Bush's popularity is sure to rise while the economy picks up steam and the stock markets begin reclaiming past losses. Newly discovered evidence of Saddam Hussein's monstrosity, these aides predict, will melt the opposition to Bush's war. After Saddam's removal, a senior White House aide says, "Iraqis will be dancing in the streets."

Bush discussed the war's aftermath in detail during a phone conversation with British Prime Minister Tony Blair last week. Among the topics: the United Nations' role in reconstructing Iraq; future efforts to "take on" weapons of mass destruction, and ways to neutralize other "rogue nations."

Just as important, Bush is intent on avoiding his father's mistake of seeming obsessed by foreign policy to the exclusion of domestic issues. At last week's cabinet meeting, he urged his senior advisers to keep working on important domestic issues, and he reiterated his support for tax cuts and other home-front priorities like Medicare reform.

If the war goes well, White House aides say, Bush will use his renewed political capital to push for a new round of tax cuts, spending reductions, and expanded prescription drug coverage for retirees.

GOOD VS. EVIL

Yet his views clearly parallel his father's in fundamental ways. Consider a poignant letter that the elder Bush wrote to his five children, including George W. Bush, on Dec. 31, 1990, just weeks before the fighting began. After explaining his concern about the deaths his decisions might cause, the elder Bush wrote: "My mind goes back to history: How many lives might have been saved if appeasement had given way to force earlier on in the late '30s or earliest '40s? How many Jews might have been spared the gas chambers, or how many Polish patriots might be alive today? I look at today's crisis as 'good' vs. 'evil'—Yes, it is that clear." He added: "Sometimes in life you have to act as you think best—you can't compromise, you can't give in—even if your critics are loud and numerous."

The younger Bush fully endorses those sentiments. In fact, his certitude has unsettled critics who see a return of the swaggering cowboy who took office in January 2001. He is so confident in the military that he feels no need to keep track of war coverage on television. Aside from watching scenes of the massive U.S. air campaign that were shown on American television Friday afternoon, aides say, he rarely turned on the TV news during the day. One aspect of the war that he *does* follow, however, is the weather, which can often limit U.S. operations. When he is relaxing in the White House residence, he sometimes tunes in the Weather Channel to check out forecasts for the Mideast, and for his beloved ranch in Crawford, Texas.

Bush's can-do attitude and willingness to take risks were illustrated during his recent meeting in the Oval Office with Italian Prime Minister Silvio Berlusconi. "It's important for a leader to lead," he said. "If you believe in something, then stand for it, and the people will follow." This is the philosophy that led George W. Bush to invade Iraq and that will guide him in the challenging days ahead.

APPENDIX OF DOCUMENTS

DOCUMENT 1: THE SPIRIT OF COOPERATION

George W. Bush addressed the nation from the Texas House of Representatives following a thirty-five-day election battle that ended with a ruling from the U.S. Supreme Court. President Bush's first speech on December 13, 2000, outlined his optimism to unite and inspire the American people after the unprecedented and divisive presidential contest.

I have a lot to be thankful for tonight. I'm thankful for America and thankful that we were able to resolve our electoral differences in a peaceful way.

I'm thankful to the American people for the great privilege of being able to serve as your next president. . . .

Tonight I chose to speak from the chamber of the Texas House of Representatives because it has been a home to bipartisan cooperation. Here in a place where Democrats have the majority, Republicans and Democrats have worked together to do what is right for the people we represent.

We've had spirited disagreements. And in the end, we found constructive consensus. It is an experience I will always carry with me, an example I will always follow. . . .

The spirit of cooperation I have seen in this hall is what is needed in Washington, D.C. It is the challenge of our moment. After a difficult election, we must put politics behind us and work together to make the promise of America available for every one of our citizens.

I am optimistic that we can change the tone in Washington, D.C.

I believe things happen for a reason, and I hope the long wait of the last five weeks will heighten a desire to move beyond the bitterness and partisanship of the recent past.

Our nation must rise above a house divided. Americans share hopes and goals and values far more important than any political disagreements.

Republicans want the best for our nation, and so do Democrats. Our votes may differ, but not our hopes.

I know America wants reconciliation and unity. I know Americans want progress. And we must seize this moment and deliver.

Together, guided by a spirit of common sense, common courtesy and common goals, we can unite and inspire the American citizens. . . .

Together we will address some of society's deepest problems one person at a time, by encouraging and empowering the good hearts and good works of the American people.

This is the essence of compassionate conservatism and it will be a foundation of my administration.

These priorities are not merely Republican concerns or Democratic concerns; they are American responsibilities.

During the fall campaign, we differed about the details of these proposals, but there was remarkable consensus about the important issues before us: excellent schools, retirement and health security, tax relief, a strong military, a more civil society.

We have discussed our differences. Now it is time to find common ground and build consensus to make America a beacon of opportunity in the 21st century. . . .

I have faith that with God's help we as a nation will move forward together as one nation, indivisible. And together we will create an America that is open, so every citizen has access to the American dream; an America that is educated, so every child has the keys to realize that dream; and an America that is united in our diversity and our shared American values that are larger than race or party.

I was not elected to serve one party, but to serve one nation.

The president of the United States is the president of every single American, of every race and every background.

Whether you voted for me or not, I will do my best to serve your interests and I will work to earn your respect. . . .

The presidency is more than an honor. It is more than an office. It is a charge to keep, and I will give it my all.

Thank you very much and God bless America.

George W. Bush, Presidential Acceptance Speech, December 13, 2000.

DOCUMENT 2: CIVIC DUTY

In his January 2001 inauguration address, George W. Bush urged citizenship over spectatorship and a sense of unity after years of poison-pen politics. Bush asked citizens to serve their nation beginning with their own neighborhoods.

I am honored and humbled to stand here, where so many of America's leaders have come before me, and so many will follow.

We have a place, all of us, in a long story—a story we continue, but whose end we will not see. It is the story of a new world that became a friend and liberator of the old, a story of a slave-holding society that became a servant of freedom, the story of a power that went into the world to protect but not possess, to defend but not to conquer.

It is the American story—a story of flawed and fallible people, united across the generations by grand and enduring ideals.

The grandest of these ideals is an unfolding American promise that everyone belongs, that everyone deserves a chance, that no insignificant person was ever born.

Americans are called to enact this promise in our lives and in our laws. And though our nation has sometimes halted, and sometimes delayed, we must follow no other course.

Through much of the last century, America's faith in freedom and democracy was a rock in a raging sea. Now it is a seed upon the wind, taking root in many nations.

Our democratic faith is more than the creed of our country, it is the inborn hope of our humanity, an ideal we carry but do not own, a trust we bear and pass along. And even after nearly 225 years, we have a long way yet to travel.

While many of our citizens prosper, others doubt the promise, even the justice, of our own country. The ambitions of some Americans are limited by failing schools and hidden prejudice and the circumstances of their birth. And sometimes our differences run so deep, it seems we share a continent, but not a country.

We do not accept this, and we will not allow it. Our unity, our union, is the serious work of leaders and citizens in every generation. And this is my solemn pledge: I will work to build a single nation of justice and opportunity.

I know this is in our reach because we are guided by a power larger than ourselves who creates us equal in His image.

And we are confident in principles that unite and lead us onward.

America has never been united by blood or birth or soil. We are bound by ideals that move us beyond our backgrounds, lift us above our interests and teach us what it means to be citizens. Every child must be taught these principles. Every citizen must uphold them. And every immigrant, by embracing these ideals, makes our country more, not less, American.

Today, we affirm a new commitment to live out our nation's promise through civility, courage, compassion and character.

America, at its best, matches a commitment to principle with a concern for civility. A civil society demands from each of us good will and respect, fair dealing and forgiveness.

Some seem to believe that our politics can afford to be petty because, in a time of peace, the stakes of our debates appear small.

But the stakes for America are never small. If our country does not lead the cause of freedom, it will not be led. If we do not turn the hearts of children toward knowledge and character, we will lose their gifts and undermine their idealism. If we permit our economy to drift and decline, the vulnerable will suffer most.

We must live up to the calling we share. Civility is not a tactic or a sentiment. It is the determined choice of trust over cynicism, of community over chaos. And this commitment, if we keep it, is a way to shared accomplishment. . . .

Abandonment and abuse are not acts of God, they are failures of love.

And the proliferation of prisons, however necessary, is no substitute for hope and order in our souls.

Where there is suffering, there is duty. Americans in need are not strangers, they are citizens, not problems, but priorities. And all of us are diminished when any are hopeless.

Government has great responsibilities for public safety and public health, for civil rights and common schools. Yet compassion is the work of a nation, not just a government. . . .

Sometimes in life we are called to do great things. But as a saint of our times has said, every day we are called to do small things with great love. The most important tasks of a democracy are done by everyone. . . .

What you do is as important as anything government does. I ask you to seek a common good beyond your comfort; to defend needed reforms against easy attacks; to serve your nation, beginning with your neighbor. I ask you to be citizens: citizens, not spectators; citizens, not subjects; responsible citizens, building communities of service and a nation of character.

Americans are generous and strong and decent, not because we believe in ourselves, but because we hold beliefs beyond ourselves. When this spirit of citizenship is missing, no government program can replace it. When this spirit is present, no wrong can stand against it.

George W. Bush, Inauguration Speech, January 20, 2001.

DOCUMENT 5: UNITY IN A TIME OF DESPAIR

President Bush will be remembered as a president who helped to heal a nation. Addressing the country in its hour of grief on September 14, 2001, during a National Day of Prayer and Remembrance, President Bush said America's character had been shown to the world in acts of kindness, generosity, and bravery.

We are here in the middle hour of our grief. So many have suffered so great a loss, and today we express our nation's sorrow. We come before God to pray for the missing and the dead, and for those who love them. . . .

War has been waged against us by stealth and deceit and murder. This nation is peaceful, but fierce when stirred to anger. This conflict was begun on the timing and terms of others. It will end in a way, and at an hour, of our choosing. . . .

It is said that adversity introduces us to ourselves. This is true of a nation as well. In this trial, we have been reminded, and the world has seen, that our fellow Americans are generous and kind, resourceful and brave. We see our national character in rescuers working past exhaustion; in long lines of blood donors; in thousands of citizens who have asked to work and serve in any way possible.

And we have seen our national character in eloquent acts of sacrifice. Inside the World Trade Center, one man who could have saved himself stayed until the end at the side of his quadriplegic friend. A beloved priest died giving the last rites to a firefighter. Two office workers, finding a disabled stranger, carried her down sixty-eight floors to safety. A group of men drove through the night from Dallas to Washington to bring skin grafts for burn victims.

In these acts, and in many others, Americans showed a deep commitment to one another, and an abiding love for our country. Today, we feel what Franklin Roosevelt called the warm courage of national unity. This is a unity of every faith, and every background.

It has joined together political parties in both houses of Congress. It is evident in services of prayer and candlelight vigils, and American flags, which are displayed in pride, and wave in defiance.

Our unity is a kinship of grief, and a steadfast resolve to prevail against our enemies. And this unity against terror is now extending across the world.

America is a nation full of good fortune, with so much to be grateful for. But we are not spared from suffering. In every generation, the world has produced enemies of human freedom. They have attacked America, because we are freedom's home and defender. And the commitment of our fathers is now the calling of our time.

On this national day of prayer and remembrance, we ask almighty God to watch over our nation, and grant us patience and resolve in all that is to come. We pray that He will comfort and console those who now walk in sorrow. We thank Him for each life we now must mourn, and the promise of a life to come.

George W. Bush, Remarks at the National Day of Prayer and Remembrance, September 14, 2001.

DOCUMENT 4: THE MISSION AGAINST TERRORISM

On September 20, 2001, President Bush called a nation to defend its freedom. He addressed a joint session of Congress and the American people from the U.S. Capitol and gave evidence that al-Qaeda was the group responsible for the September 11 terrorist attacks on the United States.

On September the 11th, enemies of freedom committed an act of war against our country. . . .

Americans are asking: Who attacked our country? The evidence we have gathered all points to a collection of loosely affiliated terrorist organizations known as al-Qaeda. They are the same murderers indicted for bombing American embassies in Tanzania and Kenya, and responsible for bombing the USS *Cole.*

Al-Qaeda is to terror what the mafia is to crime. But its goal is not making money; its goal is remaking the world—and imposing its radical beliefs on people everywhere.

The terrorists practice a fringe form of Islamic extremism that has been rejected by Muslim scholars and the vast majority of Muslim clerics—a fringe movement that perverts the peaceful teachings of Islam. The terrorists' directive commands them to kill Christians and Jews, to kill all Americans, and make no distinction among military and civilians, including women and children.

This group and its leader—a person named Osama bin Laden—are linked to many other organizations in different countries, including the Egyptian Islamic Jihad and the Islamic Movement of Uzbekistan. There are thousands of these terrorists in more than 60 countries. They are recruited from their own nations and neighborhoods and brought to camps in places like Afghanistan, where they are trained in the tactics of terror. They are sent back to their homes or sent to hide in countries around the world to plot evil and destruction.

The leadership of al-Qaeda has great influence in Afghanistan and supports the Taliban regime in controlling most of that country. In Afghanistan, we see al-Qaeda's vision for the world.

Afghanistan's people have been brutalized—many are starving and many have fled. Women are not allowed to attend school. You can be jailed for owning a television. Religion can be practiced only as their leaders dictate. A man can be jailed in Afghanistan if his beard is not long enough.

The United States respects the people of Afghanistan—after all, we are currently its largest source of humanitarian aid—but we condemn the Taliban regime. It is not only repressing its own people, it is threatening people everywhere by sponsoring and sheltering and supplying terrorists. By aiding and abetting murder, the Taliban regime is committing murder.

And tonight, the United States of America makes the following demands on the Taliban: Deliver to United States authorities all the leaders of al-Qaeda who hide in your land. Release all foreign nationals, including American citizens, you have unjustly imprisoned. Protect foreign journalists, diplomats and aid workers in your country. Close immediately and permanently every terrorist training camp in Afghanistan, and hand over every terrorist, and every person in their support structure, to appropriate authorities. Give the United States full access to terrorist training camps, so we can make sure they are no longer operating.

These demands are not open to negotiation or discussion. The Taliban must act, and act immediately. They will hand over the terrorists, or they will share in their fate. . . .

Our war on terror begins with al-Qaeda, but it does not end there. It will not end until every terrorist group of global reach has been found, stopped and defeated. . . .

These terrorists kill not merely to end lives, but to disrupt and end a way of life. With every atrocity, they hope that America grows fearful, retreating from the world and forsaking our friends. They stand against us, because we stand in their way. . . .

Americans are asking: How will we fight and win this war? We will direct every resource at our command—every means of diplomacy, every tool of intelligence, every instrument of law enforcement, every financial influence, and every necessary weapon of war—to the disruption and to the defeat of the global terror network. . . .

Our response involves far more than instant retaliation and isolated strikes. Americans should not expect one battle, but a lengthy campaign, unlike any other we have ever seen. It may include dramatic strikes, visible on TV, and covert operations, secret even in success. We will starve terrorists of funding, turn them one against another, drive them from place to place, until there is no refuge or no rest. And we will pursue nations that provide aid or safe haven to terrorism. Every nation, in every region, now has a decision to make. Either you are with us, or you are with the terrorists. From this day forward, any nation that continues to harbor or support terrorism will be regarded by the United States as a hostile regime. . . .

This is not, however, just America's fight. And what is at stake is not just America's freedom. This is the world's fight. This is civilization's fight. This is the fight of all who believe in progress and pluralism, tolerance and freedom.

We ask every nation to join us. We will ask, and we will need, the help of police forces, intelligence services, and banking systems around the world. The United States is grateful that many nations and many international organizations have already responded— with sympathy and with support. Nations from Latin America, to Asia, to Africa, to Europe, to the Islamic world. Perhaps the NATO Charter reflects best the attitude of the world: An attack on one is an attack on all.

The civilized world is rallying to America's side. They understand that if this terror goes unpunished, their own cities, their own citizens may be next. Terror, unanswered, can not only bring down buildings, it can threaten the stability of legitimate governments. And you know what—we're not going to allow it. . . .

Great harm has been done to us. We have suffered great loss. And in our grief and anger we have found our mission and our moment. Freedom and fear are at war. The advance of human freedom—the great achievement of our time, and the great hope of every time—now depends on us. Our nation—this generation— will lift a dark threat of violence from our people and our future. We will rally the world to this cause by our efforts, by our courage. We will not tire, we will not falter, and we will not fail. . . .

I will not forget this wound to our country or those who inflicted it. I will not yield; I will not rest; I will not relent in waging this struggle for freedom and security for the American people.

The course of this conflict is not known, yet its outcome is certain. Freedom and fear, justice and cruelty, have always been at war, and we know that God is not neutral between them.

Fellow citizens, we'll meet violence with patient justice—assured of the rightness of our cause, and confident of the victories to come. In all that lies before us, may God grant us wisdom, and may He watch over the United States of America.

George W. Bush, Address to Congress and the American People, September 20, 2001.

DOCUMENT 5: MILITARY ACTION AGAINST THE TALIBAN

On October 13, 2001, President George W. Bush announced his order for the Armed Services to attack al-Qaeda terrorist training camps in Afghanistan. Bush stated that the British joined in the military operation, and he warned that each of the world's nations would have to take a stand against terrorism or become the enemy of those nations that would.

Good afternoon. On my orders, the United States military has begun strikes against al-Qaeda terrorist training camps and military installations of the Taliban regime in Afghanistan. These carefully targeted actions are designed to disrupt the use of Afghanistan as a terrorist base of operations, and to attack the military capability of the Taliban regime.

We are joined in this operation by our staunch friend, Great Britain. Other close friends, including Canada, Australia, Germany and France, have pledged forces as the operation unfolds. More than 40 countries in the Middle East, Africa, Europe and across Asia have granted air transit or landing rights. Many more have shared intelligence. We are supported by the collective will of the world.

More than two weeks ago, I gave Taliban leaders a series of clear and specific demands: Close terrorist training camps; hand over leaders of the al-Qaeda network; and return all foreign nationals, including American citizens, unjustly detained in your country. None of these demands were met. And now the Taliban will pay a price. By destroying camps and disrupting communications, we will make it more difficult for the terror network to train new recruits and coordinate their evil plans.

Initially, the terrorists may burrow deeper into caves and other entrenched hiding places. Our military action is also designed to clear the way for sustained, comprehensive and relentless operations to drive them out and bring them to justice.

At the same time, the oppressed people of Afghanistan will know the generosity of America and our allies. As we strike military targets, we'll also drop food, medicine and supplies to the starving and suffering men and women and children of Afghanistan.

The United States of America is a friend to the Afghan people, and we are the friends of almost a billion worldwide who practice the Islamic faith. The United States of America is an enemy of those who aid terrorists and of the barbaric criminals who profane a great religion by committing murder in its name.

This military action is a part of our campaign against terrorism, another front in a war that has already been joined through diplomacy, intelligence, the freezing of financial assets and the arrests of known terrorists by law enforcement agents in 38 countries. Given the nature and reach of our enemies, we will win this conflict by the patient accumulation of successes, by meeting a series of challenges with determination and will and purpose.

Today we focus on Afghanistan, but the battle is broader. Every nation has a choice to make. In this conflict, there is no neutral ground. If any government sponsors the outlaws and killers of innocents, they have become outlaws and murderers, themselves. And they will take that lonely path at their own peril.

I'm speaking to you today from the Treaty Room of the White House, a place where American presidents have worked for peace. We're a peaceful nation. Yet, as we have learned, so suddenly and so tragically, there can be no peace in a world of sudden terror. In the face of today's new threat, the only way to pursue peace is to pursue those who threaten it.

We did not ask for this mission, but we will fulfill it. The name of today's military operation is Enduring Freedom. We defend not only our precious freedoms, but also the freedom of people everywhere to live and raise their children free from fear.

I know many Americans feel fear today. And our government is taking strong precautions. All law enforcement and intelligence agencies are working aggressively around America, around the world and around the clock. At my request, many governors have activated the National Guard to strengthen airport security. We have called up Reserves to reinforce our military capability and strengthen the protection of our homeland.

In the months ahead, our patience will be one of our strengths—patience with the long waits that will result from tighter security; patience and understanding that it will take time to achieve our goals; patience in all the sacrifices that may come.

Today, those sacrifices are being made by members of our Armed Forces who now defend us so far from home, and by their proud and worried families. A commander in chief sends America's sons and daughters into a battle in a foreign land only after the greatest care and a lot of prayer. We ask a lot of those who wear our uniform. We ask them to leave their loved ones, to travel great distances, to risk injury, even to be prepared to make the ultimate sacrifice of their lives. They are dedicated, they are honorable; they represent the best of our country. And we are grateful.

To all the men and women in our military—every sailor, every soldier, every airman, every Coast Guardsman, every Marine—I say this: Your mission is defined; your objectives are clear; your goal is just. You have my full confidence, and you will have every tool you need to carry out your duty.

I recently received a touching letter that says a lot about the state of America in these difficult times—a letter from a fourth-grade girl, with a father in the military: "As much as I don't want my Dad to fight," she wrote, "I'm willing to give him to you."

This is a precious gift, the greatest she could give. This young girl knows what America is all about. Since Sept. 11, an entire generation of young Americans has gained new understanding of the value of freedom, and its cost in duty and in sacrifice. The battle is now joined on many fronts. We will not waver; we will not tire; we will not falter; and we will not fail. Peace and freedom will prevail.

Thank you. May God continue to bless America.

George W. Bush, "Bush Announces Military Action Against Terrorist Infrastructure and Taliban Regime in Afghanistan," *Congressional Quarterly Weekly,* vol. 59, no. 39, October 13, 2001.

DOCUMENT 6: WHAT HAS BEEN DONE AND WHAT CAN STILL BE DONE

With war under way in Afghanistan and an investigation of anthrax scares in the United States, President Bush spoke to the nation on November 8, 2001, to indicate America's progress against terrorism. While assuring the public that the nation was acting bravely in the face of adversity, Bush informed Americans that they all had a role to play in protecting and serving their country.

Tonight, many thousands of children are tragically learning to live without one of their parents. And the rest of us are learning to live in a world that seems very different than it was on September the 10th.

The moment the second plane hit the second building—when we knew it was a terrorist attack—many felt that our lives would never be the same. What we couldn't be sure of then—and what the terrorists never expected—was that America would emerge stronger, with a renewed spirit of pride and patriotism.

I said in my speech to a Joint Session of Congress that we are a nation awakened to danger. We're also a nation awakened to service, and citizenship, and compassion. None of us would ever wish the evil that has been done to our country, yet we have learned that out of evil can come great good.

During the last two months, we have shown the world America is a great nation. Americans have responded magnificently, with courage and caring. We've seen it in our children, who have sent in more than $1 million for the children of Afghanistan. We have seen it in the compassion of Jewish and Christian Americans who have reached out to their Muslim neighbors. We have seen it as Americans have reassessed priorities—parents spending more time with their children, and many people spending more time in prayer and in houses of worship.

We have gained new heroes: Those who ran into burning buildings to save others, our police and our firefighters. Those who battled their own fears to keep children calm and safe—America's teachers. Those who voluntarily placed themselves in harm's way to defend our freedom—the men and women of the Armed Forces.

And tonight, we join in thanking a whole new group of public servants who never enlisted to fight a war, but find themselves on the front lines of a battle nonetheless: Those who deliver the mail—America's postal workers. We also thank those whose quick response provided preventive treatment that has no doubt saved thousands of lives—our health care workers.

We are a different country than we were on September the 10th—sadder and less innocent; stronger and more united; and in the face of ongoing threats, determined and courageous.

Our nation faces a threat to our freedoms, and the stakes could not be higher. We are the target of enemies who boast they want to kill—kill all Americans, kill all Jews, and kill all Christians. We've seen that type of hate before—and the only possible response is to confront it, and to defeat it.

This new enemy seeks to destroy our freedom and impose its views. We value life; the terrorists ruthlessly destroy it. We value education; the terrorists do not believe women should be educated or should have health care, or should leave their homes. We value the right to speak our minds; for the terrorists, free expression can be grounds for execution. We respect people of all faiths and welcome the free practice of religion; our enemy wants to dictate how to think and how to worship even to their fellow Muslims.

This enemy tries to hide behind a peaceful faith. But those who celebrate the murder of innocent men, women, and children have no religion, have no conscience, and have no mercy.

We wage a war to save civilization, itself. We did not seek it, but we must fight it—and we will prevail.

This is a different war from any our nation has ever faced, a war on many fronts, against terrorists who operate in more than 60 different countries. And this is a war that must be fought not only overseas, but also here at home. I recently spoke to high school students in Maryland, and realized that for the first time ever, these seniors will graduate in the midst of a war in our own country. We've added a new era, and this new era requires new responsibilities, both for the government and for our people.

The government has a responsibility to protect our citizens—and that starts with homeland security. The first attack against America came by plane, and we are now making our airports and airplanes safer. We have posted the National Guard in America's airports and placed undercover air marshals on many flights. I call on Congress to quickly send me legislation that makes cockpits more secure, baggage screening more thorough, and puts the federal government in charge of all airport screening and security.

The second attack against America came in the mail. We do not know whether this attack came from the same terrorists; we don't know the origin of the anthrax—but whoever did this unprecedented and uncivilized act is a terrorist.

Four Americans have now died from anthrax, out of a total of 17 people who have been infected. The Postal Service has processed more than 30 billion pieces of mail since September the 11th, and so far we've identified three different letters that contained anthrax. We can trace the source of infection for all but one of the individuals, and we are still trying to learn how a woman who died in New York was exposed.

I'm proud of the way our health care and postal workers—and the American people—are responding with calm in the face of this deadly new threat. Public health officials have acted quickly to distribute preventive antibiotics to thousands of people who may have been exposed. The government is purchasing and storing medicines and vaccines as a precaution against future attacks. We are cleaning facilities where anthrax has been detected, and purchasing equipment to sanitize the mail. Thousands of law enforcement officials are aggressively investigating this bioterrorism attack—and public health officials are distributing the most accurate, up-to-date information we have to medical professionals and to the public.

To coordinate our efforts we've created the new Office of Homeland Security. Its director, my good friend and former Governor, Tom Ridge, reports directly to me—and works with all our federal agencies, state and local governments, and the private sector on a national strategy to strengthen our homeland protections. For example, the Coast Guard has taken on expanded duties to protect our shores and our ports. The National Guard has increased—an increased role in surveillance at our border. We're imposing new licensing requirements for safer transportation of hazardous material.

We've passed a new antiterrorism law which gives our law enforcement officers the necessary tools to track terrorists before they harm Americans. A new terrorism task force is tightening immigration controls to make sure no one enters or stays in our country who would harm us. We are a welcoming country, we will always value freedom—yet we will not allow those who plot against our country to abuse our freedoms and our protections.

Our enemies have threatened other acts of terror. We take each threat seriously. And when we have evidence of credible threats, we will issue appropriate alerts.

A terrorism alert is not a signal to stop your life. It is a call to be vigilant—to know that your government is on high alert, and to add your eyes and ears to our efforts to find and stop those who want to do us harm.

A lot of people are working really hard to protect America. But in the long run, the best way to defend our homeland—the best way to make sure our children can live in peace—is to take the battle to the enemy and to stop them.

I have called our military into action to hunt down the members of the al-Qaeda organization who murdered innocent Americans. I gave fair warning to the government that harbors them in Afghanistan. The Taliban made a choice to continue hiding terrorists, and now they are paying a price.

I'm so proud of our military. Our military is pursuing its mission. We are destroying training camps, disrupting communications, and dismantling air defenses. We are now bombing Taliban front lines. We are deliberately and systematically hunting down these murderers, and we will bring them to justice. . . .

After September the 11th, our government assumed new responsibilities to strengthen security at home and track down our enemies abroad. And the American people are accepting new responsibilities, as well. . . .

Many ask, what can I do to help in our fight. The answer is simple. All of us can become a September the 11th volunteer by making a commitment to service in our own communities. So you can serve your country by tutoring or mentoring a child, comforting the afflicted, housing those in need of shelter and a home. You can participate in your Neighborhood Watch or Crime Stoppers. You can become a volunteer in a hospital, emergency medical, fire or rescue unit. You can support our troops in the field and, just as importantly, support their families here at home, by becoming active in the USO or groups and communities near our military installations.

We also will encourage service to country by creating new opportunities within the AmeriCorps and Senior Corps programs for public safety and public health efforts. We'll ask state and local officials to create a new modern civil defense service similar to local volunteer fire departments, to respond to local emergencies when the manpower of governments is stretched thin. We will find ways to train and mobilize more volunteers to help when rescue and health emergencies arise.

Americans have a lot to offer, so I've created a task force to develop additional ways people can get directly involved in this war effort, by making our homes and neighborhoods and schools and workplaces safer. And I call on all Americans to serve by bettering our communities and, thereby, defy and defeat the terrorists.

Our great nation—national challenge is to hunt down the terrorists and strengthen our protection against future attacks. Our great national opportunity is to preserve forever the good that has resulted. Through this tragedy, we are renewing and reclaiming our strong American values. . . .

Above all, we will live in a spirit of courage and optimism. Our nation was born in that spirit, as immigrants yearning for freedom courageously risked their lives in search of greater opportunity. That spirit of optimism and courage still beckons people across the world who want to come here. And that spirit of optimism and courage must guide those of us fortunate enough to live here.

Courage and optimism led the passengers on Flight 93 to rush their murderers to save lives on the ground. Led by a young man whose last known words were the Lord's Prayer and "Let's roll." He didn't know he had signed on for heroism when he boarded the plane that day. Some of our greatest moments have been acts of courage for which no one could have ever prepared.

We will always remember the words of that brave man, expressing the spirit of a great country. We will never forget all we have lost, and all we are fighting for. Ours is the cause of freedom. We've defeated freedom's enemies before, and we will defeat them again.

We cannot know every turn this battle will take. Yet we know our cause is just and our ultimate victory is assured. We will, no doubt, face new challenges. But we have our marching orders: My fellow Americans, let's roll.

George W. Bush, Address to the Nation at the World Congress Center in Atlanta, Georgia, November 8, 2001.

DOCUMENT 7: A CALL FOR CORPORATE ETHICS AND REFORM

President Bush created a new Corporate Fraud Task Force to reform corporate integrity and introduce fiscal accountability after a series of management abuses made national headlines. In a speech delivered July 9, 2002, in the New York financial district, Bush summarizes the response of his administration to restore confidence in corporate America.

I've come to the financial capital of the world to speak of a serious challenge to our financial markets, and to the confidence on which they rest. The misdeeds now being uncovered in some quarters of corporate America are threatening the financial well-being of many workers and many investors. At this moment, America's greatest economic need is higher ethical standards—standards enforced by strict laws and upheld by responsible business leaders.

The lure of heady profits of the late 1990s spawned abuses and excesses. With strict enforcement and higher ethical standards, we must usher in a new era of integrity in corporate America. . . .

The American economy—our economy—is built on confidence. The conviction that our free enterprise system will continue to be the most powerful and most promising in the world. That confidence is well-placed. After all, American technology is the most advanced in the world. Our universities attract the talent of the world. Our workers and ranchers and farmers can compete with anyone in the world. Our society rewards hard work and honest ambition, bringing people to our shores from all around the world who share those values. The American economy is the most creative and enterprising and productive system ever devised. . . .

We've learned of some business leaders obstructing justice, and misleading clients, falsifying records, business executives breaching the trust and abusing power. We've learned of CEOs earning tens of millions of dollars in bonuses just before their companies go bankrupt, leaving employees and retirees and investors to suffer. The business pages of American newspapers should not read like a scandal sheet.

The vast majority of businessmen and women are honest. They do right by their employees and their shareholders. They do not cut ethical corners, and their work helps create an economy which is the envy of the world.

Yet high-profile acts of deception have shaken people's trust. Too many corporations seem disconnected from the values of our country. These scandals have hurt the reputations of many good and honest companies. They have hurt the stock market. And worst of all, they are hurting millions of people who depend on the integrity of businesses for their livelihood and their retirement, for their peace of mind and their financial well-being. . . .

I'm calling for a new ethic of personal responsibility in the business community; an ethic that will increase investor confidence, will make employees proud of their companies, and again, regain the trust of the American people. . . .

Self-regulation is important, but it's not enough. Government cannot remove risk from investment—I know that—or chance from the market. But government can do more to promote transparency and ensure that risks are honest. And government can ensure that those who breach the trust of the American people are punished. . . .

Today, by executive order, I create a new Corporate Fraud Task Force, headed by the Deputy Attorney General, which will target major accounting fraud and other criminal activity in corporate finance. . . .

I'm also proposing tough new criminal penalties for corporate fraud. This legislation would double the maximum prison terms for those convicted of financial fraud from five to 10 years. . . .

Second, we're moving corporate accounting out of the shadows, so the investing public will have a true and fair and timely picture of assets and liabilities and income of publicly traded companies. Greater transparency will expose bad companies and, just as importantly, protect the reputations of the good ones. . . .

Third, my administration will guard the interests of small investors and pension holders. More than 80 million Americans own stock, and many of them are new to the market. Buying stock gives them an opportunity to build wealth over the long-term, and this is the very kind of responsible investment we must promote in America. To encourage stock ownership, we must make sure that analysts give honest advice, and pension plans treat workers fairly. . . .

The American system of enterprise has not failed us. Some dishonest individuals have failed our system. Now comes the urgent work of enforcement and reform, driven by a new ethic of responsibility. . . .

We will show that markets can be both dynamic and honest, that lasting wealth and prosperity are built on a foundation of integrity.

By reasserting the best values of our country, we will reclaim the promise of our economy.

George W. Bush, Remarks by the President on Corporate Responsibility, July 9, 2002.

DOCUMENT 8: THE UN MUST STAND AGAINST IRAQ'S DEFIANCE

On September 12, 2002, President Bush addressed the United Nations to gather a coalition of support to join the United States in forcing Iraq to comply with UN Security Council Resolutions from 1990. These resolutions called for Iraq to dispose of any weapons of mass destruction and permit UN inspectors to investigate Iraqi sites where such weapons could be made or stored. If Iraq refused to accede to these demands, Bush intimated that military action may be necessary to force Iraqi president Saddam Hussein's compliance.

The United Nations was born in the hope that survived a world war—the hope of a world moving toward justice, escaping old patterns of conflict and fear. The founding members resolved that the peace of the world must never again be destroyed by the will and wickedness of any man. We created the United Nations Security Council, so that, unlike the League of Nations, our deliberations would be more than talk, our resolutions would be more than wishes. After generations of deceitful dictators and broken treaties and squandered lives, we dedicated ourselves to standards of human dignity shared by all, and to a system of security defended by all.

Today, these standards, and this security, are challenged. Our commitment to human dignity is challenged by persistent poverty and raging disease. The suffering is great, and our responsibilities are clear. The United States is joining with the world to supply aid where it reaches people and lifts up lives, to extend trade and the prosperity it brings, and to bring medical care where it is desperately needed. . . .

Twelve years ago, Iraq invaded Kuwait without provocation. And the regime's forces were poised to continue their march to seize other countries and their resources. Had Saddam Hussein been appeased instead of stopped, he would have endangered the peace and stability of the world. Yet this aggression was stopped—by the might of coalition forces and the will of the United Nations.

To suspend hostilities, to spare himself, Iraq's dictator accepted a series of commitments. The terms were clear, to him and to all. And he agreed to prove he is complying with every one of those obligations.

He has proven instead only his contempt for the United Nations, and for all his pledges. By breaking every pledge—by his deceptions, and by his cruelties—Saddam Hussein has made the case against himself. . . .

Delegates to the General Assembly, we have been more than patient. We've tried sanctions. We've tried the carrot of oil for food, and the stick of coalition military strikes. But Saddam Hussein has defied all these efforts and continues to develop weapons of mass destruction. The first time we may be completely certain he has a—nuclear weapons is when, God forbid, he uses one. We owe it to all our citizens to do everything in our power to prevent that day from coming.

The conduct of the Iraqi regime is a threat to the authority of the United Nations, and a threat to peace. Iraq has answered a decade of U.N. demands with a decade of defiance. All the world now faces a test, and the United Nations a difficult and defining moment. Are Security Council resolutions to be honored and enforced, or cast aside without consequence? Will the United Nations serve the purpose of its founding, or will it be irrelevant?

The United States helped found the United Nations. We want the United Nations to be effective, and respectful, and successful. We want the resolutions of the world's most important multilateral body to be enforced. And right now those resolutions are being unilaterally subverted by the Iraqi regime. Our partnership of nations can meet the test before us, by making clear what we now expect of the Iraqi regime.

If the Iraqi regime wishes peace, it will immediately and unconditionally forswear, disclose, and remove or destroy all weapons of mass destruction, long-range missiles, and all related material.

If the Iraqi regime wishes peace, it will immediately end all support for terrorism and act to suppress it, as all states are required to do by U.N. Security Council resolutions.

If the Iraqi regime wishes peace, it will cease persecution of its civilian population, including Shi'a, Sunnis, Kurds, Turkomans, and others, again as required by Security Council resolutions.

If the Iraqi regime wishes peace, it will release or account for all Gulf War personnel whose fate is still unknown. It will return the remains of any who are deceased, return stolen property, accept liability for losses resulting from the invasion of Kuwait, and fully cooperate with international efforts to resolve these issues, as required by Security Council resolutions.

If the Iraqi regime wishes peace, it will immediately end all illicit trade outside the oil-for-food program. It will accept U.N. administration of funds from that program, to ensure that the money is used fairly and promptly for the benefit of the Iraqi people.

If all these steps are taken, it will signal a new openness and accountability in Iraq. And it could open the prospect of the United Nations helping to build a government that represents all Iraqis—a government based on respect for human rights, economic liberty, and internationally supervised elections.

The United States has no quarrel with the Iraqi people; they've suffered too long in silent captivity. Liberty for the Iraqi people is a great moral cause, and a great strategic goal. The people of Iraq deserve it; the security of all nations requires it. Free societies do not intimidate through cruelty and conquest, and open societies do not threaten the world with mass murder. The United States supports political and economic liberty in a unified Iraq. . . .

If we meet our responsibilities, if we overcome this danger, we can arrive at a very different future. . . .

We must choose between a world of fear and a world of progress. We cannot stand by and do nothing while dangers gather. We must stand up for our security, and for the permanent rights and the hopes of mankind. By heritage and by choice, the United States of America will make that stand. And, delegates to the United Nations, you have the power to make that stand, as well.

George W. Bush, Remarks by the President in an Address to the United Nations General Assembly, September 12, 2002.

DOCUMENT 9: IRAQ WILL BE HELD ACCOUNTABLE

Believing Iraq's use and development of weapons of mass destruction constitute a threat to America, President Bush addressed the nation. From the White House rose garden, Bush acknowledged the Congressional show of unity in favor of war with Iraq if it would ensure Iraqi disarmament or protect America from further terrorism.

On its present course, the Iraqi regime is a threat of unique urgency. We know the treacherous history of the regime. It has waged a war against its neighbors; it has sponsored and sheltered terrorists; it has developed weapons of mass death; it has used them against innocent men, women and children. We know the designs of the Iraqi regime. In defiance of pledges to the U.N., it has stockpiled biological and chemical weapons. It is rebuilding the facilities used to make those weapons.

U.N. inspectors believe that Iraq could have produced enough biological and chemical agent to kill millions of people. The regime has the scientists and facilities to build nuclear weapons, and is seeking the materials needed to do so.

We know the methods of this regime. They buy time with hollow promises. They move incriminating evidence to stay ahead of inspectors. They concede just enough to escape—to escape punishment, and then violate every pledge when the attention of the world is turned away.

We also know the nature of Iraq's dictator [Saddam Hussein]. On his orders, opponents have been decapitated and their heads displayed outside their homes. Women have been systematically raped as a method of intimidation. Political prisoners are made to watch their own children being tortured. The dictator is a student of [Soviet dictator Josef] Stalin, using murder as a tool of terror and control within his own cabinet, within his own army, even within his own family. We will not leave the future of peace and the security of America in the hands of this cruel and dangerous man.

None of us here today desire to see military conflict, because we know the awful nature of war. Our country values life, and never seeks war unless it is essential to security and to justice. America's leadership and willingness to use force, confirmed by the Congress, is the best way to ensure compliance and avoid conflict. Saddam must disarm, period. If, however, he chooses to do otherwise, if he persists in his defiance, the use of force may become unavoidable.

The course of action may bring many sacrifices. Yet delay, indecision and inaction could lead to a massive and sudden horror. By timely and resolute action, we can defend ourselves and shape a peaceful future. Together with the Congress, I will do everything necessary to protect and defend our country.

In accepting this responsibility, we also serve the interests and the hopes of the Iraqi people. They are a great and gifted people, with an ancient and admirable culture, and they would not choose to be ruled by violence and terror. The people of Iraq are the daily victims of Saddam Hussein's oppression. They will be the first to benefit when the world's demands are met. Americans believe all men and women deserve to be free. And as we saw in the fall of the Taliban [in Afghanistan], men and women celebrate freedom's arrival.

The United States will work with other nations. We'll work with other nations to bring Saddam to account. We'll work with other nations to help the Iraqi people form a just government and a unified country. And should force be required, the United States will help rebuild a liberated Iraq.

Countering Iraq's threat is also a central commitment on the war on terror. We know Saddam Hussein has long-standing and ongoing ties to international terrorists. With the support and shelter of a regime, terror groups become far more lethal. Aided by a terrorist network, an outlaw regime can launch attacks while concealing its involvement. Even a dictator is not suicidal, but he can make use of men who are. We must confront both terror cells and terror states, because they are different faces of the same evil.

I brought this issue to the attention of the world, and many, many countries share our determination to confront this threat. We're not alone. The issue is now before the United States Congress. This debate will be closely watched by the American people, and this debate will be remembered in history. We didn't ask for this challenge as a country, but we will face it, and we will face it together.

George W. Bush, "President, House Leadership Agree on Iraq Resolution," October 2, 2002.

DOCUMENT 10: SUPPORTING THE PRESIDENT

On October 2, 2002, Senator Joseph Lieberman commented on Congressional support of President Bush and why it passed the war resolution allowing President Bush the power to use military force against Iraq.

There is no more fateful, important, or difficult responsibility that the Constitution gives members of Congress than to decide when, whether, and how to authorize the President as Commander-in-

Chief to go to war. Mr. President, in your eloquent, powerful, and convincing statement this morning, you have reminded us, and I believe the American people, about why this is such a circumstance.

I have felt for more than a decade now that every additional day that Saddam Hussein is in power in Iraq is an additional day of danger for the Iraqi people, for his neighbors in the region, particularly for the people and military of the United States of America, and indeed for the people of the world. And that is why I am grateful for the opportunity to stand with my colleagues from both parties, and both Houses, and with you, Mr. President, in offering this resolution to authorize you to take military action to protect the region and the world from Iraq under Saddam Hussein, and to enforce the resolutions that are relevant of the United Nations.

There are those who say that this represents hurried or precipitous action, that we should give Saddam and the Iraqi government another chance. The record shows that for the last 10 years, we have tried—the world has tried—in just about every way—diplomatic, economic and otherwise, except military, in the end—to convince Saddam Hussein to live by the rules of international law and civilization. They've not worked.

The moment of truth has arrived. For Saddam Hussein, this is his last chance, and the best chance for the international community to come together behind the rule of law, and to show that resolutions of the United Nations are worth more than the paper that they are written on. . . .

And that, today, is the best hope for a stronger America and for a life for the American people that is safer.

Joseph Lieberman, Speech from "President, House Leadership Agree on Iraq Resolution," October 2, 2002.

DOCUMENT 11: LEAVE NO CHILD BEHIND

Listing education reform as a critical issue for America during his run for the presidency, George W. Bush was thrilled with bipartisan efforts to pass federal mandates on education in 2002. On January 8, 2003, Bush addressed the nation on the first anniversary of the No Child Left Behind Act. This landmark legislation made schools accountable to specific academic standards or face the loss of federal support funds.

[Today] marks the anniversary of an incredibly important legislative accomplishment. It was a year ago that I signed the No Child Left Behind Education Act. It was the most meaningful education reform probably ever. . . .

We can say that the work of reform is well begun. And that's—that's a true statement. The work will be complete, however, when every school—every public school in America is a place of high expectations and a place of achievement. That is our national goal.

Many schools in our country are places of hope and opportunity.

... Many schools ... are places where people can feel hopeful for the future. Unfortunately, too many schools in America have failed in that mission. The harm has been greatest in the poor and minority communities. Those kids have been hurt the worst because people have failed to challenge the soft bigotry of low expectations. ...

The time for excuse-making has come to an end. With the No Child Left Behind Act, we have committed the nation to higher standards for every single public school. And we've committed the resources to help the students achieve those standards. We affirm the right of parents to have better information about the schools, and to make crucial decisions about their children's future. Accountability of results is no longer just a hope of parents. Accountability for results is now the law of the land.

In return for receiving federal money, states must design accountability systems to measure whether students are learning to read and write and add and subtract. In return for a lot of money, the federal government, for the first time, is asking, are we getting the kind of return the American people want for every child. The only way to be sure of whether or not every child is learning is to test regularly and to show everybody, especially the parents, the results of the tests. The law further requires that test scores be presented in a clear and meaningful way, so that we can find the learning problems within each group of students. ...

Annual report cards are required to grade the schools, themselves, so parents can judge how the schools compare to others. Excellence will be recognized. It's so important for us to measure, so that we can praise the principals and teachers who are accomplishing the objectives we all hope for. And, at the same time, poor performance cannot be disguised or hidden.

Schools that perform poorly will be noticeable and given time, and given incentives, and given resources to improve. Schools that don't improve will begin to face consequences, such as that parents can move their child to another public school, or hire a tutor, or any other academic help. We will not accept a school that does not teach and will not change. ...

Some have claimed that testing somehow distracts from learning. I've heard this excuse since I was the governor of Texas—oh, you're teaching to test. Well, if a child can pass the reading test, the child has learned to read, as far as I'm concerned.

Other critics worry that high standards and measurement invite poor results. In other words, don't measure; you might see poor results, I guess is what they're saying. That they fear that by imposing clear standards, we'll set some schools up for failure, and that we'll identify too many failing schools. Well, the reasoning is backwards as far as I'm concerned, and a lot of other good people are concerned, as well. You don't cause a problem by revealing the problem. Accountability doesn't cause failure; it identifies failure. And only by acknowledging poor performance can we ever help schools to achieve. You can't solve a problem unless you first diagnose the problem. . . .

We've got to make sure the attitude changes. And the accountability systems within the No Child Left Behind Act insist that we have an attitude change in America. That's what this says.

One year ago, we met the first challenge of education reform. We passed the law. And now we've got another challenge, and that's the implementation of this law. . . . We look forward to a culture in America that understands every child can learn. And we look forward to the day that no child in this country is ever left behind.

George W. Bush, Speech on the First Anniversary of the No Child Left Behind Act, January 8, 2003.

DOCUMENT 12: A CASE FOR WAR

In his State of the Union Address to the American people on January 28, 2003, President Bush justified his case for involving the nation in a possible war against Iraq.

Twelve years ago, Saddam Hussein faced the prospect of being the last casualty in a war he had started and lost. To spare himself, he agreed to disarm of all weapons of mass destruction. For the next 12 years, he systematically violated that agreement. He pursued chemical, biological, and nuclear weapons, even while inspectors were in his country. Nothing to date has restrained him from his pursuit of these weapons—not economic sanctions, not isolation from the civilized world, not even cruise missile strikes on his military facilities.

Almost three months ago, the United Nations Security Council gave Saddam Hussein his final chance to disarm. He has shown instead utter contempt for the United Nations, and for the opinion of the world. The 108 U.N. inspectors were sent to conduct—were not sent to conduct a scavenger hunt for hidden materials across a country the size of California. The job of the inspectors is to verify that Iraq's regime is disarming. It is up to Iraq to show exactly where it is hiding its banned weapons, lay those weapons out for the world to see, and destroy them as directed. Nothing like this has happened.

The United Nations concluded in 1999 that Saddam Hussein had biological weapons sufficient to produce over 25,000 liters of anthrax—enough doses to kill several million people. He hasn't accounted for that material. He's given no evidence that he has destroyed it.

The United Nations concluded that Saddam Hussein had materials sufficient to produce more than 38,000 liters of botulinum toxin—enough to subject millions of people to death by respiratory failure. He hadn't accounted for that material. He's given no evidence that he has destroyed it.

Our intelligence officials estimate that Saddam Hussein had the materials to produce as much as 500 tons of sarin, mustard and VX nerve agent. In such quantities, these chemical agents could also kill untold thousands. He's not accounted for these materials. He has given no evidence that he has destroyed them.

U.S. intelligence indicates that Saddam Hussein had upwards of 30,000 munitions capable of delivering chemical agents. Inspectors recently turned up 16 of them—despite Iraq's recent declaration denying their existence. Saddam Hussein has not accounted for the remaining 29,984 of these prohibited munitions. He's given no evidence that he has destroyed them.

From three Iraqi defectors we know that Iraq, in the late 1990s, had several mobile biological weapons labs. These are designed to produce germ warfare agents, and can be moved from place to place to evade inspectors. Saddam Hussein has not disclosed these facilities. He's given no evidence that he has destroyed them.

The International Atomic Energy Agency confirmed in the 1990s that Saddam Hussein had an advanced nuclear weapons development program, had a design for a nuclear weapon and was working on five different methods of enriching uranium for a bomb. The British government has learned that Saddam Hussein recently sought significant quantities of uranium from Africa. Our intelligence sources tell us that he has attempted to purchase high-strength aluminum tubes suitable for nuclear weapons production. Saddam Hussein has not credibly explained these activities. He clearly has much to hide.

The dictator of Iraq is not disarming. To the contrary; he is deceiving. From intelligence sources we know, for instance, that thousands of Iraqi security personnel are at work hiding documents and materials from the U.N. inspectors, sanitizing inspection sites and monitoring the inspectors themselves. Iraqi officials accompany the inspectors in order to intimidate witnesses.

Iraq is blocking U-2 [spy plane] surveillance flights requested by the United Nations. Iraqi intelligence officers are posing as the scientists inspectors are supposed to interview. Real scientists have been coached by Iraqi officials on what to say. Intelligence sources indicate that Saddam Hussein has ordered that scientists who cooperate with U.N. inspectors in disarming Iraq will be killed, along with their families.

Year after year, Saddam Hussein has gone to elaborate lengths, spent enormous sums, taken great risks to build and keep weapons of mass destruction. But why? The only possible explanation, the only possible use he could have for those weapons, is to dominate, intimidate, or attack.

With nuclear arms or a full arsenal of chemical and biological weapons, Saddam Hussein could resume his ambitions of conquest in the Middle East and create deadly havoc in that region. And this Congress and the American people must recognize another threat. Evidence from intelligence sources, secret communications, and statements by people now in custody reveal that Saddam Hussein aids and protects terrorists, including members of al-Qaeda. Secretly, and without fingerprints, he could provide one of his hidden weapons to terrorists, or help them develop their own. . . .

Some have said we must not act until the threat is imminent. Since when have terrorists and tyrants announced their intentions, politely putting us on notice before they strike? If this threat is permitted to fully and suddenly emerge, all actions, all words, and all recriminations would come too late. Trusting in the sanity and restraint of Saddam Hussein is not a strategy, and it is not an option. . . .

The world has waited 12 years for Iraq to disarm. America will not accept a serious and mounting threat to our country, and our friends and our allies. The United States will ask the U.N. Security Council to convene on February the 5th to consider the facts of Iraq's ongoing defiance of the world. Secretary of State [Colin] Powell will present information and intelligence about Iraqi's illegal weapons programs, its attempt to hide those weapons from inspectors, and its links to terrorist groups.

We will consult. But let there be no misunderstanding: If Saddam Hussein does not fully disarm, for the safety of our people and for the peace of the world, we will lead a coalition to disarm him.

George W. Bush, State of the Union Address, January 28, 2003.

DOCUMENT 15: COMPASSIONATE CONSERVATIVE

George W. Bush describes himself and his political philosophy as compassionate conservative. Bush outlines this philosophy in an excerpt from a chapter in his book, A Charge to Keep.

We must close the gap of hope, but the answer is not found in yet another government program. The answer begins with each one of us assuming our responsibilities as parents and neighbors and citizens. I want to usher in the responsibility era, an era when every American knows with certainty that each of us is responsible for our actions, that each of us is responsible for our family and our community, that each of us is responsible for loving a neighbor as we would like to be loved ourselves.

During the more than half century of my life, we have seen an unprecedented decay in our American culture, a decay that has eroded the foundations of our collective values and moral standards of conduct. Our sense of personal responsibility has declined dramatically, just as the role and responsibility of the federal government have increased. . . .

The new culture said if people were poor, the government should feed them. If someone had no house, the government should provide one. If criminals are not responsible for their acts, then the answers are not in prisons, but in social programs. Every problem suddenly demanded a government solution.

Fathers moved out and Uncle Sam moved in. People became less interested in pulling themselves up by their bootstraps and more interested in pulling down a monthly government check. A culture of dependency was born. . . .

I am a conservative because I believe in the worth and dignity and power of each individual. My philosophy trusts individuals to make the right decisions for their families and communities, and that is far more compassionate than a philosophy that seeks solutions from distant bureaucracies. I am a conservative because I believe government should be limited and efficient, that it should do a few things and do them well. I am a conservative because I believe in a strong national defense to keep the peace. I am a conservative because I support free markets and free trade. I am a conservative because I believe government closest to the people governs best.

I am a fiscal conservative and a family conservative. And I am a compassionate conservative, because I know my philosophy is optimistic and full of hope for every American.

Compassionate conservatism outlines a new vision of the proper role for the American government. Government must be limited and focused, but it has an important job within its bounds. Government is too often wasteful and overreaching. But we must correct it and limit it, not disdain it. I differ with those who want to dismantle government down to the last paper clip—and with those who want to extend its reach. Government is neither the enemy nor the answer. The federal government has some compelling purposes: to defend our homeland, to help keep peace in the world, to help secure the retirement and health needs of our senior citizens, and to help our society confront human suffering. State and local government must educate children, put criminals behind bars, and maintain roads and basic services. But in some cases, the job is best done not by government itself, but by directing government resources to neighborhoods and parents and schools and faith-based institutions that shape values and change lives.

Compassionate conservatism is neither soft nor fuzzy. It is clear and compelling. It focuses not on good intentions but on good results. Compassionate conservatism applies conservative, free-market principles to the real job of helping real people, all people, including the poor and the disadvantaged. My vision of compassionate conservatism also requires America to assert its leadership in the world. We are the world's only remaining superpower, and we must use our power in a strong but compassionate way to help keep the peace and encourage the spread of freedom.

George W. Bush, *A Charge to Keep*. New York: William Morrow, 1999.

Discussion Questions

Chapter 1

1. In his article, "Midland Influence," Nicholas D. Kristof discusses how the values George W. Bush absorbed growing up in west Texas are critical to understanding who Bush is. Describe how growing up in smalltown Midland, Texas, developed Bush's personal and political philosophies.

2. It has been noted that George Bush looks like his father but has the spirit of his mother, Barbara Bush. Provide examples of the influence she held over her son according to George Lardner Jr. and Lois Romano's article.

3. Joe Conason notes that by Bush's father's standards, Bush was impatient in beginning his own oil drilling company. Cite examples of how Bush's personal relationships became important to his survival in this business.

Chapter 2

1. Bush became a successful businessman as general managing partner of the Texas Ranger's ball club. Give examples of Bush's management style listed in Joe Nick Patoski's article. Do you think any of these skills have been useful to Bush as president of the United States? Explain using examples.

2. In Skip Hollandsworth's article, what was the struggle Bush had in the Texas gubernatorial race against Ann Richards, and how did he overcome it?

3. Evaluate Bush's success as a governor. Why did these successes prompt the Republican National Convention to nominate him as their presidential candidate for 2000?

Chapter 3

1. What evidence did Lee Edwards use to make his case that the 2000 presidential election was not as close as it seemed? According to Edwards, in what areas did Bush best Al Gore as a campaigner?

2. James W. Ceaser and Andrew E. Busch discuss the politi-

cal climate surrounding the 2000 presidential election. Describe the atmosphere of the time and indicate how these circumstances culminated in one of the closest and controversial elections of the century.

3. Andrew Phillips notes several hurdles that Bush had to overcome as a new president. Describe these obstacles and why Phillips considers the surmounting of them to be political triumphs for Bush.

CHAPTER 4

1. What skills did Bush demonstrate during the ten-day hostage standoff with China according to William Schneider? What did the American people learn about Bush during this incident?

2. According to Siobhan Gorman, why does Bush have a passion for education reform? Describe what Gorman says the real test of the Bush reform package will be.

3. According to Richard Cheney, what are some of the economic stimulants Bush put into practice to facilitate long-term economic growth in America?

CHAPTER 5

1. From Robin Wright's viewpoint, explain why international respect for Bush increased based on his handling of the terrorist attacks of September 11, 2001. Discuss why the Bush administration could face larger hurdles once initial retaliation in Afghanistan ceases.

2. The national agenda changed with the terrorist events of September 11, 2001, according to Jeffrey H. Birnbaum. Consider these changes and cite examples to support his view that the nation is headed in a new direction.

3. Jeffrey H. Birnbaum also explains how Bush's leadership style developed throughout initial terrorist attacks. Compare Bush's management style after September 11 to the presidential characteristics he displayed before September 11, 2001. What similarities and differences are apparent?

4. Using Tony Carnes's article, describe how Bush's faith and politics led the nation in healing from September 11, 2001, terrorist activity in America.

CHAPTER 6

1. Kenneth T. Walsh examines Bush's actions following the September 11, 2001, terrorist attacks against the United States and his plan to eliminate terrorist activity around the world. Explain what role Iraq, Iran, and North Korea play in Bush's plan.

2. T. Trent Gegax outlines Bush's approach to the war against terror. Once a plan was devised, what methods did Bush choose to explain his mission to the world?

3. Bush originally kept his administration at a distance from the Middle East conflict, according to Michael Duffy. Yet Bush eventually changed his mind over involving America in the conflict between Israel and the Palestinians. Describe the events that took place to make Bush reevaluate the situation and stake his presidency on peace in that region.

4. Why was the war with Iraq unprecedented? According to Kenneth T. Walsh, what was Bush's philosophy behind the coalition's attack?

CHRONOLOGY

1946

George Walker Bush is born in New Haven, Connecticut, on July 6.

1948

The Bush family moves to Odessa, Texas.

1953

Bush's sister, Robin, dies in October.

1961

Bush enters Phillips Academy in Andover, Massachusetts.

1964

Bush works as a campaign aide for his father's Senate race and enters Yale University in September.

1968

Bush joins the Texas Air National Guard on May 27 after graduating from Yale. On June 10 he leaves for one year of flight training at Moody Air Force Base in Georgia.

1973

Bush enters Harvard Business School.

1975

Bush graduates from Harvard and heads to Midland, Texas, to work in the oil industry.

1977

Bush organizes his first company, Arbusto, then runs for Congress. He meets and later marries Laura Welch on November 5.

1978

Bush wins the primary election for Congress but loses the general election.

1981

Bush's father becomes the vice president of the United States. Laura gives birth to twin daughters, Jenna Welch and Barbara Pierce Bush, on November 25.

1985

Bush discusses religion with the Reverend Billy Graham and finds renewed religious conviction in his personal life.

1988

George H.W. Bush becomes president of the United States.

1989

Bush purchases the Texas Rangers baseball club in April with a group of investors.

1994

Bush defeats Ann Richards in the Texas gubernatorial race.

1998

Bush is reelected governor of Texas.

1999

Bush enters the presidential race.

2000

Bush becomes the forty-third president of the United States.

2001

January: Bush is inaugurated on January 20.

April: Bush negotiates the release of twenty-four U.S. prisoners in China after the U.S. surveillance plane collided with a Chinese fighter; he implements a tax relief bill and issues refund checks to tax-paying Americans.

June: Bush introduces a patients' bill of rights, ensuring medical review; dedicates a D day memorial in Virginia; and visits Europe.

August: Bush approves federal funding of stem cell research only within federal limitations.

September: Bush proclaims a National Day of Prayer and Remembrance after planes crash into the World Trade Center, the Pentagon, and a field in Pennsylvania; he assembles an international campaign against terrorism.

October: Bush creates the Department of Homeland Security; he begins an antiterrorism war in Afghanistan.

2002

January: Bush passes Brownfield legislation, helping cities clean up industrial sites; he signs a landmark educational reform bill; he implements legislation to aid victims of terrorism.

February: Bush launches the USA Freedom Corps, an expansion of the Peace Corps serving and mentoring in local communities in America; he increases funding for bioterrorism research, defense, and test protocols; he meets with Israeli prime minister Ariel Sharon to discuss peace in the Middle East and eliminating world terrorism.

March: Bush signs the Corporate Responsibility Act, requiring business leaders to adhere to a code of ethics.

May: Bush signs a treaty with Russian president Alexander Putin to reduce nuclear arsenals to their lowest levels in decades.

September: Bush addresses the UN General Assembly, challenging it to enforce disclosure and destruction of weapons of mass destruction for Iraq according to Security Council resolutions from 1991.

October: Bush gets the House's approval to use force to impel Iraq to comply with UN Security Council resolutions to eliminate weapons of mass destruction.

2003

January: Bush assembles a multinational coalition to force Iraq to adhere to UN Security Council resolutions from 1991.

February: Bush attends memorial services for *Columbia* astronauts killed in flight; he sends Secretary of State Colin Powell to address the UN, requiring it to enforce previous mandates against Iraq.

March: After giving Iraqi leader Saddam Hussein forty-eight hours to leave power, Bush authorizes a military strike against Iraq. War with Iraq ensues.

April: Bush declares the United States has military control of Iraq; he addresses the Iraqi people by radio, promising the return of the country's power to the people.

May: Bush announces that combat operations in Iraq are over; he removes sanctions imposed by the United States against Iraq under Saddam Hussein; Bush signs the Jobs and Growth Tax Relief Reconciliation Act offering tax relief.

June: Bush signs an agreement with the EU to stop the proliferation of nuclear, biological, and chemical weapons; he outlines am agenda for U.S.-African relations.

July: Bush travels to Africa offering terrorism, education, and AIDS initiatives.

FOR FURTHER RESEARCH

BY GEORGE W. BUSH

George W. Bush, *A Charge to Keep.* New York: William Morrow, 1999.

BOOKS ABOUT GEORGE W. BUSH

Frank Bruni, *Ambling into History: The Unlikely Odyssey of George W. Bush.* New York: HarperCollins, 2002.

Barbara Bush, *Barbara Bush: A Memoir.* New York: Charles Scribner's Sons, 1994.

George H.W. Bush, *All the Best, George Bush.* New York: William Morrow, 1999.

David Frum, *The Right Man: The Surprise Presidency of George W. Bush.* New York: Random House, 2003.

Bill Minutaglio, *First Son George W. Bush and the Bush Family Dynasty.* New York: Time Books, 1999.

Bill Sammon, *The War on Terrorism from Inside the Bush White House.* Washington, DC: Regnery, 2002.

Bob Woodward, *Bush at War.* New York: Simon and Schuster, 2002.

BOOKS ON THE 2000 ELECTION

James W. Ceaser and Andrew E. Busch, *The Perfect Tie: The True Story of the 2000 Presidential Election.* Lanham, MD: Rowman & Littlefield, 2001.

E.J. Dionne Jr. and William Kristol, *Bush vs. Gore: The Court Cases and the Commentary.* Washington, DC: Brookings Institution, 2001.

Martin Merzer and the Staff of the *Miami Herald, Democracy Held Hostage.* New York: St. Martin's, 2001.

Dana Milbank, *Smashmouth: Two Years in the Gutter with Al Gore and George W. Bush—Notes from the 2000 Campaign Trail.* New York: Basic Books, 2001.

New York Times, Thirty-Six Days: The Complete Chronicle of the 2000 Presidential Election Crisis. New York: Henry Holt, 2001.

Richard Posner, *Breaking Deadlock: The 2000 Election, the Constitution, and the Courts.* Princeton, NJ: Princeton University Press, 2001.

Jeffrey Toobin, *Too Close to Call.* New York: Random House, 2001.

PERIODICALS

Michael Beschloss, "How Bush Rates: Does He Measure Up to Other Wartime Presidents?" *Time*, December 31, 2001.

Jeffrey H. Birnbaum, "Bush's Growth Spurt: George W. Has Found His Presidential Authority and Voice Since September 11th," *International Economy Publications*, 2001.

Robert J. Bresler, "Bush, War, and Iraq," *USA Today*, November 2002.

Tony Carnes, "Bush's Defining Moment," *Christian Reader*, March 2002.

Joe Conason, "Notes on a Native Son," *Harper's*, February 2000.

Michael Duffy, "After Several False Starts, George W. Bush Commits Himself Fully to Ending the Bloodshed in the Middle East. The Inside Story of His About-Face, and the Risks He Confronts," *Time*, April 12, 2002.

Lee Edwards, "The Closest Presidential Election Ever—Bush Won, Barely, by Offering a Slightly to the Right, Limited-Government Presidency," *World & I*, February 2001.

T. Trent Gegax, "Bush's Battle Cry: Drawing on Prayer and a Sense of Personal Mission, W Becomes a War President," *Newsweek*, October 1, 2001.

Nancy Gibbs, "Person of the Year: George W. Bush," *Time*, December 17, 2000.

Siobhan Gorman, "Bipartisan Schoolmates," *Education National Journal*, 2002.

Fred Greenstein, "The Contemporary Presidency: The Changing Leadership of George W. Bush: A Pre- and

Post-9/11 Comparison," *Presidential Studies Quarterly*, June 2002.

Skip Hollandsworth, "Born to Run: What's in a Name? How About the Republican Nomination for Governor," *Texas Monthly*, May 1994.

Nicholas D. Kristof, "A Boy from Midland: A Philosophy with Roots in Conservative Texas Soil," *New York Times*, May 21, 2000.

George Lardner Jr. and Lois Romano, "At Height of Vietnam, Bush Picks the Guard," *Washington Post*, July 28, 1999.

————, "Bush Earned Profit, Rangers Deal Insiders Say," *Washington Post*, July 31, 1999.

————, "Bush Name Helps Fuel Oil Dealings," *Washington Post*, July 30, 1999.

————, "Bush's Life-Changing Year," *Washington Post*, July 25, 1999.

————, "Bush's Move Up to the Majors," *Washington Post*, July 31, 1999.

————, "So-So Student but a Campus Mover," *Washington Post*, July 27, 1999.

————, "Tragedy Created Bush Mother-Son Bond," *Washington Post*, July 26, 1999.

————, "Young Bush a Political Natural, Revs Up," *Washington Post*, July 29, 1999.

Ryan Lizza, "White House Watch—Future Tense," *New Republic*, September 2, 2002.

Dana Milbank, "What 'W' Stands For," *New Republic*, April 26, 1999.

Adam Nagourney, "White House Power Grows Under Bush," *Seattle Times*, December 22, 2002.

Joe Nick Patoski, "George Bush's Career Running the Texas Rangers," *Texas Monthly*, June 1999.

Andrew Phillips, "Victory at Last," *Maclean's*, December 25, 2000.

Ramesh Ponnuru, "Bush at One Year," *National Review*, January 28, 2002.

————, "The Front-Runner: Is It George W. Bush Already?" *National Review*, December 1997.

Harold C. Relyea, "The Law: Homeland Security; the Concept and the Presidential Coordination Office—First Assessment," *Presidential Studies Quarterly,* June 2002.

Jon Sawyer, "President's Leadership Gets High Marks, but Test Looms," *St. Louis Post-Dispatch,* December 28, 2002.

William Schneider, "Bush Wins 'Let's Make a Deal,'" *National Journal,* April 21, 2001.

Kathryn Dunn Tenpas, "The Bush White House, First Appraisals," *Presidential Studies Quarterly,* September 2002.

Michael Waller, "A Wartime Window of Opportunity," *Insight on the News,* September 2, 2002.

Kenneth T. Walsh, "W, as in War," *U.S. News & World Report,* February 25, 2002.

WEBSITES

Republican Party, www.georgewbush.com. This site highlights George W. Bush and his presidency. Information on Bush, his 2000 election campaign, and where he stands on current issues are some of the topics offered.

Texas, http://gotexas.about.com. This site focuses on information on Texas. Search "George W. Bush" to find family history, biographies, his role as president, and his campaign and work as governor of Texas. Photos and links to other sites are provided.

Texas Monthly, www.texasmonthly.com. This site keeps archives of George W. Bush, especially his life as governor, his biography, and information about his life in Texas and his family.

Washington Post, www.washingtonpost.com. This site has archives that focus on George W. Bush and issues at large during his presidency.

The White House, www.whitehouse.gov. This site provides information on George W. Bush as president. Speeches by Bush as well as photos, press releases, presidential time lines, and links to other sites are available.

INDEX

abortion, 77, 84
accountability, as campaign theme, 20, 68, 128
Adams, John Quincy, 110
Afghanistan, 23, 144, 146, 158–62, 164
AFL-CIO, 94, 95
airline industry, 165
Ameen, Michael, 47
Americans for Tax Reform, 76, 87–88
Andover, Massachusetts. *See* Phillips Academy
Arafat, Yasser, 170–73, 175
Arbusto Energy Co., 13, 14, 43
Arlington Hispanic Advisory Council, 57
Arlington Sports Facilities Development Authority, 50
Armey, Dick, 149
Ashcroft, John, 165–66
Atwater, Lee, 14–15
Austin American-Statesman (newspaper), 86
"axis of evil," 158–59, 162

Bahrain, 47–48
Baker, James, III, 44
Baker, Ross, 159, 179
Ballpark, The (Arlington, Texas), 49–50, 52, 56–58
Bar. *See* Bush, Barbara
Barak, Ehud, 172
Barksdale Air Force Base, 160
Barnard, Brandon, 80
Bartlett, Dan, 161–62
Bath, James, 44
Bayh, Evan, 122
Beck, Paul Allen, 100
Bennett, William, 175

Berger, Sandy, 159
Berlusconi, Silvio, 182
Bernstein, Tom, 46, 54
Betts, Roland W., 45–46, 53–55
bin Laden, Osama, 141, 144, 146, 149, 172
bipartisanship, 98, 114, 120, 122, 149
Birnbaum, Jeffrey H., 145
Black Tuesday, 168
    see also September 11 attacks
Blair, Tony, 165, 174, 181
Blake, Charles, 153
Boehner, John, 123
Bolten, Josh, 82, 167
Boskin, Michael, 82
Bradley, Bill, 83
Breeden, Richard, 48–49
BR Rangers, 54
    see also Texas Rangers
Brzezinski, Zbigniew, 176
Bullock, Bob, 73, 108
Burka, Paul, 73
Busch, Andrew E.
Bush, Barbara, 13, 16, 31–32
    parenting by, 29, 37–40, 63, 64
    political encouragement by, 18
Bush, Dorothy (grandmother), 44
Bush, Dorothy (sister). *See* Koch, Doro Bush
Bush, George H.W. (father), 9, 31, 64, 65–66
    childhood of, 28
    letter by, prior to Persian Gulf War, 181
    New World Order and, 177
    parenting by, 30–31, 39
    political ambition of, 61, 64, 82
    presidency of, 149
    presidential campaigns of,

14–15, 45, 66
Bush, George W.
  on abortion, 77, 84
  childhood of, 27, 30–32, 37–38,
    41–42, 63
  education of, 10–12, 40, 42
  family legacy of, 9–11, 77
  as governor of Texas, 16–18,
    74–76, 81, 84
  historical records set by, 25
  image of, 61–63, 73–74, 77,
    145–51, 179
  leadership style of, 15, 53–54,
    140–41, 159, 166–67, 179, 182
  marriage of, 13
  nicknames for, 11, 17, 150
  oil career of, 13, 14, 44–49
  as owner of the Texas Rangers,
    15–16, 45–47, 49–50, 52–58,
    63, 72
  political ambition of, 61, 64,
    66–67
  radio address to Iraq by, 180
  religious beliefs of, 152–56
  in Texas Air National Guard,
    11–12
  as world leader, 140–41, 146
  see also campaign, for governor;
    campaign, for president;
    campaign, for U.S. Congress;
    election of president; religion,
    government and; September
    11 attacks
Bush, Jeb, 36, 38, 68, 115
Bush, Jonathan, 44
Bush, Laura, 13, 16, 18, 34, 62, 64,
  73, 165
Bush, Marvin, 35, 37, 39, 41
Bush, Neil, 39, 41, 49
Bush, Pauline Robinson. *See*
  Bush, Robin
Bush, Prescott S., 9, 31, 64
Bush, Robin, 10, 35–39, 53
Bush administration. *See*
  *individual names of
  administration members*
"Bush Doctrine," 159, 162,
  164–65, 167, 171, 179
Bush Exploration Oil Co., 44
Butts, Roland, 58

Calio, Nick, 147–48
campaign
  for governor, 60–62, 67
    education policy, 69–70

  home-rule plan, 69
  juvenile crime, 68–69
  for president, 92–93, 101–103,
    154
    campaign issues, 19–20, 81,
      86–87, 89, 96–97
    candidates' campaign styles,
      83–85, 95–96
    decision to run, 18
    funding for, 94–95
    media and, 97–98
    partisan faithfulness and,
      100–103
    popular vs. electoral vote and,
      106, 110
    postelection campaign and,
      20–21, 107
    see also election of president
  for U.S. Congress, 13–14, 43,
    64–66
Card, Andrew, 160, 162, 178
Carnes, Tony, 152–56
Castellini, Bob, 53
Ceaser, James W., 99
Chadderdon, Liz, 81
"Charge to Keep, A" (hymn), 156
Cheney, Dick, 88, 141, 161, 170,
  173
  on economy, 130–38
  on Israeli-Palestinian conflict,
    172, 175
  reaction of, to September 11
    attacks, 146
  on war against Hussein, 178
  as war minister, 167
Chiles, Eddie, 15, 53
China, 21, 117–19, 172
Chirac, Jacques, 166
Christian Coalition, 94–95
Church of the Nativity
  (Bethlehem), 169, 175
CIA, 161
Cizik, Richard, 152
Clinton, Bill, 60, 75, 81, 92, 150
  Bush's criticism of, 171
  on Elementary and Secondary
    Education Act, 121
  communitarium movement,
    82–83
  "compassionate conservatism,"
    33, 77, 80, 92
Conason, Joe, 43
corporate integrity, 133–34
Cottrell, Comer, 54, 57
Craig, Mark, 18

crime policy, 70
  faith-based rehabilitation for
    prisoners and, 33, 80, 81, 86
  in Texas, 68–69, 86
Crosby, Austine, 32

Daley, William, 106
Dallek, Robert, 178, 179
Davis, Lanny, 83
death penalty, 17
death tax, 135
defense policy, 89, 90, 160
DeLay, Tom, 114, 149
Delta Kappa Epsilon fraternity,
  43
Democratic Party, 108, 149
  "New Democrats," 84, 85, 122
  presidential candidate of, 74
  see also election of president;
    individual names of politicians
Dettmer, Jamie, 20
DeWitt, William, Jr., 44, 45, 53
Dorn, Lacey Neuhaus, 42
Draper, William, III, 44
Duffy, Michael, 169
Dukakis, Michael, 45

economy
  federal spending and, 135–36
  growth of, 133–35
  policy of, 131, 134–36, 151
  recession and, 131–33, 151
education policy
  block grants and, 122, 123
  "tough-love" academics and, 70
  vouchers and, 75, 122–23
Edwards, Lee, 92
Egan, Edward, 153
Egypt, 150, 173
election of president, 20–21,
  92–98, 108–109
  effect of, on Bush's presidency,
    110–11, 114–15
  election night events and,
    103–107
  events following, 112–13
  in Florida, 100, 103–105, 111–13
  media coverage of, 98–99,
    103–105
  public opinion about, 109–10
  tied votes of, 99–103
  U.S. Supreme Court decision
    about, 108–14
  see also campaign, for
    president; Gore, Al

electorate, 100–101, 106, 110
Elementary and Secondary
  Education Act (ESEA), 120–21,
  125–29
  failing schools, defined, 124
  partisanship and, 123–24
  requirements of, 126–27
  state compliance and, 127–29
Ellis, John, 38
embargo, oil (1979), 14
energy plan, 136
Ernie (family cat), 10
Evans, Donald L., 106–107, 168

failing schools, 124
Fege, Arnold, 127
Feldstein, Martin, 82
Financial World (magazine), 58
Finn, Chester, 75
Fleisher, Ari, 155
Florida
  ballot recount in, 111–13
  Jeb Bush as governor of, 68, 115
  presidential election results
    and, 103–105, 112–13
  Supreme Court of, 100
  U.S. Supreme Court decision
    about, 109–14
  see also election of president
foreign policy, 88–90, 117–19
  on Afghanistan, 23, 144, 146,
    158–62, 164
  on China, 21, 117–19, 172
  on Egypt, 150, 173
  international coalition and, 24,
    144, 173
  on Iran, 159, 170
  on Iraq, 23–24, 48, 159, 170, 173,
    177–82
  on Israeli-Palestinian conflict,
    169–76
  on North Korea, 159, 178
  on Russia, 142, 172
  on Saudi Arabia, 150, 165
  on Syria, 170
Fort Worth Star-Telegram
  (newspaper), 55
Free Trade Area of the Americas,
  137

Gaylord, Edward, 54
Gegax, T. Trent, 163
Gelb, Les, 144
Gerson, Michael, 155, 161
Giuliani, Rudolph, 165

Goeglein, Timothy, 152
Goldsmith, Steve, 85
Gore, Al, 20, 74, 81, 92
    comparison to Bush and, 83–84
    election conceded by, 105,
        109–10, 113
    image of, 95
    reaction of, to election results,
        21, 106, 112
    on U.S. Supreme Court
        decision, 111–12
Gorman, Siobhan
    on education policy
        compromise, 123–24
    on Elementary and Secondary
        Education Act, 120–21, 125–29
    on vouchers and block grants,
        122–23
Graham, Franklin, 153, 154
Graham, Rev. Billy, 19, 153
Greene, Richard, 49, 50, 56
Greenspan, Alan, 165
Greenstein, Fred, 22–23
Greenwich Country Day School,
    28, 40, 63
Gregg, Judd, 124
Grieve, Tom, 56
gubernatorial campaign. *See*
    campaign, for governor
Guelzo, Allen, 155–56
Gutierrez, Mrs., 79–80

Hance, Kent, 66
Hannah, Douglas, 41
Harken Energy Corp., 14, 44–49
Harris, Katherine, 112, 113
Harvard Management Company,
    45
Harvard University, 12, 27, 43,
    149
Hayes, Rutherford B., 100
Hayes-Tilden presidential
    election (1876), 100
Hernandez, Israel, 61
Hickok, Eugene, 127–29
Hicks, Tom, 58
Hizballah, 175–76
    see also Israeli-Palestinian
        conflict
Hockaday School, 62
Hollandsworth, Skip
    on Bush's crime policy, 68–71
    on Bush's image, 61–63
    on Bush's sincerity, 63–64
    on campaign for governor,
        59–61
    on George H.W. Bush's
        campaign for president, 66–68
Homeland Security office, 23, 166
Hostler, Charles, 47
Houston, Texas, 40
Houston Post (newspaper), 48
Hubbard, Al, 81, 82
Hubbard, Glenn, 87
Hughes, Karen, 77, 83–84, 161,
    167–68, 174–75
Hussein, Saddam, 23–24, 48, 173,
    178, 181
    see also Iraq
Hutchinson, Kay Bailey, 17, 70
Hybels, Bill, 153

immigration policy, 77, 80
international trade, 137–38
investment protection, 134
Iran, 159, 170
Iraq, 159, 170, 173
    Bush's radio address to, 180
    international coalition and, 24,
        146, 173
    war with, 23–24, 177–82
Islam, 143–44
Israeli-Palestinian conflict,
    169–71
    Bush's position on, 174–75
    diplomacy and, 171–73

Jakes, T.D., 153
Jeffords, James M., 128
Jennings, John F. "Jack," 125, 129
Jiang Zemin, 140

Keller, Tim, 154
Kennebunkport, Maine, 40
Kennedy, Anthony, 111
Kennedy, Edward M., 122, 128,
    145
Kennedy, John, 93
Kidde, John, 37
Kieschnick, Gerald, 154
Kimmitt, Bob, 82, 88
Kinkaid School, 40
Koch, Doro Bush, 39, 41
Koizumi, Junichiro, 140–41
Kress, Sandy, 124, 126, 127
Kristof, Nicholas D., 27
Kristol, William, 175

Langdon, James, 87
Lanzillo, John "Zonk," Jr., 55

Lardner, George, Jr., 35
Law, Bernard, 164
League of United Latin American
   Citizens (LULAC), 57
Lehrman, Lewis, 44
Lichtman, Allan, 109
Lieberman, Joseph I., 122
Lieberman-Bayh bill, 122
Lilley, James, 118
Lindsey, Larry, 82, 87
Lucado, Max, 153
Luce, Tom, 56

Mahon, George, 64
Malek, Fred, 53
Malley, Robert, 176
Marcus, Jess, 54
Mathes, Curtis, 57
McCain, John, 88–89
McClure, Fred, 60
McKinnon, Mark, 73, 81
media
   Bahrain oil contract reported
      by, 47–48
   election coverage by, 98, 99,
      103–105
   *see also individual names of
      media outlets*
Meyer, Fred, 67
Midland, Texas, 12–13, 63, 64
   Bush's childhood in, 27–34
   image of, 27, 33
   racism in, 29–30
Milbank, Dana, 79
   on Bush as presidential
      candidate, 81–86
   on Bush's economic policy, 87
   on Bush's foreign policy, 88–90
   on Bush's social policy, 86–87
Miller, George, 121, 123, 128
Millie (family dog), 55
Minutaglio, Bill, 33
Monroe, James, 177
Monroe Doctrine, 177
Moody Air Force Base, Georgia,
   11
Mubarak, Hosni, 173
Musharraf, Pervez, 142
Muslims, 143–44

Naim, Moises, 143
National Assessment of
   Educational Progress (NAEP),
   125
National Association for the

Advancement of Colored People
   (NAACP), 29, 57, 94
National Day of Prayer and
   Remembrance, 22
National Education Summit, 125
National Federation of
   Independent Business, 95
National Security Council, 23
Nixon, Richard, 93
Noonan, Peggy, 155
Norquist, Grover, 77, 88
North Korea, 159, 178

O'Beirne, Kate, 93
O'Connor, Sandra Day, 111
Odessa, Texas, 30
oil industry
   Arbusto Energy Co., 13, 14, 43
   Bush Exploration Oil Co., 44
   Harken Energy Corp., 14, 44–49
   1979 embargo and, 14
   Spectrum 7, 14, 44
   Zapata Petroleum Corp., 38
Olasky, Marvin, 82–83
O'Neill, Joe, 27, 40
Organization of Petroleum
   Exporting Countries, 14

Paige, Rod, 126
Palau, Luis, 153
Palestinians. *See* Israeli-
   Palestinian conflict
Patient's Bill of Rights, 21, 148
Patoski, Joe Nick, 52
Pauken, Tom, 77
Pentagon. *See* September 11
   attacks
Peres, Shimon, 176
Perle, Richard, 88
Perot, Ross, 126
Petty, Marge, 32
Phelps, Gerry, 86–87
Phillips, Andrew
   on Bullock's influence, 108–109
   on Bush as governor, 109–10
   on Bush as president, 114–15
   on election results, 109–14
Phillips Academy, 10–11, 28, 42
Ponnuru, Ramesh, 72
Powell, Colin, 93, 114, 143
   on China, 118
   on Israeli-Palestinian conflict,
      170, 172–73
   role of, in international
      coalition, 146

prescription drugs for seniors, 114
presidential election. *See* campaign, for president; election of president
private-sector solutions, 84
Proctor, Michael, 29, 40
Project PULL, 12
Putin, Vladimir, 142
Putnam, Robert, 85–86

al-Qaeda, 23, 144, 146, 161
see also Afghanistan
Quasha, Alan, 47

Rainwater, Richard, 46, 53, 54
Rather, Dan, 103, 104
Rea, Paul, 45
Reading Is Fundamental (RIF), 16
Reagan, Ronald, 172, 177
Rector, Robert, 74
Reeves, Jim, 55
Rehnquist, William, 111
Reilly, Mike, 54, 57
religion, government and, 152–56
Bush's beliefs about, 18–19
Christian Coalition and, 94–95
church-state cooperation and, 86
faith-based rehabilitation for prisoners and, 33, 80, 81, 86
school vouchers and, 75
Republican Party, 15, 72, 75, 78, 81, 148
Bush's control of, 114, 149
Bush's vision for, 85–86
on education, 122
on immigration, 30
see also individual names of politicians
"responsibility era," 33
Reynolds, Mercer, 44, 53
Rice, Condoleezza, 82, 114, 160, 167, 170
on Bush's foreign policy, 119
on Bush's leadership, 162
on Israeli-Palestinian conflict, 175
war with Iraq and, 178
Richards, Ann, 17, 50, 62, 67, 73
campaign of, for governor, 58–60
on juvenile crime, 68–69
Ridge, Tom, 23, 166, 167, 174

Roden, Randall, 30, 39
Romano, Lois, 35
Rose, Edward "Rusty," 15, 46, 53, 54
Ross, Dennis, 176
Rove, Karl, 28, 150, 159, 166
Rumsfeld, Donald, 88, 170, 173
on Israeli-Palestinian conflict, 172–73, 175
role of, in international coalition, 146
on war with Iraq, 178
Russert, Tim, 104
Russia, 142, 144, 172
Ryan, Nolan, 55

Sam Houston Elementary School, 29, 35
San Jacinto Junior High, 28, 40, 63, 72
Saudi Arabia, 150, 165
Sauls, N. Sanders, 113
Scalia, Antonin, 111
Schieffer, J. Thomas, 54, 56–58
Schneider, William, 117
Schwartz, David, 57
Securities and Exchange Commission, 48
Security Council, 24
September 11 attacks, 22–23, 124, 132–33, 146, 152
economic impact of, 165
public support for retaliation for, 140–44
war in Afghanistan and, 23, 146, 158–62, 164
Sharon, Ariel, 170, 172, 173, 176
Shreve, David, 128
Shultz, George, 89
Sibley, David, 73
Sidey, Hugh, 65
Sierra, Ruben, 55
small businesses, promotion of, 136–37
Smith, Fred, 84
Smith, Marshall S., 126, 128
Souter, David, 112
Spectrum 7, 14, 44
Spot Fletcher (family dog), 10, 55
Stapleton, Craig, 53
Steinberg, James, 143
stem-cell research, 149–50
Stevens, John Paul, 111
Stone, Ann, 77
Sununu, John, 66

Swetnam, Monte, 47
Syria, 170

Taliban, 23, 146, 147, 150
taxes
    Americans for Tax Reform, 76,
        87–88
    death tax, 135
    reform plans for, 21, 132, 135,
        148–49
Taylor, John, 82
television. *See* media
Tenet, George, 170, 178
terrorism. *See* September 11
    attacks
terrorism risk insurance, 135
Texas Air National Guard, 11–12
Texas Daily Newspaper
    Association, 84
Texas Education Agency (TEA),
    69, 75
Texas Healthy Kids Corporation,
    76
Texas Observer (newspaper), 58
Texas Rangers, 15–16, 45–47, 63,
    72
    The Ballpark and, 49–50
    Bush as managing general
        partner of, 15–16, 55–56, 58
    financing of, 53–54
    sale of, 58
Thomas, Clarence, 111
Throckmorton, Terry, 31
Tilden, Samuel J., 100
Time (magazine), 47, 170–71
"tough-love" academics, 126
trade, international, 137–38
Trakatellis, Demetrios, 164
Truman, Harry, 177
Truman Doctrine, 177
"Turn Around Texas" program,
    86

Ueberroth, Peter, 45, 53
United Nations, 23
    diplomacy and, 175–76
    Israeli-Palestinian conflict and,
        174
    weapons inspectors from, 24
U.S. Congress. *See* campaign, for
    U.S. Congress; *individual names
    of congressmen/senators*
U.S. News (magazine), 178
U.S. Supreme Court, 21, 97–98,
    100, 111–13
Uzielli, Phillip, 44

Vandergriff, Tom, 56
Vietnam War, 11
Voter News Service, 103

Walker, Elsie, 11, 37
Walker, John, 38
Wall Street Journal (newspaper),
    48
Walsh, Kenneth T., 158, 177
Washington Post (newspaper), 61
weapons of mass destruction. *See*
    "Bush Doctrine"
Weekly Standard (magazine), 118
Weiss, Peggy Porter, 30, 34
Welch, Laura. *See* Bush, Laura
Wellstone, Paul, 128
White, John, 12
Williams, Clayton, 64, 67
Wittmann, Marshall, 149
Wolfowitz, Paul, 82, 88
World Trade Center. *See*
    September 11 attacks
Wright, Robin, 140

Yale University, 11, 28, 30, 43

Zapata Petroleum Corp., 38
Zinni, Anthony, 173
Zogby, John, 96